MY LIFE WITH HORSES AND HOF

BY

SAM HUMPHREY

Best Wishes
Sam Humphrey
2022

THIS BOOK IS PROTECTED BY COPYRIGHT

My Life with Horses and Horse People text© sam humphrey 2021

By Sam Humphrey

Book cover

This is a photograph of a collage of photographs of some of our favourite horses and horsey moments that hangs in our office. I look at it on a daily basis and enjoy those memories.

Dedications and Thanks

I dedicate this to my wife Louise (Lou) who has been my rock and anchor for the past forty-seven years. Without her help and support many of the events in this book would never have happened. I also dedicate this book to my three granddaughters Katherine, Florence, and Georgina all riders and carrying on the Humphrey riding tradition. All my three autobiographical books have been primarily written for my grandchildren so they will know something of our family history. Although I can remember all four of my grandparents, they all died when I was young and I wish that I had pressed my parents for more details of their lives before they also passed away.

The unsung heroes of this book are my grooms who looked after my horses, checked the safety of my tack, and put up with my nervous tantrums. Every time I went out to compete, I put my life in their hands, they never once let me down. My heartfelt thanks to Sally, Brian, and Jackie.

Also, I owe a debt of gratitude to all the owners that allowed me to compete their horses. Sadly, most of them are not with us anymore and I regret not writing this book earlier so at they could read this.
I could not have written any of my books without the help and patience of my wife who helped cross check my memory and read this book several times over, looking for typo's and other mistakes. This whole series of books has been produced by family and friends so if you find the odd mistake, please forgive us.

I big thank you to Vanda Craig for editing the book all the way from Turkey where she is stuck thanks to COVID-19. Although I must say, I can think of worse places to get stranded. Sometimes we moan about technology but it has been a marvel during this pandemic. Also, to my wife Lou (Louise) and granddaughter Katherine for re-reading the final proof.

Finally thank you to all the people that have phoned, emailed, or just took the time to say how much they have enjoyed my books. It means so much to me, you have given me the energy to carry on.

Other Books by Sam Humphrey

The Knights Errant (Bunny Hill Chronicles Trilogy Book 1)2017

Boy Gone Feral on Bunny Hill (Bunny Hill Chronicles Trilogy Book 2)2019

Available on Amazon Books in eBook and paperback

Contact: - email samhumphrey2@gmail.com

Contents

Dedications and Thanks 3
Prologue 8
Glossary 10
Chapter one 12
Early Days 12
Chapter Two 17
Pony Club Days 17
Chapter Three 23
Show Jumping 23
Chapter Four' 26
Hunting 26
Early Days 26
The South Notts Hunt Derbyshire 32
A Bit of Bladder 46
The Quorn Hunt 48
Chapter Five 62
Visiting other packs 62
The Belvoir Hunt 62
The Cottesmore Hunt 65
The High Peak Hunt 67
The Meynell and South Staffordshire Hunt 69
The South Durham Hunt 71
The Pytchley Hunt 72
The Bicester with Whaddon Chase Hunt 74
Chapter Six 77
Racing 77
My First Race 77
My Second Race 82
The rest of my first season 85
Wetherby 91
A Journeyman Jockey 105
Dick Benson 116
Victory 123

The Road to Cheltenham 125
A Little Foreign Adventure 129
Chapter Seven 139
Drag Hunting and Bloodhounds 139
The Readyfield Bloodhounds 139
Drag Hunting 141
The Cambridge Universities Drag Hounds 141
The Mid Surrey Farmers Drag Hounds 142
The Welsh Borders Drag Hunt 147
Chapter Eight 151
Ireland 151
Chapter Nine 172
Riding Abroad 172
Chapter Ten 183
Team Chasing 183
Chapter Eleven 203
Field Master 203
Chapter Twelve 215
Teaching 215
Chapter Thirteen 220
The Melton Hunt Club 220
End of Book Reflections 226
Thank you and What's Next! 228
The Raggedy Bush Girl 228

Prologue

It was a hot sultry afternoon in a field near Market Rasen. The field was close to a river and surrounded by willow trees, a sign that this was wetland. Our empty flatbed lorry left ominously deep tracks as we entered the field. Unlike the surrounding lush green fields this field was yellow and dotted with small oblong hay bales, it looked like hundreds of other hayfields that I had spent time working in. The air was so hot and heavy it made sweat ooze from every pore in my body and that was before we had started to load the bales.
In the distance huge blue-black clouds rose into the sky like distant mountains, a stark contrast to the cloudless sky above us with its oven-like sun beating down on the damp sheltered meadow. It was a natural sauna.

Dad pulled the engine stop and said, "right, best get started before that lot arrives" as he pointed to the distant storm clouds. At this point you may well be thinking, what on earth were we doing collecting hay in a small water meadow near Market Rasen, some fifty miles from where we lived. For me this was not unusual, it was the way dad did business.

Dad was a likeable person and made friends wherever he went. He loved to buy and sell horses. To do this effectively, he had to travel over a large area to find good horses. You needed a network of people around the country to inform you of suitable horses that were coming up for sale. Mum called these people his cronies. Dad was good at what he did, a good eye for a good horse and some very high-class clients. When things went well, dad made good profits on his horse sales, but as with all dealing businesses you win some, and you lose some. These modern reality television shows such as Wheeler Dealers for cars and Salvage Hunters for antiques make me laugh with their earnings figures. No mention is made of time or overheads in their profit and loss statements, without the television company covering these they would be bankrupt in weeks.

Dad was like these shows, he always justified his passion by stating how much he had bought a horse for, and how much more he had sold it for. There was no mention of other costs, such as time, traveling, collecting, delivering, keeping, shoeing, vets and more. He hardly ever took a holiday in his life and looking back now, dealing was probably his hobby and holiday from the farm and the riding school.

When I went to pick up the first bale, I found that the two sisal strings holding the bale together were not as tight as they should have been. Alarm bells immediately started to ring in my head. There were two reasons for loose strings, one was that the baler had not been set up correctly or that the hay had not finished drying when it was baled and judging by the weight of the bales it was the latter. If a farmer baled hay too early, he would ease the tension on the strings to allow the bales to breath and continue to dry after baling. This rarely worked, usually the damp hay heated up and turned the hay mouldy. If you were lucky and the bale did dry out the strings became even looser when the moisture was lost making it exceedingly difficult to pick up the bale without it breaking.

I was seventeen and a lot of water had passed under the bridge since I had left school at sixteen, nine months working as a bricky's labourer with my later to be brother-in-law had changed me from scrawny youth into a strong muscular young man. We were halfway through loading the bales, the black storm clouds were inching ever closer, dad glanced across at the horizon and commented that we should have brought a tarpaulin with us. My hackles rose, it was never his fault when things went wrong. I had been pressed ganged into helping him collect these bales and now I was getting fifty percent of the blame for forgetting to bring a tarpaulin. We were sweating our guts out loading bales of hay of which fifty percent would probably be inedible come winter due to mould, now to cap it off another chunk was going to be ruined by the approaching storm.

I dug my pitchfork into another bale and hefted it into the air. Just before it reached dad who was on the lorry stacking, the hay slipped out of the strings and came crashing down onto me. I had stripped to the waist and hay seeds stuck to my sweaty body making it itchy and horrible. It was the fourth bale that had done this and I was well pissed off!

Then dad just had to say it didn't he? "Watch what you're doing you stupid bugger that's another one pound you've cost me". I exploded, slammed my fork into the ground and told him I had had enough of trying to load these shitty, damp, badly baled bales. We proceeded to scream and threaten each other until we were both exhausted. A distant rumble of thunder brought us to our senses. Dad never admitted he was wrong but would often offer a conciliatory gesture to end an argument he knew he could not win. This time he said, "as soon as we make a bit of money, I'll buy a couple of nice horses and we will go hunting with the Quorn. That will make all this seem worthwhile ''.

The storms passed, the one in the sky and the other between dad and me. We finished loading the hay, roped it down, and trundled off home. Not long after, I gave up working with dad and riding. I got a job at British Gypsum in their Research Department and I left home soon after, glad to see the back of dad, the riding school, and horses.

Now at this point you may wonder, why I started this book about my life with horses, when I was nearly eighteen years old. It is because it was a watershed moment in my life. I was constantly having blazing arguments with my father that went on for thirty minutes or more. Nobody ever won these arguments, we just disengaged when exhausted, to fight another day. These arguments left me totally drained, both mentally and physically, I would slink off to find a secluded place, usually my bedroom, collapse sobbing with frustration and embarrassment. Frustration, because dad always took an opposing view to everything I proposed, embarrassed because of the cruel things I had said to him. He was my father and I loved him and looked up to him. The problem was that I was becoming a man and he was not allowing this to happen. Looking back with all those extra years of knowledge, I now understand that this goes on in many families with both sons and daughters.

I hardly rode for the next three years. When I did return it was on my own terms, I was ready, and keen to start riding again.

Glossary

Hunting Stock............ A white or cream cravat that wraps around the neck and is then knotted. Part of traditional hunting attire

Stock pin................... An ornate clasped pin usually made of gold that holds the stock in place.

Field......................... The mounted followers of a hunt or the runners and riders of a race.

A Brace...................... Hunting and shooting term for a pair of the same species

Martingale................ A device that stops a horse throwing its head dangerously high.

Hunt Button............. A mark of honour earned by giving long service to the hunt. Presented by the Master. The buttons are engraved with the Hunt motif. You have to buy the buttons which will set you back just shy of £100. These days you can often get your buttons if you just subscribe for a couple of years.

Covert.......................Pronounced cover. A small patch of wood used for holding game.

Jorrocks................... A famous fictional hunting character of the writer R. S. Surtees

Chapter one
Early Days

Although I was born in West Bridgford, I moved up to Bunny Hill when I was three, just before my fourth birthday. Mum and dad already owned a horse when they moved to the hill. I can only vaguely remember seeing the horse a couple of times before we moved to our new abode, as it was kept near Adbolton on the Ratcliffe on Trent side of West Bridgford, known as Trent Fields.

From the age of four I was regularly plonked on the horse and led around. Looking back now I was an extremely late starter compared with my siblings, children and grandchildren who have all been on the back of a pony or horse before they could walk. At the age of five I was taken hunting on the lead rein by my father. It was not a pleasant experience. Hunting in the 1950s still retained a strict class system. Titled people had a strict dress code. Ladies rode mainly side saddle, dressed in navy blue riding habits either wearing a bowler hat or top hat with their faces covered by a net veil. Gentleman wore silk top hats, red tailcoats, white breeches made from buckskin with a matching apron and long black boots topped with mahogany leather, and of course spurs. Nearly all of the men smoked and it was not uncommon to see a top hatted man galloping down the road smoking a cigarette in a cigarette holder. There was also the occasional outrageous avant-garde lady who wore breeches and boots and rode their horses astride but these ladies were hard core hunters who often hunted four or five days a week during the season.

Riding attire was always very formal as was everything in the nineteen fifties. Children wore thick jodhpurs with tight narrow legs and voluminous baggy wings at the thighs that looked like giant cauliflower ears, along with tweed hacking jacket, shirt, and tie. You rode either bare headed or wore a cloth cap. Girls were by the mid-fifties riding astride, if they had long hair, it was always plaited. Again, no head protection was worn, just a silk headscarf like you still see the Queen wearing, when she rides.
If it was really hot in the summer, you were allowed to ditch the jacket and maybe even the tie if you were riding at home. But you always had to wear your hot itchy bloody jodhpurs that were so coarse that they always rubbed you raw. If you look at First World War pictures of military officers or indeed right up to the beginning of the Second World War, both sides wore these stupid looking things as they denoted that you were from a cavalry background and the cavalry were mainly drawn from the aristocracy.
The only time you wore a riding cap was if you were hunting or show jumping. The riding cap was covered in black velvet for male and blue for female. They were made from shellac which gave you a small amount of protection but if they got wet or were old, they became very flexible and more like rubber. They had no means of attaching them to your head, you just crammed them on. Some people sewed an elastic band on them that fitted under your chin to help hold them on. This was extremely frowned upon and considered very sissy. I only mention hunting and show jumping because during the fifties these were the only equestrian sports unless you were mega wealthy and could afford to play polo. Hacking out

on the roads was always done bare headed or in a flat cap for men or a headscarf for girls and ladies.
The only thing for children to do with their ponies was hunt, hack, show or join the Pony Club.

The Pony Club was founded in 1929 and during the early fifties it was still very much rooted in pre-war mentality with all the branches being linked to fox hunts. Stuffy and stuck up is how I would describe them. The class system of the thirties was still very much alive and kicking and I hated my early days in the Quorn Pony Club.
Then in nineteen fifty-seven the modern thinking, sport, and action loving Prince Philip presented a perpetual challenge cup to the Pony Club. It was for team mounted games. All the branches in the UK, over three hundred of them, were invited to send a team to compete. First area, then regional knockout competitions. The final six teams would then compete at the Horse of the Year Show which in those days was held at Wembley Pool in north London.
This was the catalyst that started the craze of gymkhanas, that would dominate the summer activities of junior riders for many years. It would also bring in a new class of rider. By the end of the fifties the Country was starting to recover economically from the Second World War and a working middle class was developing with money to spend on leisure.
Children from ordinary backgrounds started to ride and compete, and like so many other things of that period, swept away all the stuffy old-fashioned conventions. The swinging Sixties had arrived!
My life changed from loathing riding to loving it. Showing declined, and gymkhana games along with show jumping boomed. There was a competition every weekend during the summer and it was a family day out.

I mention my first day's hunting in the next chapter which did not go well at all and started my dislike of horses and all that went with them. Over the next few years my parents unwittingly went out of their way to reinforce my view that horse riding was an unpleasant painful pastime and should be avoided at all costs.

My parents to their defence were well meaning, as all parents are, and it was beyond their comprehension that I did not want to ride. When I tried to tell them, mum would say, "don't be silly, riding horses is lovely, you will have lots of fun."
Dad's response was, "get on that bloody pony and do as you are bloody well told!" so I suffered.

The next thing they came up with to humiliate me with was lead rein pony showing. How could anyone in their right mind could think that a boy would want to do this is beyond me. To this day I cannot bear to look at a showing class.

Dad's knowledge of horses soon became well known and through his work in engineering, he came into contact with some wealthy people that kept horses as a hobby. One of these families was keen on showing ponies and somehow, I got put forward as a lead-rein rider. To become a lead-rein rider, I discovered that you had to be scrubbed clean in the bath and then I was dressed in smart riding clothes that I was told to keep spotlessly clean under pain of death. The smart riding clothes included a thick black jacket, usually worn for hunting in the depths of winter; however, for showing you had to wear it mid-summer in 80 degrees Fahrenheit. I also had to wear a white shirt and a tie. The tie was constantly retightened to the point where I could not breathe, and it made my neck sore. The final insult was I had to wear a rose in my buttonhole.

Even when I was on the pony, I was still being brushed to remove specks of dust from my clothing and having my shoes re-polished for the tenth time. However, I think the most painful and degrading thing was people taking out their handkerchief, spitting on it and then scrubbing my mouth or nose and saying, "there you are dear, just making you look spic and span." Finally, we got to enter the ring along with twenty or more other poor souls, we were led or should I say dragged around the arena. A man in a suit and bowler hat was accompanied by an overdressed woman, who sported a large hat, bedecked with feathers that was enough to frighten even the quietest of ponies, let alone put the fear of God into the poor riders. After much pointing and debating from the judges, one by one we were called into the centre of the ring to line up. We were then inspected, and both the riders and ponies were poked and prodded as we came under intense scrutiny. We then had to do a show one by one, which involved being dragged around the arena in various directions and at various speeds. Finally, after more debate they reshuffled the line and slowly gave out the prizes. I always seemed to be at the wrong end of the line to get a nice red, blue, or yellow rosette, I always got a pale pink one, that said commended or sometimes even highly commended. The entire process felt like it had taken half of my short lifetime. As soon as I got out of the arena, I was dragged off the pony and discarded whilst the adults debated how blind and biased the judges were, and was not the winner somehow related to one of the judges?

Unfortunately, although I never won anything for the owners, the next year I was promoted to the first ridden which meant I was out there on my own. Nobody explained why I had to do the set of walk, trot, and canter movements and as I never saw the pony except on show days, I never got the opportunity to practice them. Luckily, I was never asked to go first so I just copied what the others did. I hated it and sulked all through the ordeal and slouched when sitting in line but still they wanted me to ride the next week.

Thankfully, the new craze sweeping the horse-show world would save me from further ordeals in the show ring. The craze was Gymkhana games. It attracted enormous numbers and the games ran quickly with many separate age groups. They were extremely exciting to watch and as showing was less exciting than watching paint dry, it soon started to push showing off the schedule of many smaller local shows. However, showing still continues to this day at the large agricultural shows. Finally, the best thing about gymkhana games was that it made lots of money for the organisers, and for kids who were good at them, as each class had generous prize money down to fourth place.

Suddenly, there was a quantum leap from the sedate showing classes dominated by wealthy families to these brash working-class games competitions. The other tremendous change was that it was not primarily private owners competing, the majority of the owners were riding school proprietors or owners of horse dealing yards. These people were also making good money out of hiring ponies to the competitors taking part in the new craze! The riding school owners would bring lorry loads of games ponies to the shows along with their riders who were generally stuffed into an overcrowded cab and the Luton part of the lorry that protruded over the top of the cab. What went on in those Luton's cannot be written in this book, except to say a lot of teenagers gained their first sexual experiences in a horsebox either going to or returning from a gymkhana.

The other equestrian sport that was becoming exceedingly popular was show jumping. So, by the early sixties the traditional showing classes were fading away and the new format for shows was gymkhana games and show jumping classes. During the late fifties and early sixties, most show jumping competitions were B.S.J.A affiliated but, like games, as its popularity grew, cheaper unaffiliated club-based competitions started to spring up which undermined the viability of small local shows to put on top class show jumping events or games competitions giving large prize money. We are starting to see the same thing happening today with the latest "In" sports of dressage and eventing. During the late fifties and early sixties, most of the villages would hold a gymkhana every year, often combined with a fete or a vegetable show. Many of these started to die out as the sixties progressed and were replaced by the riding schools running their own shows. Eventually, riding clubs were formed and they ran shows for people in a specific area. However, with the shows becoming more prolific, the class numbers dwindled, clubs stopped giving prize money for games in order to reduce the entry fees, and only gave rosettes. This well-meaning decision brought about the end to the heyday of gymkhana games because, without the prize money to fund the keeping of ponies, both the top riders and the riding schools lost interest and started to look for other avenues to make money from their horses.

.
I had two gymkhana ponies, but as we were still struggling financially from expanding the business, my ponies were cheap, and both came with a quirk. Omo was my first. He was about 13.2hh and a flea bitten grey and his quirk was that you couldn't catch the little bastard. Some days you could walk up to him and catch him no bother at all but on important days, like show days, he would trot around you in a circle about 10 yards away just taunting you. Other times he would just gallop off as soon as you entered the field and you just knew that you didn't have a cat-in-hells chance of catching him that day. This meant my planned weekend of games competition never happened on a fairly regular basis. We tried hobbling his front legs (a leather version of the old convicts' leg irons that restricts the movement of the front legs). This failed spectacularly after a week or so, when he learnt to bound like a kangaroo and travel at a similar speed as a gallop. Our next trick was to tie a long rope around his neck and attach a large car tyre to the other end. He could drag the tyre around grazing, but I could sneak up and grab the tyre before he realised that I was close enough to catch him. Sadly, it didn't take long for him to work this out as well and I discovered that he could gallop just as fast dragging a tyre behind him as without one. In fact, it didn't even make any difference with me attached to the tyre! I would often return cut and bruised after being dragged on my belly through nettles and thistles like an Indiana Jones film. On the upside, he was a good games pony and won a lot of prizes if you could actually manage to get him to the event. Eventually, I would catch him midweek and then tether him in the orchard until the weekend.

My next pony was the best games pony I ever had, but again she had some flaws as do most products purchased from the bargain basement. Her name was Pigeon and she was a black mare, slightly larger than Omo. She tended to rear and sometimes to go completely over backwards. She was also hopeless when she was in season as she would refuse to start and either rear or plant herself and urinate. Despite her faults, she was brilliant on her day and was picked for the Quorn Hunt Pony Club Prince Philip Cup Team. The PPC, as it was known, is still a very prestigious national games competition for branches of the Pony Club that culminates in a final at the Horse of the Year Show. The team successfully progressed through the area competition, but we were beaten by the Atherstone Pony Club in the regional finals. There was some consolation in that the Atherstone won the cup at the Horse of the Year Show that year.

I had one other problem with Pigeon. Because she was much bigger than most games ponies, I struggled to vault on her. I have never excelled at vaulting onto a horse, unlike my two younger brothers who were very adept at all the differing types of vault. In the games that you had to dismount to pick something up and then vault back on at the gallop, my success rate was about fifty percent. If I missed the vault, I would be pulled over flat on my face at the gallop. Although I was now about eleven years old and enjoying the camaraderie of the games circuit, there was not a lot going on to change my view, that horses and riding was something to avoid if at all possible.

In my early days of riding, I had one other pony that I was allowed to call my own and his name was Robin. He was a very pretty 12.1hh bright bay gelding similar to the pony that my granddaughter had a couple of years ago. Robin was very sharp and prone to whipping around. One day when he whipped around, I was ejected very violently, my foot got hung-up in the stirrup. This panicked Robin and he shot off at the gallop with me being dragged along bouncing around his hind legs. Luckily, he didn't kick me as so often happens in these situations, but I was pretty battered and very shaken. This experience really convinced me that there was nothing to like about horses or riding and it was only strong words and threats from my father that got me back in the saddle. Robin introduced me to another flaw that horses and ponies have and that was their ability to injure themselves. I was riding in our home field when Robin did a buck and a skit sideways. The next moment a fountain of blood was spurting out of his lower front leg. It made me go very weak and wobbly, but I knew I had to get him back to the yard as quick as possible. Dad quickly stemmed the fountain of blood by making a pad of cotton, out of an old bed sheet, but the cut was very deep so reluctantly the vet was called to stitch up the wound. I of course got the blame and a strong lecture about how expensive it was to have a vet come out to stitch a horse, I would be expected to do extra jobs to help cover some of the cost.

Chapter Two
Pony Club Days

I joined the Quorn Hunt Pony Club when I was six, not because I wanted to but because Mum and Dad thought it was the thing to do, now that we were land owning horse owners. As with most early riding activities, I was not keen. I was taken to random fields around the county and balled at by junior army officers or people who thought they were sergeant majors. All we ever did was trot circles whilst someone in the centre bawled sit up straight, heels down, keep your chin up, put your lower leg back. It didn't matter who was instructing, they all shouted and said the same thing. The instructors never explained anything, they just shouted orders. I think those days were the divining moments that were to form my style of teaching riding in later years. If instructors had explained the reason why we had to change the way we rode, I could have accepted their instructions more readily. The problem was nobody's fault, as everything to do with riding was so intricately linked to the army and in the army, you gave and obeyed orders without question. When the British Horse Society was formed in 1947, their Manual of Horsemanship was virtually a carbon copy of the military cavalry handbook and throughout the fifties and early sixties cavalry officers dominated teaching, judging, and sitting on equestrian committees. It was the same within the hunting world where Masters of Foxhounds often carried a military title. Thankfully, things are much more enlightened these days.

My pony club days of rallies in fields moved on to training for the Prince Philip Cup Team. This took place in Gaddesby, early on Sunday afternoons, and was run by a lovely kind lady who never balled or shouted at us. There were only ever about six of us and it was great fun practising bending and jumping off our ponies at the canter. The downside of these days was that towards the end of the practice sessions, the lady's husband would return from the pub. It was obvious that their marriage was not in a happy place. It was very clear by his manner that he had always had a lot to drink and he had a very florid complexion. He would stagger into the field and start screaming and shouting at our instructor, using the vilest and most degrading swear words, wanting to know as to why she was wasting her time with stupid children and not at home cooking his Sunday lunch. Their screaming matches could go on for thirty minutes or more and very often heralded the end of our games practice. It seems unbelievable that events such as this could happen in front of children these days but happenings such as these were commonplace in the fifties and early sixties. I do not know whether it was the war or our society still clinging onto Victorian values, but women were still very much second-class citizens and were expected, like children, to be seen but not heard. Looking back, I can see that there was a real battle going on. Men wanted things to go back to how they were before the war, whereas women had been empowered during the war, proving that they could do the jobs that had been considered only suitable for men and perform them equally as well.

Each Pony Club had a DC (District Commissioner) at its head. The title itself conjures up visions of colonial Africa. How on earth they came up with a title like that, for a national children's riding organisation I cannot comprehend. However, it does give you another insight into the people who were running equestrianism in the fifties and sixties. The Quorn Pony Club had Mrs Wheldon as their DC. She was a short grey-haired lady, always dressed in a tweed suit. She would appear without warning at rallies, putting the fear of God into both the instructors and the riders alike. All the children attending the rally would be formed into lines for inspection. Then, with hands clasped behind her back, she would start her inspection, closely followed two steps behind by the relevant troop instructor. All very military! Every unpolished shoe, unbuttoned shirt or not straight tie was pointed out harshly, making the recipient feel totally inadequate. Your nervousness increased as she made her way relentlessly down the line towards you. I cannot understand why anyone joined the Pony Club of their own free will and I think most of us were put there by our parents, who saw it as a social must, a bit like being sent to a good boarding school.

The saving grace to all this purgatory was pony club camp. I attended my first camp when I was eleven. The Quorn pony club camp was always held at Stapleford Park, the family home of Lord Gretton. Our accommodation was in large marquees, one for the boys and two for the girls, plus several bell tents for the members in their later teens.

For Mum and Dad, sending me to camp was a big strain on the family budget. Not only was there the cost of attending, but there was a huge list of obligatory items that had to be taken, including a folding camp bed, a torch, a wash bag and so on, the list stretched to two pages. There was a similar list for your pony too! One mandatory item on the pony list was that the pony must be freshly shod. As Dad did all his own shoeing in those days, it was another unwelcome job for not only Dad but for me as well, as I had to turn the handle that powered the fan, that made the coke fire into a furnace, for making the horseshoes.

Lord Gretton not only gave us the use of his estate for the week but also the use of his magnificent stable yard. There were endless loose boxes and standings for our ponies, all set around a square gravelled courtyard that was accessed through a grand gateway. The horse accommodation was as grand as everything else on the estate. The loose boxes were massive! The lower part of the box was varnished mahogany with the upper part being cast iron railings surmounted with brass globes. The floors were just as grand, made from special blue bricks that had a chequered non-slip surface. There were also matching blue-brick gullies to drain away the urine.

The standings were of matching style but only had three sides. The open end was onto the main internal passageway that ran around the whole complex. Standings have all but died out in the horsey nanny state environment that we find ourselves living in today, but they were exceptionally efficient. The horse is tied to the front of the standing in a good leather head-collar, a long rope that passes through a ring about four feet from the ground, above the built-in manger. The rope is attached to a special round wooden ball with a hole in it for the rope to pass through, and secured with a quick-release knot. The wood ball was often referred to as a noggin and they were often quite ornate. This allowed the horse some movement including lying down. The noggin kept a light tension on the rope so that the horse could not get tangled up. The other great advantage of standings was that all the droppings were in one place at the back of the box, right on the edge of the service passageway, which made mucking out very quick and easy. The standings also had a slight slope from front to back so that any urine drained into the gully that ran along the back keeping the straw dry and saving waste. Most of the children at camp schemed to get a big loose box but I always volunteered to have a standing as we had them at home, and I knew how much quicker they were to muck-out.

The tack room was also beautiful, boarded completely in varnished mahogany, including the ceiling. The bridle and saddle racks were also very decorative. There was a large table in the centre of the room for tack cleaning and a long mahogany saddle horse. It was what every serious horse owner dreamt of having.

The downside of these beautiful stables was that they had to be kept in immaculate condition during our stay, so there was endless sweeping up and polishing of the brassware. We had two inspections per day, one after morning stables before riding and another after evening stables. Nobody was allowed to go for their evening meal until everything had passed inspection. The large gravel yard in the centre of the stable courtyard also had to be raked every day and then we all lined up shoulder to shoulder, and handpicked every bit of hay and straw up, right down to pieces the size of chaff that the rakes had missed.

Our days were filled with mucking out and skipping out, tack cleaning, grooming, and riding our ponies, plus the manicuring of the stable yard. None of this really appealed to me but it was a necessary evil that I had to suffer to get to the fun bit. After our evening meal, we were left to our own devices. We explored the woods and the rest of the estate, raided tents, and tried to ward off raids from other tents. The latter of these activities went on well into the early hours. I became a bit of a legend, making my way to other tents avoiding the sweeping torch beams of our elders, who patrolled late into the night, trying to keep us in order. I soon discovered, whilst hiding in bushes to avoid the adult patrols, that it was not only the children that were up to mischief! Patrolling the grounds at night was a good excuse for meeting up with a secret lover. By my second year at camp, I had worked out that most of the adults in charge of us were having a secret affair with another member of staff. Many of the junior staff were in their late teens or early twenties and often aided some of our mischief, such as providing transportation so that we could raid the Belvoir pony club camp that was being held a few miles up the road at the Garthorpe racecourse. This of course brought about retaliatory attacks from the Belvoir camp. It was all good, "Swallows and Amazons", style fifties fun and I loved it!

It was at camp that I started to find something else that I liked about riding other than Gymkhana games. Towards the end of each camp week, we would go out and gallop around the estate as a group jumping cross country fences. As we got older, hedges got added into the rides as well, I found I loved jumping hedges. When I progressed into my teens, I also noticed that the ratio of girls to boys riding was massively in the girl's favour but for a male teenager starting to take an interest in the opposite sex, riding was starting to have some very positive advantages!

My last year at camp was when I was fourteen. My previous three years of adventurous behaviour had not gone unnoticed and my parents were contacted by the powers that be, to inform them that I would not be allowed to go to camp, unless I mended my ways. After strong words from my parents and the fact that I loved my time at camp, I agreed to mend my ways. As with a lot of things in my life, once I commit to a project I do it with almost manic dedication. In this case I changed so much, that I was awarded the camp belt for best boy during the camp. It was a very prestigious prize, a bit like the belts you win in boxing, and showed me that if I channelled my energy, I could achieve things that I had always thought were beyond me. Dad was always trying to motivate me by telling me how useless I was, and I had started to believe that I was truly totally useless and would never achieve anything. Looking back, I now see that this was the catalyst that made me change and it triggered a remarkable improvement in my schoolwork shortly afterwards.

Winning the belt was not easy and it was never my goal, I just wanted to prove to the powers that be, that I would not let them down. An example of this was that after a lecture on 'Haute turnout of horse and rider' I polished my pony's clenches twice every day before inspection with Brasso. Now that was.
 dedication!

That year I was fourteen and found that I had become a senior member of the camp and was allocated one of the prized bell tents which I shared with Kenneth Clawson, who would later become the senior show jumping coach for British Eventing. I was always trying to get him to come out at night to meet up with some of the girls, but he always refused. I just thought that he was being a goody-goody. However, many years later, after the legalisation of homosexuality, all became clear. In the early sixties, it was something I had never heard of and I now realise how blissfully naïve I was on certain matters.

Although I didn't know it then, this was to be my last camp. Winning the belt had given me status and a lot more friends. I left camp that year excited by the prospect of returning next year to defend my belt. As was the norm after camp, I promptly fell asleep in the horse box on the way home and slept all that day and night after unloading my pony, catching up on six days of very little sleep. I always smile when parents tell me that their children have slept all day on returning from Pony Club Camp but refrain from explaining why they are so exhausted.

I was all booked in for camp the next year, but then Dad was asked by a friend if he could do some welding for him at Pedigree Pet foods in Melton Mowbray. Dad's friend had secured a contract to erect a new steel structure in the plant during the summer shutdown period. What started out as a two-day job expanded to six weeks. It was the management who were so impressed with the quality of the work that they kept asking my father's friend if he could do extra projects. Unfortunately, he didn't have the staff available for the extended period and he also didn't want to upset his new and very large customer. The money was excellent, and Dad was put in charge of finding enough people to form a team to carry out the new jobs. Although I had just turned fifteen, I suddenly became a sixteen-year-old and a new apprentice for the duration of the summer holidays. Working at Pet Foods was like entering a new world. It was a Dutch company and was part of the Mars Group. I had been in several factories before but never anything like this.

For the first two weeks during the shutdown period, we worked as outside contractors but when production restarted, we became temporary staff with all the staff benefits, such as the use of the staff canteen, which was out of this world. Something that was really strange and that I had never heard of in England at that time was that workers and management sat down together and even shared tables together for their meals. It was in this canteen that I tried a food that I had never heard of but seemed to be very popular: it was called yogurt! When I tasted it, I thought it had gone off, so I tried another, which tasted just the same. It was not until ten years later that I discovered that all-natural yogurt actually tasted like that. Other innovative things were changing rooms, fresh overalls every day and individual hot showers. If you got very dirty you could even have a shower and fresh overalls at any time during the day. Becoming official did have its problems and I had to take a year off my date of birth when signing a whole load of forms to become temporary staff. I had a wonderful time working all my summer holidays there and saved up enough money to buy a motorbike later in the year.

This was the reason I missed my last Pony Club Camp, but I came up with a crazy idea to meet up with my old camp mates. On the Friday night of the camp, I came home from work and had an early tea. I then set out on my old bike to cycle over to Stapleford Park. My bike had no gears as they had broken the previous year. I had no puncture repair kit or repair tools as this was a last-minute decision. I had no idea how far it was but estimated that it would take about one and a half hours. What I had seriously underestimated was the number of hills and long steady upward gradients that sapped the energy out of you, especially on an old one geared bike. I set off at 6pm and didn't arrive until nearly nine. Being mid-summer, it was still light. I hid my bike and made my way towards the campsite down the back-lane but to my surprise there was security on the gate. I quickly beat a hasty retreat and went into the woods and made my way to the campsite that way. Secreted at the edge of the wood, I studied the campsite, but it seemed devoid of life except for two adults patrolling around the tents. I waited for about thirty minutes but there was still no sign of life, except for the two adults. The campers were obviously off doing organised activities. It was then that I noticed the light starting to fade. It was at that moment I realised that I had no lights on my bike, so I decided to abandon my fruitless adventure and headed for home.

It was dark by the time I reached Melton Mowbray. I had no problems in Melton as the road was fairly well lit right through to the far side of Asfordby. By the time I got that far it was pitch black. I could see alright as I was used to roaming the woods at night and using my peripheral vision to see where I was going. But having no lights, I had to constantly look over my shoulders for cars. Every time I saw car headlights approaching, I would jump off my bike and wheel it onto the grass verge. I was particularly worried about the police, as in those days you got regularly fined for riding a bike without lights. My progress home was considerably slower than going and my legs were exhausted. I ground to a wobbly halt about a quarter of the way up Saxelbye hill. I dismounted and started to push my bike, but my legs had completely gone. I made it to halfway up but could go no further. I knew I had to rest, so I hid my bike under the hedge and climbed over a gate into a cornfield. I walked about ten yards into the field and then lay down and fell fast asleep almost instantly. Some hours later, I woke up much revived and restarted my journey. It must have been the early hours of the morning by then and there was no traffic on the roads, so I made better time and once I reached Saxelbye crossroads, there were some long downhill stretches that helped as well. I reached home a little after dawn and slipped quietly into the house and my bed. I told nobody about my futile journey, and nobody asked what I had been up to that night. Except for a couple of close friends, I have never told anyone about my crazy bike ride, until writing this book. It was also the end of my association with the Quorn Pony Club.

During the latter years of my Pony Club days, things were not good within the Quorn Pony Club. Most of the committee members lived in Quorn Friday Country which lies between Melton and Leicester and stretches out to Twyford. Consequently, most rallies were centred in this area. People living in the north of the area, around Nottingham and Ashby, felt they were being side-lined and campaigned for more rallies in their area. The committee were set in their ways, which was par for the course in those days and this eventually led to the formation of a new Pony Club called the South Trent. Things got very bitter running up to the split, with both sides canvassing parents and children to join one side or the other. I was torn between the two but decided to stay with the Quorn. My two brothers also stayed with the Quorn, as did my daughter in later years.

By a twist of fate, I became the trainer of the South Trent show jumping team in the nineties, which won the pony club national show jumping championship at Hickstead. Since then, I have had a long and happy relationship with the South Trent. Their DC was an old pupil of my father's and much more enlightened than the DC's of old. Life moves on and changes. My granddaughter Katherine became a member of the South Trent Pony Club.

Chapter Three
Show Jumping

In my second year at Rushcliffe Grammar School, I got an unpaid regular job show jumping in junior pony classes. I am not sure how it came about but it was probably a friend of a friend of my dad's. The man's name was Stan Mellor and he was the father of the then famous champion steeplechase jockey also called Stan Mellor. Before becoming a jump-jockey, Stan was a phenomenally successful junior show jumper, competing at major venues such as White City, Harringay arena and Wembley Pool. His father lived and breathed show jumping and wanted to return to the glory days that he had had with his son. He lived near Quorn and had a small farm where he kept his horses. The ponies that I was jumping were all 14.2hh and he had quite a few of them. Stan was a dealer, so my string of show jumpers changed constantly. Sometimes I had ponies that had done some jumping but often they were totally green with no jumping experience.

When I started, I was told we were going to be aiming for Wembley and other top class shows but that never happened! Every time one of my ponies started to do well, it was sold on and new ponies appeared for me to train on. This was exactly what had been happening at home with dad, but the enormous difference was that when I was jumping for Stan, I didn't have to look after the ponies, I just had to turn up and jump them. However, I didn't have it as easy as I thought it was going to be, you could say that I served my apprenticeship with Stan Mellor senior. Over the weekend, we would often attend two shows in one day. Stan was very thorough and planned his weekends to the minute. He would contact all the show secretaries and find out what time the 14.2 class was due to start and very often he would be able to find a class in the morning and then another class at a different show in the afternoon. We travelled with all the ponies tacked up and ready to go, often travelling several hours between shows. I sometimes had four or even six ponies to jump at two different shows, so I was jumping at least twelve rounds per day and then there were the jump off rounds as well!

More often than not, shows also had two or more suitable classes that I could jump the ponies in, so I was doing an enormous number of show jumping rounds every week. I did manage to keep one pony long enough to compete at the larger shows, such as the Moorgreen and Derby County shows. These larger BSJA shows were so well-run and the courses were a joy to jump.

The world of show jumping in those days was a rough tough world with little regard for the welfare of the horse or rider. Although many will be shocked by what I am about to write, everything I mention was commonplace in the sixties. Firstly, it was the norm to rap a horse both at home, training and just before you went into the ring. This was done very openly and shows would provide a rapping pole in the collecting ring for everyone to use. As the horse in front of you jumped their round, two people would hold the pole usually between three and four feet off the ground. You would then jump your horse over the pole. As they jumped it, the pole holders would jerk the pole up higher, so it hit the front legs. You then repeated the exercise but this time it was the hind legs that were rapped and then it was off into the ring to jump your round. Safe rapping took great skill from the pole holders but newcomers to the game often caused the horse and rider to fall when they miss-timed lifting the pole. When schooling at home, it was often a metal scaffolding pole. Another fabled training device was a pole with hedgehog skins nailed to it so that it pricked the horses legs if they brushed the pole. I say fabled because I heard a lot about them but never actually saw one personally.

One day before a big competition, I was being schooled over a solid cross-country style fence. After jumping it a couple of times, Stan nailed some steel fencing wire to the railway sleeper stands six inches above the top pole. He then told me to jump it! Both myself and the horse had a crashing fall. Stan rushed over and picked me up saying, "Well that's a b**ger, didn't think it would fetch you both down. Any road it'll make him pick his feet up tomorrow." Then as an afterthought said, "Not hurt yourself, have you? Big day tomorrow."

Rather than making it pick its legs up; the pony showed a distinct reluctance to jump in the big competition the next day. The pony did jump a clear-round, but he hesitated before each fence and I had to kick him every inch of the way. I would say that the training session, had a profound negative effect on the confidence of both the horse and rider. Shortly after this incident, I was schooling a hot wayward mount, when my rein broke on landing. It had never happened to me before and for a brief moment, that at the time seemed to be an eternity, I could not understand what was happening. I was out of control and galloping extremely fast, we narrowly missed several large trees, and I was beginning to think my time was up! It was only a couple of seconds, but it seemed to be a lifetime before I worked out that one of my reins had snapped close to where it attached to the bit. Pulling on the other rein was pulling the bit-ring into the pony's mouth and causing it to panic, so I forced myself to stop pulling with my good rein and lean forward in order to grab the bit ring on the broken side. After a couple of attempts I managed to grab the bit ring and pull it through the mouth and then get a balanced pull. All these things along with me lying up the neck caused the pony to check briefly but long enough for me to bail out and use my rein like a lunge line to bring him under control. Thankfully, both of us were unscathed but after the recent events some of the gloss was starting to fade on this job!

Not long after these events, I started my fourth year at Rushcliffe School and the two years course work that led up to the GCSE exams. I just didn't have the time to carry on show jumping with Stan and do my course work. It was a wonderful experience and I wouldn't have missed it for the world. Although I had a few scary moments, we had some great times together and I learnt a lot about show jumping, I would not have missed it for the world. We parted on good terms, but as my mother was always telling me, schoolwork must come first. I continued to show jump until I started to Point-to-Point in the 1970s. In fact, my first point-to-pointer was originally my show jumper but that is another story.

Chapter Four
Hunting

Hunting has been a big part of my life from an early age, until I was 66. Sixty-one years, where did they go to! Over those sixty-one years I have seen many changes. The worst without doubt was the change in law banning hunting with dogs. The fact that most of the foxhound packs still survive to this day is a testament to its popularity, both with the farmers and the followers. As I write this section of the book it is the wettest winter in memory, much of my local area has been flooded over and over again since autumn. Yet hunting has continued with few cancellations. I was Field Master of three hunts during my time hunting. First, was the Trent Valley Drag Hounds, then the Atherstone Hunt, and finally the South Notts Hunt. It was through those roles that I met many farmers and landowners clearing country, (gaining permission for the hunt to go across their land). The warmth and hospitality that I received from many of them was amazing, and those years were some of the happiest years of my life. They were also some of the most stressful. Dealing with the farmers and walking their land brought me great joy. Dealing with Hunt committees and managing hunt days brought me great stress, but more of that later.

Early Days

My early years hunting did not really induce me to like the sport at all. If you have read my book "Boy Gone Feral on Bunny Hill" I apologise for repeating my early hunting experiences but for this book to work it is a necessary evil.

The first time that I went hunting was in the autumn of 1956, it was a Saturday, I was five and a half years old. My riding experience amounted to occasionally being led around on the back of, Mum and Dad's horse and being told to stand up and sit-down.

The Quorn Hunt were meeting at Costock Manor and dad had acquired a pony to take me on the lead rein. He had also managed to get a riding cap, jodhpurs, and tweed jacket. I think that they were all borrowed, as we had no money to spare for such luxuries at that period of my life, I think my cap (the fee you paid to the hunt) was waived, as dad had become friends with a local farmer who hunted regularly, and owned land that the hunt would cross on that particular day.

The meet was overwhelming. We were squashed into a corner by huge horses ridden by men in top hats and scarlet tailcoats. The ladies were riding on side-saddles, again wearing top hats or bowler hats and a strange net veil over their faces, which I found very frightening. Added to this, they all spoke very loudly and did not sound like the people that I had known in my short life. Drinks on silver trays, were being handed around by smartly dressed waiters but none came anywhere near our corner. I got the distinct feeling that I was not welcome: the riders looked down their noses at me as if they had nearly stepped on a freshly steaming dog turd. Their huge unruly horses backed into us wedging us ever tighter into our little corner. They would then turn around and shout, "Get that bloody pony out of my way, you have no bloody business being here!"

At last, the hounds moved off and we were able to escape from our corner. Dad dragged me along at the trot at the back of the hunt, bouncing me around all over the place, as it made its way along the road towards the next village of East Leake, before turning right towards the back of Bunny Hill. It was at this point that my legs started to go wobbly and I asked if we could go home now! This caused my dad to explode, shouting that I was an ungrateful little brat, and did I not realise all the trouble that he had gone to, for me to have this incredibly special day. I thought, but didn't dare say, that I had not actually asked to go hunting or in fact if I even wanted to ride a pony. By the time we got to Bunny Hill I was in tears, but things suddenly got a lot worse, we left the bridleway and set out over some grass fields and the horses in front started to jump the hedges. We managed to find gateways that kept us moving in the right direction, but then there were no more gateways. I now realise that we had come to a boundary hedge, luckily the hedge had been obliterated by the time we got there. This left a convenient hole for us to go through. Unfortunately, the ditch on the other side of the hedge, was far more resilient. To a small child with little to no riding experience, the ditch might as well have been the Grand Canyon, there were also the remnants of the hedge to contend with. I just bawled my eyes out saying, "I can't do it, I will fall off." Dad just shouted at me for being such a wimp and making him look a fool. Eventually, we jumped the fence, I fell off in the mud and got scratched all over by the thorns. I vowed never to go hunting again!

Over the next few years my riding improved and I started to go cub hunting whenever the hounds met, close by. In those days, the Quorn hunted at Bunny, Bradmore, Keyworth and Plumtree, all within safe hacking distance from our stables. At that time, a lot of sugar beet was grown in this area, known as the Moors. The large sugar beet leaves made it a favourite place for foxes to layup in. It was not unknown for ten or more foxes to be found in just one field, keeping the hounds very busy. Although all the spit and polish the day before was a real fag, as was getting up at the crack of dawn, I did find that watching the sun rise at the dawn of the day was something quite special. The air was fresh and still, allowing the music of the hounds to echo off the hills. I cannot think of anything better than waiting at the side of a covert in utter silence, and then hear a lone hound speak to be followed by another and another as they find the scent of a fox. It slowly builds until it is like a hundred peeling church bells sending shivers down your spine.

When it came to Dad teaching me to ride, Dad passionately believed in leading by example, Dad's only words were always "follow me". Unfortunately, neither me nor my mount of that moment had extraordinarily little desire to follow him as he powered his large horse over a huge hedge. Sadly, it was always me that got the bollocking for not following him, never my mount.

I think I was about ten when I had a pony named Omo, and one day Dad announced that he was taking me cub hunting with the Quorn Hunt at a place called Ragdale. We were cub hunting because we couldn't afford to hunt in the proper hunting season, and in those days, children could go cubbing for free and it was only a minimal cap (fee) for adults. This was an excellent way for Dad to showcase horses that he wanted to sell. I had a sneaking suspicion that he wanted to showcase Omo in the hope that someone would want to buy him. Although I had many ponies during my early life, I only mention three because these stayed with me long enough to remember them and that was only because they had quirks and were difficult to sell.

All went well to start with. We worked late into the evening preparing our steeds and then got up in the early hours to do more preparation. Whenever we went hunting, Dad was at his worst. Nothing was ever right, and he would rant and rave at everyone and everything including the dog. My mother and Dawn my sister, dreaded hunting days. This particular meet was at Ragdale Hall which is ten miles from Bunny and a place I had never been to or heard of, but I'm sure there was an ulterior motive on Dad's behalf for the choice of that particular meet. It must have been late in the cubbing season because after about an hour or so of standing around several coverts and tapping our saddle flaps with our whips, the hounds were allowed to go away and hunt a fox which caused great excitement from everyone and we all set off at a mad gallop. Dad turned to me and said, "Push your hat down hard and follow me." This was an order rather than fatherly advice.

At first it was genuine fun, we galloped across several grass fields and I managed to jump a broken post and rail fence. Dad turned several times and shouted at me to keep up and then we came to a hedge! Dad kicked-on hard and sailed over it, never to be seen again that morning, Omo stopped and slid into the hedge causing both of us to come out of it scratched and bleeding. I made several attempts to get him to jump it, but he was having none of it and I was soon exhausted trying to force him to jump. Thankfully, I was not alone and a group of us tried in vain to find a non-jumping way to follow the hounds but to no avail. It was then that people started to notice me and that I didn't appear to be accompanied by anyone. Who was looking after me?, they asked. I explained my predicament and enquired if they knew where we were. Apparently, we had run towards

Leicester and were close to a village called Thrussington, another village I had never heard of! A kindly lady took pity on me, she suggested that I accompany her back to where the hounds had met earlier that morning. Along the way she asked my name and where I lived. It was very worrying when she told me that she had never heard of a place called Bunny Hill. When we arrived back at the meet field, there was not a sight or sound of the hunt. The lady apologised, that she could not stay with me, but she was sure that my father would come back to find me. I was not so sure so asked for directions home. As she did not know where Bunny Hill was, she started to ask about other villages that I had heard of. After saying the names of many villages, she mentioned Wymeswold, which I was sure we had passed through on our way to the meet. She gave me directions to Wymeswold, and suggested that when I got there, I asked my way again.

I started the greatest adventure I had ever had in my short lifetime. I set off from near Ragdale Hall, I turned left when I got to a road and this took me to the Fosse Way Road crossroads at the Durham Ox Pub. Thankfully the Fosse Road was only a single carriageway road in those days and was not the busy high-speed dual carriageway that it is today. I had been told to cross the Fosse and stay on the lane which the lady thought would take me to Wymeswold. A short time, after passing the Durham Ox, I came across a signpost that had half fallen over into a ditch, it was hard to read, but I was fairly sure it said 'Wymeswold'.

The lane was very narrow and there was grass growing up the middle of the road. The lane twisted and turned constantly. The sun had come out and it became stifling hot due to the high overgrown hedgerows and I suddenly felt very thirsty in my thick jodhpurs, tweed jacket and tie. There seemed no sign of Wymeswold and I started to wonder if I had misread the sign. As I rounded a bend, I came across two people standing in a gateway, they were a man and a woman that were dressed very strangely. They both wore wide-brimmed straw hats similar to those worn by beekeepers and strange clothes that looked like they came from another century. I was going to ask them if I was on the right road for Wymeswold but lost my nerve as their strange dress scared me to death. I murmured good day to them, but they just stared silently at me, so I kicked Omo into a sharp canter and put as much distance as fast as I could between them and me. Writing now it reminds me of a scene from the film Deliverance. I rode on and eventually started to see wisps of smoke rising in the distance; my mood cheered!

Riding down a hill I came to a cottage on my right and a brook on my left. A small sign said Brook Street. I had found civilisation at last but had no idea if I was in Wymeswold or some other village. I rode along Brooke Street until I came to a grass triangle where the road split three ways. I didn't know which road to take so I stopped and let Omo graze whilst I pondered what to do. As I rested, the church bell sounded and that made up my mind; I headed towards the sound. After only a few yards, I saw a shop, a pub, and a main road. When I arrived at the main road, there was a signpost that said Rempstone. I knew Rempstone was near Costock, so I followed the sign. Riding through the village on the main road was very scary as it was terribly busy, and cars were parked at the side of the road forcing me into the middle of the road. Thankfully as I left the village there was a wide grass verge and as I looked back towards the village, I saw a sign that said Wymeswold, so I knew I was on the right route.

I later found out that the wide grass verges that surrounded Wymeswold dated back to the days when livestock was herded on foot from Ashby-de-la-Zouch market to Melton Mowbray market. Wymeswold was one of the overnight stops where herds of animals would be rested and grazed overnight on the wide verges. Apparently herding livestock was very thirsty work as Wymeswold boasted nine thriving pubs during the late 1800s.

I rode on and after a while was cheered up to see Rempstone Garage that lay on the edge of the village: the garage was well known to me as Dad often stopped there for fuel, and, better still, they sold ice creams. Sadly, I didn't have any money with me because an ice cream would have gone down very well at that moment in time. The road dropped steeply from the Garage into the village and my ride became quite scary as there were steep embankments on either side of the road, leaving me nowhere to go when I met traffic. Thankfully at the bottom of the hill another signpost pointed to the villages of Costock and Wysall, so I turned right and was soon on another quiet country lane with wide verges. Now that I knew I was getting into home country; I decided to have a canter and soon came to a farm. I recognised the farm from earlier in the year, when we had collected grass cut on the roadside to save as winter feed for our horses. Another forty minutes and I was home.

It was after lunch when I arrived home and mum was horrified to see Omo and myself covered in scratches and dried blood. These superficial wounds always look worse on grey horses. When I told her my story, she was furious that Dad had left me to my own devices. When Dad arrived back sometime later, he just shrugged off her complaints by saying, "I knew he would be alright, he's home safe isn't he?" End of story.

During my early years, going hunting was spasmodic, mainly free cub hunting. As I entered my teens, our fortunes were on the up and Dad decided that I could be quite useful show casing horses that fell into the ladies hunter bracket i.e., 14hh-15.2. Mum and dad were now hunting regularly on Tuesdays with the Quorn. We hadn't got enough money to afford the high cap fee for Dad to hunt Monday's which was one of their best days. However, he always seemed to manage the odd free day courtesy of his farmer friends. The Quorn Tuesday country was mainly up in Charnwood Forest to the south and west of Loughborough. Even today it is beautiful piece of countryside, with its high rocky hills, stonewalls and woodlands. Today many of the small farms have been bought up by the wealthy, and turned into mansions with small estates, but in the early sixties it was still a wild untouched area of small livestock farmers. This was where I jumped my first stonewall and I loved it. Although the stonewalls were great fun to jump they harboured a sinister hidden danger. A lichen grew on the stones of the walls and if your horse cut itself jumping one of these walls it often became fatally infected. In those days vets did not have the range of antibiotics that are available today. Although I am not sure whether even today there is a cure for the poisoning. We lost a horse that had cut his knee to this poison. It was a horrible slow death; we poulticed the cut and the vet used everything at his disposal but after a week we had to have him put down. It was such a problem that the hunt started to make small sections of the wall into what were called hunt jumps. The jagged coping stones were removed and replaced by wooden railway sleepers. Many of those jumps are still intact to this present day sixty years on. The Forest as it is known in hunting circles has always been a fun place to hunt. Foxes scamper from covert to covert, so you don't get the long-sustained hunts of the more open countries of the Quorn Monday or Friday meets where hounds can travel several miles very quickly, and if you are not bold and well mounted may never see the hunt again that day. On the Forest however hounds are never far away, although getting back to them can be quite a challenge as sounds tend to echo around the hills and valleys. Sadly, during the mid-sixties, the M1 Motorway sliced through the middle of this beautiful patch of countryside and made parts of it unsafe to hunt. I am probably one of the few people still alive that can lay claim to following the hounds across the M1 near Nanpantan. It was just before the motorway opened, the tarmac was laid, but the finishing touches were still being worked on. The hounds checked just as we started to cross the motorway and we waited on the motorway for about ten minutes before the hounds picked up the line again. It was a sad day as we all knew that this would be the last time, we ever hunted this beautiful patch of the country. My lasting memory of that time on the motorway was a poor young child whose pony got down and rolled in a huge puddle of yellow water at the side of the Motorway. The yellow colour came from the crushed stone that had been laid at the side of the road. The poor child went right under and came up screaming covered in bright yellow mud as did the naughty pony. The last thing you want to happen on a cold winters day.

It was always a treat to hunt up on the Forest but was restricted to school holidays. I jumped at a chance to go to the Boxing Day meet that in those days was held in Loughborough marketplace. Dad constantly reminded me that both my horse and my personal turnout had to be immaculate as this was the most important meet of the year. Dad got very worked up before a day's hunting and would always explode into a terrible rage over the slightest thing. The family and everyone at the yard dreaded hunting days. If I got the chance, I would disappear off into the woods and hideout until the horsebox left the yard. However, I was usually caught and given a task that I knew would not be completed to his exacting standards. I was once given the job of polishing his riding boots and I did not know that you had to polish the stitching that attaches the sole to boot. Wow did I get a roasting.

The Boxing Day meet was attended by over a hundred mounted followers and over a thousand spectators. We just stood around at the meet for what seemed like for ever and a day. Finally, we moved off and I started to fizz with excitement. It was a long hack out of the town up to the priory pub along Forest road towards Nanpantan. Just past the pub we turned left onto Woodhouse lane and then into a field by a small reservoir. The hounds scampered around but were not allowed into the woods, after ten minutes of the adults sharing their hip flasks the master thanked everyone for coming and wished us a happy new year. That was it! No hunting, just purgatory! All that work for nothing, I sulked and fumed all the way back to our horsebox which was on the opposite side of Loughborough. It took us an hour to hack back and I vowed never to hunt on Boxing Day ever again. It was a vow I kept for over forty years until my Field Mastership duties made it an unpleasant necessity.

Most of my spasmodic childhood hunting was carried out on Saturdays. Our land was on the border between Quorn Monday and Saturday country, and the South Notts Hunt still had meets at Tollerton, Flawforth Lane Ruddington and Cotgrave. I hacked to all these meets often on my own. I never knew the name of the huntsman of the South Notts but the Master was Major Bob Hoare - more about him later. The Quorn in my early days had the long serving huntsman George Barker who after a few years of me starting to hunt was succeeded by his whipper in Jack Littleworth. Sadly, Jack had health problems and the new young whipper in had to stand in for him and he showed great skill and sport with the hounds. His name was Michael Farrin and I was present when he first took the huntsman's horn on a Saturday meet at Kinoulton. He was only twenty-five when he was officially given the full time role of Huntsman of the Quorn Hounds in 1968 following Jack Littleworth's retirement, and continued in that role for 30 years.

The South Notts Hunt Derbyshire

From the age of fifteen until I was nineteen, I hunted a lot with dad. I was a useful asset to him as I was light enough to ride small horses and even well put together 14.2hh ponies and show them off in the hunting field. Although I had hunted with the South Notts since a child I never ventured up into high Derbyshire until I was sixteen. I went with Dad, as it was definitely not within hacking distance. The meet was at the Puss in Boots at Hazelwood near Duffield. We were as usual late arriving at the meet and looking at my watch I thought that the Hunt would be long gone. It was already twenty past eleven and we still hadn't found a place where we could park as the lanes were so narrow. After asking a very friendly local we found a spot not far from the pub. It was gone eleven thirty by the time we arrived at the pub but the mounted followers were still in the car park, quaffing drinks and casually chatting. This was nothing like the Quorn who met at eleven and were often gone by ten past. The meet had a market day feel about it with loads of foot followers all mingling with the horses telling jokes to the riders and roaring with laughter.

I was not over impressed - had we just come all this way for a social gathering? Hunting with the Quorn was a serious business with no time wasted on socialising, just a quick good morning greeting and a quick stirrup cup if you were one of the favoured few, and then off down the road at a spanking trot to the first cover. On Mondays and Fridays there were one hundred plus mounted followers Tuesdays and Saturday slightly less.

At the Puss in Boots there were barely thirty mounted followers. Eventually the master shouted casually "Come on everybody drink up we really must make a start". We trotted up a steep narrow lane and went into a small field. Within minutes the hounds had found a fox in the thick hedgerow and we were off! All the fields were exceedingly small and the fences came thick and fast, a mixture of stonewalls and hedges some with big drops on landing. The hunt was over almost before it had started but I lost count of the fences I had jumped in just a few minutes. This was great fun, as soon as we checked, huge saddle flasks were pulled out and passed around again accompanied by loud laughter and chatter. These hunters were different people to the ones that hunted with the Quorn or on Mondays with the South Notts. On those days red tailcoats and top hats were the norm. Up in Derbyshire nearly everyone wore black or tweed jackets many of which sported sewn up tears and looked several generations old. Many of the horses were unclipped or just trace clipped, likewise not all the horses were plaited. A bit scruffy they may be, but both horses and riders knew their job and covered the trappy country with ease. Swearing was the order of the day from both sexes. It was the first of many memorable days that I would have in this beautiful small patch of hunting country. There were many firsts for me that day, seeing predominantly local people doing a necessary job of culling a predator that killed their chickens and their lambs, and having some fun jumping both their own fences and their neighbours. Dad and I were welcome not as hunt visitors but as visitors to the local farming community. Towards the end of the day hounds pursued a fox through the local churchyard and the followers jumped in and out of the graveyard in a corner by a tree where there were no graves. Today if such a thing happened it would be sacrilege and front-page news for days. But here those lying beneath the earth were probably related to many out hunting that day and would have rejoiced at the hounds hunting across their graves and the followers popping over a quiet unused corner, after all it was their local Church. Things are so different today, the constant flow of urbanites into the countryside has changed everything, taking away the cherished values and pastimes of the people who have lived and worked there for generations.

It was four thirty when the huntsman blew for home, and dark by the time we reached our horsebox. We wished everyone a heartfelt "Good Night" as they made their way home. A good friend of Dad's, Herbert Richardson, passed us and we wished him the same farewell. He reined up and said "What you're not thinking of going home yet are you? We always have a drink in the pub as a thank you for putting on the meet for us". Dad pointed out it was over an hour until the pub could re-open and that we could not wait that long as we had a long drive home. "Don't be silly, you are in Derbyshire now they don't bother about the law up here".

The pub looked closed from the outside and only when you got into the car park could you detect a slight chink of light emanating through the closed curtains. We opened the pub door with a little trepidation but were presented with a packed smoke-filled room full of noise and laughter. We fought our way to the bar and an hour later fully rehydrated and thawed out we returned to the lorry and made our way steadily home. What a great day!

The South Notts master for Derbyshire on my early visits up there was Major Bob Hoare. He was fanatical about hunting and he was not only master, but he hunted the hounds as well. Although he loved hunting, he hated the mounted field as he felt that they impeded the hunt. Consequently, he had a habit of not blowing gone away when the hounds left the covert, leaving the field patiently waiting for the signal to follow. He always tried to place the field when drawing a covert in a place where it was hard for them to see or hear anything. The field master tried sending out spies to see if he was still drawing or had slipped away with his hounds. Unfortunately, the Major had a terrible temper and had sent home several spies for being in the wrong place. Because I was usually the youngest follower I got sent out on recognisance on a regular basis. The reasoning being I could get away quicker on my smaller mounts and that he was less likely to give me a bollocking because of my age. However, I believe it was simply that I was dumb enough to say yes when asked.

I had so much fun up in High Derbyshire. There was none of the etiquette of the Quorn, just the raw joy of good friends enjoying good food, drink and sport. In the sixties the country was incredibly open and there were very few no-go areas.

Having said all that, it was a dangerous country to cross, full of nasty surprises and you soon learnt the meaning of look before you leap. We always looked forward to the last meet of the season as it provided an entirely different kind of sport. The sport was 'toff' watching. Because the Quorn and the other shire packs always finished hunting a week or sometimes two weeks before the High Derbyshire country closed, we used to get a lot of the red coat brigade coming up to visit us. It was welcome income for the always cash strapped South Notts. and a form of great amusement for the regular field. They stuck out like a sore thumb in a field that dressed in black and tweed coats, a bit like a wealthy member of the family visiting his poor relations, wanting to show off rather than engaging with them. The high Derbyshire country held many unforeseen surprises. One of the biggest problems were large stones that had been dislodged from the wall and lying-in wait for you, unseen on the landing side on the wall. I suffered several, really nasty falls from these hidden traps and they often did serious physical and mental damage to your horse. Another thing that was common was for farmers to park their tractor implements at the back of a wall - another danger for the unsuspecting rider. All these and many more hazards awaited our gallant, red coated knights as they charged the stonewalls as if they were hawthorn fly fences of the shires. We stood back sharing our hip flasks and watched the slaughter. There was never any need to rush in Derbyshire as hounds rarely ran long distances due to the abundance of good cover for the foxes.

Both Dad and I succumbed to Derbyshire surprises in our early days up there. I was following Dad on his famous palomino stallion, Amber Solaire, on a good run that we were having high up behind The Bulls Head pub where we had met earlier at Belper Lane End. The fields were quite large and we were having great fun picking off stonewall after stone wall, all white and gleaming from the sun in a clear blue sky. Everything was so perfect, such a joy and privilege to be there. Suddenly, a huge plume of white erupted around dad as he landed over the stonewall in front of me. I reined back hard but could not stop in time, so I pulled out to my right garnering shouts and swearing from other riders spread out on the wings. I regained control of my horse and circled around to peer over the wall to see what had befallen my father. It was like an illustration from "Jorrocks". Dad and Amber Solaire were both clambering out of a Dew Pond, both with water dripping from them. They were soaked, and despite the sunshine, it was a bitterly cold day high up on the tops. By this time, several other followers had pulled up to render assistance. Seeing that neither horse nor rider were seriously injured they started to see the funny side of Dad's fall. Unfortunately, Dad never had a sense of humour when he was the butt of the joke. I shouted to him to ask if he was ok and got the inevitable reply "Don't just sit there. Jump the f**king wall and catch my f**king horse." Somebody had already caught his horse, and desperate to get away from everyone laughing at him, he snatched up his hat that was serenely floating in the pond and crammed it on his head. Unfortunately, in his temper he failed to notice that the hat was half full of water when he crammed it on his head. The icy cold water poured down over his head and face as if he were being baptised. The onlookers treated him to another round of uncontrollable laughter. That night when I told Mum the story while Dad was at the pub, she smiled and whispered "Oh my! I would have paid to see that", which rather shocked me as Mum never wished ill on anyone.

I had several similar near misses with unexpected things on the other side of walls. I nearly jumped into a set of chain harrows neatly parked on the other side of the wall, spikes all protruding skywards. Only a warning shout back to me from the guy on my right who was a few strides ahead of me saved me that day.

My cockiness nearly led me to another potentially bad outcome and it was only some nimble footwork from my point to pointer Dadda Boy that saved me. I was approaching a nice stonewall and there was a queue to jump it as someone had fallen off in front of the wall. Quick as a flash I assessed the wall, saw no problems, so I pulled out and jumped it 20 yards to the right. We met the wall on a perfect stride and I sailed over with a big grin from ear to ear glancing smugly at the others queuing. A nano second later my face had turned to horror. The queue was caused because the horses were having to land on a road, this was making both horses and riders nervous. The problem with jumping onto roads is that they are very hard and jar the horses joints, tarmac roads are also very slippery and can cause the horse to slip over, which is one of the worst falls that you can have next to a rotational fall. If it is an unmade road such as a farm track, protruding bricks or stones can do serious damage to the horse's feet. My problem was much worse, I was jumping into a sunken tarmac road and the drop was about eight feet and it was also a narrow single-track road. Thankfully, it was a farm drive and there wasn't another stone wall on the other side, just a grass bank. In that nano second so much flashed through my mind as we descended towards the tarmac. My plan, made on the fly, was keep it simple, keep my horse straight and balanced and kick on! We didn't quite bounce it (when a horse lands and takes-off without taking a stride) but he landed changed legs and scrabbled up the bank on the other side of the road. We survived thanks to my horse's nimble footwork but it could have ended horribly. Twenty yards further up where everyone else was jumping there was no drop. That is the thrill of the chase, I was clean away leaving the others still queuing. In the pub later people were congratulating me on a superb feat of horsemanship. I took their compliments but felt a bit of a fraud, it was more good luck and clever horse, rather than the horseman.

I mention the pub after the hunt. In Derbyshire, the pub was an integral part of the days hunting. People would arrive at ten o' clock for an eleven o' clock meet otherwise you could not find a parking space. The pub was already open and had been since about nine o' clock, two hours before the legal opening time. It would be so packed that you had to fight your way in through the door and getting to the bar was impossible. To get a drink you shouted someone near the bar with your order and then you passed the money via several hands to the bar. Then a short time later the drinks and change were handed back over the heads of the other customers. The drinking was serious, it was not unusual to drink six to eight large ports before leaving the pub to mount your horse. The poor Master would spend a good fifteen minutes shouting at the riders to leave the pub usually to little avail. When mounted, trays of whisky, sherry and port, along with sandwiches and sausage rolls were handed out. Hounds rarely moved off before eleven thirty after which we had to rely on hip and large saddle flasks to see us through until the huntsman blew for home. At the end of day, it was back to the pub for a few pints to rehydrate before ordering a substantial meal, after which most drove home, although there were tales of some staying until closing time before taking their horses home. This was before drinking and driving laws were brought in.

After the breathalyser took its grip, the after-hunting drinking diminished but the early morning drinking at the meet remained the same.

I heard a story that when one of the riders had a bad fall and was rushed to hospital the doctor asked if they had been drinking alcohol, as it affected certain treatments. The rider was uncertain in his reply so the doctor changed his approach by asking which Hunt he had

had been following. When the rider said the South Notts Hunt the doctor replied "Oh! Then you most definitely have been drinking".

Dad and I had an hilarious incident once when hunting up in Derbyshire. We decided to take our own line during a good run and jumped a wall that was back fenced with barbed wire and we found ourselves wired in, as it is known in hunting circles. We rode around several fields, opening and shutting gates, listening to the music of the hounds get ever fainter. Dad, like me hated missing out on a good hunt and things got more and more frantic. Finally, we found a small area not back fenced with barbed wire. I shouted Dad who without a second glance launched himself at the narrow bit of unfenced stonewall and disappeared from view. The only way I knew that he alright was hearing the words "Jesus Christ!" shouted out in shock. I peered over the wall and saw a massive drop that landed you in a load of small scrubby thorn bushes. I turned my horse and followed Dad. At least I was prepared for what was waiting for me on the other side. After the usual argument of why I had not told him that there was a f**cking great drop and me countering that he didn't give me time to even look over the bloody wall before he jumped it, we settled down to finding a way out of the small paddock. Going back the way we came was not an option. We soon spied a cottage tucked neatly into a fold in the ground at the bottom of the next paddock, smoke was rising from the chimney so hopefully someone was at home. As we crossed the home paddock complete with geese and a donkey, we saw a lady working in the garden. When she saw us approaching, she quickly looked up and then ran into the house. We assumed two riders coming out of nowhere had given her a bit of a shock. Dad shouted, "Excuse me, can you tell us how to get back to the nearest road". This was standard practice if you became detached from the main body of the hunt. You were supposed to retrace your steps but the big drop had made that impossible. Suddenly, the door flew open and the woman charged at Dad swinging a broom at him and his horse. Dad tried in vain to explain it was an accident that we had got where we were, but to no avail, and after several near misses to his head from the broom we beat a hasty retreat to a lane that I had located during Dad's skirmish with the wild woman. We were still laughing when we finally caught up with the hunt. Our story caused great mirth, apparently, we had found the only anti-hunting person in the area and she was well known for attacks on unsuspecting fox hunters. It was my first ever encounter with an "anti". I found it hard to believe that anyone would hold such views because having been brought up on a chicken farm foxes were top of the list for must kill vermin. Oh, how things have changed!

The weather up in High Derbyshire can really catch you out. On two occasions, beautiful sunny days turned into whiteout blizzards without warning and on many occasions, I have hunted over snow covered fields when most hunts would have cancelled. The South Notts. Hunt motto was always that we will meet whatever the weather and if it is really too bad to hunt there is always the pub.

It gave me great pleasure and pride to take my daughter Emma up to Derbyshire with her exceptionally talented little horse Cassy. Cassy was bought as a dressage horse and came with a posh dressage name "Knabhall Cascade". Unfortunately, he was a very lazy dressage horse, he had the movement to be a great dressage horse but trying to get him to show off that movement was like getting blood out of a stone. We tried to liven him up by taking him hunting and to our surprise he suddenly came alive and jumped everything that was put before him, much to his young owner's delight. I say young owner because we did not buy Cassy, Emma did! From an early age she started to buy ponies to school and sell on at a profit. Her entrepreneurial skills did not stop with horses, she also ventured into the cattle business at the tender age of six. She managed to persuade a butcher friend of ours, Roger Jalland, to purchase two calves for her, she grew them on until they were ready for slaughter. When it came to buying and selling them, she used her sweet innocence to get the best deal from even the hardest dealing farmer. It was the cattle that gave her the capital to buy bigger and better ponies to school and sell.

The trips to Derbyshire with Emma were fraught with unexpected incidents and it is a wonder that she didn't give up on hunting and go back to dressage. However, unbeknown to us at the time Emma met a friend of mine who lived up in Derby and was a keen foot follower of the hunt. Many years later he would become her long-time eventing sponsor. His name was Cyril Embury.

On Emma's first visit to High Derbyshire, I went to introduce her to the Master who at that time was Brenda Dutton. Brenda had been a long-standing friend of the family and so I was proud to introduce her to the third generation of hunting Humphrey's. For Emma's education I addressed Brenda formally by saying "Good Morning Master. May I introduce my daughter Emma, who is hunting up in High Derbyshire for the first time today". Brenda turned towards me and gave me a strange look. What she said next astounded me.

She looked me up and down saying "Oh it's you. Have you got one of those bloody rings in your cock as well!"? I was absolutely flabbergasted and so was Emma. After a few seconds that felt like an hour I retorted "Brenda what the hell are you talking about. I've never ever had a ring in any part of my body". She stared at me long and hard then said "Sorry got you mixed up with someone else ". The meet was at the Malt Shovel pub high above Wirksworth and was probably the highest altitude meet in the South Notts. calendar. Emma always seemed to end up going to this meet year after year, probably because it always fell during the Christmas school holidays.

My mother had given Emma her old side-saddle jacket with a cutaway front - it was a beautifully cut jacket that probably dated back to the early nineteen hundreds but unfortunately, its cutaway front made it less warm than a regular hunt coat. One year, hunting was abandoned because of heavy snow that swept in midway through the day. Luckily when the master called a halt to hunting, we were only a couple of miles from the meet. We arrived back at the pub looking like snowmen. I still have a great picture that someone took of me, Emma, along with Emma Brown and Andy Brown as we arrived back at the horseboxes, we were almost completely white. On that occasion Emma complained of being cold and we had to take her to the pub and sit her in front of the fire to thaw out.

On another occasion we had a new master who opened up a lot of new country to hunt. We moved quickly from the meet onto ground that was several miles away. Nobody had ever hunted this area so remembering how to get home was exceedingly difficult. Suddenly an unexpected snowstorm hit us in the middle of this unknown country. Hounds were running and we galloped on into a whiteout. We crossed a river by means of a narrow rickety bridge high above a noisy gushing river, soon after Emma and I found a body lying in the snow. We stopped to help the poor unfortunate person. They were badly dazed but they were able to tell us that a friend had gone off in pursuit of their horse. By the time we had managed to get the person on their feet their friend had caught the horse and found us. The fallen person had been laying in the snow for several minutes or more and was very stiff and cold. It took an immense effort from all three of us to get the person remounted. Visibility was down to less than two yards. There was already a good covering of snow on the ground probably about three inches already. We listened for the sound of the hounds to give an idea which way to go. We could not hear a sound except for howling wind and snow. After a short discussion we decided that the only course of action was to try and find our way back to the road and then try to find the hunt. If you have ever been out in a blizzard, you will know how disoriented you can become. Even though we were only half a field from the narrow bridge it took us some time to locate it. Over many years of hunting, I had developed a system of noting features even when galloping along on a run. Sadly, this is not much help when you can't see more than a yard in front of you. The only thing that we could do was to find the hedge or stone wall and follow it around the field until we found the gate. A slow laborious job but it was the only thing that worked. At first, we had tried using our sense of direction but got hopelessly lost in the relatively small field for about ten minutes until we found a fence line. From the bridge to the road was only four fields, which under normal circumstances would have taken about two minutes on horseback. In these conditions it took twenty. We constantly looked for hoof prints but the snow had obliterated everything. We kept stopping to listen for traffic noise but all we could hear was the low growl of the wind and the muffled sound of driven snow whacking into us. When we finally found the road, we understood why we couldn't hear the traffic, there was none!

By now we were very cold and so were our clipped-out horses and although it was very slippery, we forced our mounts into a slow trot. Our joints were cold and stiff but we had to get moving or get hypothermia. It was at this point Emma said, "Dad I am cold". "Yes, we all are but we must keep moving and get back to the horseboxes as quick as we can" I told her. It is heart-breaking when you know someone you love is suffering and you cannot do anything to help them. Progress was terribly slow as the conditions were treacherous under foot, our eyes and faces were sore from the wind driven snow. When we reached the road, we thought all our troubles would be over but the road had not been gritted and a healthy covering of snow made even proceeding at walk hazardous. Our attempt to trot only lasted a few strides. Thankfully, all traffic on the road had disappeared, but zero visibility and the howling wind made us painfully aware of our vulnerability, should a car or lorry come along the road.

The good thing was that we now knew where we were going even though it was several miles back to the box. Emma was constantly telling me that she was really, really, cold and the heart-breaking thing was that I could not offer her any solace. Even with thick woollen hunting gloves I could not feel my hands and holding the reins became a nightmare. We slithered and slipped our way forward always with the fear that your horse might lose its footing and come crashing down on top of you. I was really worried; I had no doubt that we could find our way back to the meet but time and the cold was against us. Somehow, I had to keep Emma going, she was now crying with the pain. We tried trotting because our horses were now shivering but had to stop immediately as the horses legs splayed all over the place.

Finally, we reached Wirksworth, a small town of only five thousand people that sits on the side of a steep hill. On the other side of the town and a bit further was the Malt Shovel pub and our horsebox. As we entered the town the snow suddenly stopped and we could see our surroundings. People were emerging from shops where they had sought shelter from the storm and gawped at us as we suddenly materialised. We must have looked very strange plastered from head to toe in snow. Thankfully, the town roads and paths had been salted and although it was very slushy the horses seemed to have a good footing so we pushed on into a trot to try and warm up both ourselves and our mounts. We all started to cuss as our hands and feet started to throb painfully as the blood tried to force its way into our numb limbs. Even our knee joints had seized up!

We arrived at the top end of the town still cold but at least our circulation was working and our mounts were now steaming after trotting up the very steep hill. Our elation was short lived because as we reached the top end of the town there had been no gritting so it was back to walking on snow covered roads. Up on the high hilltops the wind was vicious and we were peppered by short sharp snow showers. Eventually the pub and the horseboxes came into view. I tried to cheer Emma up promising a hot chocolate at the pub in front of roaring fire as soon as we got back, but the cutaway front of her hunt coat was giving her no protection from the snow and freezing Derbyshire wind.

We finally arrived at the horseboxes. The main body of the hunt field had already arrived back at the boxes having hunted in a circle that brought them back much closer to the meet when the day's hunting was abandoned. I slithered off my horse and collapsed in a heap as my numb legs hit the ground. As I forced my way up off the ground Emma said "Quick Dad! Grab Cassy". Emma had passed out with the cold. Bless her she had hung on grimly until we reached our horsebox. Luckily, the people who had arrived before us had put their horses away and were heading for the pub. We were a tight knit group and were always there for each other. Within seconds of my cry for help people were running to our aid. Somebody said, "Give me your horses we will put them away for you!" Another voice said, "Here let me help you get her into the pub and the warm". We carried Emma into the pub and everyone was marvellous, an area was cleared in front of the roaring fire and a comfortable armchair found. We managed to get her boots off and covered her with a blanket. A mug of hot chocolate appeared and we managed to wake her long enough to get her to drink a couple of gulps before she passed out again. The consensus of opinion was that we let her sleep in front of the fire until she warmed up. I warmed up with a large scotch and a bowl of hot soup and waited. I have never been offered so many drinks in my whole life, but I could not take advantage of them as I had to drive the lorry home.

I was getting very worried about Emma; I was checking her every five to ten minutes but after an hour she still had not come around. Her breathing was steady and her body now felt warm. After an hour I decided to wake her. After a bit of gentle shaking, she became conscious and we then moved her to sit at a table where she demolished some hot soup and sandwiches which seemed to perk her up.

It was time to make a move and although the horses were rugged up the temperature was dropping. We set off very slowly and had an arduous first part of the journey as the road was still covered in snow. The road from the Malt Shovel down to Hazelwood is steep, narrow, and full of bends. Although it is only six miles it felt like twenty-six. Once down to Hazelwood the roads had been salted, thankfully I was the only idiot driving down that lane. I don't know what I would have done if I had met something coming the other way. Emma was wrapped up in a horse blanket and fell soundly asleep after less than half a mile and never stirred until we arrived home, she was now fully recovered and full of energy. The tables had turned and it was now me who was exhausted, the bitter cold seemed to sap all your energy from your body.

Although high Derbyshire was my favourite there was also low Derbyshire which was mainly on the outskirts of Derby City. These were small patches of grassland that had a mixture of hedges and stonewalls. My favourite meet in this area was Coxbench on the north east of the city. When the A38 was upgraded into a busy high-speed dual carriageway, Coxbench, was effectively cut off from the rest of the lower part of the country, and it was feared that hunting would have to end and the meet would be lost. However, South Notts. Huntsmen were all masters of providing good sport on a postage stamp and I also think that having three pubs in the village might have had an influence on the decision to keep meeting at the village.

This little patch of land gave us some great fun especially a nice line of hedges and also some trappy fences just to keep you on your toes.

As I said at the beginning of my stories about the South Notts. It was not all about the hunting but having a good day out and lots of fun! To this end close by to the Coxbench country was a huge holly hedge, and on a quiet days hunting we would migrate to the holly hedge for a bit of fun. Not only was it high but it had a massive drop. The Field would position themselves on the landing side of the hedge with saddle flasks withdrawn generously sharing the various powerful cocktails that they contained, whilst the daredevils of the hunt took it in turns to pitch themselves and mounts at this formidable obstacle. As each rider rode at the hedge the field would start an ascending chorus of Whooooo! Followed by hoots of laughter if the rider hit the deck or loads of cheers if they made it. This hedge gave the South Notts hours of entertainment and was a legend.

I remember one very wet day at Coxbench when farmers didn't want us and the master of the day finished hunting at two o'clock but we still didn't leave the pub until six.

Oh, the good old days!

Derbyshire both upper and lower provided me with many misfortunes of my own. Once in my late teens, I was riding a lovely big thoroughbred that belonged to one of dad's clients at the stables. I was feeling immensely proud to be riding such a stunning horse. We had just crossed a brook that was fast flowing and stony. As I emerged and clambered up the bank another member of the field turned to me and said "Excuse me, but I think your horse is bleeding rather badly from his front leg" I look down and to my horror saw blood spurting from his near fore. Whether he had cut it on a sharp submerged stone or his hoof had struck into his opposite leg I will never know. Whatever had happened it had cut an artery and with the exertion and excitement of hunting his heart was pumping strongly causing the blood to spurt out. I was distraught, it was early days with the South Notts, and one of the first days that I had driven myself to the meet on my own. Blood was everywhere and for a few moments panic set in. Someone had stopped to help me and was holding the horse while I examined it. All I had was a handkerchief to try and stop the bleeding. I Looked up at my kind helper and cried "I can't stop the bleeding all I have is my handkerchief". "Use your Stock" came the calm reply "That's one the reasons we wear one. You can use it as an emergency bandage".

I ripped off my stock, used the handkerchief as a pad and then bandaged it on using my stock. My helper told me to wait for a few minutes until the blood congealed and that would stop the bleeding. I waited horrified as the blood seeped through my stock turning it from pristine white to crimson red. True to her word the bleeding stopped, she gave me directions back to the horsebox and told me to leave the stock in place until I got home. It felt like the longest walk of my life, as did the drive home. When I arrived home, I half expected to find the horse dead but I was treated to a bright and cheerful horse when the ramp came down. When we removed the stock, we could not even find the cut and it didn't even need a stitch.

From that day on I always carried an elasticated bandage and a lint pad sealed in a plastic bag in my hunt coat pocket. In later years, the bandage was replaced by Vetwrap. I also made up a comprehensive first aid box that I always kept in the horsebox. It soon became common knowledge that I carried a bandage in my pocket and I helped many a distraught hunter over the years. Despite profuse thanks at the time and promises to replace the bandage they never did. When I swopped to Vet-wrap it became quite an expensive service but well worth it.

The problem with hunting in Derbyshire was that often the weather was totally different up there and without the benefit of mobile phones, texts and email you had to set off to the meet totally oblivious of what conditions would be like at the meet. Fog and frost were the biggest problems although unexpected snow as I have already mentioned was another problem.

I once arrived late for the meet and the fog had come down. There was not a soul about just empty horse boxes but undeterred I set off to find the hunt as I could only be a few minutes behind them. At first it was extremely easy to follow their route, steaming horse droppings and scrawks on the tarmac left by the horseshoes made it easy to follow. Every now and then I bumped into lone foot followers who gave me extra directions. The lanes up there are like a maze, and sign posts an object of great rarity so it wasn't long before I was completely lost. Occasionally a ghost of the sun appeared through the mist giving me hope that the fog might burn off but they were very fleeting glimpses so weak that sometimes I thought my mind was playing tricks on me.

Suddenly I heard something, was that the sound of hounds hunting? It was very faint and seemed to come from every direction. I rode this way and that desperately trying to get a fix on the beautiful sound. Finally, I decided I had a fix on it and rode positively in that direction although the sound still seemed to move around as if it were teasing me. No, it was gradually getting louder and I spurred my mount on into a steady canter hoping to god I did not meet a car or lorry looming out of the fog. Yes, it was getting even louder I was definitely on the right track. Then a village name sign loomed out of the mist giving me a quick fright. Strange that hounds were hunting through a village I thought, but not unknown up here. As the sound got louder something did not sound quite right. As I entered the village it hit my like a ton of bricks, "You stupid bastard" I thought as I realised that the sound was not hounds but children playing in the school playground of the village school, the sound distorted by the fog.

By the time I found my way back to the meet all the horseboxes had gone. I found out later that the hunt had soon been abandoned due to the quickly worsening conditions. As I returned home, the sun was shining by the time I reached Derby. Needless to say, I became the butt of many jokes when I related my tale of woe.

Another time it was a clear blue sky almost right up to the meet, but when I arrived it was pea soup fog. A man called Graham Arm was the master on this occasion. Now Graham loved drinking as much as hunting which went down well with the South Notts.

Not long after I entered the pub Graham banged his glass on the bar and stood up to make an announcement. He announced that it was not fit to hunt at this present time because of the fog, but was confident that the fog would lift soon so we would wait it out in the pub. To ease the disappointment, he announced that he was buying everybody in the pub a drink. This was welcomed with cheers from the packed pub. The fog still had not lifted three hours later, by which time most of the followers were not fit to ride or drive so we all sat down to a late lunch and lashings of black coffee before we drove home.

In the seventies we saw the first Anti Hunt Protesters. We only saw them once and then never again for many years to come. Legend has it that after making a thorough nuisance of themselves a group of local farmers captured them and stripped them naked on this cold and frosty morning.

Some years later they reappeared but found it impossible to follow the hunt down the narrow single-track lanes surrounded by a hostile local population. It wasn't unknown for tractors to block both ends of a lane and leave them trapped for hours.

On another time I had been sent out on point while the huntsman drew a large covert. The hounds found and went screaming away. Unfortunately, I was on the wrong side of the covert. It was too far to retrace my steps as that would mean going in the opposite direction to which the hounds were running. I decided to take my own line. I found a green lane and it seemed to run in the general direction of the hounds. After a short while I realised that I was running parallel to the hounds so I needed to leave the lane and cut across country to my left. My only problem was barbed wire back fences on the far side of the walls, and to make matters worse the ground was covered in a blanket of snow. I passed field after field all back fenced by the hunters nemesis barbed wire. The hounds were screaming with these almost perfect scenting conditions. With every wired-up field I became more desperate to get with the hounds. Then at last a wire free field. The field seemed to have a lot of humps and hollows but that was par for the course up in Derbyshire. I brought my horse to a screeching halt, turned, sat back, and attacked the wall out of the lane. Two strides and we were sailing over the wall and off we galloped. Suddenly I saw a red flag! Shit! I'm on an army firing range! I quickly came to a halt by the red flag, a number was on the flag and then the full horror dawned on me as I realised what the strange humps and hollows were. No not a military firing range it was a bloody golf course. Luckily, I had not set a hoof an any of the greens. I looked around and could not see a living soul so I crept back to the wall and popped back into the lane. It was then I noticed the silence, the hunt was over, I had missed it. I retraced my steps and found the main body of the hunt. I never told anyone about my indiscretion.

The problem with the South Notts Country in Derbyshire, was that it was so small and so were the farms. Farmers had a hard life up on the hills and could not afford a lot of damage to their grassland from hunting. Fields of about thirty people were fine and damage was minimal because nearly everyone was local or a long-time dedicated hunter who understood and respected the land and the farmers. Over the years I got to know a lot of the farmers up there and would always have a chat to them in the pub and offer to buy them a drink. They really appreciated this and all the other hard-core regulars did the same as me. Farmers and hunters had their own little community.

Unfortunately, thirty people hunting was not financially viable for the hunt which has always been strapped for cash. So, over the years I have seen a constant cycle of two types of masters. There were the masters that provided stunning sport and crazy jumping days. They attracted many visitors from other packs and helped fill the hunt coffers with regular fields of sixty to seventy people. They worked incredibly hard entertaining the farmers and repairing damaged walls. Unfortunately, some of the visitors thought that they had bought the right to roam here, there, and everywhere when they paid their visitor's cap. They could never understand that the man in muddy overalls holding the farm gate open for the hunt was the landowner. A red coated visitor who galloped passed without the courtesy to say thank you was enough for the farmer to question if all the damage and upheaval that the hunt brings was really worth it. Chip by chip no matter how hard the master worked on public relations; farmers would start to refuse the hunt permission to cross their land. I remember my good friend Richard Brooks when he was Master telling me that he had to visit about eighty people to put on a day's hunting in Derbyshire, whereas with the shire packs such as the Quorn twenty visits would secure a much larger area as the farms were much bigger.

Just a few no-go areas in Derbyshire could severely hamper a day's hunting. As the sport became less, the number of visitors dropped, and the fields dropped, to what once again became a manageable thirty odd, then a change of Mastership and lot of hard work on public relations most of the country would be reopened and the sport would get better. Another new master would come along and the number of visitors would start to rise again and so the cycle repeated itself.

I was getting very frustrated one day because hounds were running and the only way out of the field was an awkward trappy stone wall that was blocked by several riders whose horses were consistently refusing. Whenever I hear hounds speak excitement builds like a volcano inside me. I have to be up and away galloping and jumping to try and be with them. I started to look for another way out because the hounds were getting further away and it was doing my head in. Many followers do just that! follow! but for me it was a race and a point of honour to be with the valiant few at the end of the hunt. I thought that I had found another place to jump and was about to set sail at the wall when a hand clasped my shoulder and a voice said "If you are thinking of jumping that wall don't! Because it will be the last thing you and your horse will ever do. Walk slowly to the wall and look over it". I could not see anything wrong but this was Herbert Richardson speaking, now well into his sixties and he had hunted up here all his life. He was a man that I had great respect for. I wandered over to the wall. The rule in Derbyshire "Look before you leap" I had forgotten the golden rule! When I got to the wall I gasped in horror; on the other side of the wall was a quarry two hundred feet straight down. Just writing about it makes my stomach turn.

I went back to Herbert and thanked him profusely. He went on to tell me that he had accidentally jumped into a quarry when he was much younger and it was not an experience, he would wish on anyone. Luckily, his quarry was in the south of the hunt country where they mined sandstone and gravel. The base of the quarry had been flooded with deep mud and this broke his fall. His horse sank up to its belly and had to been extracted by a crane. Both he and his horse survived with only minor injuries.

So, remember always "Look Before You Leap"!

Still on the subject of Herbert Richardson or "Richo" to his friends, he once stood alongside me in a wood of tall pine trees. He looked up at the tall trees and said "My, these trees have grown well, I remember riding through here when they were just six inches high back in 1947" I was speechless I just love things like that.

He told me about some tales from the wartime. He related how he used to make cider from the apples in his orchard in an open top barrel. One day a horse took a long drink from the barrel. Not long afterwards the horse was seen galloping around the orchard in a very erratic manner and finally galloped head on into a tree and knocked itself out. At first, he thought it was dead but then noticed that it was still breathing. Some hours later the horse came to and was fine. He also claimed that a rat had fallen into the barrel of cider and drowned. When they bottled the cider, they found no trace of the rat, not even its bones. Even worse they still drank the cider. Perhaps that is why I cannot stomach cider or could it have been that I got very drunk on it when I was about twelve. Who knows?

A Bit of Bladder

Something that is a regular problem when hunting with the South Notts in Derbyshire is affairs of the bladder. Copious pre-hunting drinks always means that by the time you had hacked to the first cover despite the last minute wee before mounting you are always busting for another. Country people have never had a problem about relieving themselves in the open air unlike our city dwelling cousins.

I was always reminded of a friend who took a fall with a full bladder causing the urine to be forced back into his kidneys and causing an infection that made him extremely ill. I always remind clients to make sure that they have an empty bladder before riding.

Occasionally, I would take a livery owner up to introduce them to the delights of the stone wall country. On one occasion I took a lady to a meet at the Bear Inn at Alderwasley. It was always a good meet for hunting but also for pre- and post-hunt drinking. As we got to the first covert, the men started to leap off their horses and hand them to a friend to hold before running across to the nearest wall to relieve themselves. All very proper in country circles always turn your back towards the ladies before peeing. The lady was so naive that she asked me what they were doing. I told her that it was a special ritual and that they were praying for a good, safe days hunting. When she enquired why the women were not taking part, I had to own up to what they were really doing. She was horrified by such uncivilised behaviour and even more when I asked her to hold my horse while I popped over to the wall. Inevitably she had to ask what the women did. I told her to ask someone to hold her horse and then go behind a conveniently large bush. Aghast she announced that she could never do that. I smiled and said, "you will before this day is out".

I once took a lorry load of clients up for a hunt ride during the summer. Again, a lady asked where she would find the ladies toilet. My wife Lou said, "In the back of the horsebox". The lady smiled and said, "Really I never knew that you had a toilet in your horsebox, where is it hidden". Lou replied "Oh we have six, just choose any partition that's empty" the lady laughed and thought that she was joking. She must have asked six other people before she accepted that Lou was not joking.

Once when out with the Quorn two very wealthy well-known ladies had quietly dropped back from the field to relieve themselves. Unfortunately, a few minutes later the hounds put up a fox that ran back towards where we had just come from. Over one hundred riders galloped past shouting and whistling at the unfortunate ladies squatting down, breeches and knickers around their ankles. It is amazing how many swear words well to-do ladies know. We certainly heard every one of them that day!

My personal embarrassment was out in Derbyshire. I was busting for a pee but we were constantly on the move. Eventually I could wait no longer, I dropped back from the field and dismounted, I had considered trying to pee mounted but I had tried it once before with disastrous consequences. I was riding Wetherby my point to pointer who was not happy about leaving the field. The place I had decided to stop was on a track that bordered a wood of mainly silver birch trees. The trees were growing on a very steep cleft in the ground, at the bottom over one hundred feet below was a fast-flowing stream. It was beautiful, just like a picture you would get on a countryside calendar. I think I was in a bit of a daydream watching urine cascade through the air down the steep slope. Bang! Something struck me solidly from behind and sent me flying down the bank. I tried in vain to keep hold of the reins but Wetherby pulled back and reared, frightened by my sudden jerk on the reins. Down I tumbled bouncing off silver trees and going head over heels until I landed in the icy cold brook. Although dazed the cold water quickly brought me to my senses. It was then that I realised that my willy was still hanging out. Stupidly I looked around to see if anyone was looking at me. Why I imagined that anyone else would be wandering around at the bottom of a ravine that was impossible to access, except by the unusual way that I had got there. I looked up hoping to see my horse but he had gone off to join his pals. I decided now was a good time to finish what I had started. That ticked off my to-do list, I started to try and climb back up the bank, I was on my hands and knees all the way. When I got to the top I painfully straightened up. I was cold, covered in mud, and had no idea how long I would have to walk until I caught up with the hunt. It was now that I suddenly realised what had happen to me. My dear horse, impatient to re-join the hunt had head butted me in the back sending me skedaddling down into the ravine.

Thankfully, I only had to walk a few minutes before two friends rounded the bend leading my nag. They laughed when they saw me in such a sorry state and laughed even more when I told them my tale of woe. When we caught up with the hunt, my story spread like wildfire and so the whole field was laughing at me. I rarely fell off, so this was even sweeter for my friends.

The Quorn Hunt

My early experiences with the hunt didn't get much better. In the fifties and sixties, the Quorn was very much a club for the wealthy, and locals were a necessary evil. The majority of male riders wore top hats and white chalked breeches made of buckskin leather surmounted by a similar apron that protected the breeches from mud, many ladies rode on side saddles.

I remember going out on my own when I was thirteen for the first time dressed in a tweed jacket and all turned out very smartly. The hounds were at the end of Bunny woods on the Wysall road that used to be called Windmill Hill, when I was accosted by the hunt Secretary John Ingelsant who enquired who the hell was I and where had I sprung up from, in a tone that made me feel like a leper. He went on to ask me if I knew that I had to pay to join the hunt. His tone softened when I answered in the affirmative and I produced the children's cap fee. The money was taken as if it was a poor tip and stuffed into the leather satchel slung across his shoulders that was stuffed to full of paper money. He looked me up and down distastefully and parted company by saying "If you are thinking of ever coming out again make sure you get your bloody haircut, it's a disgrace, it's almost touching your collar". I felt grubby and out of place and I certainly did not feel welcome. If I hadn't just parted with what to me was a vast sum of my parents cash, I would have gone home straightaway. The Secretary's final words were "Stay at back and DON'T! Get in the way".

Happy Days!

All my rare appearances with the Quorn over the next few years were met with the same overt unwelcome. I found hunting exciting but other than that a horrible experience. I think the only words ever spoken to me were "Get that pony out of the way, you stupid bloody child".

Dad was desperate to be accepted into the Quorn so I was dragged along as a sign that his whole family were ardent supporters of the hunt. My love of going hunting only really got going when we started to visit Derbyshire.

However, Dad's persistence and horsemanship was breaking down barriers, especially as he was building a name, for having good horses to hire for a day's hunting. The people who could afford to hire horses were very wealthy and often titled. Once these people started to deal and speak to you, the barriers came tumbling down.

However, it was the mid-seventies before I got to hunt on the best days Mondays or Fridays. I only hunted Fridays on rare occasions as they were on the opposite side of the Quorn country from where we lived. To hunt on these days was still beyond our means but I was making a name for myself as a schooling jockey, and my days were paid for by the owners of the horses that I was schooling. This was great fun, just rock-up at the meet and get on the horse and then at the end of the day hand the horse back to the groom and drive home. Not one finger lifted in preparing the horse or cleaning it afterwards. Happy Days!

After my second-year racing, both the jousting and the riding school were doing well and dad with the help of Geoff Brooks, who was a large landowner in the Monday country managed to strike a deal with the hunt, that allowed me to qualify my point to pointers and share the day with dad. The way it worked was dad would drive me and my horse to the meet and then at change of horses which was usually about one o' clock dad would arrive back with his horse. Dad would hunt in the afternoon and I would drive back to pick him up at the end of the day. This arrangement varied depending on our work schedules, and sometimes the box would be left with the other horse left on at second horses and Lou or mum would drive over to pick up the driver and then pop back to assist with changing horses. This meant that one of us would then hunt two horses in one day. Dad by this time was suffering from Angina and if there was a cold wind, he became very breathless, and so on these days I got to ride two horses for the full day.

The Quorn has been blessed with long stable masterships throughout its long history that dates back to 1696. But that was severely disrupted first at the end of the 1980s and early 1990s by the Lloyds of London crash and then again by the financial crisis in 2007-2008

I was lucky enough to hunt during the last of the glory days of big fields and jumping up to one hundred fences in a day. The fields of this era were well over one hundred mounted followers every Monday. There was supposed to be a maximum cap of one hundred and twenty for field numbers but that was a running joke. The cost of a day's hunting changed every season but if you chose a modest figure of £100 per person for a day, you get to understand the vast amount of money being turned over. Although Tuesdays and Saturdays had smaller fields Fridays had similar numbers to Mondays.

The field was like a who's who of Society and the Equestrian world. Visitors would fly over from America to hunt with the Quorn. His Royal Highness Prince Charles was a regular follower, as was champion jockey of the day Willy Carson and famous flat racehorse trainer Barry Hills. From the world of Pop music, there was Malcom Allured drummer with the Band Showaddywaddy and Mickey Dolenz of the American group The Monkeys, interestingly he was also a drummer.

The master for Mondays was Capt. Fred Barker. A charismatic leader and a bold fearless man to follow. His horses were also superb, they had to be with over one hundred other good riders behind him there was no room for errors.

Monday country was had with many good lines of hedges where the field could spread out often up to four fields in width and riders taking their own line. Taking your own line is the ultimate joy when hunting, keeping one eye on the hounds and huntsman if you were lucky enough to be that close. The Quorn Monday hounds were usually all bitches and were renowned for their speed.

The other eye was employed working out the route you were going to take and making a calculated guess as to where the fox was headed. A large number of the field were visitors and followed the Master, but the regulars would often wait and let the main body of cavalry go while deciding which route to take. You could only do this if you knew the country with great intimacy. You had to know where there was a barbed wire back fence or had that nice cut and laid hedge got a strand of barbed wire hidden along the top, waiting like a wartime sea mine ready to spring a terrible fall on the brave but unknowledgeable rider. Where to jump a hedge was also critical. Jump it in the right place and the ditch lurking behind is no problem a few feet to the left and it is a yawning chasm. These are but a few of the considerations to be made before taking your own line.

Whether it was Walton Thorns, Ella's Gorse, Muxloe Hill, High Holborn or one of other well-known runs, the field would muster behind the Captain waiting in anticipation for him to lead the charge. The first rank was made up of the thrusters the do or die brigade. If you fell at the front, you had another hundred behind who were going to gallop over you, this was a place for only the brave.

I remember being on point once at Walton Thorns and looking down on this formidable line of big hedges and ditches. To watch probably one hundred and thirty horses move forward as one at the gallop was awesome. It was like the tragic charge of the Light Brigade. It was as if there were hidden machine guns mowing them down. The landing side of each fence was littered with the bodies of fallen horses and riders but still they came on the later ranks being brought down by the fallen of the leading ranks. On one occasion two fallers remounted onto different horses in the carnage. It was not until they returned their hired horses at the end of the day did, they discover that they were not riding the horse that had been hired. Luckily all the horse hirers knew each other well and it was not long before the two horses had been reunited with their correct owners.

In less than five minutes it was all over. The survivors of the front rank twenty to thirty gathered around Capt. Fred, laughing, joking, and taking a swig from there hip flasks as they waited to be joined by the stragglers. Strangely the hounds always seemed to lose the fox at this point and the horse and riders were able to catch their breath while Michael Farrin cast his hounds. If you fell you needed to get remounted as quick as possible because the Quorn never hung about, you were always on the move. Even change of horses was like a Formula one tyre change. Like many other great huntsmen Michael never got off his horse his groom would bring his new horse alongside his tired horse and horn in hand would step off his first horse onto his second in one smooth motion. It looks easy but if have two safe horses try it sometime.

Unlike my days with the South Notts I do not have the same number of recollections. In fact, when I wrote the chapter heading for the Quorn, I didn't write anything for several days because it was just a blur of fast action, very enjoyable at the time but too much for the brain to clearly log. Now I am writing snippets, the memories are starting to come back.

My hunting pal on Mondays for many years was an old family friend Roger Jalland. Our association with the Jalland family went back to when we moved to Bunny Hill and Roger's uncle Percy used to call twice a week with his butcher's van which was a small Austin or Morris 5cwt if my memory serves me well. In those days we had no refrigerators so meat had to be bought and eaten within a few days. The nearest thing that we had to a refrigerator was what was called a meat safe. This was a large tin box with lots of exceedingly small holes drilled through it to allow air to flow through but too small for flies to get in. It was fixed to the north facing wall of the bungalow as that was always the coolest place.

Percy was a great character always had a tale to tell you and was well known for his love of beer. His nephew Roger was of the same character and I spent many wonderful times with him. He kept his horse with us and I would pick him up from his house at Wymeswold in the horsebox on the way to the hunt meets. He was always extremely excited and even before we had left the village, he would produce a large hip flask of whiskey which he would hand to me and say here have a swig of this it'll make those f**king fences look smaller.

Roger was a big raw-boned man with huge hands that by all accounts had knocked out several men in his early days. In his younger days he had been a Speedway rider and had been involved in a high-speed crash and suffered terrible injuries and the doctors had replaced his palate with a metal plate which he could take out. His party trick was to show my children Mark and Emma how he could take it out. They were mesmerised by this and always demanded that he perform this grotesque ritual every time they saw him. It was Roger that brought Emma's Calves for her.

By the time we got to the meet Roger had always drunk half his flask and found it great fun to swoop on friends when they had their flasks out and snatch it from them with his big strong hands and gallop off guzzling it dry. It got so bad that you used to look to see if Roger was in the vicinity before offering friends a drink.

One day I decided to get my own back. The father of Lou's best friend Vanda was Polish and I asked him to get me some of their strongest vodka. He sourced some, that I think was home made by the polish community. It was rocket fuel! Well over 100% proof. On the following Monday I filled two hip flasks one with the neat vodka the other with sloe gin. While the hounds were drawing a covert, I separated myself from Roger and started to pass my sloe gin around to a group of friends, all the time keeping a watchful eye on Roger. My friends were in on the prank and knew about the other flask that I casually held opened in my hand. Like a fish unable to resist the fisherman's bait he swooped in and grabbed my flask and galloped away draining it as fast as he could. He only got twenty yards before coming to an abrupt halt. His eyes were bulging and his mouth was opening and closing like a freshly caught fish, but no sound was coming out. The group were all beside themselves with laughter. Roger rode up to me and was obviously trying to say something but only a little squeak came out. Realising that he had been well and truly done over he handed me back my flask forced a grin and rode off shaking his head. After that he never tried that trick again. Whenever I got my flask out after that he would always say "Now Mr Humphrey may I enquire as to the contents of your flask today before I partake. He repeatedly told people about what I had done to him and told me it was the best trick anyone had ever pulled on him.

Roger and I were great pals and had some great times together out hunting. Whatever was happening good or bad he could put a smile on your face.

He loved his hunting and once he had his adrenaline up, he was absolutely fearless to the point of being dangerous.

One day we were at Willoughby, the Melton Hunt Ride had taken place there in the Morning and I had ridden in it. I had changed from my racing colours into hunt dress and had hunted my other horse in the afternoon. It was the first time that I had an extra horse available to hunt. It had always been a pipe dream of mine to do this and now I had actually done it.

Roger and I were hacking back across the fields towards our horsebox parked on the Wysall lane. Our route took along part of the Melton course and I was relating to Roger how each of the fences had jumped. As we rode down the side of Willoughby Gorse, we approached a hunt gate, to the right hand-side of the gate was a set of post and rails that we had jumped during the ride. The rails were not massive but the ditch on landing was! Suddenly Roger pulled his horse out from the side of the covert and announced that he was going to have a crack at it there and then. Now, I have always had a strict rule that when I decided to leave a hunt, I would never re-join however tempting it was. Also, that I would never jump anything on the way home unless it was the only option to get home. Jumping on the way home was known as "Larking about" and was very frowned upon, but more importantly once you and your horses adrenaline had gone down you were much more likely to have an accident.

Because of this I pulled my horse across the front of the fence and told Roger he must not jump the fence. Roger was determined to jump the fence and an aggressive stand-off pursued, it was the only time we had ever had an argument and I was scared. Roger could easily have laid me out with just one punch. We stood facing each other in the middle of nowhere all on our own like two gunfighters in a western. I was just about to give in when he said "Ok you miserable bastard, have it your own way. We will go through the gate."

As I turned around, I suddenly saw that the barbed wire back fencing had been reinstated by the fence mending crew. If Roger had jumped it would have ended very badly for both Roger and his horse. Suddenly I was his best friend who had just saved his life. After that if he introduced me to somebody he always started with "This is the man that saved my life." We never had another cross word between us ever again.

Dad was always running late especially on hunting mornings and he was always in a foul mood. I can only put his bad moods down to adrenaline. Having spent my life living on adrenaline I have observed the many different effects it has on people. Personally, I go noticeably quiet and weak in my whole body, others chatter endlessly, often called verbal diarrhoea, some like dad become temperamental, flying off the handle at the smallest thing. When we were jousting, I was like this in the mornings before a show but this was stress adrenaline and perhaps dad found it stressful trying to get all his jobs done before going hunting, who knows. All I know is that it was best to make yourself scarce on hunting mornings. When we started to hunt regularly on Mondays it worked well because I used to hunt mornings and dad the afternoons. We only met briefly at change of horses.

One day we were changing horses on Bridegate Lane between Hickling and Hickling Pastures. As I fought my way through the melee' of horses and people that covered the narrow lane loading and unloading horses, I spied dad pacing up and down in the middle of the road. He was obviously very agitated, I took a deep breath and prepared to face the music. His first words were "Those stupid F**king girls have forgot to put my horse in the horsebox". I had sort of guessed that this might have happened so was prepared. This was third time that this had happened the other two times had been on Tuesdays with mum, after the second time mum refused to go with dad ever again both had blamed each other and terrible rows had ensured. Luckily for me it had been a very warm morning and there had been no scent so we had just hacked from covert to covert and only had a couple of scampers around quickly losing the fox, so my horse was still fresh. As dad drew breath for his second explosion, I said "No problem, we've done nothing this morning. You can take my horse". I dismounted and helped him mount "Hope you have a good afternoon" I shouted as he trotted away to join the others.

When I returned home the yard was in shock. One girl had gone home rather than facing dad. My mum and Lou greeted me with trepidation, shocked that dad was not with me. They both breathed a sigh of relief when I told them he was riding my horse.

What had happened was that the grooms could not undo the catches on the ramp to lower it and put the horse in. They had been waiting for dad to come out and undo the catches. Unfortunately, he had dashed out and driven straight off before they could tell him. Both of the girl grooms wanted to hand their notices in and leave before dad came back but I promised them that I would explain to him what had happened. Lou had already suggested that they hide. Although dad would rant and rave once it was over it was forgotten. By the time he returned he was in high spirts the temperature had dropped producing great scenting conditions and they had had a fantastic afternoon. I explained what had happened but it went in one ear and out the other as he gave me a fence-by-fence account of the hunt.

He never said a word about the missing horse to the girls in the yard, much to their relief! I asked Jackie Clarke our head groom if she was working for us when this happened. She replied "Oh yes! I will never forget that day".

There were many characters that hunted with the Quorn and I am sure that is the same for all hunts. For some it takes over their whole lives. Because hunting requires the goodwill of farmers and landowners to exist all hunts give them special concessions. The Quorn Hunt allowed all farmers to hunt for free on the hunting day that there land was in. There was one farmer near Upper Broughton who would come out on a scruffy pony, covered in mud, he would be wearing an old dark suit also covered in mud and other things picked up around the farm, a pair of old wellies, an old velvet riding cap complete with several large rips in the velvet, and to complete his ensemble a stick freshly picked from the hedgerow that morning. He seemed oblivious of his dress and happily chatted to the top hat brigade as if he were one of them. People always looked forward to him joining us whenever hounds were in that area.

Another character was Malcom Allured who was the drummer in the pop band Showaddywaddy and also owned a night club just outside Osgathorpe. Malcolm was a great character and hunted most weeks on Mondays. We became good friends and joined the small group of locals that hunted on Mondays as the vast majority lived outside the Monday area. We tended to hunt from the back as it was definitely the safest place to be. We knew the country inside out and could use short cuts that were not available to the huge field that followed the Quorn on Monday.

One day I was on gate shutting duty with Malc, we were several fields behind the main body of the hunt and having a very social time sharing our hip flasks. We were in the vicinity of Hickling Standard and had secured the gate at the bottom of a hill. We were galloping up the hill keen to catch up with the hunt when suddenly over the crest of the hill in tightly packed formation came the whole of the hunt at full gallop. More than one hundred and twenty horses were bearing down on us at an alarming rate. I shouted "F**cking Hell Malc prepare to meet Cavalry" Malc's mind as usual was somewhere else but then saw what was coming at us. I am sure the front rank all wore sadistic grins. There was no way that they were going to be able the stop given the steep gradient that they were coming down and the greasy conditions under foot. We wheeled our horses and rode for our lives as fast as we could. We could hear the rumble of over four hundred hooves just behind us. As we reached the gate the field came to a screeching halt and enveloped us. I leapt off my horse and opened the gate. Capt. Fred the Master with a big grin on his face shouted "Thank you very much. Bet that put the shit up you" and galloped away chuckling to himself. Malc and I closed the gate and drained what was left in our hip flasks.

Finally, we saw the funny side of the incident.

Another great character was Doc. Connors who was a practicing medical doctor and lived at Upper Broughton. He originally hailed from Ireland and was passionate about Fox hunting and everything to do with horses. There was a running joke that it was no good being ill in Upper Broughton on a Monday during the hunting season. Doc. Was a fearless rider across country and attacked every fence with the attitude of through it or over it. He was also exceptionally good at training horses to jump well and he would bring horses over from

Ireland, school them on in the hunting field and then sell them. He was renowned for the quality of his horses throughout the hunting world and often demand out stripped supply.

The big problem he encountered when hunting was that people were always hurting themselves and he was always being called on to help on what was his day off. My friend John Cook was kicked by a horse once and it broke his leg. Doc arrived, checked him out, announced that he had broken his leg and told him he needed to go to hospital. He quickly despatched someone to go to the nearest call box and phone for an ambulance (no mobile phones). He checked they knew the correct location for the ambulance to find them and then instructed friends to use their jackets to keep him still and warm. Finally, he gave him something for the pain. He scribbled his diagnosis and what pain relief he had given him on a note instructing the people with John to pass the note to the ambulance crew. Within a few minutes he was back on his horse and galloping after the hounds. His philosophy was that once he had done all he could do for a victim it was much better to stay with the hunt to be on hand for the next casualty.

Doc. Connors owned much if not all the land on Muxlow Hill. It was all grass and hedges with an abundance of foxes. The Quorn hunt made regular use of this land and the ground suffered a lot of damage because of such regular use. I once asked Doc Connors if it upset him to see the ground so cut up and he said, "Not at all he I bought the land for people to enjoy. Not to make money out of it". The Quorn Hunt Teamchase was first held at Muxlow Hill. I think it was in 1975 and was sponsored by the Bunny Club of Great Britain. Thanks to Doc Connors it became the venue for the highly popular event for many years to come.

After twelve glorious years Capt. Fred Barker retired and he was succeeded by Jim Bealby.

Jim was a vastly different Master from Capt. Fred but equally as good. Jim was a much quieter man but still had the air of authority to control the huge Quorn Monday Field. He was the only Master to send me home but also gave me my prized Quorn Hunt Buttons. What I liked about Jim was his horsemanship, he was an incredibly quiet calm rider who seemed to slide across the country with the greatest of ease. Early on in his Mastership I noticed that when he was deciding when to sally forth after the hounds, he would hold his hands high above his horse's withers. As he made his decision to go, he would drop his hands onto the withers. I would watch his hands like a hawk and as soon as they started to move downwards, I would kick on gaining at least two strides on the rest of the field. This gave me the coveted back-pocket position one stride behind him. Why was this so important? Because in that position you get a great lead from top class rider and no interference from others in the field.

We were hunting in the late afternoon on the edge of Upper Broughton on the Melton side and on this occasion, I was towards the back of the field. I was annoyed at being bottlenecked at several gateways and was trying to push on to get back towards the front before the hounds found a fox. I was making good progress forward when I saw Jim launch himself at a huge hedge some three hundred yards in front of me. There was a strong wind that day and with the speed that I was travelling it was roaring in my ears. I heard nothing but the wind but saw several people attempting to jump the hedge but their horses were all running out. I saw a clear run at the fence. I was mounted on Oggie, Dick Benson's racehorse who was one of the best jumping horses that I have ever ridden. I saw a perfect stride, it was time to make a spectacular show, the only rider to follow Jim over this big hedge. As we sailed through the air I was bursting with pride. As I landed, I turned and grinned at Jim so proud to be the only rider in this high-class field to be able to join him. My joy was noticeably short lived as I received the biggest bollocking that I had ever had. The riders in front of me were not refusing but had pulled out because Jim had accidentally jumped into a field that had just been reseeded. He a personally guaranteed the owner that no horse would go on that field and as soon as he realised what he had done shouted back to the field not to jump. I had not heard that instruction. I tried to explain but to no avail. I was sent home and ordered to go that very evening to visit the landowner and apologise. Having taken on the duty of a Field Master I now understand why he had to do it to maintain his authority.

Unbeknown to Jim his punishment was not as severe as he thought. The landowner was Mrs Wynn Reese a good friend of the family and she always loved a good laugh. I rang her and asked if I could come over and see her and received an enthusiastic yes of course. I related my tale of woe and apologised profusely over several generous drinks. She laughed her head off at both Jim's and my mistakes and thanked me for coming over and cheering up her evening. I wrote to Jim explaining how I came to disobey his instructions and apologised for my actions.

Nothing more was said but the next season he presented me with my Hunt Buttons. Earned not brought as so many are today by generous donations. I still have the handwritten letter that he wrote.

I was incredibly lucky to have had access to so many good horses to ride out hunting although as a schooling jockey I also had my fair share of appalling rides. Most of my unpleasant rides came from home rather than other owners, a lot from dad, who was buying horses that had little schooling and probably never seen hounds but also from me as I schooled youngsters and gave them their education.

Sadly, most of the people that I rode for and who gave me the opportunity to ride such lovely horses out hunting are no longer with us, but I mention them as a thank you. Starting, roughly in date order there was David Wilson, Charlie Brown, Cyril Embrey, Mike Elvin, and Dick Benson. I had many more one-off rides for people whose names are now lost in the mists of time.

One of the scariest rides that I had out hunting was on a grey thoroughbred mare called Wilma that dad had brought as a possible teamchaser. I took her out on a Monday with the Quorn from a meet at Cedric and Jill Ford's

house on Bridgegate lane just outside Hickling. Right from the start she took a fierce hold and pulled like a train. It took every bit of my knowledge and strength to contain her. There was no reasoning with her and I was starting to have my doubts that I would survive until change of horses. Most of the morning was spent on the flat land towards Kinoulton which was quite helpful as it involved going slowly one behind the other around the headlands of ploughed fields. It was late in the season very warm and sunny. The hunt was basically wasting time as there was no scent due to the heat. We finally crossed over to Hickling Standard but did not draw Parson's Thorns surprisingly, I guessed that they were leaving it until the afternoon when hopefully the scent would improve. As we cantered up the steep hill towards the top of the Standard, I eased my grip and let her attack the hill to try and burn off some of the pent-up energy. That hill brought most fit horses to their knees if you rushed it. Many a cocky visitor has passed me going up that hill at full gallop only to be found a few minutes later in a heap on the ground, claimed by the telegraph pole Hunt Jump at the crest of the hill.

The hill appeared to do the trick and I was able to relax a smidgen as we made our way to Green Lane that led us back towards Hickling Village. I had kept well to the back of the field all morning and by the time I got onto the lane the hounds were about half a mile in front of me. As I went through the gateway, I looked back towards the rider following me and shouted "Gate Please" the recognised signal throughout the hunting world that the last person through the gate secures it. The mare seized her chance as I was distracted for a split second, she snatched the rein whipping a couple of inches through my fingers hooked her jaw and was gone! We hurtled down the lane at full gallop. We were going down a fairly steep hill and it was terrifying. I tried everything single trick I knew but it had no effect, we were hurtling down a slippery narrow tarmac lane, in front of me two riders were happily chatting away in the warm midday sun, whilst crossing a narrow bridge that was just wide enough for the two horses to cross side by side. "Look Out I can't stop" I screamed over and over again, at the last moment they heard me and kicked on clearing the bridge and started to move apart. I split them like an axe splitting a straight grained log. One flew to the left and the other to the right. To my horror I realised that one of the gentleman that I had just knocked into the ditch was Major Charlie Humfreys (no relation) Secretary of the Hunt who shouted "Try turning it into that big hedge" as I flew past. I decided to give it a try just to humour him but I had already tried and failed further back up the lane. I pulled on my left rein as hard as I could but her neck was locked against me. What it did do was to deflect her off the lane into a very deep bramble filled dyke that ran alongside the lane. I thought we were going to come down but after the initial shock she came up and galloped through the dense brambles tearing her skin and my clothes. All I could think about was my hand made Horace Batten boots that were being scratched all over. We finally came to an abrupt halt when we hit a culverted gateway across the dyke which she breasted. Wilma suddenly stopped in a state of shock and for a few moments refused to move. After much cajoling I managed to get her out of the dyke and went over to make my apologies to the Major and his friend for knocking them for six. Major Humfreys just laughed and said "I've had a lot worse happen. No harm done. Although, galloping in a ditch full of brambles to stop your horse is a new one on me!". After more apologies I promised to take Wilma home immediately but he just smiled and said, "Looks like you are back in charge now why don't you hack along with us we are only going back through the village to change horses".

Dad was waiting at our horse box ready to swop over with me. The first thing dad said to me was "Well how did she go?". "Terrible, nearly killed me" I replied as dad mounted and rode off to join the hunt.

Dad was convinced that all we needed was a change of bit and then Wilma would be fine. After two more outings on her where she galloped through several sets of post and rails turning them into match wood and then when I finally got her airborne, she ballooned over a set of rails going away from Ella's Gorse with a big ditch behind. She landed with both front feet in the ditch giving me one of the worst falls that I have ever had out hunting. Two falls later in that day and I had had enough. Shaking like a leaf and almost in tears I told my good friend Roger Jalland that I had total lost my ability to ride and that this was the last day I would hunt. He told me not to be so stupid. He said he always admired my riding and would give his right arm to be able to be able to ride one tenth as well as me. It was a nice compliment but it didn't help.

I didn't know it at the time but this would turn out to be a game-changer and influence my career as a coach. Everything I tried with this mare went wrong, we even tipped up jumping a plain innocuous open ditch. Major Humfrey even commented to me that I seemed to have found a love for being on the ground.

When I returned home, I made my announcement to dad. I had expected him to explode and belittle me but instead he told me he understood and that he would help me. He actually apologised for giving me a string of difficult rides and that a couple of rides on his best horse Frenchy would sort me out. It helped but didn't completely cure me. I was over thinking everything when it came to jumping fences. We didn't have the internet back in those days so it was a matter of going to the library and talking to people about it. Talking about it was the hardest part but it helped more than anything but more about that sort of stuff later in the book. The hunting season ended, summer came along with jousting and by the time we got to September and the start of the Teamchasing season I was back on form.

Another scary ride I had was on a lovely horse called Emily. Dad had been on a trip to Ireland and had bought a lorry load of horses. When he returned, he told us that he had bought twelve but when they arrived there were thirteen of them.

A good hunting friend of mine John Bayliss was interested in buying a new hunter so dad asked me to take the mare out and show her to John. She was a lovely ride and we jumped many jumps in fine style. We were hunting on what is called Dalby Top. Late in the day a fox took us over a line of hedges at the back of David Chandlers Turkey Farm towards the A6006 Melton road. They were big, black, and cut square with a wide flat top. The mare was keen and willing as we approached the huge hedge. We sailed into the air perfectly. I was already thinking if this does not sell the horse to John nothing will. Then the strangest thing happened she seemed to land on top of the hedge. Somehow, we managed to get to the other side without falling. I turned to John and said "I don't know what happened there, we met it on a perfect stride. Perhaps she didn't realise how wide it was". A few moments later the mystery was solved when a chuckling Doc Connors slapped me on the back saying "I bet thank that gave you a surprise young Sam. She must be Irish, she thought that big black hedge was a bank and tried to bank it. She won't make that mistake again. A grand horse you have there". The Doc was right we sailed everything else that day in fine style. John bought Emily and I think if you ask him, he will probably say it was the best horse he ever had.

You can never predict what a horse will do even in competent hands. One Monday near the end of the season I was following the Quorn in the car. I was not riding because I was starting my point to pointing and spring teamchasing season. The hounds had run from Ella's gorse and swung up to the Ashby to Melton road between the turn-off towards Willoughby and Birkles farm. Jim Bealby was master and I watched as he approached a gate onto the wide lane and gracefully popped the post and rails at the side off the gate. His horse clipped a protruding flat reinforcing stake and it flipped his horse over in corkscrew fashion. A horrible, unexpected fall. Thankfully, he was not hurt but his horse jumped up and galloped off down the road towards Wymeswold. His son Ashley was dispatched to go and retrieve his father's horse. For some unknown reason Jim's horse went into full panic mode and bolted towards Wymeswold about a mile away. It is almost unheard for a horse to run away from the herd. Lou and I followed at a safe distance behind Ashley in the car so as not to exasperate the problem and to be there to give assistance when the horse was caught. As we approached Wymeswold I became aware that Ashley's speed was increasing and that he was making strenuous attempts to stop the horse but to no avail. Just before they got to the village Ashley did an amazing thing. He threw himself off his horse into some thorn bushes at full gallop. How he managed to do it and to survive I do not know. We paused our chase briefly to check that he was ok but he was already getting to his feet and waving us on. By the time we got into the village there was no sign of the horses. Every corner we turned I had a dread of a dead horse wrapped around the front of a car or lorry but thankfully there was none. There were two junctions in Wymeswold which meant the horses could have gone one of three ways. They galloped nearly three miles including just under a mile along the main A60 Nottingham to Loughborough road before turning up a lane to Canaan Farm Riding Stables. How they avoided a major pile up I will never know. It made no sense that two horses should bolt away from over one hundred horses. Somebody once said that you are always just a tenth of a second away from sitting on a wild horse if it is badly frightened. How true!

The excitement of fox hunting as against drag hunting is that with drag hunting the organisers know where they are going and organise the day so that it finishes close to where the horse boxes are parked. With fox hunting they try to do the same but after Xmas you get what are called travelling dog foxes that have come from a different area and that's when you get an extraordinary hunt that takes you to places unknown. We had changed horses at the Durham Ox Hotel on the A46 near Ragdale. As the temperature dropped, we got what is called a breast high scent when cold air pushes down towards the warmer ground trapping the fox scent about eighteen inches to two feet off the ground which is simply perfect for the hounds and they fly. These hunts are often known as the four o' clock fox.

 On and on we galloped desperately trying to keep up with the hounds from Ragdale to Old Dalby and on towards Grimston before swinging down into the Vale of Belvoir finally running the fox to ground on the edge of Nether Broughton. It was about three thirty, I assumed that we would all head back to Ragdale but everyone seemed to be just hanging around and I was starting to worry as in an hour or so it would be getting dark. I finally managed to grab a word with the hunt secretary to find out what was going on. It was not good they had finished hunting and sent a car back to The Durham Ox to tell the grooms to bring the horse boxes down to Nether Broughton because they didn't think that they could get back before dark. I didn't have a groom and this was pre- mobile phone era. When I thought through my options non were good. The Durham Ox was probably the quickest but when I got there I would have to try and load my horse in the dark all on my own. Not a pleasing prospect.

Hacking home was probably a little longer but probably the safer option. Having just googled the two routes I was a little out on my calculations. The Durham Ox was six miles, and home was ten miles. I knew time was against me so I set off wishing friends good night, when I told them that I was hacking home they were gob smacked. My route took me along the A606 to Upper Broughton then I took the lane to Willoughby. I stopped at the phone box in Willoughby and called home to let them know what I was doing. In those days you always carried phone money in your hunt coat pockets for emergencies. First my mum and then Lou would always say to me as I rushed out of the house on hunting mornings "Have you got your phone money?" It was not easy to use a call- box with a horse as the heavy strongly sprung door was always trying to close and trap your reins. You had to spread your legs wide to keep the door open, talk to your horse to keep calm so that it didn't pull-back, balance the phone on your shoulder while dialling the number and pushing the money in to answer. The last bit was the hardest as when you pressed the A button to speak there was a loud clunk followed by a lot of clattering as your money fell through the mechanism. This nearly always spooked your horse and you were dragged out of the phone by the horse running back leaving the phone dangling and a voice saying "Hello, hello, is anyone there".

On the second attempt I managed to get through to Lou and tell her what I was doing. I then proceeded on to Wysall the light was fading fast by now and as I left Wysall it was completely dark.

And so, started on of the most terrifying rides of my life, three and a quarter miles riding a dark bay horse. To make matters worse I was wearing a long black hunt coat and black boots. We were as near too invisible as you could get. There was hardly any safe grass verge so I was forced to ride along the edge of the rode which was a narrow lane barely wide enough for two cars to pass. It was rush hour and drivers were speeding along with only home on their minds. I had so many near misses and cannot believe we survived once I got onto the main A60 the traffic was almost bumper to bumper and the closely packed headlights illuminated me enough to be seen but it didn't stop many of them sounding their horns at an idiot dressed all in black riding up Bunny Hill at rush hour. As I turned off the A60 onto Bunny Hill top I breathed a huge sigh of relief. How we had survived the last forty-five minutes without a serious accident I do not know. The only thing now was to be drive back to the Durham Ox and retrieve the horsebox. It was gone seven by the time I arrived home. An exceptionally long and tiring day's hunting. The aftermath of my experience was the I went to a cycle shop and bought a florescent Strip that you could wear diagonally across the body and added to my hunt coat pocket along with the other emergency items such as the bandage and money for the phone. Nowadays the horse rider is blessed with every manner of reflective kit, even red and with sidelights that strap to your boots.

What I would have given to have some of that on my ride home!

Chapter Five
Visiting other packs

This is a short chapter, and I regret that greatly, but sadly time and money were not available to go gallivanting off all over the country fox hunting. There is an old saying "Work. The curse of the fox hunting man"

I joined the Melton Hunt Club when I started racing and you will hear more about that Club later on in the book. Its importance to this chapter is that as a member you could buy a ticket that allowed you to visit one of the participating packs at a much-reduced fee. Originally, it was only the main shire packs that had country touching Melton Mowbray, the Quorn, Belvoir and Cottesmore, but over the years other packs have joined the scheme when they have hit hard times.

The Belvoir Hunt

I had several very enjoyable days with the Belvoir who I found to be a really friendly pack. They have a large, varied country with superb grass and hedges in the Vale of Belvoir, and wide deep open ditches out in the Lincolnshire part of their country. I first hunted with them when Joey Newton was master. Joey was one of my point-to-point adversary's, a top-class jockey, and a quiet competent master to follow across country. I will always remember jumping a gate off the road on my home bred horse Mitten who was out of my dad's great hunter Frenchy. Hounds were running and Joey turned to the field and said "I'm going to jump the gate it is chained and padlocked. Only follow me if you are sure, you and your horse are capable. If you break the gate, you will be charged £100". Not only was it off a narrow slippery lane you had to jump it at an angle to get enough run up at it. A large proportion of the field decided to take the longer easier road route. I could not bear to lose face so I went for the gate. The short approach suited Mitten and we sailed cleanly over the gate, Quorn honour was retained and my meagre bank balance breathed a sigh of relief. I met up with two old friends that day, one was Sally Spence, daughter of Stuart Spence the farrier. Stuart and our family have a long association, both my brother Phil and later my son Mark served their apprenticeships with this great farrier. His forge is on the edge of the village green at Hose in the Vale of Belvoir. It is probably the only forge in the country that is still left in the centre of a village on its green, and it goes back for generations. I was mortified to hear that newcomers to the village wanted to have it closed down and moved out of the village. Morons!

Stuart and his son Richard run a big yearly shoeing competition and for many years my dad supplied the horses for the competition. Sally and my daughter Emma were of similar ages and we met the family at lots of Pony club events when they were younger. The other person was Joey Newton's wife Emma who I knew from racing days. I asked if he was still racing as, I had lost touch with that scene. He stopped about the same time as me. Joey is a big, tall guy and she told me that his natural weight was near to fourteen stone and it had been purgatory trying to keep his weight down to eleven stone. I struggled and my normal weight was about twelve stone. Hats off to him, that's serious dedication.

Another visit to the Belvoir was when Martin Brown was master. The Brown family like the Spence family have been family friends for generations. Dad and myself were good friends with Martin's parents Ann and Charlie, Martin is roughly the same age as my two brothers Phil and Stuart and spent a lot of his school holidays at Bunny Hill. Later Martin joined the Jousting Troupe and travelled all around the world with us for many years. I think Martin is about eleven years younger than me, I was still Point to Pointing when he started to race and we rode against each other for a couple of seasons. We also hunted together in Ireland which is why I got to be out that day.

Martin had invited a big group of his Irish hunting pals over for a few days hunting and partying as the Irish do.

They had brought all their own horses over in two huge lorries. Many of the horses were being stabled at Richard Chandler's farm which is just outside of the village of Long Clawson. Richard loves his hunting and was a great open team chase rider, riding with many of the top teams. His farm was the venue for the Belvoir Team Chase. The course was my favourite and was definitely one of the best in the country. Personally, I would say it was the best but I'm sure others would disagree.

I met up with the visitors for an evening meal at the pub in Long Clawson. The night before hunting.

Much beer and wine was consumed as I caught up with a lot of my old Irish friends. It was a great night and we were all a little delicate as we made our way to the meet at a beautiful house in Buckminster. It was late in the season and I recall an Irish lady saying that she was regretting wearing a pullover. Like a lot of spring mornings, it was very cold first thing but it was a lovely sunny day and now it was getting decidedly warm as we made our way down the long drive to the meet. Not a good omen for scent.

After some restorative drinks at the meet, we moved off to draw some lovely old woodland. Hounds soon found and hunted well in the large tract of woodland and we had great fun, scampering around, jumping a few post and rails in and out of the woodland and several streams that ran through the wood. Unfortunately, as soon as the hounds left the damp woodland and got out into the sunny fields the scent disappeared. It was very frustrating for Martin as he was desperate to give his visitors a good day. However, Martin had anticipated the bad scenting conditions and saved the best of the country for the end of the day when it was forecast for the temperature to drop. Warm ground, cold air, hopefully a magical breast high scent to end the day. Martin kept us busy until about three thirty when the temperature started to drop. Martin sidled up to me and quietly said "Got a bit of a long hack now but it will be worth it. Don't go home yet".

One of the unexpected surprises was to ride underneath the massive Waltham on the Wolds, television transmitter mast that soars to a stunning height of 950 feet. As I looked up from its base my stomach flipped and I went very giddy. It really is an awesome piece of engineering.

Shortly after passing under the tower, we came to a dense thorn covert and the hounds were put in to draw. Martin looked across to me gave me the thumbs up as he silently mouthed "This is it". We all waited for the hounds to speak trembling with excitement. But all was quiet not a whimper from the hounds, the last dregs of hipflasks were shared and drained. As the long wait continued Martin addressed what was left of the field which now only amounted to me the Irish and a few Belvoir diehards. He explained that he had organised a photographer to capture us all jumping this huge bloody hedge all together as a memento of the visit. We all had to line up as close together as we could and jump between two specific points, so that the cameraman could get us all in the shot. Martin gave us a great lead and everyone was laughing and joking as we galloped towards the hedge all packed so close together, we were like sardines in a can. By the time, the photo-shoot was over hounds were out of the covert and we finished the day with a good hunt.

The visit was concluded with another evening meal/party this time the venue was the Sugar Loaf pub at Ab Kettleby just outside Melton Mowbray. To the racing mad Irish Ab Kettleby was like visiting a shrine as it had been the home of Desert Orchid the famous grey steeplechaser who achieved cult status during his glittering career.

My brother Phil and his band, "Growling at the Badger" played after the meal and it was a wild night of singing, dancing, and of course drinking. Again, I met yet more long-lost friends. It was especially nice to meet up with the Dobson family who like our family were all into riding and also had a riding school in the early sixties at Ashfordby before moving out to Cold Newton near Oakham when we started to lose contact with them.

I did not know all the Irish visitors personally but one of the prime movers of the trip was Pat Loughlin who I had recently bought a horse from. Pat is a very colourful character not only does he deal in horses, but he also supplies hirelings for hunting, has his own pub Loughlins in the Village of Gowran and is the local undertaker. Michael Brannigan and John Dollard were also over in the party and were long-time hunting friends.

I spoke to Martin just before writing this piece and he reminded me of a tale from our racing day's together. I had completely forgotten the incident. We were both riding at the Fernie point to point which is held at Dingley. It is one of the last hunt point to points of the season before the grand finale of the Melton Hunt Club meeting.

Martin was riding a horse owned by his friend Bill Halliday in the race before mine. I think it was the horse's first race because it ran out at one of the fences and crashed through the wings ejecting Martin straight over his head so violently that he took the bridle with him. Apparently when he came to in the ambulance, he was still holding the bridle. I was just about to go out to ride in my race when he staggered into the changing room blood all over his face and still clutching the bridle. He slumped down and looked very groggy. I went over to him and said "You alright mate, you don't look so good" just then we got the "Jockeys out for the next race" call from the paddock steward just as he mumbled "Yeah, I think I'll be ok when I've had a bit of a rest" he said that my last kind words to him as I left the changing room was "You'd better be! Don't forget that I'm picking you up at eight in the morning. We are jousting down in Hounslow tomorrow". True to the racing and jousting spirit he was on parade next morning albeit a bit stiff and crotchety. We were performing at Hounslow Festival; it was one of the biggest shows we ever did. The organisers wrote a letter of thanks afterwards and said that the attendance for that day was 37,500 people.

The Cottesmore Hunt

The hunting world is small and wherever you go you will meet someone who knows a mutual friend. This gives you confidence to chat with complete strangers. My visit to the Cottesmore started badly I arrived in good time but finding somewhere to park our large jousting horsebox proved exceptionally difficult. Eventually I found a place but it was some distance from the meet. It was 10:50am by the time I was mounted and set off at a cracking trot confident that I could make the meet on time. At two minutes to eleven I entered the long drive up to the house where the meet was being held. I slowed to a walk to allow my horse to cool down as it is not good form to arrive at the meet with your horse in a muck sweat. The drive was considerably longer than I had expected and in was about five past eleven when I arrived. There was not a sole about. There were horse droppings everywhere so I was at the right place but now not a sight or sound of horses. Eventually a gardener appeared with a wheelbarrow to start cleaning up after the horses. I asked him where the meet was. He laughed, "You must be a visitor" he said. Didn't they tell you we meet at 10:45 the Captain likes to be hunting by eleven. He gave me directions to the first covert that they were going to draw. I thanked him profusely and cantered off leaving him chuckling into his wheelbarrow. I thought, I like the sound of this master but I better get a wriggle on or he could be in the next county before I catch up. Sadly, a lot of my visits to other packs were at the end of season and so scenting conditions were never great. But to be out in different country and face fences that you have never jumped before makes it all worthwhile. I came around a clump of trees next to some old farm buildings and wham! There was the field quietly waiting at the side of the covert. Relief washed through my body I was not going to miss the hunt after all!

As I looked around for the hunt secretary a man dressed in a tan hunt coat with a dark brown velvet collar smiled and nodded to me. His face looked familiar but before I could make my way over to speak with him, I was accosted by the secretary. What puzzled me was the colour of his coat and collar. I had it in my mind that it might be the collar of the Readyfield Bloodhounds but his face was familiar I just could not place him. As I paid my dues to the secretary, I took the opportunity to ask him who was the man in the brown coat. Hunt secretaries are always a mine of information as it is their job to know the status of everyone who is following on a given day. He informed me that he was part of a group of Irish who were all members of the Scarteen Hunt better known as the Black and Tans. Now I knew who he was Dickie Power. He was my chaperone from the last time I visited the pack when I was over in Ireland on a hunting trip. Every time I hunted with a new pack in Ireland Patricia Brennan would arrange for someone to be my buddy for the day in case I got injured or lost.

The Irish party was led by Chris Ryan a legend in his own time as Master and Huntsman of the Scarteen Hounds it was like a mutual royal visit, because Capt. Brian Fanshawe Master and Amateur Huntsman of the Cottesmore Hounds was also considered to be one of the greatest huntsmen in England. There was no ceremony about visits as they were both modest people. Sadly, it was a bad scenting day so no great hunts but plenty of scampering around over mainly hunt jumps.

My friend Dickie from the Scarteen seemed to be chief cameraman for the party using a small camcorder which he even used while sailing over the jumps one handed. When I finally caught up with him and had a chat I asked if any of the footage he had shot would be usable because when I had tried to video off horseback the picture was terrible due to camera shake. He explained that this model had just come out and it had an image stabiliser built into it giving a crystal-clear picture at all times. I was amazed, how things have come on, nowadays every camera has that technology. He was extremely pleased to meet-up with me again and he told me that this was their last evening over here. They were having a meal, followed by Chris Ryan giving a talk and showing a film of the Scarteen in action to members of the Cottesmore Hunt as a thank you. The venue was the Barnsdale Hotel. The hotel sits on top of a hill overlooking Rutland Water. He invited me and Lou to join them. I readily accepted and hoped Lou hadn't made other plans for the evening.

It was a good hour's drive from our house to the hotel and the meal was at 7pm. It was a bit manic when I sprang the news on Lou as didn't get back to the yard until five and we needed to leave before six. That didn't give Lou long to sort out what to wear and then there was the matter of the meal she had prepared. Anyway, Lou understood we owed a debt of gratitude to Dickie. So off we raced. We were slightly late arriving but we were made very welcome, it was a hot buffet and people were still queuing to be fed, so no problem. We had a wonderful evening and even managed to have a nice chat to Chris Ryan.

What a lovely man!

The High Peak Hunt

My next story is about the High Peak Hunt which hunts in north Derbyshire known as The Peak District. Its country lies between Ashbourne, Bakewell, and Buxton. It is without doubt the most stunning country I have ever laid my eyes on. It just takes your breath away. Most of their country is over 1,000 ft above sea level. It is a sea of grass and white stonewalls. Just writing about it sends a shiver down my spine.

I am writing this section of the book during the corona virus lockdown. The week before the lockdown started, we were supposed to be visiting the Alhambra Palace in Granada Spain but we cancelled as flights to Spain were already shutting down. Having gone to a lot of trouble to arrange for animals to be looked after and Lou's father who is ninety-one to go into a care home for a week we decided to have a few days up in Derbyshire. We have a horsey friend who owns a hotel just outside the village of Hope. With time to kill we decided to take a scenic route along narrow B roads from Bakewell to Hope. It was a corner of the Peak District we had never explored. We rose up out of Bakewell and seemed to be climbing forever, up narrow tree covered valleys, then suddenly we burst out onto the tops. A huge vista of reasonably flat grassland covered in white stone walls that sparked in the sunshine from a cloudless blue sky. Lou and I both uttered the words WOW! In unison. I then said, "This is high peak country, and it is just as I remember it". A wave of emotion swept through my body as I remembered that day and wished I had made the effort to make the long journey to visit them again.

As I said earlier, I love stone walls!

The story of how I got to be invited to hunt with the High Peak really belongs in another chapter but like so much this book many of the doors that opened opportunities for me came about through riding horses one way or another.

It was 1984 and we had made a big breakthrough into television drama. The series was a BBC production about a family split by the English civil war called "By the sword divided". We were hired to do the cavalry scenes and took the parts of both royalists and parliamentarians. It was filmed at Rockingham Castle near Corby in Northamptonshire. We were on set for six weeks in September and October. There was a lot of publicity surrounding the series and the film and television industry is a close-knit community. Early in December we got a call from the High Peak Hunt. They had been asked to provide horses riders and hounds for a hunt scene in a film called "Lady Jane Grey". They were struggling to get enough Hunt members to commit to several weeks of filming just before Christmas and asked if we had any horses and riders that could come and work on the film. It was our second big break in a year. We ended up working on the film through most of December and into early January. We did more sitting in a catering tent than filming as we were waiting for it to snow. During these long boring days, I met Martin Brocklehurst who was amateur huntsman with the High Peak. His father John was Master of the Hunt so it was a real family affair. Their business was country clothing as is still flourishing today. If you visit any big agricultural show or equestrian event you see their trade stand, Brocklehurst's. I always pop in when I am at Burghley Horse Trials and have a quick chat with Martin to this day. It is a super stall full of great quality clothes.

Our friendship flourished and he invited me up for a day hunting.

I was extremely excited about this day's hunting as their stone walls were legendary. Then disaster struck. I was training a new jousting horse to halt from canter, gripped hard with my legs and got a searing pain at the top of my leg. I had done my groin muscle. They call it the riders injury. When I dismounted, I realised that it was worse than I thought. I could not pick my right leg up to walk. The only way a could walk was by taking hold of the front of my breeches and lifting my leg and swing it forward. I was supposed to be hunting with Martin in five days' time, I was devastated. There was no way I could ride my usual hunter I had no grip in my right leg nor could I kick with it. I was so down at the thought of missing my day with The High Peak. I can't remember if it was dad or Lou who suggested that I take Sniper. I was mortified at the suggestion. Sniper was one of our riding school horses, she was a coloured cob that had been pulling a milk float when dad bought her. She wasn't a stuffy Cob; in fact, she was extremely forward going and was superb jumper. However, the thought of me turning up on a coloured cob was more than my pride could take. I gave it a lot of painful thought; she was used to novice riders and was used to sorting everything out herself when it came to jumping. She was very much a point and shoot jumper. I could just hang onto the neck strap and she would do the rest. As the days ticked by my groin was no better, I had to decide! Did I miss something that I had been looking forward to for weeks or did I swallow my pride and take Sniper. I swallowed my pride.

It was just under a two hour drive up to the meet and I now thought how lucky it was my right leg that was injured because there was no way I would have been able to push the lorry's heavy clutch in if it had been my left leg.

The High Peak are a harrier pack and I fell in love with the hounds as soon as I saw them, they were beautiful and oozed personality. Although they were a Harrier pack, they also hunted fox. The hunt livery was dark green which I thought was very smart. During our first hunt I noticed a lot of barbed wire in front of the stone walls and was musing to myself on how this would affect the hunting. I need not have worried as soon as we approached a wired wall a gallant gentleman leapt from his horse and threw his hunt coat over the offending wire and we all sailed on, over hunt coat and wall. The gently rolling hills gave some lovely views of these beautiful little hounds working, they were so quick. The hunt were very respectful of their country and if you rolled a stone off a wall you had to dismount and replace it. Luckily for me Sniper jumped clean as a whistle all day including a massive wall without any help from me. I think we must have jumped over fifty walls that day and I loved every minute of it as did Sniper. As I hacked home, I recalled the old horse saying. "Handsome is as handsome does".

It was a glorious day, thank you Martin!

The Meynell and South Staffordshire Hunt

My visit to the Meynell Hunt was again courtesy of the Melton Hunt Club. Although they were not a regular member of the hunt club ticket scheme they did join for a few seasons. The Meynell borders the South Notts. in high Derbyshire and the Atherstone in the south. Their country is rugged and trappy and is not for the faint hearted. The huntsman at the time was David Barker who had been a top class show jumper in his younger days. His equestrian skill was a wonder to observe as he effortlessly jumped what many would have deemed un-jumpable obstacles.

As always on visits to other packs I was greeted by the hunt secretary, not really greet me but to relive me of my cap money or in this case my pre-paid Melton ticket. The unusual thing about this hunt secretary was that he smoked a pipe and this intrigued me for the whole day as he never seemed to take it out of his mouth except when he was having a long conversation. Galloping and jumping he kept it firmly clenched between his teeth.

The hounds were much smaller than our local hounds and I was informed by a friendly local that David Barker had been deliberating breeding smaller hounds because the country was full of thick hedges and the larger hounds found it difficult the get through them. It certainly seemed to be working as they crossed the difficult country with great speed and agility. Early in the day I witnessed the huntsman's jumping skills. Hounds had just found and were quickly away but we soon found ourselves wired in as everyone crammed into this small paddock making almost impossible for the hunt staff to get through the packed horses. The way everyone needed to go was barred by an extremely large hedge with a wide scoop ditch in front of it that was protected by two strands of horrible sagging barbed wire. Our intrepid huntsman turned to his whipper in and ordered him to take off his jacket and lay it over the barbed wire. As this was being done, he shouted at the field to give him some room which was nigh impossible in such a compact space. After much shuffling and shouting we managed to give him barley four strides approach for this massive leap, seconds later he was gone and we were left shuffling about trying to turn around and find another route. During this mayhem I found myself wedged next to the whip who had now retrieved his jacket and was trying to button up his jacket one handed. I offered to hold his horse reins so that he could use both hands to do up the buttons which he gratefully accepted. As he buttoned up his coat I said, "your governor takes at bit of following". He just sighed and said, "Yes he's a f**cking nightmare".

We had a good hunt, jumping some big holly hedges and some had a good drop on landing, all of which I noted were jumped by the secretary while still puffing on his pipe. Later in the day I saw David Barker jump a large set of rails that had a very low bough hanging down in front of them somehow, he managed to duck under the bough and jump the post and rails, his poor whip tried to follow him and took a crashing fall.

I had a great day with the Meynell, some great hunting and a very friendly field. Many years later our lifetime friend Vanda and Lou my wife went hunting with Meynell. Vanda's partner Ian had bid for them at an auction held during the Atherstone hunt ball. She hadn't hunted for many years but was determined to go. As her partner didn't ride, she chose Lou to accompany her. They made them very welcome and when they found out she had not hunted for many years told her not to worry they would look after her. Everyone was so friendly and Vanda had a great day she will remember for the rest of her life. However, I believe she did have trouble walking for a couple of days after the event. Vanda is editing this book for me locked down in southern Turkey during the Corona virus epidemic so this memory will be a nice surprise.

The South Durham Hunt

The furthest I have travelled to go hunting was to visit the South Durham. Both Lou and I were invited by Dick Watkin a colleague of Lou's father who worked for Price Waterhouse as a consultant partner. Dick lived in Sedgefield and had taken up riding as relaxation from his busy work that took him all over Europe. Dick is a man full of energy and had set his sights on going hunting. This led to him coming down to Bunny Hill with his horse to improve his cross-country skills. As his old pal Rex, Lou's dad lived just down the road and also had taken up riding it made sense as a short break holiday.

Dick lived in a large farmhouse with plenty of out buildings for his horses and horsebox. Except for a few acres of grazing for his horses he had leased the rest of the land to a local farmer.

Dick was incredibly pleased with the outcome of his training visits and we became good friends, culminating in an invitation to come up to stay with him and his wife Barbara who also had an interest in horses. Also included was an offer for Lou and I to have a day's hunting with the South Durham Hunt, horses provided.

After an excellent evening, the night before, and substantial breakfast in the morning, we drove over to the meet which was being held in the centre of a large village. The village was beautiful with a very wide main street lined with trees planted on a wide strip on grass. The meet as with so many hunts was at a pub. The pub welcomed us with generous stirrup cups and excellent food before we moved off. Dick wasn't hunting as he had generously donated both of his two hunters to us.

The field were extremely friendly both in conversation and their hip flasks.

Again, as with so many of my visits it was late in the season a lovely sunny day with spasmodic scent. You may wonder why I did most of my visiting late in the season when sport tends to be not quite so good. It came down to two factors, first was qualifying my pointers which often dragged on into January and the other factor was up to Christmas we could usually get on the fields to do work, but in January they became bottomless and all work had to stop until early May. This made Feb/ March the ideal time to by away from home.

We had lots of short hunts and although there were no swathes of grass and hedges, the country was trappy not unlike Derbyshire and it certainly kept you on your toes. The great thing about visiting is riding new country, always learning new skills, and of course meeting new people which I love more than anything. At the end of a busy and most convivial day our chauffeur awaited us. Dick was a little apologetic that we could not go straight home and soak in a hot bath but the Hunt master had a strict rule that everyone who was out that day had to return to the pub and have at least one drink as a thank you to the landlord for putting on the meet. He also asked that, if possible, they also have a meal as well. What a brilliant idea a man after my own heart, so many people these days take and never think about giving something back. I was always taught if somebody lends something or helps you always give something back.

You may be surprised but both Lou and I were both happy to defer the hot bath to obey the master's request. Later after our hot bath we were treated to another great meal and lively banter.

Thank you, Dick!

The Pytchley Hunt

The Pytchley Hunt was dad's local hunt before he was married. Their kennels were at Guilsborough just two miles up the road from the village of Ravensthorpe where he lived with his family before moving to Nottingham. Dad talked a lot about the hunt and I always dreamed about having a day with them. It was not until my daughter Emma moved down to that area did the opportunity arise to make that dream come true.

Emma moved her event horse's to Aston le Walls Event Centre after she finished training with Tiny Clapham. The Centre is situated close to the border of the Pytchley and the Bicester with Whaddon Hunts.

I hunted with the Pytchley just before the ban probably in 2003/4 season on one of Emma's young eventer's, the countryside was beautiful with rolling hills. As usual everyone was very friendly. It was a busy day but recent heavy rain had restricted where we could go. My overriding memorable moment was when the horse I was riding got agitated when we got very squashed together on a narrow lane. My horse suddenly started to run backwards trying to get out of the tight cram. Once in reverse gear he just kept walking backwards, intermixed with the horses were a lot of expensive cars and as looked over my shoulder I saw we were moving relentlessly towards the bonnet of a brand-new top of the range, Range Rover. It is times like this that you start to realise how important insurance is. I was having a quiet panic attack as I could not recall if mine had been renewed. Thankfully just as we were about to sit on this car's bonnet the hunt moved forward again and I breathed a big sigh of relief. When I related the incident to Emma she just laughed saying "Oh, did I not tell you about that. Yes, he does tend to do that when he gets worried".

My second visit to the Pytchley was just after the ban. The meet was at Charwelton and we were late arriving. The first thing that I saw when we found the hunt was an impeccably dressed man in a sort of hunt livery, but he was not mounted, he was holding a magnificent golden eagle. This was one of the loopholes in the hunting ban that allowed you to flush a foxes with hounds to be hunted by a bird of prey. It was a very lively morning and we had checked on the side of the cover. Everyone was chatting away enjoying the late autumn sunshine and sharing hip flasks. I was catching up with a friend from the Quorn Stuart Morris who had moved away some years before and we had lost touch.

Suddenly mayhem broke out and horses shot here, there, and everywhere. Several bodies hit the deck. This all happened in a matter of seconds, horses senses are far better than ours. Without warning a large stag with a full set of antlers burst out of the wood, leapt over the wire fence that surrounded the covert and landed a few yards from where I was standing. He seemed as surprised to see us as we were to see him. He landed and paused; it would have appeared that he was surrounded by horses. For a few seconds I was mesmerised by his magnificence, even though I knew more mayhem was about to happen. A loud authoritative voice shouted "Quickly clear a way for him to escape. Move! Now! Quickly". This man saved us from what could have been a nasty incident as we were hemmed into a small paddock. The paused stag looked around accessing his situation, time stood still. People started to move back and open up an escape route for him. He looked around, dipped his antlers ever so slightly as if giving a royal salute and then trotted down the pathway we had cleared for him. As he exited our pathway he broke into a slow graceful canter and calmly disappeared. It was as if he understood we presented no threat to him. It was one of the most moving things I have ever seen.

We had a great day with lots of jumping. Sadly, a lot of post and rails had had their top rails removed to make the jumps smaller so that all the followers could cross the country. For me it was so sad. I had been brought up to the saying if you cannot follow hounds wherever they take you, don't hunt.

Unfortunately, the times were changing, hunts were suffering financially and needed more followers. It was not the hunting ban although that wasn't helping. It was a complete change in the equestrian and general mind set of the nation. It was extraordinarily complex but put simply the nation lost its balls. In the seventies and eighties and more so in the years before, we took risks in business life and sport. In hunting, racing and team chasing we expected injuries and wore them as a badge of honour. Many of us rode and competed with plastered arms, or a stirrup leather around our body and an upper arm to hold a dislocated shoulder in place. I even fabricated an extra-large stirrup so that I could ride with a full leg plaster. Concussion was something you got on a regular basis but you didn't stop riding or competing.

Health and safety was a big cause but the sharp recession of the mid-nineties really shook people's confidence, jobs became precious, employers did not take kindly to their staff injuring themselves doing risky sports. People became more careful with their money, the spend, spend, mentality of live life today, tomorrow will look after itself vanished. New rules appeared regarding safety. Even little village horse shows were required to have medical cover. Skull caps and body protectors became mandatory for virtually everything. The list goes on I suppose it is progress in some people's minds.

The Bicester with Whaddon Chase Hunt

The Bicester and the Whaddon Chase hunts amalgamated in 1986/7 and the hunt is now mostly referred to as the Bicester for no other reason than it is easier to say. The Bicester was Emma's other local pack and when Emma suggested that I come down and have a day I jumped at the chance.

I was accompanied by Mark Milner whose wife Helen was a joint Master of the Atherstone Hunt. I had taught Mark to ride and we had become great friends. I thought it would be good for him to see how other hunts work and experience some other hunting country. As usual when visiting other packs finding somewhere to park close to the meet is always a problem and we ended up parking further away from the meet than we would have liked. It was just after eleven when we arrived at the Butcher Arms in Priors Hardwick, thankfully the hunt was still at the meet. Emma had warned us that the Bicester had changed from normal colourful hunt livery to tweed jackets. This applied to everyone including the hunt staff so we were dressed in tweed as well. After paying our dues to the secretary we moved on to introduce ourselves to the master. It was quite a challenge to find him, as everyone looked the same. When we did locate him, he welcomed us and asked the usual questions such as, which hunt do you belong to and where do you live. When I told him the Quorn, he immediately asked me if I knew the village of Widmerpool. I told him I knew it very well as it was about five miles from where I lived. He was delighted and ask if I knew his father Major George Valance. I had known George and his wife for many years as he had been Master of the South Notts when I was qualifying my point to pointers with them. He was a lovely man and after he retired, he and his wife would regularly follow both the Quorn and South Notts in an incredibly old Land Rover that was full of enough booze to give everyone following a drink. Whenever the hunt checked, the Land Rover would appear like magic and George and his wife would be instantly handing out generous portions of whatever tipple you fancied. I never knew he had a son but again just goes to show what a small world the hunting world is. He was so pleased that I knew his father and we were warmly welcomed.

Something had gone very wrong at the meet which accounted for the delay in moving off. The pub or perhaps I should call it a restaurant was not open. The restaurant was a great favourite of the local equestrian and farming community and would never have deliberately not offered hospitality. I had eaten at this excellent restaurant several times and knew the owner would have been mortified at the mix-up. We waited patiently until someone arrived to open up and hand out stirrup cups.

When we finally moved off, we were quickly galloping across large grass fields and jumping small fences. The countryside was fabulous, big, rounded hills and stunning views. Although I love my jumping seeing new vistas is almost as thrilling. The morning was taken up with lots of dashing backwards and forwards but everything changed as we came down a steep track and before us lay much flatter ground. There was an air of anticipation creeping though the field. It was then that I noticed that the large majority of the field were going off in a different direction to the way the master was heading. I asked someone what was happening, why were all these people going home? He went on to explain that they had two masters these days, a jumping master, and a non-jumping master. I was dumbfounded. Not only about the non-jumping master but that the non-jumping section of the hunt was the largest. I thought the Pytchley were bad having lowered some of the jumps but to have an official non jumping section beggared belief. It went against everything that I believed hunting was about. Even sadder, was I realised that this was the future of hunting if it were to survive. We were changing from expresso to latte and I never could stomach latte.

In their defence what came next was pretty serious. Large hunt jump after large hunt jump. This was sheep country and all the lovely hedges had been back fenced with stock wire and barbed wire. It would have been uncrossable without hunt jumps. I hate hunt jumps but these were seriously good and not for the faint hearted. Bolt upright big thick telegraph poles with four sheep rails underneath giving them a slight false ground line, all were a metre plus in height not massive but if you made a mistake, they were very unforgiving, built so solid that a tank would bounce off them. The good thing was that the take-offs and landings had all been stoned with soft stone so at least you were not jumping out of deep mud, that would have been really scary! We had a great run over these unforgiving fences and during a brief check I commented on the sturdiness of their hunt jumps to a man that looked as if he had hunted most of his life. He told me that some years ago the hunt had a financial crisis and one of the biggest outgoings was fence repairs. They decided to invest in these solid hunt jumps, they had cost a lot of money at the time but now the cost of repairing fences was a negligible cost. We hunted back to the steep hill that we had come down earlier it was about two thirty in the afternoon and as we only had one horse decided to call it a day because the last thing you wanted to be doing was jumping those fences on a tired horse.

It was a couple of miles hack back to the horsebox. After seeing to our horses, we ate our packed lunch and relived our lovely day out before driving home. It was a long day but well worth the trip.

Chapter Six
Racing

My First Race

It was Easter Monday, my first point to point race. As we circled at the start, a bitterly cold wind blew across the flat fenland chilling my body to numbness. I looked up at the sky hopefully wishing that the sun would break through the high flat cloud but all it could manage to do was to turn the cloud a pale sallow cream. It was late March. Easter was early that year and Spring had yet to show itself. How was I going to be able to ride a race when all my body was numb? All I was wearing was a pair of thin nylon breeches and a thin loose knitted pullover which bore my racing colours, they were navy blue, lemon hoop and lemon cap silk. Underneath my pullover was a back protector, a strip of high-density foam that ran down my back and widened at the bottom to protect the kidneys. It was held in place by a broad piece of elastic that used the new fastening method called Velcro.

I was jerked out of my stupor by someone asking if I needed my girth checking, "Yes Please" I answered glad to have somebody to talk to and break the tension. We continued to circle as everyone else had their girth checked and then suddenly a man started to shout out numbers and one by one my fellow competitors shouted out, "Here Sir". Nobody had told me about this as I nervously checked my number cloth and waited for my number to be called. Why hadn't anyone told me about calling the officials sir? I was just thankful mine was not the first number called. When he had finished his role call the starter studied his watch with a deliberate intensity before raising his head and announcing, "Three minutes gentlemen. Continue circling until I call you in". The three long minutes ticked slowly by and the cold bit ever deeper.

The starter, flag in hand, slowly mounted the steps to his rostrum while his assistant appeared in front of the first fence holding another flag high above his head, even at seventy-five yards away you hear the rattle of the flag in the cold stiff breeze. "Right let's be having you. Make a line and walk forward! Steady, steady, keep that line. Go on then!" he yelled as he brought the flag down and the nine jockeys kicked their mounts forward.

The starter's assistant paused for a moment to check that the starter was happy that it was a clean start, he then lowered his flag and marched at double time off the course to the safety of the course running rails.

The silence was broken instantly by a mixture of snorting from the horses as they launched themselves from a walk to a gallop in one huge bound intermixed with shouts of encouragement from their riders. A sharp crack like a rifle shot could be heard from our rear as the starters assistant cracked his hunting whip just in case any horse was reluctant to join the fray.

A sound like distant thunder grew from beneath us as the hooves pounded the turf and my stomach turned as I focused on the formidable black birch fence in front of me. In a blink of the eye the fence vanished! No, I had not jumped it, I was just slow off from the start and a wall of horses had closed in front of me obliterating any sight of the fence. Oh my god this is the end, I was hurtling towards a big fence that I couldn't see, I mentally prepared myself for the forthcoming pain and carnage. All that sweat and toil training, why hadn't someone told me about the start. The line of horses packed together as tight as sardines in a can rose out of the ground to jump the first fence followed by a loud cracking sound, as dust and birch twigs flew into the air. I knew I had milliseconds left before a crashing fall of both me and my beloved horse. Oh, what an arrogant idiot I was to think I was good enough to be a jockey.

Then to my amazement my horse rose into the air, the fence was still hidden by the horses and jockeys in front of us but we were in the air. It must have been an instinct that horses have and humans don't. We sailed through the air - it was the greatest thrill of my life! As we touched down my knees took the impact but even after all my training, they were not strong enough to stop my bum smacking the saddle knocking the air out of my lungs. Time stopped for a split second, that dead in the water moment, thinking but not doing. I jumped back into action as I realised that my opponents were now some ten lengths ahead of me and increasing their lead by the second. I sat up and kicked on, we didn't gain on the leading pack but the gap didn't get any bigger. "At least I will be able to see the next fence before I have to jump it" I thought. My view at this moment was something I had never seen before. A line of horses back ends so close to one another that they appeared to be one giant monster that was hurling clods of earth at me. It was like following a muck spreader and to make it even weirder this monster was surmounted with a line of bottoms in white breeches bobbing up and down to the rhythm of the monster. A clod of earth hit my face and brought me back to reality as we approached the second fence.

I was lagging behind the main bunch of horses and this gave me a clear view of the second fence. It looked smaller than the first fence and I started to relax just a little bit. We met the second fence on a good stride and sailed into the air. For a few seconds that felt like a minute or more I felt that I was flying. I had never jumped so far between take-off and landing, the drug that was going to get me addicted to this sport coursed through my body. It was Adrenaline! I was about to get another shot of it because in my euphoria I had forgotten that the fence was located on a sharp bend into what would be the home straight after two more circuits. My horse turned sharply on landing to follow the other horses throwing me violently to the right. For a heart stopping moment I thought I was going to be unseated. I was so cross with myself for not remembering the turn. As I regained my balance, I said to myself "Wake up you dozy bastard, concentrate or else we are going to end up in hospital". My heart pounded in my chest and for a brief moment I considered pulling out of the race, I had got left behind at the start and now nearly fallen off at the second fence. I was out of my league big time. As we galloped down the straight, cheering from the crowd brought the argument with myself to a close, or were they laughing at my pathetic performance? Several more fences passed without incident, and everything was starting to settle into a rhythm, except for my body which was showing signs of exhaustion even though we had covered less than a quarter of the race.

How could this be happening, I thought that I had prepared myself well for this day. I had run endless miles at long distance racing pace interspaced with sprint work, ridden endless gallops, and schooled over numerous single steeple chase fences. My solution was to try and take deep breaths especially after landing over a fence as that seemed to have a similar effect as being punched in the stomach knocking the air out of your lungs. I also tried but not very successfully to relax my muscles between fences. Several more plain fences passed without incident and then the open ditch loomed into view quickly changing my priorities. I remembered walking the course only an hour and a bit ago and feeling reasonably confident until I reached the open ditch! It was like no other fence I had ever encountered; the birch brush was not sloping like the other fences but stood up thick and square almost three times thicker than the plain fences. The ditch was not real, in that the ground had been dug out but was formed by a very substantial small wooden fence about 60 cm high that was built approximately one metre in front of the fence giving the effect of a ditch.

This was the fence I was dreading! I was about fifteen lengths behind the leading pack as we approached the open ditch, suddenly as they rose into the air over the ditch a pair of hind legs rocketed skywards followed by an explosion of birch twigs. My first view of a falling horse. I mentally logged where the horse appeared to go down and altered my course accordingly. My heart was pounding as I kicked into the strides before take-off. To my relief my horse Dadda Boy sailed into the air and never touched a twig. As I went over the top of the fence, I saw the fallen horse was back on its feet galloping off after the leading bunch of horses. I looked down to see where it's jockey was and was relieved to see he was off to the right of me just starting to sit up, he glanced up at me, his face and eyes pleading at me not to jump on him. Suddenly my elation fell out of the bottom of my stomach as the grim reality of this sport dawned on me. Thankfully, we landed safely about a metre to his left. I gave him a quick last glance, forgot him, kicked on and set myself to the job in hand.

Shortly after we passed the start and I realised we were starting the second circuit of the course. Like magic I got a second wind, finishing the race was starting to feel like a possibility. After jumping the first fence for the second time I saw a horse in front of me veer off the course and slow to a trot. For a split second, I was confused as to what was happening and then it dawned on me that he was pulling up and leaving the race for whatever reason. My spirits soared as I realised that I was still in the race although still some way behind the leaders and my horse was jumping like a stag clearing the fences with a foot to spare. I would later discover that jumping big over race fences was not a good thing as time in the air lost you ground, but all that was in the future, I was a novice and sort of enjoying my first race and glad to be still on board my horse.

We galloped down the finishing straight for the second time and started our last lap. As we rounded the left-hand bend heading towards the back straight there was another faller and another two pulled up at the fence before the open ditch. It was, as I landed over the fence before the open ditch, that I looked up at the leading pack that was now nearly a fence ahead of me and realised that there were just three left. "Oh my God! If I get home in one piece, I'm going to be fourth", I thought. The thought was quickly erased from my mind as the open ditch loomed up before me for the second time and I saw another horse and rider go crashing down. It suddenly dawned on me why the other jockeys were pulling up their horses - they were exhausted. It was at that moment I realised that my horse was also getting tired and he had only lasted this long because I was not going as fast as the others. If I could just manage to get home, I would be third and in the prize money, that however was a big "IF".

It was then that my dad's instructions came back to me. Don't try and mix it with the big boys, go your own pace and if he or you get tired just hunt around.

Five strides out from the open ditch I sat up and checked my horse to rebalance him before kicking hard on those last strides before take-off. He made a good jump but his legs were as tired as mine so he didn't rise quite as high as the last time and his legs brushed through the top of birch. The sudden deceleration shot my tired body forward up his neck causing him to peck (stumble) on landing. I went further up his neck and saw the ground looming up towards me. So close to finishing yet so far. I struggled hard not to go out the front door. For those that don't ride falling from your horse is often described as going out the door. In the main a horse has four doors one forward one at the back and two at the side left and right - it's just like an aeroplane's emergency exit layout.

Just as I was making my arrangements to have a meeting with Mother Earth when my horse recovered his balance, came up out of the ground and threw me back into the saddle. *Thank you, horse!* I thought and then just to show my gratitude I slapped him with my whip down his shoulder and shouted pick your bloody feet up or else we will be both on the ground. *No time for pleasantries.* However, I didn't immediately push on as we both needed to catch our breaths before the next jumping test. Four strides out I gave him another slap down the shoulder and shouted at him to focus his mind on putting a good jump in. Thankfully, it worked. It was a tired jump but we were over without incident. Just two more fences and we would be home but the fuel in his tank was getting exceptionally low and we were starting to wander, he was a bit like a sailing yacht that had lost wind from its sails. I shook him up and got him together for the penultimate fence which was jumped but not in great style. We plodded on towards the last fence. I was having to work harder to keep forward momentum but my energy was falling as much as my horse. The last fence didn't seem to get any closer it was as if time was standing still. I started to shout at my horse and myself, I slapped both the horse and me with the whip to summon up those deep reserves of energy that our brain keeps hidden from us. Finally, the last fence was in front of us, it was the only thing that now barred me from getting that second place. As my horse's power dwindled the fence seemed to grow bigger. I saw my stride four out and kicked and shouted as hard as I could. I don't know whether it was my tired weak body or the horse's but the stride I saw didn't happen. He was too far from the fence to take off, tried to add an extra short stride but that brought him too close. We crashed through the top of the fence. My body was thrown, here, there, and everywhere but this was not like the open ditch when I was caught napping. I had approached the last fence in the old-fashioned hunting seat leaning back with legs stuck forwards. My horse had learned a thing or two at the open ditch as well and instead of pecking on landing he stretched his front legs out forwards and up; this took much of the energy out of the messy landing. Together we had survived a bad mistake at the last fence we recovered and crossed the finish line at more of a fast canter than a gallop.

I was met by Louise and my dad running down to greet me with beaming smiles. I was also met by a bowler hatted steward who raised his hat, congratulated me, and informed me that as I had been placed, I was required to weigh in. I immediately jumped off my horse in order to remove my saddle and weight cloth that had to be weighed with me. As my feet hit the ground both my legs buckled underneath me and I crumpled in a heap much to the amusement of the crowd gathered around the winners enclosure.

My Second Race

After my unexpected success in the South Notts Hunt members race Dad decided to enter me into the South Wold Hunt point to point, as their secretary was at the South Notts meeting taking entries for their race meeting the following week. I however was not consulted about this and I think somebody may have suggested it to him while he was celebrating in the bar. Anyway, I was excitedly informed that I was entered in the Adjacent Hunts Race at the South Wold Hunt Point to Point which was being held at Revesby Park the following Saturday.

At this point I must explain that I had never heard of The South Wold Hunt or Revesby Park and hadn't a clue what an adjacent hunts race was. To make matters worse I don't think that my father was very much wiser than me.

After much intelligence gathering by Dad, again most of it done in the bar or sampling the delights of various car boot picnic hampers offered by well-wishing friends, he discovered that the meeting was taking place at a place called Revesby Park near Horncastle in Lincolnshire some fifty miles to the east of where we lived. When I enquired what an adjacent hunts race was, I was told that it was just the same as the race that I had completed except that people from hunts that adjoined their country could also enter. I was fairly ok about that and was starting to look forward to Saturday just five days away. However unbeknown to me the description of what an adjacent hunts race was not entirely correct.

Early Saturday morning we trundled across into deepest Lincolnshire in our old Bedford Tk horsebox in search of Revesby Park. Thankfully, the hunt had put out direction signs off the main road so we found it with ease. I found the park fascinating; the whole park was covered in a light mist and was illuminated by a low early spring sun which gave a golden glow like a scene from a romantic film, set in the eighteenth century. In the background were the scant remains of a once grand house. The park itself was old grassland on low wide rigg and furrow dotted with mature wide spreading parkland trees. Even as we pulled through the park gates you got the feeling of a real old-fashioned rural occasion.

Unlike the previous course at Thorpe where my first race was held there were no rails to mark the course or keep the crowds back except for some rope and stakes from the last fence and the finish line. As I made my way from the horsebox parking area with all my kit towards the declarations tent and the jockeys changing tent, I passed the refreshment tent and was delighted to observe a large wooden cask of real ale set up at the back of the bar. I made a mental note to give that some hammer after my race. I also noted that the mist was not lifting and if anything was getting a little thicker. It did not trouble me as there was nearly two hours to go before the start of my race. What I didn't know was that the racecourse was less than twenty miles from the east coast.

The adjacent hunts race was the second race so after walking the course and declaring to run in the race I returned to the jockeys changing tent to change into my racing clothes and then get weighed out. Weighing out involved being dressed in your racing clothes and colours and carrying your weight cloth and saddle. At most point to points, you sat on a chair or stood on an Avery weighing machine, but the South Wold had an old wooden sack weigher with cast iron weights to determine the weight. The simple scales must have been over one hundred years old. The designated weight for my race was twelve stone seven pounds. In the changing tent everyone seemed to know each other and there was much banter and play fighting. The valet greeted me by saying "Good morning Sir. New are we Sir?" I nodded shyly as he scanned his eyes around the tent and said "Right, let's put you over here in this nice quiet corner shall we. Now does Sir have everything he needs and which race will Sir be riding in?" This was my second encounter with a jockeys valet and I quite liked all this Sir malarkey. Nobody else spoke to me in the changing tent and I sat quietly in my corner staring at the coconut matting floor twiddling my whip though my hands and thinking about the forthcoming race. My trance was sharply broken by a dark suited man in a bowler hat who barked out the order "Right then! Jockeys out!". My stomach turned as I stood up and followed the other jockeys out and into the parade ring where my family and horse awaited me. After several wishes of good luck Dad gave me a leg up onto the horse and I was led around the parade ring to be gawked at by Joe public until the mounted huntsman dressed in all his finery blew his hunting horn and led us off to the start.

Down at the start it was hugely different from the previous week. The jovial banter turned sharper with comments such as "Hey, Harry keep that f**king horse straight today or I'll cut your f**king balls off when we are finished". As we circled at the start the jockeys glared at each other like prize fighters before the start of a fight. This was not the jolly hockey sticks of last week's start. I was bluntly informed to keep out of the bloody way or else. I felt like someone who had just walked into a London Gentleman's club dressed in jeans and a sloppy jumper. Definitely not welcome! As we came into line there was much pushing, shoving, and swearing. As soon as the starters flag dropped, they jumped forward so fast that they were almost over the first fence before I even got going. This was very much a different league from last week's race. The horses did not jump the fences they punched through the top eighteen inches like a high-powered rifle bullet through soft tissue.
I felt forlorn and embarrassed as I kicked on trying to close the gap between lonesome me and the rest of the field. The only thing that cheered me up was that both me and my horse were jumping the fences much better than the previous week and by fence four of our allotted eighteen I was having the ride of my life even if I was tailed off. I was enjoying my first circuit despite the rolling ridge and furrow that made it difficult to hold a rhythm or get a good take off stride at the fences. I think my slightly slower speed was helping with the jumping as I passed several jockeys on the ground. I did however feel somewhat uncomfortable as I rode passed the home straight to boos and laughter. This I concluded was not so much about my poor riding but down to the fact that my second place the previous week had prompted many people to wager their hard-earned money on me to win. Dad told me after the race that I had started third favourite with the Bookies.

As I started the final circuit a bank of fog suddenly rolled across the racecourse obliterating my fellow competitors and even the fences. Fences and trees suddenly loomed out of the fog in front of me. Several fences later I passed an unconscious jockey lying at the base of a tree. That tree almost got me as well. I learned later the jockey had been in the lead and had decided to snatch a quick look over his shoulder to see where his nearest opponent was. It was only a split second but enough for a tree to jump out in front of him. His horse saw the tree and dived sideways hurling him into the base of the large tree. It was a miracle that he wasn't seriously injured or worst still killed.

I plodded on through the fog that must have rolled in off the North Sea following the hoof prints of the other horses. Eventually I came to the last fence and jumped it nice and cleanly. There was not another horse in sight I just wanted to run away and hide. A huge roar and clapping erupted from the crowd vaguely visible through the fog. The cheering and clapping made me think "Now you are really taking the piss out of me".

It was not until I saw the family running towards me after crossing the finish that my spirits lifted. Why were they so happy about my dismal performance I enquired as we reached each other? "You have come second again; you are the only other horse to finish!" All those cheers were from the punters who had backed me and we're now going to get paid out for my second place. It was a life changing experience to be thanked by complete strangers for seeing the race through to the end and saving their money. To me the race was all about my opponents, I had never thought about the betting public who funded our sport. After this race I always finished the race unless the horse was distressed or I fell. It was something that built me a large loyal fan base over my racing career.

Post-race I learnt that the adjacent hunts were not just hunts whose borders were adjoined but a number of the other local hunts as well. It was also usually one of the most hotly contested races on the card. Oh well you live and learn. The race that Dad should have entered me in was in fact the adjacent hunts maiden race for horses that hadn't won a race before. After this revelation I took over deciding which venue and race we would enter.

The rest of my first season

For the next six weeks I travelled the length and breadth of the midlands point to point area competing in maiden races. A very respected horseman came up to me at the start of one of these races whilst my girth was being checked and said "That's a good horse, you have there, my boy. If you get one good horse in your lifetime then you are incredibly lucky. Look after him and keep at it, he will win you a race by the end of the season. Good luck today ". These words were very prophetic and have brought a tear to my eye as I write them down this day.

During those six weeks I learnt a lot and became fitter and stronger. With every race I learnt about pace and rhythm when to attack and when to sit tight and wait. How to pick a horse up out of the ground when it had pecked on landing and most of all to stick my legs forward, slip my reins to the buckle end and throw my body back if a horse hit a fence low and hard.

My big disappointment of that day at the South Wold was by the time we had eaten our picnic lunch and I had recalled all the dramas of the race for the umpteenth time, the lovely wooden barrel of ale had been drunk dry by the thirsty race goers. I was so looking forward to tasting that beer.

So, by now you must me wondering why I took up point to point racing and where did I get my racehorse from. For those of you not acquainted with the sport of point to pointing I think that a brief history of the sport would be beneficial.

In the eighteen hundreds fox hunting was the sport of the gentry and the very wealthy. Racing also known as the Sport of Kings was also extremely popular with this group of people. For a large group of the hunting fraternity hunting itself was a race as the first rider to arrive at the kill gained great kudos. This aggressive riding naturally led to arguments as to who had the fastest and boldest horse. Gambling was yet another favourite pastime of the gentry and so it was a natural progression that people would wager each other to race their best horses against each other. Many of these races were impromptu affairs with one rider betting another an amount of money that he could get from one point to another faster than his rival, hence the name point to point race. As church steeples were clearly visible landmarks in those days many races were from one church to another hence the name steeplechase. The races were of no fixed distance but were usually about three miles as this was considered a good test of stamina. So, these races acquired two different names point to point races, or steeple chases, but they were basically the same and these sort of amateur races to this day still continue to be called by both names depending in what area you live in.

These races became exceedingly popular and started to attract large numbers of spectators and many of them were keen to have a wager on which horse would win. Gradually these races developed into group races from point to point and then into a more circular route so that spectators could see both the start and finish of a race. Eventually the hunts saw an opening to make money out of these events and make a social event for their followers and farmers at the end of the hunting season. At first these were over natural fences and my dad told me that even in the late forties and early fifties some courses still included the odd ploughed field. These days many of the hunt point to point courses have disappeared due to costs and the change in farming practices. In the East Midlands area three courses host most of the races. These are Dingley near Market Harborough, Garthorpe near Melton Mowbray, and Thorpe near Newark. Although all these courses have their unique characteristics it is not the same as going to many different courses. Dingley is unique in that it is the only point to point course that has a water jump.

National Hunt Steeplechases are a vastly different game. This is the professional side of the sport that you see on television such as the Grand National and the Cheltenham Festival. This type of racing takes place all over the country with usually two meetings per day throughout the season which starts in the autumn and finishes in late spring. It is highly regulated and all jockeys have to have a licence. Most of the jockeys are professionals but amateurs can compete if they can prove that they have sufficient experience in point-to-point races. Amateurs can obtain two different licenses. One allows you to compete in races for amateurs only, these are called Hunter chases. The other is a license that also allows you to ride in professional races. If a jockey in a professional race has the prefix of Mr, Miss, or Mrs to their name this denotes that they are an amateur.

If you listen to the commentary of the Grand National many of the fence descriptions hark back to the 1800s when Beechers Brook was a hedge with a brook on the landing side. You did actually jump across the Melling Road and I have seen an old painting showing a five-foot stone wall as one of the obstacles.

My association with the horse I rode in my first race started about eighteen months before my first race. His name was Dadda Boy a 16.3hh chestnut gelding. He was not a full thoroughbred but was registered at Wetherbys in their general stud book and that allowed him to take part in races. He was not bought by my dad as a racehorse but as a good quality horse with a bit of a problem. Dad saw a good profit in the horse if this problem could be sorted out, he believed that he or me could solve the problem with some tough riding. Dadda Boy's problem was that his former owner could not get him any further than the end of the farmland where he lived. He would suddenly stop and then spin round so quickly that he flung his rider off. In the horse world this is called napping and means that they refuse to leave home or other horses, or just refuse to move forward.

I was tasked with sorting this out, my dad was so kind! It required lightning-fast reactions and forceful riding. The art of besting a nappy horse is not to let it happen. That is far easier said than done. You need to get to know the little things that the horse does as it prepares to be naughty. It is like a gunfighter knowing little things that his opponent does just before he goes to draw his gun and then beating him by a split second. I had some hairy moments as I learnt Dadda Boy's little quirks and we had some fine old battles before I learnt all of his tricks. Horses are creatures of habit and they tend to nap in the same places which gives you an edge, they also often drop the contact between the hand and the bit in their mouth which gives you that split second to perform a pre-emptive strike. Even if the horse does not give any indications, if you are approaching a favourite napping point, I find that leaning back strengthening the leg and a sharp tap with the whip about five strides before that point, usually dissuades them from trying it on. The reason this is so effective is I believe that the horse thinks you can read it's mind.

I always tell clients with nappy horses that you can control nappiness but you will never cure it. The horse is just waiting for you to drop your guard. I sorted Dadda Boy's nappiness out and never had any trouble for two years. That was until one morning after a late-night partying I rode out with a major hangover. I got to the bottom of the slip road just two hundred yards from the stables and quick as a flash I was flat on my back before I knew what had happened. He had waited all that time and he knew I was not up to par that morning. As I looked up from the ground checking over my body for any serious injuries I just smiled and said, "You got me that time you bastard!" He never did it again! However, perhaps I should rephrase that to, I never allowed him to do it again.

Dadda Boy's stable name was Wetherby, a strange name to give a horse you might think but dad was prone to giving horses a name that related to the area from where he purchased the horse. Wetherby had a good jump in him so I naturally started to show jump him. At this period in time show jumping was the main adult equestrian sport, it had a huge spectator following and was regularly shown on television. Even at the lower levels there was good prize money to be won. Show jumping was an elite sport in the sixties and seventies with the entry level starting at about 1metre 10cm and even local club shows would start adults at about the 90cm mark. I still remember winning a puissance in our indoor school on Wetherby when show jumping was still held on a regular basis at Bunny Hill. My winning height was five feet which in today's money is approximately one metre fifty-two centimetres.

Wetherby's show jumping talents soon got noticed and dad sold him for almost three times what he paid for him, the princely sum of £750. In those days that was serious money. All went well until the vetting. The vet was unknown to us, which was strange as we knew most horse vets within a fifty-mile radius. The Vet concluded that an old scar on the coronary band was side bone and failed him. Side bone in horses is the ossification of the collateral cartilages in the foot. The collateral cartilages are just above the coronary band on each side of the lower pastern and ossification can cause lameness.

It would be an understatement to say that Dad was angry. This was more because it affected his reputation as an honest horse dealer rather than the loss of the sale. Although he got a second opinion from our vet who reaffirmed Dad's opinion that it was scar tissue from an old injury. It was just one word against another's. There was no X ray or scanning equipment for horses in in those days so it was impossible prove the matter one way or the other.

There are no secrets in the horse world, and word of a high priced, well known horse failing the vet spread like a wildfire. Dad had to come up with something to prove that his horse was sound and that he was trustworthy. What he came up with would change my life as much as jousting, and tie me to the horse world for the rest of my life. I will always remember the words that he said to me that day. "Right, this is what we will do to prove to those bastards that I am right. You have always fancied a go at point to pointing, so you can take him hunting, qualify him and then race him". That was it, a life changing statement.

We were still short of money at this time, building the indoor school and clubroom had meant large borrowing coupled with debts from our misadventures of Dad's partnership with Major Ritchie and our jousting at Gwrych Castle had left us severely stretched. To qualify a horse to point to point you had to subscribe to a registered pack of hounds and hunt the horse a minimum of six times. You had to show your horse every time to the master and could not go home until he decided that the horse had done a fair day's hunting. This was usually until change of horses which occurred approximately two to two and a half hours after the meet at 11am. Our shortage of money ruled out our most local pack, the Quorn Hunt. It was one the most prestigious packs in the country and its subscription fees reflected that, so we opted for the South Notts Hunt who were our next nearest hunt and had much more reasonable subscription fees. We had hunted with them off and on for many seasons when we had suitable spare money. They were a very friendly pack and I knew many of the regulars through Dad's horse dealing and competing in gymkhanas and show jumping competitions. These visits had always been to the high Derbyshire area where Dad and I had some great fun.

Because the Derbyshire country was further away than the rest of the South Notts country and commanded a higher subscription fee I qualified Wetherby in the Monday country, which was cheaper and much closer. It was a decision that almost stopped me hunting ever again. It was so boring. The country was intensively farmed arable land and, in those days, there were no headlands around the fields. So, although hunt staff and hounds were allowed over most of the ground, the field (mounted followers) were restricted to roads and tracks. Not a jump in sight anywhere. Usually, I never wanted a hunting day to end but when qualifying on a Monday with the South Notts I was always looking at my watch and praying that they would change horses early.

Our family connections with the South Notts Hunt went back almost to the time of moving up to Bunny Hill. Dad rode horses in point to points that belonged to someone who lived in Lowdham and I can remember going to watch Dad ride in a race when the South Notts point to points were held at Cropwell Bishop, before they moved to Thorpe near Newark. I remember becoming a race programme seller from an early age. Dad got me the job; it was unpaid but there was a prize for the seller of the most programmes. My allocated partner and I never won the prize and after a few years realised that it was the selling area that you were given that mattered and all the good areas went to children of landowners or subscribers. I also have a strong suspicion that Dad got a free car park pass for supplying me. Although program selling was boring, we were freed of our duties after the second race. The South Notts point to point was always held on Easter Monday and it was the highlight of our year and was the place to be and be seen if you were in the horse world.

At the Cropwell Bishop track all the cars were parked on a steep hillside so you had a bird's eye view of the course. The car boots would be packed with picnics and lashings of alcohol. Everyone tried to outdo each other in the grandness of their offerings. Each year we had a long list of invitations to visit people's cars and by the end of the day there were a lot of very drunk drivers, but in those days nobody cared. As soon as I was freed from program selling, I would wander off on my own and walk around the course watching each race close up from a different fence. The fences in those day were not the mini portable National Hunt style fences that we see today but natural hedges that had been cut to size and trimmed with greenery a little like the Grand National fences. So, it was at an early age that I started to aspire to take part in this daring sport. However, I never really believed it would happen as I could tell even at an early age that the people taking part were vastly different to me. They had wealth and belonged to a different class to me, my only chance of riding in a race was to become a good enough rider and be offered a ride on someone else's horse just like Dad. These ambitions of course quickly faded after the race day but like seeds discarded by a plant, they lie dormant for years and then suddenly for no reason burst into life!

This is how my racing career started. I had completely forgotten my childhood pipe dream and then out of nowhere in a blink of an eye I was riding my own or should I say Dad's horse. Actually, I think we should say the Humphrey family horse. Talk about fairy tales.

After my incredibly lucky, two second places everyone was on board to continue right through to the season end which was the end of May. In those days, most hunts still had their own courses and it was a real adventure travelling around the Midlands riding at so many different venues. Each course needed to be ridden in a different way and it was a steep learning curve for me. Only the courses at Dingley and Garthorpe held multiple meetings and it was on these two courses that I started to learn about tactical racing. How to set a pace and when to make an attacking move to step up the pace in the closing stages of the race. I learnt to relax for the first circuit and a half and let the race unfold then if things were going well move up to join the horses that I believed were in contention to win the race. It was then a game of cat and mouse until someone decided to make a break and go for the finish.

After my first two races I started to enter the correct race for my horse's standard, which was the maiden race for horses that had not won a point to point or any other race. However, I was extremely glad that I had gained some experience before competing in a maiden as they were not an easy race for a novice rider to compete in. The number of horses in these races were much higher than other races with the number of starters being usually between eighteen and twenty-two depending on the safety number for the maximum number of horses allowed to take part in a race. Each racecourse had its own safety number depending on widths of fences and sharpness of bends. To make matters worse these novice horses were highly unpredictable and often jumped sideways across the fences. On one occasion I had the front leg of a horse come across my horse's withers and knock the reins out of my hand just as we landed over a fence. From a distance things would look very ordered but it was more like a rugby match out there in the thick of it. I quickly learnt how to stay out of trouble and soon was finishing in the top six and that quickly became the top four.

Our consistent form although not actually winning started to get us a strong group of followers throughout the midland area and we started to get phone calls from complete strangers asking which racecourse we would be competing at next. At this time, I was a bit unique and along with our consistent form I was the only person not riding in a race saddle and that stood out like a sore thumb to race goers. I just raced in my hunting and show jumping saddle. We just could not afford a racing saddle. In fact, thinking back I don't know how we managed to even find the money to go racing every week.

I finally won my first race right at the end of that first season. It was at the Fernie point to point which is held at Dingley near Market Harborough. I won by several lengths. I just could not believe it! Winning a race is fantastic because you not only win it for you and your team but also everyone at the racecourse who bet on you. You have ten minutes of hero worship from the race going public before they start thinking about who to bet on in the next race.

I received a lovely silver perpetual challenge trophy and a memento in the form of a Waterford Crystal brandy glass from the Master of the Fernie Hunt Colonel Murray-Smith who had been joint master of the Quorn hunt with his wife Ulrica. Sadly, the marriage did not last and as fate would have it, their last hunt as joint masters was from a meet at our stables on Bunny Hill. They had a blazing row in front of the field. The hunt had just spent a lot of money opening up the area putting in a series of hunt gates on the hill. Mrs Murray-Smith vowed she would never hunt that ground again and all that work went to waste. It was many years until the Quorn would meet on Bunny Hill again.

The track at Dingley seemed to suit Wetherby (Dadda Boy) well and we won the adjacent hunts race there the next year. This time I won a Waterford Crystal claret wine glass. It is in a Georgian era style. Along with the Brandy Goblet they are two of my most treasured possessions. Every time I use them, I relive those two glorious days.

There is a twist to this tale. After winning the claret glass I tried to purchase another so that we had a pair. I visited numerous Waterford Crystal shops but none of them had it in stock nor could find it in the Waterford catalogues. I was starting to think that that perhaps my prizes were not Waterford after all. Many years later we met Jim and Patricia Brennan who lived in Kilkenny Ireland. We became incredibly good friends and on one visit to see them they took us to the Waterford Crystal factory for a guided tour (We always tried to do something cultural before getting down to the serious drinking. Those of you who have friends over the water will know what I mean). The beginning of the tour was a short film a about the history of the company. The first picture that appeared on the screen was my claret glass. I was so excited, I jumped up and shouted that's my claret glass! Much to the shock of all the other people in the small cinema. All through the tour I explained the significance of the claret glass and how I had been trying for years to purchase another one. At the end of the tour, I was desperate to find out if it was still available to purchase. To my great dismay Jim announced that he had booked lunch at a restaurant and we were already running later, so there was no time to make enquiries. He did however promise to make some enquiries at a later date on my behalf. Some weeks later I called him to see if he had any news. He told me he had made enquiries at Waterford Crystal but sadly it was no longer available. I was deflated, but not surprised. My quest to make a pair was over and at least I now knew that it was definitely Waterford Crystal. The quest was over and I never gave it another thought. Six months later Jim and Patricia came over to visit us and as usual arrived bearing a host of gifts. This time it was a bottle of rare Irish whiskey and Clonakilty back-pudding my favourite. After opening the presents and thanking them Jim suddenly said, "Oh I almost forgot I thought this might interest you". He handed me a medium sized plain cardboard box with no ceremony as if it was just a small afterthought. When I opened it, I could not believe my eyes. Wrapped in tissue paper was an identical claret glass. Not just one but three identical claret glasses. When I thanked him profusely with tears welling up in my eyes, I told him one would have made my year but three was unbelievable. Jim gave a dismissive wave and said "Ah 'tis nothing. I couldn't bear to be sitting drinking wine whit you and Lou with your fancy big glasses and me and Patricia with shitty little ones". As ever generous to a fault.

Wetherby

I raced Wetherby for four seasons and he allowed me to learn my trade as a jockey. The great thing about him was his versatility. Not only was he a great racehorse but I also teamchased him, Dad did a dressage competition on him two days after a race, he was a brilliant hunter and a particularly good show jumper. I am sure that if eventing had been a mainstream sport in those days, he would have risen to the highest levels. He will be mentioned later as I cover other equestrian disciplines but now it's back to the racing.

We were all fired up for our second season and keen to start much earlier in the season than our Easter Monday debut the previous season. In those days, the point-to-point season started on February the first and finished at the end of May. There was no internet in those days to find out the date that each hunt ran their point to point. However, the Horse and Hound magazine published a full list of every hunts' point to point date, venue along with the secretary's address and telephone number. This was usually the first edition published in the new year.

Armed with a list of point-to-point dates I started to plan my campaign for the new season early in January. To my dismay I discovered that there were no early point to points in the Midland areas but my racing mentor ex jockey John Cook recommend that we go to Cottenham just north of Cambridge. He told me it was an easy flat course and the jumps were not big. Ideal for a first run of the season. He also advised me to enter the open race as they tended to have less runners. I was about to learn an important lesson of life. That a little knowledge is a dangerous thing. I was also about to learn about half lengthening.

It was a good journey down to Cottenham as the A1 and the A614(now called the A14) had recently been upgraded to dual carriageway and it was also a lovely bright sunny day with a light early morning frost. I was extremely excited about starting the new season and with a win under my belt at the end of last season I was also a bit cocky. The course was just as John had described it with the fences far less formidable than at Garthorpe or Dingley. I can still remember how very cold the jockeys changing tent was, although the sun was shining the tent was in the shadows and the tent was still sub-zero inside. There is nothing worse than having cold muscles when you are about to take part in a three-mile steeplechase. I didn't know any of the other jockeys as I was a long way out of my area so I got changed in a quiet corner and avoided eye contact with the other jockeys.

Once out of the fridge like tent and mounted, the late winter sunshine soon warmed my cold muscles, it felt good being led around the parade ring before going down to the start. The field was small, only about eight or nine of us and I was feeling very confident, quite cocky in fact. We set off at a steady ordered pace and Wetherby skipped easily over the fence. The going was good and the sun was shining, it felt so good to be racing again. The open race was so ordered compared with the melee of the maiden races. Wetherby was enjoying himself as well, putting in huge jumps at every fence. Oh, what a feeling you get as you fly through the air on the back of a good jumping racehorse. Wetherby's bold jumping also put us at the front of the field. It is very strange when you go into the lead steeplechasing. When you are in the middle of the field the noise is deafening, the drum of the galloping hooves, jockeys shouting at their horses or at other jockeys, the slap of leather and the cracking of horses nostrils as they gallop. It's like watching a live heavy rock band coming to the end of their performance, pandemonium. Then you hit the front and it's like the band has finished, absolute silence, it's really spooky, just the wind whistling in your ears.

We sailed over the fence in silence, no sound of the other horses at all. Six fences from home I started to think that I could maybe win this race, so I thought I would pick up the pace a little and put some clear water between me and the rest of the field. As I approached the fifth fence from home, a horse suddenly loomed up alongside of me and then overtook me just before I was about to take off. I thought nothing of it! The next moment I was catapulted forward my head smacking into the top of Wetherby's head as it flew up and backwards, simultaneously I heard a crashing sound. In what seemed an age but was only a few milliseconds I saw, horse, ground, sky, horse and then Bang! I was on the ground, every jockeys nightmare a fall when leading the field. I instinctively curled into a ball and shook with fear as the ground shook to the sound of thirty-two horses hooves approaching the fence that I was laying behind. My hands were on top of my head pulling my head into my body desperately trying to make it smaller, one eye glancing into the blue sky above so I could see what was coming. Then it came the sound I had been dreading, the cracking off horses hooves punching through the top of the tightly packed birch at the top of the fence. The sky disappeared and was replaced by the underbellies of horses flying through the air front legs stretched out in front of them, hind legs trailing. First four came over tightly packed together as one, quickly followed by three together then silence, was it all over? Then I heard the sound of a lone horse approaching. A slightly slower beat than the first seven. This must be tail end Charlie I waited with trepidation. The horse was tired and landed much shorter right where I was lying, but thankfully a few yards to the left. The other horses had sailed right over the top of me and not one of them had touched me!

The St. John's Ambulance men came and checked me over on the ground and then it was the long walk of shame back to the jockeys changing room. It was made all the worse by the crowd cheering the winning jockey as he received his prize. When I emerged from the jockeys changing room, I was met by my mentor John Cook, he took my saddle and weight cloth to lighten my load before giving me one of the most memorable bollockings of my life. I had been expecting sympathy and that made it all the more shocking. He started by congratulating me on giving the field such a fantastic lead around the course and ending it by saying that they must have thought that I was the biggest fool in the world. When I told him, I thought I had a chance of winning the race he just laughed and told me I was the biggest fool in the world if I had thought that. To me it was just another race to try and win. My end of season win had made me cocky and I hadn't done my homework on the opposition nor had I ridden to orders, which was to use it as a warmup schooling run for both horse and rider. John finished off with a devastating question. "Why had I allowed myself to be half lengthed". I asked him what he meant by being half lengthened. His mouth dropped open in shock and said "You are kidding me, surely you know about half lengthening" "No I haven't a clue" was my reply. John shook his head in disbelief and started to explain that it was one of the oldest tricks in the steeplechasing game. If you were upsides another horse approaching a fence and you suddenly put on an extra spurt so that you are in front of the other horse by half a length the other horse will instinctively take off at the same time causing the horse to hit the fence and most likely cause the horse and rider to fall. Wow and here was me thinking that this was a gentleman's sport. This was the most important thing that I learnt in my racing career. From that day on I never again thought of the jockeys in a race as competitors but rather as enemies prepared to do anything no matter how dastardly, to win the race. He went on to tell me about other tricks to watch out for down the far side of the course out of the stewards view. These included giving your opponent a push mid-flight over a fence to unbalance the horse and rider on landing, pulling a rider's whip out of his hand again usually mid-flight over a fence and finally to flick an opponent's bridle off over its ears, very nasty. There were also verbal distractions like shouting something to your opponent just before his horse was about to take off. I never had anyone try to remove my bridle but came across all the others but as the saying goes, for-warned is for-armed. As I thought about half lengthening, I realised that I could use that knowledge as a defence or as a weapon.

That was my first fall of my racing career, I had come out of it relatively unscathed but next day every bit of my body was aching. However, it was my stupidity in my attitude to the race and realisation that winning a race did not instantly make me a competent jockey that hurt the most. The old saying "You are only as good as your last race" put me most definitely at the bottom of the pile. From that day on I started a new regime. I watched how my opponents rode in other races, studied the form of the horses that I raced against, I entered more than one race at a meeting and delayed making my declaration to run until the last few minutes and if the race had a strong field I would declare for another race. I got fitter running morning and night and riding with my stirrups shorter, keeping my bum out of the saddle at trot for miles at a time bringing tears to my eyes as my legs screamed with pain.

We travelled far and wide during February and March to get our early runs in and because we were running out of our area, we had to enter something called a Restricted Open race which was for horses that won a maiden race but nothing else. These proved to be quite successful always finishing in the top six of large fields of up to twenty-five runners. My racing guru John Cook decided Wetherby had stamina but lacked speed at the finish so he announced that we needed to find longer races to enter so that we could use his stamina to our advantage. Unfortunately, all the point-to-point races seemed to be run over virtually the same distance of around three miles give or take the odd furlong. However, John was a racing addict and after much research discovered a race that was four miles and one furlong. The race was part of the Middleton Hunt point to point card and was held at a place called Sheriff Hutton near Malton in Yorkshire. By this time Mum, Dad and my wife Lou were all enjoying having a racehorse so although it was a long expensive trip, they were all up for this adventure. Again, my lack of in-depth knowledge of racing allowed me to get swept away with the enthusiasm and agree to take part in this race. Looking back now I was so naïve not to see that I was totally not ready to take on such a challenge. Yes, I lengthened my training regime for me and my horse to up our fitness but I only had three weeks before the race. Again, in those days with no internet, knowledge was hard to come by so I went to the race believing it was just another point-to-point race but a bit longer. As word spread that we had entered the race, a well-wisher referred to the race as the point to point Grand National - alarm bells started to ring in my mind. What had my racing naivety allowed me to get talked into this time.

The day of the race finally arrived. It was an early start and a long drive in our old TK Bedford up to Malton, just over three and a half hours. We encountered some big hills on the latter part of our journey and our speed dropped to just a few miles per hour as we ground up the hills in first gear and the engine temperature gauge rose ever closer to the red. Would the old lorry even get us there, I thought, ever the worrier about unnecessary things. When we finally arrived, I was surprised how small and rural the point to point was. Hosting such a famous race I had expected something grander. The racecourse was in two halves, the parade ring, changing tents, secretary's tent, etc. was on top of the hill and the actual racecourse was lower down at the bottom of an escarpment. As I walked the course, I was pleasantly surprised to find that the fences were unlike Garthorpe well-built to maximum height just how we liked them. Some courses had smaller, softer fences and these favoured the lighter weight thoroughbreds who were much quicker than us. The course was not as open as some of the modern course with trees and hedges dotted around the course. Not only was the course an extra mile longer but you also had more fences to jump the usual number was eighteen for three miles but for the Gold cup it was twenty-seven or maybe it was twenty-eight.

The runners and riders left the parade to cheers and applause and were led down the steep hill to the start by the Middleton Huntsman. It was all extremely exciting. The first half of the race was run at a cautious pace which suited Wetherby perfectly. I was out of harm's way and picked off the fences one by one taking care not to get in a half lengthening position. As we reached the three mile point my legs were starting to ache but Wetherby felt good. I had no idea when to step up the pace so I just kept myself handy and waited for the more knowledgeable to make the move. When it came, Wetherby rose to the occasion and I stayed with this ever-decreasing pack as one by one horses faded away or fell. Two fences from home Wetherby ran out of steam but was still jumping well so I eased back and nursed him home past more bodies on the ground. Although I would have loved to have won the race, just finishing this race was as good as winning for me. We almost fell over the last fence and I trotted over the line. Wetherby's legs had gone all wobbly and I jumped off him shortly after crossing the finishing line. This fabulous horse had not put a foot wrong throughout the whole race. As I descended towards the ground, I had tears in my eyes from all the emotions. My feet hit the ground and I collapsed into a heap; my legs had gone as well. A steward quickly came to my aid and helped me back into the saddle saying "Well done sir, you have come fourth. We need to get you up the hill to weigh in". Although there is no prize for fourth place you still have to weigh in just in case any of the first three are disqualified.

I ended the day elated just to have taken part in that great race and totally exhausted. I slept most of the way home.

The race had exhausted both me and Wetherby but it also brought our fitness on by a giant leap. The four-mile race had taught me to relax more keep out of trouble and watch the race unfold. Conserve both the horses and my energy for the last tenth of the race.

The following weekend was Easter and it was back to where it all started, the South Notts Point to Point on Easter Monday at Thorpe near Newark. I started the race as second favourite. What a change in a year. This was a momentous race for me and it was the first race that I had ever made a tactical plan for. There were two other horses in the race that I thought could beat me. My weakness was that Wetherby was not a fast horse, so the flat galloping track of Thorpe was not in our favour. However, he was a superb jumper and had great stamina. My race could not be won battling it out over the last fence and dashing for the finish but rather by out jumping my opponents and hoping that they made a mistake.

I set off and settled in at the back of the pack staying out of trouble. My two major rivals both wanted to lead so were racing from the word go. In Members races you are playing in front of your home team so it is easy to get carried away putting on a good show. I sat quiet for the first circuit keeping in striking distance but not posing a threat. As we landed over the first fence after passing the finishing post for the second time, I made my move. I pushed on and joined the leaders just before the next fence but didn't overtake them, then two strides out kicked on and asked Wetherby to take off early. The horse next to me tried to keep up with me but I had caught the jockey napping, he hadn't expected me to attack so early and I had half lengthed him. The combination came crashing down and hampered the other leading horse allowing me to gain several lengths lead. It took him until the last open ditch to catch up with me. I knew he would try same the tactic on me so I was ready for the duel. My advantage was that I had been cruising while he had been pushing to catch me. He came along side me four strides from take-off. I knew he was coming and so did Wetherby. We both pushed hard to take off first but my horse was fresher because I had only been cruising. Even so I only managed to get a head lead at take-off. We took off further than I would have liked but I knew It was well within Wetherby's scope. The other horse matched us. We sailed through the air and landed well out from the fence and I kicked on hard as my horse's feet touched the ground,the race was on. My opponent hit the top of the fence; his horse's legs had lost a bit of spring. However, it was a good horse and jockey, they didn't fall but had knocked the wind out of their sails while I was kicking on and gaining more ground. They continued to threaten but the four-mile race had brought both mine and Wetherby's fitness on and we galloped on holding our opponent at bay all the way to the finish line.

We won a lovely solid silver perpetual challenge cup that was incredibly old with all the past winners names engraved on the wide silver band on its base. I cherished that cup with all of its past winners. I went on to win it three times back-to-back and became extremely attached to it. I had a pipe dream that they might let me keep it as nobody had ever won it consecutively three times and the silver band was now full of names. Of course, my dream never came to fruition - the cup was worth a fortune.

The competition was stiffer in the restricted open races but not as stiff as the Adjacent Hunts, or the open races but both horse and jockey had improved greatly and we were placed in every race. We did however pick up a minor injury that kept us out of a couple of races mid-season. I finally won my restricted open race at the end of the season again at the Fernie Races. This time I won a lovely Waterford crystal brandy goblet. We liked the Fernie Races!

The last race meeting of the season was the Melton Hunt Club held at Garthorpe it was held at the end of May, the going was nearly always good to firm, the weather was nice and much warmer than the early spring meetings. Because the going was better the horses jumped better and galloped much faster. Best of all it attracted the best horses and jockeys from all over England. It was the unofficial point to point championships. I loved riding there, the speed, muscles warmed by the sun, wearing tinted goggles riding against the best horses and jockeys, the huge crowds, it had it all. I never won a race at any of these meetings but again was placed every time and that was an achievement in itself.

I have never been a betting man on horses or on anything else, and the reason for this was that when I started racing things never turned out as I expected. I concluded that if I owned, trained, and rode, a horse and still got things spectacularly wrong what was the point in betting. Louise and Dad would always have what they described as a good luck bet on me and I remember Louise telling me how ashamed Dad felt when placing a £10 bet on me to win after the man in front of him had just placed a £600 bet on me to win.

That race was at the Atherstone point to point which had a long uphill finish which suited Wetherby's staying power. It was a large race and because the going was heavy the race was run at a steady pace with everyone tightly bunched. We picked up speed as we steamed down the steep hill for the second time and I dropped back a bit in the field as I wanted to conserve my horse's energy for the extremely heavy going at the bottom of the hill. I was not worried as there was only five lengths from the leader to tail end Charlie. As we got to the bottom of the hill, we hit the heavy going and it was like hitting a traffic jam at high speed and we all compressed into a tight bunch and then, to my horror saw the four lead horses break away and make their race for the finishing post. I was wedged in like a sardine in a can, I shouted, swore, pushed, and shoved to get out of the pack as my opponents streaked away into the distance. When I finally managed to break free, they were a full fence ahead of me. Part of me said pull up and fight another day, but anger got the better of me and I kicked Wetherby on and started to make the chase. The ground was getting better by the stride and my slow progress meant that I had not taken so much out of my horse. By the time we turned to climb the infamous hill we hit good going and Wetherby's stamina started to shine and I realised that the fourth horse being pegged back with every stride we took and there was real hope of getting home in fourth place. By the time I jumped the fence at the bottom of the hill which had been the first fence at the start of the race I had caught him and passed him a couple of strides after landing. This seemed to give both me and my horse a great boost. I looked up and set my sights on the third placed horse, was it my imagination or was that horse slowing and coming back to me as well. I pushed on and we rapidly closed the gap much quicker than expected. The hill was killing my opponents and it changed my nightmare into a fairy-tale. I cannot truly describe the feeling. It was as if everything in front of me was in slow motion and I was still travelling at normal speed. The only other thing that seemed to be at normal speed was how quickly the finishing post was coming towards me and that was the bad news, we passed the third horse with ease. The second horse was now ten lengths ahead of me, my legs were burning but adrenalin was keeping the pain at bay. I think the jockey didn't know I was coming as he made no effort to push his horse on, or maybe the horse was just exhausted but we swept passed him as if he was standing still. Oh my God! I was in second place and I was gaining on the leader every stride but the finishing post was nearly upon us. I came up alongside him as we crossed the line. Had I done enough it was too close to call. There was a long delay before the judges announced the winner. This was not fantasy but reality, I lost the race "on the nod" as they say, a short head. One more stride and we would have won easily but it was not to be. Even though I did not win, I had had the ride of my life and my horse had proved just how great he was.

As a consolation, I got a write up in the Horse and Hound magazine describing my ride up that hill. It read, Sam Humphrey and Dadda Boy almost caused the biggest upset of the day catching the favourite on the line when they came up the Atherstone hill with a wet sail".

When people ask me, what was your greatest race, greatest competition or who my greatest horse was? I can never give them a definitive answer as there are many in every category, each with their own special merits. The Atherstone was definitely one of my most memorable races, as was my first race and my first win, although funnily, I cannot recall that race in detail, it just happened. Other races that stand out are my first fall, and the four-mile race at the Middleton Point to Point. There were two more notable races with Wetherby that stand out and I will recount them in a moment but first I would like you to take note that most of my really memorable moments in my life have not been winning but more about achieving new goals and learning from my mistakes. Winning is usually easy on the day and the ecstasy lasts only until the next day, only if you win from adversity does it become memorable. To me the journey to winning is more important than the actual winning. As soon as I become successful on a regular basis, I lose interest and need to find a new challenge. I suppose that has been the story of my life.

Because I had won my restricted race that season it qualified me to enter a Hunterchase at Leicester Racecourse. This means that you are riding on a professional racecourse over much bigger and stiffer fences. There are much stricter rules and you need to apply for an amateur licence from The Jockey Club which is the ruling body for all horse racing. I had qualified for a similar race the previous season by winning the maiden race. Because I was new to the sport, I had not realised that I needed an amateur licence to ride in it. Looking back, I now realise, that I didn't really have enough experience that first year to ride over the bigger fences. I did however get the offer of some help from an unexpected quarter. The encounter has stuck we me for the rest of my life. Mrs Ulrica Newton was the owner of Garthorpe racecourse, she also owned a large area of land. She was the daughter of Lord Rank. Her deceased husband had revived the defunct and now world-famous Melton Hunt Club and of which she was now chairman. Her son Joey was one the leading amateur jockeys in the country. She was very forthright and outspoken and a lot of people were frightened to lock horns with her. So, when she hailed me down at the Melton Hunt Club point to point, I quaked in my boots, no, actually I nearly shit myself. I had never spoken to her but I had watched her verbally tear wealthy and powerful men to shreds publicly. Before I could open my mouth, she told me how pleased she was that I had won my maiden race and, as that qualified me for a Hunter chase at Uttoxeter why! had I not entered it. I explained that this was all new to me and that I didn't have a licence and that when I had contacted the Jockey Club, they told me it would be impossible for me to get one issued in time for the race. I failed to mention that I could not afford the cost of the licence, or the entry fee for the race, nor that I didn't own a proper racing saddle. She simply went on to say that I had earned the right to take part in that race and if I had any trouble getting the licence in time, I was to give her a call and she would soon sort out those stupid little buggers out down at the Jockey Club, and with that she strode off! It was a spontaneous act of kindness that I will never forget. Our paths crossed many times in the future. I also met her regularly when hunting on Mondays with the Quorn and we always had a pleasant chat.

After winning my Restricted race in my second season I applied for my Amateur licence straightaway. It was like applying for a driver's licence, question after question, then a full medical. That was a cost I hadn't budgeted for! Things at home were going better and Dad announced that he was going to take me to Milner's, the saddlers in Leicester town centre and get me measured up for a proper racing saddle. I don't know where he managed to find the money from but he did. It was like going to the tailors. I was measured, sat on various racing saddles, and asked how heavy I was. Because I was barely ten stone, they decided on a seven-pound weighted saddle so that I didn't have to carry so much lead in my weight cloth. Apparently, a horse carries weight easier in a saddle than the dead weight in a weight cloth.

The race was held early in June just after the end of the point-to-point season.
What awaited me at the racecourse astounded me and turned me into a quivering jelly. You needed passes to get into every different section of the racecourse. Where you got those passes from seemed to be a state secret. Everybody except me seemed to know where to go and what to do. It started at the gate of the horsebox park then at the stable yard. Everywhere was guarded by people that had been told not to let anyone in without a pass on pain of death, full stop. In the end we had to buy an entry ticket in order to get access to the secretary's office. After showing my new shiny rider's licence to prove who I was and being double checked that I was actually riding that day I was told that I should have received all the passes with my entry confirmation. It was said in an accusing manner as if I had given all my passes away and was trying to pull a fast one. Oh, how I hate the foot soldiers of authority!

Finally, I had the paperwork to gain entry and got Wetherby off the lorry and into the stable yard. The stable yard was like Fort Knox with only a groom and the trainer allowed access, so I set off in search of the jockeys changing rooms. Wow these were something else. Varnished wood panelled walls and benches with ornate cast iron coat hooks above for your clothes. The room was a hive of activity almost like a battlefield command centre except it was full of men in various stages of undress. As soon as I entered the door, I was apprehended by a man wearing a green apron who said, "Good morning sir, who normally does you sir?" I explained that this was my first race under rules and didn't have a regular valet. "No problem Sir, I'll put you here and get Fred to look after you". He then shouted to Fred "Oy Fred got a new gentleman here; will you look after him".
Fred appeared introduced himself and explained that this was my place for the day and that I could safely leave all my kit with him. He then asked me which race I was riding in and if I needed any kit for the race. Although I had everything with me that I needed, I was intrigued to discover what he could supply. The answer was everything except a bridle, saddle, weight cloth, lead, girth, surcingle, breeches, riding boots of various weights, racing mitts, neck stock and ladies tights. All you had to bring, was your hat, jockstrap, and racing colours. That sounded great but he then explained that each item had a hire charge per race and although these charges were not high, collectively they added up to a tidy sum if you wanted everything. My race was at three thirty-five so he said that if I returned around an hour before that would be plenty of time to get ready and weighed out. Finally, he took my saddle and kit bag and informed me that everything would be laid out ready for me when I came back. Nice!

I left the changing room and went to a prearranged point to meet up with my team, no mobile phones in those days to help you find people. I left Lou, Sally, my groom, and John

Cook to look after the horse side of the day, arranged various meeting times and locations before going off to walk the course with Dad. At this point I would like to explain the roll of the groom which is so often understated although it is now getting more of the recognition that they deserve. They are a vital part of any equine competition team. Not only do they look after your ride on a daily basis, muck out, feed groom, and often do basic exercise, they also monitor the wellbeing of the horse as they spend more time with the animal than anyone else and often notice subtle changes in health long before they become apparent to others. Competing horses is like being in charge of a costume department for a theatre production. Each horse needs all its own rugs, bandages, travelling boots, water, hay, feed, first aid, electrolytes, cooling gels and if eventing, several different sets of tack and studs for the three different disciplines. Then there is all the travel paperwork, passports, and veterinary records. I always said to my grooms that my life was in their hands because before every competition they checked every stitch on the leatherwork of my saddlery. The stress that is exerted on stirrup leathers, girths and reins must never be underestimated. A good groom allows the rider to do their job of planning and riding the horse to the best of their ability. Three cheers for the grooms.

Walking the course was a real eyeopener. The first shock was getting access to the course with passes having to be shown several times. This was totally different from point to points where access was open to all at any time. The second unexpected surprise was that there was a golf course inside the centre of the racetrack and people were still playing as the race was happening. My final shock was the size and width of the fences. They were significantly bigger and much wider. Brush through the top of these and you had better be sitting tight. The open ditch really made me gulp as I stood in front of it! Also, the water jump was significantly wider than the one that I had jumped at Dingley.

Time flew by and I was soon returning to the changing room to get ready for the race. When I returned, I was amazed to find my bag had been completely unpacked and my colours were all hung up with breeches and boots laid out underneath. My saddle and weight cloth were on a saddle rack next to my colours, everything very shipshape. My valet, Fred, welcomed me back and told me I was in good time and to get changed at my leisure. He would be back to help me weigh out just as soon as he had got his jockeys out for the next race. There were about six to eight valets all dashing backwards and forwards with great efficiency getting all the jockeys ready for the next race. There is only about forty minutes between races. The race itself takes about six to seven minutes with another five minutes to walk back to the paddock. The first four have to remove their saddles, grab a quick few words with the owners and press before weighing in. The jockeys are called out to the parade ring approximately fifteen minutes before the start of the next race. Simple maths show that the valets have about ten to fifteen minutes to help change the jockeys into their next colours and weigh out for the next race. Muddy breeches and boots had to be replaced with clean shiny new ones and battered bodies checked over by the course doctor. There could be twenty plus riders in the next race and every second counted as the powers to be accepted no excuses for being late. The immaculately dressed parade ring Steward arrived and announced "Jockeys out" in full military fashion as if they were being ordered to charge the enemy head on.

Peace descended on the changing room. The valets took a swig of lukewarm tea, took a deep breath and sprung back into action. I was changed by now except for my stock which I asked Fred to tie for me. "We don't use those here sir" he told me and produced a Velcro pre tied one. "Make you look like a proper jockey for the punters out there" he said. He had already prepared my saddle and weight cloth based on my weight and the weight that I had been allocated for the race. He took my saddle and escorted me to the test scales. My weight was almost bang-on just a couple more ounces of lead and it was perfect. Then it was into the weighing room to present myself before the Clerk on the Scales, another ex-military man who barked, race, name, and number. Fred said the race, I gave my name and number. He peered at the number cloth draped over the top of my saddle and studied it intently, why I do not know, as the black number on the white cloth was huge and designed to be clearly seen at fifty yards or more? He then checked my weight and announced that it was correct followed quickly by the barked order "Next". I passed my saddle to John Cook who was waiting at the barrier at the side of the weighing room along with the other trainers for horses in the next race.

I returned to the inner sanctum of the jockeys changing room and waited. I had come to love the changing rooms as you were protected from the hustle and bustle of the racecourse outside and well-meaning well-wishers. Absolutely nobody except the valets and Paddock Steward were allowed in and the Steward only came to the entrance. I always thought of it as the jockeys church, peace, and tranquillity before the battle. A place where many a prayer was muttered, religious or not.

The race was the highlight of my season. It was a field of top-class horses and I was the rank outsider. It is fabulous to race against good horses and riders. Everyone rides straight and with discipline. Wetherby rose to the occasion sailing over the bigger fences with ease although I had a few dodgy moments on landing until I got used to the extra G-force. The only real wobble we had was at the water jump, Wetherby stood off and dropped a hind leg in the water, we soon recovered but it cost us a couple of lengths. After a few milliseconds of recovery, I looked up to see three golf trolleys trundling across the track in front of me. I was in complete shock but nobody else seemed bothered so I kicked on. Like everything else in racing their crossing was timed to perfection and they were long gone by the time we arrived at the crossing point. To my delight I finished fourth and the elation that I felt far outweighed winning the restricted open. If you had seen us in the owners and trainers bar post-race you would have thought that we had won the race. Although it was a huge extravagance, we all clubbed together and bought a bottle of champagne. This was to celebrate not only our first run under National Hunt Rules but also to celebrate a truly remarkable season. We had not won the race but had moved up to the next level in style. That is what matters most, not winning, although winning is nice.

I returned to the changing room to pick up my saddle and kit bag and to pay my valet. The last surprise of the day was to discover that all my racing kit had been washed and dried. Even my boots had been cleaned and polished. A true day to remember.

Wetherby gave me two more memorable races - both were at Garthorpe. The first was an open race and was full of top-class horses. At least five were rated several points above Wetherby. As I circled at the start, I concluded that I would be lucky if I finished in the first six. The race was run at an unusually slow pace as these top horses and jockeys played cat and mouse with each other. I sat in about sixth or seventh for the first circuit and a half just behind the top horses, keeping out of trouble. The ground was good and Wetherby was loving the pace and jumping superbly, I was loving it too. As we approached the last fence at the top of the hill the jockeys in front of me made their move and I went with them. As I kicked Wetherby, he surged forward with hardly any encouragement from me. I caught, and half lengthed the back marker of the bunch. The jump was so good I landed alongside the next rider who look surprised to see that it was me, as I had come from nowhere. I was now up with the leading bunch matching their pace. I was also wondering how long I could hold my own against these top-class horses. As we rounded the top bend and started to run down Garthorpe's famous hill all but one fell back leaving me to dispute the lead. I assumed that the others were taking a breather and waiting until we had jumped the notorious downhill fence that had put paid to so many a jockey's winning aspirations before delivering their final attack. I knew that this fence was my weakness as I usually played safe and looked for an easy stride. Today was different I was matching one of the best horses that I had ever raced against, and my horse was jumping superbly. As the adrenaline coursed through my blood, I attacked the fence as hard as I could and Wetherby responded with a thrilling leap. It was so great it is making me tingle all over just writing about it. We out jumped our opponent and took the lead. I kicked on as hard as I could hoping to hold onto the lead over the last two fences and onto the finishing line. As we hurtled down the hill, I hugged the inside rail knowing that anyone trying to pass me would be forced out onto ground that sloped away to the outside of the track on the tight final bend. I had watched three horses slip and fall in front of me on that bend at a previous meeting.

It was my day! I was never challenged after that downhill fence and I won comfortably. I was astounded, if ever there was a day, I was going to get stuffed it was that day and here I was riding into the winners enclosure.

After the all the razzmatazz of weighing in and the prize giving, I got changed and was making my way back to the horsebox park to celebrate with the team. I had only gone a few yards when I saw Brian Crawford running towards me. Brian was a good friend. He was a fellow jockey who farmed near Aslockton. This was South Notts country so we qualified our horses together and had become good friends. He was a very good jockey and rode for other people as well as his own horses. He was a great friend and mentor to me during my racing period, always cheerful in a quiet way, very thoughtful and knowledgeable. It was very out of character for him to be half running, half skipping towards me grinning like a Cheshire Cat.

He grabbed my hand shook it profusely and slapped me on the back. "You have made my day! When I saw you coming down the hill in front of all those top horses it made my day. It just proves that money does not always buy success. You have given us poorer chaps the confidence that we still have a chance at this game despite them buying expensive horses we could never afford". It was then I realised how great my achievement was. I remember being told that Peter Greenall now Lord Daresbury and a regular in the jockeys changing room during my racing period had spent over £30,000 at the sales to strengthen his string of pointers in a bid to win the amateur championship. This equates to approximately £165,000 in today's money whereas Wetherby had cost a mere £268. I do not say any of the above with malice or jealously, all the jockeys that I beat were friends of mine in the changing room but not socially. Whether it was in the hunting field or racing it was a dangerous game and no place for airs and graces. Peter Greenall gave me great advice during my racing career. Although he was The Honourable Mr Peter Greenall on the race card, he was just Peter to the jockeys.

That win was one of those great moments for the little guys. Money does count massively in all equestrian sports but every now and then a lowly amateur with not even two halfpennies to rub together comes along and turns the tables upside-down and gives all those other not so well-off enthusiasts the boost they need to carry on at all costs.

My last memorable race on Wetherby was again at Garthorpe our favourite course. The race unfolded almost the same as the previous race I have just written about. I made my move just before the last fence at the top of the hill and took the lead but almost instantly I was joined by another horse and jockey. We matched each other stride for stride as we screamed down towards the downhill fence at brake neck speed just kicking and hoping we got a stride at it. We both smashed through the birch quite low down, our mounts both going too fast to jump any height. The stride after landing we turned and glared at each other. I didn't know the jockey but he did look vaguely familiar. It is hard to make out facial features when wearing a skullcap and goggles and going lickety split down a steep hill. He had come up on the inside of me out in the country where there were no rails. I was so taken up with trying to keep up with him I gave it no thought but as we landed, I realised that the crafty bugger had got the inside rail. I should have pushed him out before the wings but I had been caught napping. We were going as fast as our horses could go and faster than I had ever been down that hill. I knew that I faced the adverse camber of the sharp bend at the bottom of the hill unless I could get past him. We were so close to each other our legs were constantly crushed against each other and our elbows hit each other's body. My opponent growled, swore, and shouted at me to move over and give him some room. For a split second I was tempted to move over and give him a bit of room because for me this was uncharted territory, I had never been in a battle like this before. In an instant I realised all his shouting at me was just gamesmanship. I held my line and swore back at him. I felt sure that our horses would entangle their legs with each other or strike into each other but battle had been enjoined and the red veil had come down. This was do or die. As we hurtled around the bend, I could feel Wetherby's hooves slipping sideways on the bend and visions of the three horses that fell in front of me the previous year flashed up in my mine. I clearly relived that terrible moment that had unfolded in front of me the previous season. The lead horse going down on its side, which brought the next horse down and finally the third horse down in a domino effect. Three horses and jockeys sliding across the track all jumbled up together. The play back seemed to be in super slow motion.

I lent on my opponent and held the line as close to the rails as possible, my adversary elbowing me and shouting to be given more room. Even stronger swear words were exchanged. It probably took less than ten seconds to get around the bend but I could write a whole chapter about it. Suddenly we burst out the corner and saw the penultimate fence in front of us. It had been the first fence at the start of the race and along with the next fence which was the last fence, the only two fences that were jumped three times. We remained glued to each other as we both kicked hard to get a good stride out of our tired horses, the front legs of our mounts touched down in perfect symmetry on landing. As soon as the front legs touched down, we screamed at our horses and kicked on. We were both crouched low on our horses to cut down any wind drag. My thighs burnt like a furnace. At the last fence, my adversary got a slightly better jump and gained maybe two feet on me when we landed. We continued our battle all the way to the finishing line bumping into each other whips and legs hitting each other as much as the horses. The verbal abuse never ending. I was starting to hate this man and I am sure that he hated me. He beat me by a short head, the jump at the last fence was the only thing that could separate us. As we pulled up to a trot, I steeled myself for a strong dressing down by the jockey and Stewards over my aggressive riding. We both pulled down our goggles and turned to face one another. To my surprise I was met with beaming smile, or perhaps it was a cheeky grin. He extended his hand to shake mine saying "Well done, what a battle. That was great fun, I can't remember when I have had such a long fight to the finish. Marvellous!" We shook hands and I agreed with him. We rode back to the winners enclosure side by side to cheering and clapping from an appreciative crowd.

My adversary that day was the legendary Dick Saunders who didn't ride in our area very much. It was the next season that he rode Grittar to victory in the Grand National becoming the oldest rider ever to win the race and one of only three amateurs to have won the race in the last fifty years.

Dick was always immaculately dressed, with gentlemanly manners to match, always lifting his trilby when he met the opposite sex and greeting people with a good morning or good afternoon. He was always so kind and obliging it was hard to believe he could transform into this aggressive jockey with nerves of steel. I suppose he was the consummate English gentleman from a bygone era when a man was judged by the way he dressed, his manners, along with his physical and daring prowess.

I rode against both him and his daughter Caroline quite a few times mainly at the Dingley race meetings. It was at one of these meetings that I first came across Grittar in his fledgling days. I clearly remember circling at the start of a race at Dingley waiting to be called in by the starter. It is in those few minutes as we wait for the appointed time that jockeys decide who is going to make the running and who is going to be sitting it out at the back. On this occasion Caroline turned to us and said "Hey listen up lads. This horse is some machine. He will go off like shit off a shovel, don't try and keep up with us or you will kill yourselves".

I thought she was bluffing or that it was a bit of gamesmanship but she wasn't. He did set off like shit off a shovel and all any of us saw was Grittar's and Caroline's backsides. They won by a distance!

The horse world is a small world and I learnt recently that Caroline trains point to pointers in a village close to Ravensthorpe where my father was born and grew up in Northamptonshire. Dick Saunders became master of the Pytchley Hunt after his retirement from racing which was also my father's local pack. Staying on the small world theme at the time of writing this piece, Lou and I attended a wedding in Kilkenny Ireland and as we arrived at the back entrance of the Club House Hotel the first person, I saw was Graham Smith, a farrier who lives about five miles from us and was also a fellow jockey back in the day. I walked into the bar and the first person that I met was Martin Brown, who used to joust with us, and was a fellow hunting enthusiast and keen Point to Point rider. They along with Graham's wife Holly who show jumps for Team GB were over in Ireland for the

Goresbridge Horse Sales and were also staying in the hotel. A little later on that evening I bumped into Steve Barnes now a horse dealer in north Nottinghamshire who I have known since my early show jumping days, also over for the sales and staying at the Club House Hotel. Small World!

At the end of my fourth season, I was starting to feel that I had done all that I could with Wetherby. We could only run in Adjacent Hunts and Open races both of which attracted the best horses. Although I pulled off a couple of spectacular wins and was nearly always placed in the top four, I was having to ride him ridiculously hard to get those places. It did not sit well with me continually using the whip in the latter stages of the races on such a horse that always gave his best.

In my third and fourth seasons I was starting to ride for other people. This helped me greatly to improve my strength and fitness. Sometimes riding in back-to-back races forced me to relax during the early part of the race and conserve my energy for when it mattered. I became fitter in the mind as well as the body. When you are competing you always believe that you are as fit as you can be but it is only when you move up a level do you realise that you need to get even fitter.

At the end of that season, we were approached by the Greenall family's stud groom enquiring if we were interested in selling Wetherby. They of course referred to him as Dadda Boy, his registered racing name. The Greenall family were looking for a school master for Peter's younger brother Johnny to start his racing career. The offer was generous and after much soul searching, I agreed to the sale. By this time Dad and Lou were both enjoying the racing game and it was agreed that all the money from the sale would go towards buying other racehorses.

I do not know whether we were lucky and sold at the right time, or that Johnny never had the same rapport with him that I had, but he failed to shine as bright the following season. He certainly taught Johnny his trade but was soon sold on to the Master of the Fernie Hunt where he had a glorious racing retirement ending his days being ridden by the master's wife, after leading the Fernie for several seasons. A great horse who really touched my soul.

With the money from Wetherby's sale, I purchased two young horses Stanford Mill, and Vanter Play, both were lovely horses but I had been spoilt by having such a good horse to begin with. I obtained minor placings with both but I knew that they were never going to be another Dadda Boy and so I sold them both after a season. Unfortunately, the price of racehorses was starting to rocket and although I sold both horses at a good profit, by the time I found a replacement all that profit and more had been eaten up by inflation.

My two younger brothers had by this time also started racing, and they along with Dad and myself had also started teamchasing. Just having me racing had stretched the family finances. Now despite our business doing really well, the finances could not sustain all this, plus hunting with the Quorn on Mondays. Dadda Boy's profit rapidly frittered away and although we had some good horses in the riding school it would be killing the goose that laid the golden egg if we constantly took them away, not to mention the risk of serious injury to them. Thankfully, many wealthy people like to own horses and watch them being ridden by others. They are the competitive rider's saviours and everyone is happy.

A Journeyman Jockey

During my last season on Dadda Boy I had started to ride racehorses belonging to other people and John Cook my racing mentor provided me with my first outside ride on a horse called Tudor Abbot. It made me appreciate the risks journeymen jockeys take at every meeting. I understood that racing was dangerous from the start and anyone who thinks otherwise is a fool. But when you start climbing onboard horses that you have not schooled, ridden or in some cases never even seen before, then the risk factor multiples massively.

Tudor Abbot was a good-looking horse, black with a small white blaze, about 16.1hh but lighter in build than Dadda Boy. John worked for Lord Crawshaw who lived at Whatton Hall on the edge of the village of Long Whatton. I first met John when Dad contacted Lord Crawshaw to see if we could hire his gallops and schooling fence. Lord Crawshaw was an enthusiastic follower of racing and told us we were welcome to use the gallops free of charge. John was sent down to the gallops to meet us and supervise the schooling session. We instantly got on and he gave me some great advice and was my racing mentor for the whole of my racing career. John had been a professional jockey and ridden for Lord Crawshaw as a jockey. He was now stud groom for his lordship and lived in a flat over the stable yard adjacent to the Hall. His position as Stud Groom gave him considerable autonomy on the estate and he arranged many more schooling sessions over the coming years.
Lord Crawshaw was an ex point to point rider himself, who had tragically broken his back whilst riding in a point-to-point race when he was in his late teens or early twenties and was now confined to a wheelchair. Perhaps confined is the wrong word because he spent a lot of his time zooming around the estate on a specially modified quad bike. This quad bike also had a modified seat that swivelled and enabled him to take part in Game Shoots. I got to know Lord Crawshaw very well but more about that later.

John had done all the qualifying and basic fitness work on Tudor Abbot himself, and I only did the final few gallops and jump schooling with him to get to know him. Only riding Dadda Boy had allowed me to forget what it was like to ride a young novice horse again and it was quite a culture shock. Tudor was a bit iffy with his jumping to start with but soon seemed the be getting the idea.
Our first race proved just how schooling on your own is no guarantee of what might happen in a race. The race was at Garthorpe and was the maiden race. This was another culture shock as I had got used to rocking up at the racecourse at about noon and riding in either the open or the adjacent's race usually number two and three on the card, all done and dusted by three o' clock, then eating and drinking my socks off. My usual routine was not to eat or drink after supper on the evening before race day and abstain until I had finished racing. As soon as I had finished, I stuffed my face with beer, food and a variety of other alcohol beverages that were offered from various car boots. I would normally put on about eight pounds in weight by the time I got home. Going back to maidens made me have to wait until the last race of the day by which time most food and drink had already been scoffed by others and everyone was packing up to go home.

The race was a large field of about 24 horses and I jumped off at the back to try and keep out of trouble but Tudor had other ideas and panicked at being left behind and we were right in the thick of it by the time we reached the first fence, so much for race planning! As we took off over the first fence Tudor veered left and proceeded to run sideways along the top of the fence. I took off on the outside rail and landed in the middle of the course, to screams and shouts from my fellow jockeys who called me many things, none of which can be written in this book. I think a few painful death threats were also thrown in for good measure. That first race really shook me up and I felt incredibly lucky to get back into the changing room in one piece. Although his jumping did slowly improve, he always jumped to the left throughout his career. I used to warn all the jockeys at the start after that first race and this seemed to reduce the number of death threats during the race.

One of the hardest things that I had to deal with during my racing period happened in my second season and that was starting a family. My son Mark was born in March and seeing Lou holding our tiny baby by the exit of the parade ring as we set off to canter down to the start always tugged at my heart strings and made me ask myself should I really be doing this and what would happen to them if I got severely injured. Although I share these thoughts with you now, I have never shared them until now. Sometimes in the changing room before a race, mates might touch on what they think about before going down to the start but usually everything is kept securely in the privacy of their own minds.

I always suffered from nerves going down to the start. As I left the parade ring all my strength would drain from my body. I could not grip the reins and my legs went to jelly so that I could not even do the rising trot and barely stay on board as we cantered down to the start. As the starter called us into line a calm came over me and my strength came back. I learned to live with this phenomenon and one day someone said something that was a game changer. It was one of those extremely rare moments when riders bare their soul to a fellow compatriot. I cannot remember who said it but they told me that they had been told not to fear nerves or a touch of the collywobbles because it was just the side effects of your body preparing itself to do great feats. Nerves are the side effects of the adrenaline being pumped into the bloodstream. It's like feeling a little sick after an injection. Whether that is true or not, from that day on I made nerves my friend rather than my enemy.

Riding for other owners had its advantages and disadvantages. The advantages were that all the costs for the horse were met by the owner as well as all the responsibility of entering races and all the other necessary paperwork related to racing a horse. Qualifying the horse in the hunting field was also done by the owner or by somebody employed by them. If the horse was sane and sensible this could be a pleasurable experience if you could spare the time. However, most racehorses are not sane or sensible in the hunting field and it can often be a nightmare. A sensible jockey will usually try to ride a gallop or better still jump a few schooling fences to get a feel of the way the horse goes before the day of the race, although this often has no reflection on what happens on the racecourse.

The disadvantages are the expectations of the owner or even worse the owners if it is a syndicated horse. Nearly all owners believe that their horse will win even if the form ratings put their horse as the lowest rated horse in the race. Having purchased a racehorse, the owner often believes that his judgment has been besmirched if his horse does not win or get placed, and so a scapegoat has to be found. First in line is the stupid, inept jockey, quickly followed by the trainer. If a horse falls or jumps badly it is never the horse's fault always the jockey's. In order to keep their jobs, trainers and jockeys must invent plausible excuses for the horse not performing like a super star, for example the ground didn't suit him or the race was run too quick or too slow and so on and so on, the excuses never end!

All my hairy rides were on other people's horses that I hadn't trained, and all but one of my falls were on rides for other people. I had relatively few falls in my career and only two injuries of any significance.
I fell at the last fence on one of John Cook's horse's at Dingley when I was disputing the lead with another horse. We hit the last fence hard, the horse's head snapped back and I was thrown forwards. The horse's head hit me full in the face and knocked me unconscious. When I regained consciousness, I was choking and I felt a heavy pressure on my arms and chest. Gradually as my faculties came back to me, I realised that my body was being held down by two St. John's Ambulance men who were constantly telling me to lie still and not move. I could not speak because something warm and sticky was blocking my throat. It was also making it extremely hard to breath. As my head cleared a bit more, I realised it was blood from my nose that was choking me. I tried to tell the St John's men but I could only gurgle and they only pressed harder and told me not to move. They seemed oblivious of me choking to death.
In the end, I decided that drastic action was required, I closed my eyes and relaxed as much as possible. I felt the pressure of them soften. I think they thought I had passed out again. I summoned up what little strength that I had and suddenly pushed up and rolled over catching them by surprise. Before they could react, I had coughed out a huge jelly like lump of congealed blood that was blocking my throat and felt cool clean air rush into my lungs. By this time, they had recovered and were trying to force me down flat on my back again but now that I had my voice back and I shouted "Get off me you stupid buggers! I'm fine you were forcing me to choke on my own blood "

I feel sorry now for swearing at them. In those days they gave their services free and were at every fence for us, but they were not the paramedics that are on hand at today's meetings. Some were truly knowledgeable but others had only basic first aid training which in those days was far less than we have to have as riding instructors today.

I rode several horses for John Cook, some of these were jointly owned with friends. One of these jointly owned horses was called The Vacationer and the co-owner was Paul Maine. Both Paul and John liked a good bet. At home, The Vacationer showed good promise and I should have realised that they were up to something when John informed me that he was going to run The Vacationer at a course called Mollington near Banbury well outside our Point-to-Point area. John announced that he thought that the track would suit him. To me it seemed a crazy idea as I had never seen or heard of the course. I thought that it was a long way to go and a lot of expense for a first run. I was even more perplexed when I walked the course, which was set on the side of a hill not unlike Garthorpe but the track was left-handed and the uphill and downhill sections were much more severe than at Garthorpe. This was a strange choice of track for a first time run but then I was only the jockey who had to do as he was told by the trainer.

An interesting turn of fate was bumping into an ex-jouster who I hadn't seen for about ten years. His name was Steve Harrison. He used to work for us at the stables and did the jousting for several years. He was also a particularly good singer and was lead singer in a successful local band. He left the riding world to pursue a career in the pop industry, and we had not seen or heard of him since. Apparently, his singing career didn't flourish and so he had returned to the horse industry.

My instructions for the race were to try and win the race but if I thought I couldn't do that easily, I was not to push him hard and to give him an easy race. It was hard to ride a good race on a track that you have never ridden before. You need to know the subtleties of a track to have that winning edge.

As it turned out he ran a better than I expected race. Three fences from home I was still with the leading pack, his jumping had been impeccable and I thought that I might be in with a shout. I moved up to fourth but quickly realised his stamina was fading with no chance of winning. Riding to orders I did not push him any further and finished a distant seventh.

I was aware that I could have run a better race because not knowing the course as well as the local area jockeys I had made a few minor tactical errors. John Cook had a good eye for things like this and was always saying things like you went a bit too early or you needed to be a bit more handily placed at that point in the race. So, I was expecting quite a long post-race discussion, but to my surprise got a short well done excellent! He then preceded to inform me that he had entered us for a race at another racecourse that I had never heard of. I had also never heard of the Hunt that was holding the point to point. This time we were travelling south east.   All very strange.

When we arrived at the course whose name, I cannot recall I was again surprised as it was the exact opposite of the last course. It was a right-handed course whereas the other was left-handed, this course was almost flat with just a slight rise to the finish whereas Mollington had a bloody great hill. All very strange. Looking back now it all made sense. Point to points are run in areas and you usually run in your own area every week because it keeps travelling time and expenses down to a minimum. Both these runs on The Vacationer were out of our normal area and they were in two different areas as well. In both of the race cards all the horses had a rating number next to their name which related to their form based on previous performances. The Vacationer only had NR next to his name which denoted no rating, if you were betting this translated to, don't touch it with a barge pole. Amazingly even our run the previous week had not been recorded. We started the race as 50-1 rank outsiders.

Watching the races before mine with John it was clear that this was a fast-galloping course and all the winners were close to the front from start to finish. My instructions were jump off quickly at the start and try to stay near to the front. The race was run at a cracking pace right from the word go and my mount seemed up for it. The fences had a good slope on them and jumped well at speed. Five or six of us were in a group at the front and I was having the ride of my life, all my competitors were jumping well as we skimmed over the fences at a blistering pace, nobody was giving an inch. I was at the top of my game as a jockey, riding two horses every race meeting and doing some Hunter Chases over the bigger fences as well.

You could throw a blanket over the leading bunch; it was if we were welded together. Then at fence fifteen we clipped the top of the fence I think the fierce pace was taking its toll. The Vacationer's front legs crumpled on landing and we went down. Unlike my early falls my reactions were now razor sharp. I flung myself back and pushed my feet towards his ears and slipped my reins to the buckle end. I cursed to myself, everything had been going so well, I really thought I had a chance of winning. We slid along the ground. The Vacationer's head had completely disappeared from view, bent underneath him sliding face down along the ground. The momentum of the fall subsided after about ten yards of sliding, I instinctively whacked him with the whip and to my amazement he came up out of the ground and was back on his feet in a flash. By this time, I had pumped so much adrenalin into my bloodstream I was up for anything. My fall or maybe I should say hiccup had cost me at least ten lengths and any chance of winning gone as the leading pack were now approaching the third last fence. I was so annoyed that I resolved to ride as hard as possible and finish the race. I was astonished how well he recovered from the fall and we quickly got back into our rhythm and to my amazement we were closing on the leading pack and quickly past the back markers in the race. When most horses go down it knocks the wind out of them and they never get going again. I had really enjoyed my first ride on him and thought he could be something special but now I knew he was special and my thoughts drifted to his next race when hopefully all would go to plan.

The leading pack were falling apart as the blistering pace of the race started to take its toll and my mount rather than having the wind knocked out of him seemed to have used the time on the ground to get his second wind. We caught the leading pack just before the second last fence and swept past them. From the second last fence it was a long downhill run around a long sweeping shallow bend and I was leaving my competitors standing. Was this really happening or was it just a dream? I glanced over my shoulder about halfway around the bend just to check it was real. I broke the golden rule of racing which is never look back. There were no running rails around the bend just a couple of hurdles staked out on the inside of the bend as turning points. Looking back took only a second or so but it took my concentration and as I looked forward again, I realised something was wrong. I had lost my line on the final part of the bend. I was drifting out to the left on the final right-handed bend. I tried to correct it, but nothing was happening the ground fell away slightly to the left and the further I drifted the more it fell away. The Vacationer was just not responding although I was pulling hard on my right rein. Perhaps he was napping back to the horses box park. Movement appeared in my peripheral vision. It was a horse closing down on me making good use of the ground I was giving away. In desperation I swapped my whip over and gave him three good whacks down his left shoulder to which he thankfully responded. The ground I had lost going wide on the bend cost me dear and my comfortable ten to fifteen length lead had been lost and I jumped the last fence with barely half a length lead. Thankfully, I still had fuel in the tank but I had no idea where it came from. I won by two lengths, starting price 50-1!

To this day I still do not understand John and Paul's reaction. To have a 50-1 winner is a once in a lifetime achievement especially with all the things that happened that day. It was tradition that if you had a good win then the owners would give the jockey a memento and have a celebratory meal. None of this happened and everything was subdued. Perhaps they did not expect the horse to run so well and were kicking themselves for not wagering more. Sadly, it soured the day for me.

The reason I had run wide on that last bend may have had something to do with John avoiding me. When Lou untacked The Vacationer, she noticed that there was something wrong with the rubber bit. The right-hand bit ring was connected to the bit by only a single strand of well stretched rubber, no thicker than a heavy-duty elastic band, like the postman uses to hold a bunch of letters together. If I had taken another pull on that right rein and not swopped my whip over it would have snapped. Game over! When we examined the bit more closely the metal safety chain that runs through the centre of a rubber bit and holds the two-bit rings together had completely corroded away. The bit must have been twenty to thirty years old and should have been thrown away years ago and never ever used in any sort of riding let alone a race. Writing about it now still makes my blood run cold and realise how lucky I was that day. I have already praised my grooms for always going through my tack with a fine-tooth comb before every race, when you ride for other people, you are putting your life in the hands of someone you do not know and have often never even met. If you use a rubber bit my advice is to check it and check it again.

Another horse that John Cook brought at the sales was a horse that had run in a top-class chase at the Cheltenham Gold Cup meeting. This should have rung alarm bells for me as John was not a wealthy person. I never found out how much he paid for the horse and was too excited about riding a top-class chaser to delve into the why and wherefore of the purchase but looking back now, I think the old adage of, if it sounds too good to be true it probably is!

When I schooled John's new purchase, I stopped asking questions. I cannot recall the horse's name but I have never ever sat on such a powerful jumping machine in my life. It stood off its fences further than I thought was possible and soared into the air as if it had a missile up it's backside. This horse, without a shadow of a doubt, gave me the biggest thrill I have ever had jumping a horse and believe me, I have had many. Looking back, it was just like the Vacationer. I asked questions but the subject changed and I never got any answers. Easy to see now but like taking drugs, people know they are bad for them but the thought of the high makes them ignore the risks.

There was obviously a gamble being planned as I was told that I must not carry any excess weight. I was to diet really severely and ditch my beloved 7lb saddle and racing boots for a valet supplied postage stamp sized saddle and paper boots. Paper boots are not made from paper but are made from thin leather and have no heel or sole just chamois leather instead. We were entered in a Hunterchase at Warwick and I remember painfully feeling ever bit of gravel as I walked from the changing room to the parade ring. Worse was to come when I mounted and put my feet into the stirrups. I might as well have ridden barefoot! I broke into a cold sweat as I tried to get my head around the thought of riding three miles with stirrup treads sawing into the balls of my feet. Unlike other jockeys I never mastered the art of riding with my whole foot thrust through the stirrup. Luckily, the excitement of riding such a stunning horse seemed to numb the pain. Down at the start as we circled waiting to be called out onto the course by the starter, my whole body buzzed with excitement, the pain in my feet gone completely. I knew this horse was going to take a strong hold so I positioned him behind the front rank so that I could hold him up and conserve his energy for later in the race. The starter's flag dropped and the elastic bungee tape flew back across the track clearing the way for us to leap forward and gallop down towards the first fence. All the horses in the race had to have won a point to point or a national hunt race to qualify to run in this race so jockeys and horses all knew their job.

As we approached the first fence, I was nicely tucked in behind one of the leading horses just where I wanted to be, as we approached the wings of the first fence the front rank opened up a bit so I edged sideways to give myself and my mount a clear view of the fence. It is always nice to see what you are about to jump. I was a good half a length behind the horse in front of me so that there was no chance of being half lengthed. The horse in front of me started to take off and shit! Oh my god I was in the air. My horse had taken off about ten to twelve yards before the fence. In the next nano second a thousand and one's thoughts flashed through my mind, mainly about the extent of my injuries that I was about to receive, and my wife and children. We thrust forward and upwards like a scrambled fighter jet and to my amazement cleared the fence, sailed past the leading horse and landed in the lead. Wow! This was in another dimension; in all my riding career I had never experienced a jump of this magnitude. I tried to contain my horse's exuberance as I did not want to be in the lead at this early stage of the race but then I realised that he was not running away with me, this was his normal pace. He was just bowling easily along eating up the ground. Another big jump at the second added to our lead as we made our way past the stands, I felt high as a kite, this was the best horse that I had ever sat on. What a privilege. The pull on my arms slackened a little and I thought that he was settling down into the race. The next fence was jumped with less exuberance and as I picked him up on landing, he felt as if the spark had gone out of him, but I must be imagining it. I kicked and pushed but it was like a car spluttering as it ran out of fuel still moving forward but without any power. The field swept passed me and even with the other horses in front of me he didn't improve. With tears in my eyes, I pulled him up and walked slowly back to the exit. It was like falling out of a plane without a parachute at 10,000 feet. In less than a minute I went from the greatest high to the deepest low.

As I exited the course my mind was in a turmoil trying to make sense of the last few minutes. I undid my chin strap to try and ease the nausea that I was feeling. I was snapped back into reality by a horrid little man in a bowler hat who screamed at me shouting "Get that bloody chin strap done up or I will have you up before the Stewards. You have no business on a proper racecourse, galloping of into the lead and then pulling up like that. What the hell do you think you are playing at. Bloody amateurs shouldn't be allowed on a proper racecourse!" Unfortunately, most minor officials at racecourses seemed to be ex-military with a chip on their shoulders. The Jockey Club is a law onto itself, run on military lines and even has its own sort of police force. It just seems to attract officious little prats that like to make every day, normal people's life hell.

When I returned to the changing room, I was summoned by the Clerk of the Course to explain why I had pulled up so early in the race after such a strong showing. I explained what had happened and told him I pulled up because I feared for the welfare of the horse. Like me he found the incident very strange but accepted that I had acted in the best interest of the horse. He was a nice man with common sense as are most senior officials.

I told John Cook exactly what had happen and asked him if the horse had been vetted when he bought the horse. He quickly changed the subject and I never got a definitive answer but I did urge him to get the horse checked over by a vet.

The horse was entered at Dingley the following week but I could not ride it as I had a previous engagement so my brother Stuart took the ride. The horse dropped dead early in the race I think it was just after the second fence. I assume it must have suffered a heart attack or a brain aneurysm but although I asked many times, the answers were not forthcoming.

Another of John's super bargains was a horse called Artea. He was a 16hh chestnut gelding nicely put together. His sire was Articulate. I have never been a big follower of breeding but certain events made me remember this stallion. Not long after John purchased him, he was sent to our stables for me to get fit for racing. This should have set alarm bells ringing as John couldn't really afford livery and always prepared his horses himself but as usual, macho pride and being cocky blinded me. Shortly after Artea arrived John sent a vet from what was then the premier horse veterinary practice in our area, Oakham Vets. As the vet studied his passport prior to updating his vaccinations he uttered these profound words which I have never forgotten to this day, "Ah I see he is by Articulate, he throws some incredibly talented offspring. I am glad he has come to your yard as they all need to be kept in a knowledgeable yard". At the time I took it as a compliment but as events unfolded, I realised that it was a very candid warning. Everything to do with horses is a gamble and when you race them it is the biggest gamble of all. I was a poor boy trying to make it in a rich man's world and I could not afford to think too hard about risks, as every cheap horse I rode had the potential to be my next Dadda Boy.

I rode Artea in two races his first race went very well. It was right at the end of the season and he jumped and ran very promisingly. We were keen to get another run into him before the end of the season but all the local races had finished. However, John's research found a new meeting called the Point-to-Point Owners Association who were holding their first meeting on an entirely new course. It was for members only so John joined the association and off we went.

When we arrived, I was surprised to see that all of the fences were of the new portable type. I had come across the odd one or two but never a full course. I was not a fan of this new invention. The new course was a tight, flat galloping course. We started well and were nicely placed in the leading bunch. The pace was very quick and although he was keeping up easily with the other horses, he was having to jump much faster than he was used to. We flew the first five fences and I was starting to think that we had a new rising star. The pace of the race was more like a hurdle race and at the seventh fence his inexperience caught us out. He dived at the fence going through the brush at the guard rail. Normally hitting a fence that low would somersault the horse but these new portable fences were so soft we went straight through and barely checked our pace. We went so low through the brush my legs were ripped back out of the stirrups. I was still up with the leaders but now had no stirrups but thankfully it was a long run to the next fence and I managed to get them back before the next jump. Like a lot of talented horses Artea was very clever and he had just learned something terrible. He had learned that he did not have to bother jumping these stupidly soft fences! He just ran through the next fence; the brush came up to my knees as we went through at guard rail height. I adopted a position of laying back and trying to get my feet up as close to his ears as possible at every fence. Amazingly, he managed to stay on his feet and keep up with the leaders but every fence was a near death experience. I hoped and prayed that the others would leave us behind so I would have a reason to pull-up, but I was wedged in the middle of the tightly packed leading group. The rules of racing, because of betting are that you must ride your horse to try and achieve the best possible placing. If I had pulled up whilst in the leading pack, I could have faced a fine and lengthy ban. The nightmare continued until the bitter end. I think I came a close fifth at the finish. After going through the general routine of getting changed back into street clothes and meeting up with the rest of the team for a picnic I went into shock as I debriefed the race with John. I suddenly stopped talking went into a cold sweat and started to shake. I told everyone I felt unwell and needed to leave immediately. They put me into the back of the car while everyone quickly packed up our picnic. Someone passed me a three-litre wine box and a glass, it wasn't full but still had quite a lot left in it. During the two-hour drive home, I drank the lot, I had pumped so much adrenaline the wine seemed to have no affect at all.

A few days later I had another debriefing with John and we decided that we needed to re-school Artea over some fixed fences to get him jumping properly again.

Shortly after, one Tuesday evening I was taking my usual two classes in the indoor school. In those days I always taught mounted and it was an efficient way of giving some of my horses some light exercise while I was teaching and so killing two birds with one stone. At the end of the second class, I set up a small double jump across the diagonal. I was riding Artea and as usual set off to demonstrate how it should be ridden. Artea jumped the fences perfectly. However, on landing over the second element he put in a massive corkscrew buck - it came so quick it caught me stone cold and sent me spinning out of the saddle. That was bad enough but as I exited the saddle my left thumb got caught in the martingale neck strap. As I regained my senses, I became aware of a terrible burning pain in my shoulder area. Luckily one of my clients on the ride was a doctor at the QMC hospital in Nottingham who diagnosed that I had dislocated my shoulder in the worst possible way. The doctor was great - she called for an ambulance and arranged for me to be fast tracked into casualty. The pain was excruciating, my body was drenched in sweat and I was drifting in and out of consciousness. Thankfully, the doctor's fast track instructions worked and I was whisked straight into a cubical with no checking in and waiting to be seen by a triage nurse. Little did I know that this was just the beginning of a nightmare. In the cubicle, with its curtains closed I lay curled up shaking violently and pouring with sweat, no matter which way I positioned myself I could not relieve the terrible burning pain. I kept thinking that any moment a doctor would come and see to me. Luckily, Lou had come in the ambulance with me so she was there to keep me company. I sent her out several times to beg for some pain relief and help but she told me that there had been a major traffic accident and there were trollies everywhere with really seriously injured people on them, nurses and doctors were running everywhere. Finally, after nearly two hours the curtains were flung back and a doctor asked if I was Mr Humphrey. Lou answered for me. The doctor apologised for the long wait explaining that they had had a terribly busy night and because we had not been checked in there was no record of where we had been put and he had been searching everywhere for me. He quickly gave me an injection and the next thing I remember is waking up feeling very pleasantly woozy, no pain and my left arm was bandaged to my body. My shoulder was back in place and I could go home as soon as I was able to walk. This was my first experience of morphine, amazing stuff and thankfully I have only needed it on one other occasion but more about that later!

It took a long time to recover from this injury and I still cannot lift my left arm up above shoulder height and the pain is excruciating if I accidentally move it too high.

Artea went back to John and was sold on. I never rode him again.

I also rode briefly for another friend of John Cook's who I also knew from hunting on Tuesday's with the Quorn up on Charnwood Forest. His name was Butch Caylliss and he and his wife bred high quality show hunters on their small farm up in the forest. He had bred a lovely thoroughbred chestnut mare and I think John had talked him into running her in a point to point. The mare showed great promise and was a lovely ride. Her first race was at

Cottenham near Cambridge and she gave me a great ride. Unfortunately, she cut herself brushing through the birch. A fairly common occurrence but unfortunately, she nicked a small artery and when I pulled up blood was spurting from high up on her hind leg near her stifle. It wasn't serious and the vet soon had it under control but it looked horrific with her back leg covered in blood. Poor Butch's wife was beside herself; she loved the horses that she had bred like her children.

It was several weeks later that the mare was ready to run in her second race. The race was at Garthorpe and it was the first week in May. I will never forget that day. It started out as a chilly sunny day very much the norm for early May. Our race the Maiden Race was the last race of the day at 4.30pm. As we mounted in the parade ring the sky darkened and the temperature dropped dramatically. The horses quickened their pace around the parade ring, suddenly there was a sense of urgency in the air. As we cantered down to the start snowflakes started to fall, just tiny icy ones that stung your face. In the short time it took to reach the starting area it was snowing and the wind was cutting through our flimsy racing clothes chilling us to the bone. We circled and froze, hoping to be called in by the starter, our teeth were chattering and our hands so cold it was hard to hold the reins. Normally jockeys do not address the starter but now we were pleading with him to start the race. He answered us and explained that he was missing one horse and did not know what had happened. There were no mobile phones or Walkie-Talkies in those days. Finally, a car arrived at the start and we were told that the saddle on the missing horse had slipped causing the jockey to fall but everything was now sorted and the horse and jockey should be with us in a few minutes. We were delayed at the start for over ten minutes by which time the snow shower had turned into a blizzard. Both horses and jockeys were chilled through to the bone making muscles tight and inflexible, the last thing in the world that you wanted at the start of a three-mile chase. There was a lot of disquiet and grumbling from the jockeys, but we were mere cannon fodder in the eyes of the stewards and so no order came to abandon the race.

The starters flag went down and off we went, we couldn't see either the starter's assistant in front of the first fence because we couldn't see the first fence. We galloped into a white wall of snow, suddenly a vague grey apparition loomed up in front of us that darkened with every stride of the horse. Instead of flying over the fence the horses ran deep into the bottom of the fence and show-jumped it, their stiff cold muscles stifling their athleticism. I think every jockey swore and cursed the Organisers with unrepeatable words. We ploughed on, the snow cut into our faces like razor blades, the horses twisted their heads to try and avoid the blizzard. None of the horses were jumping well and after only the third fence a couple of jockeys pulled up. As we climbed the hill, we were doing no more than a fast canter and clambering over the fences. Every fence we jumped we were fewer. I jumped the first fence a second time and pulled up having completed just one circuit both me and my gallant little mare were shaking. Butch's poor wife was distraught and vowed there and then that she would not allow her mare to ever race again. They took their horse and John helped me sort of slide off the saddle, I staggered across to the changing room, my body shaking with a mixture of cold and shock. There was a stunned silence in the changing room, hardly a word was spoken, people were undressing and dressing in slow motion, heads down, even the winner, and the very few who finished the race just silently staggered into the room.

As I rose to leave the changing room, I suddenly realised that my friend David Christian was not there. Dave was a farmer and did everything himself, drove himself to the races in an old lorry and had the minimum help with his horse. The general consensus of opinion was that he had gone back to his lorry to look after his horse first before coming back to get changed. Thankfully, I decided to report the matter to the Clerk of the Course who immediately sent out a search party to find him. Having checked the lorry park to no avail they sent a landrover out to search the snow-covered course. They found him about fifty yards after fence No 15, lying unconscious in the snow.

We later found out that he had hit the fence hard and as so often happens the horse's head hit him in the face. Dave was a real tough character and had hung on for several strides before finally passing out. Because of the blizzard none of the jockeys or the St John's Ambulance staff at the fence saw him fall. Being the tough guy that he was he soon recovered after he had thawed out. He then drove himself and his horse home in his old lorry!

Every time I saw him after that he would slap me on the back and announce to the world in his deep gravelly voice that here was the man that saved him from freezing to death at the top of Garthorpe Hill.

Unsurprisingly Butch and his wife decided that racing was not a sport for them or their horses. Although we rarely see them these day's we remain good friends.

The race in my opinion should never been allowed to go ahead.

These days the St John's volunteers had been replaced by fully trained Paramedics at every fence.

Another bizarre incident happened when I took an outside ride for Jeremy and Annona Young. I had been and galloped their horse a couple of times in a field just outside the village of Hoby. I can't recall the name of the horse but he was a big strong horse who took a fierce hold and took a lot of pulling up. He was entered at Southwell races in a Hunterchase. Both Southwell and Nottingham racecourses are now flat racing only courses but in my time as a jockey they were both dual purpose, hosting jump racing in the winter and flat during the summer.

At Southwell all was fine until the groom let me go on the racecourse to canter down to the start. As I started towards the start, he bolted with me. I went flying past my fellow competitors, past the start and halfway around the racecourse in the wrong direction. I must have gone nearly a mile before I could stop him. I finally got him back to the start and everything was going fine, we jumped about four fences fine but at the first fence in the home straight he hit the top of the brush, it was nowhere near as hard as many other occasions with other horses. However, if one leg is a little lower than the other it can be like a judo throw and flick you over with the greatest of ease. I think it was because he was such big horse, seventeen hands plus, didn't help. To my amazement he came crashing down like a felled tree. It was a hard fall and I was at the front on the inside of the track, the worst place to have a fall. Miraculously I didn't get trampled on at all, as the runners were packed tightly together. It is incredible how much goes through your mind in a nano second. I clearly remember thinking "You stupid bastard horse you cannot be falling because of such a small error." Somehow although it was a crashing fall, when I started to get my senses back, I realised that I was not injured. I think I might have blacked out monetarily but that was all. In the racing game you never mentioned being knocked out or blacking out because if the course doctor got a whiff of it, he would ban you from racing until a doctor signed you off as fit to ride again. This was usually a week to ten days and would cost a professional jockey a fortune in lost rides. A friend of mine broke his wrist in a fall and calmly smiled at the course medical officer as he twisted his wrist this way and that claiming that he could feel no pain at all, because he was booked to ride the favourite in the next race. In the changing room most of the jockeys bodies were covered with a mixture of yellow and purple bruises from falls.

As I heaved myself up into a half sitting position, I became aware of my horse doing the same a few yards away from me. We were both badly winded and needed a few more moments to get our breath back before trying to stand. We seemed to recover at exactly the same moment and as I started to rise from the ground, so did he. If you have ever observed a horse getting up from lying down it is an ungainly affair with the front legs splaying out wide to form a sort of A frame to stabilise its body so that the more powerful back legs lift the body up. It was during this manoeuvre that one of his front legs hit me in my side. To be correct it was a hoof that struck my ribs and broke them, although I did not know this at the time.

Ribs are funny things to break. Often, they do not hurt too bad at first, but next day you are in agony. Whenever you have a fall racing it is mandatory that you be examined by the course doctor immediately on your return to the changing room. My ribs were sore but it was only like I had bumped into a door handle and I categorically denied blacking out for a moment. I smiled and did my absolute best to look happy and chipper. My acting skills paid off and I was passed fit to ride. When I picked up my kit bag that included my saddle and weight cloth full of lead, I noticed a bit of a twinge from my ribs. I was aware of this twinge on several occasions whilst I was finishing off the yard that evening.

At home Lou and I had a rota for taking the kids to school in the mornings as we both ran the bar at the stables every evening and did not get home until about 11.30 at night, it allowed one of us to get a lie-in every other day. It was my turn to take the children the day after the race. I always wake first and when I tried to get out of bed a stabbing pain took my breath away. After a couple of attempts at moving I was struggling to breathe so I woke Lou and explained my problem and told her that she would have to take the kids to school this morning. In one quick motion she rolled me out of bed and onto the floor. I screamed with pain and gasped for breath. Lou just laughed convinced that I was play acting to get out of the school run. I think it must have been a good minute before she started to take me seriously. My doctor, yes, we used to get the same doctor every time in those days, he had the same sympathetic nature as my wife, carefully running his hand over my ribs, he suddenly stabbed with his finger. I let out a scream and he casually said "Yes you have broken your ribs, we can't do anything. Just take painkillers and stop doing all these dangerous sports. Goodbye!"

My ribs plagued me for a good six weeks both at work and trying to sleep at night. Luckily, Southwell was my last race of the season so it didn't affect the racing. My ribs still plague me to this day. If I turn and reach for something low down, I get an extremely sharp pain that takes my breath away. It really frightens people as they think I am having a seizure.

Dick Benson

One Saturday afternoon a man and his wife walked into our clubroom to enquire about riding lessons. At that time of day, the bar was always terribly busy with riders who had pumped a lot of adrenalin, and locals enjoying a relaxing weekend drink. The room was full of cigarette smoke and laughter. The gentleman was small, extremely polite and well spoken. He decided to book some lessons for himself and his wife. As he concluded his business, he looked around the bar and said, "I realise that this is a club bar but is there any chance that we could have a drink while we are here." I told him that I would sign him in as my guest and that it would not be a problem. He seemed delighted and stayed for about half an hour soaking up the jovial ambiance of the little bar. The man's name was Dick Benson, little did I know at that time but he was to become a particularly good friend and give me some of the happiest moments of my riding career. Dick and his wife both started to learn to ride with us and quickly bought themselves horses. Dick's first horse was a steady cob called Garth. This allowed Dick to participate in hacks through the woods, and later to join Dad on his famous Sunday morning rides around the cross-country course, this was in the fields across the road from the stables known as Cooper's fields. Garth being a cob would try to avoid anything like hard work at all costs and came up with many ingenious ways of depositing his new owner onto the ground. His favourite one was to accelerate dramatically when approaching a jump. His novice rider would then stop riding him forward as he felt that the horse was going rather too enthusiastically into the fence. As soon as Dick stopped riding forward Garth would either stop dead or duck out at the last moment, either way Dick was ejected from the saddle and soundly deposited on the floor. Dick never got angry about this. He was a barrister and he likened his dual with Garth to duelling verbally with his barrister colleagues in court. You win some and you lose some. Dick never blamed Garth and found it amusing that a horse could outwit Dick's razor-sharp mind. Dick's motto was that there was always another day and with persistence he would finally better him.

Although he worked in law, he accepted the stupidity of many laws often made hundreds of years earlier with no relevance to modern day. One Sunday morning he staggered into the clubroom covered in mud caused by several visits to ground, courtesy of Garth, but still smiling and flushed with adrenalin. He enquired in his very formal and proper English if it would be possible to have a large brandy as he felt he had earned it that morning. He went on to say, "Being a man of the law I realise that this is totally illegal for you to sell alcohol on a Sunday before twelve noon but these are extenuating circumstances. I think that if you were to give me a brandy for medicinal purposes, that could be construed as first aid and I could argue that you have not broken the law". I laughed and agreed that he looked in need of a medicinal brandy and I poured him a large one. The following week Dick was joined by two pals, Mike Elvin a local solicitor and Terry Richardson who was a director of Boots pharmaceutical company, all in need of medical drinks after Dad's hairy cross-country ride. After this the three of them came in most Sunday mornings for their medicinal drinks and happily swopped their near-death experiences of the previous hour in the corner of the closed bar while I prepared for opening at twelve o' clock. They were doing no harm to anyone, thankfully we now have much more lenient drinking laws.

One day after Dick had been riding with us for about three years, he told me that he had made an exciting discovery and he was clearly extremely excited to be passing the news onto me. What he told me astounded me, it was something that I had never heard of despite all of my years in racing. His exciting news was that he had discovered that there was a point-to-point race exclusively for members of The Bar, in other words judges and barristers. Dick thought it would a marvellous goal to set and wondered how many more years it would take before he would be good enough to buy a racehorse and compete in the race. My first question to him was. "How old are you?", to which he replied forty-three. I felt really mean saying what I did but this was a seriously dangerous project that he was proposing. I pointed out to him that most jump jockeys had retired long before that age, so if he was serious about this, he had to start training for this goal today as time and age were already against him. Rather than being downhearted and after long pause for thought, he just said "Oh gosh I never thought about age. Well, you had better draw up a list of what we need to do and get started." I spent the next hour in a quiet corner of the bar out of earshot from everyone, trying to dissuade him from this mad adventure and what all the pit falls were and believe me, there were many.

However, I had done crazy things and I had met many true amateur people in the riding world who had started riding late in life who took incredible risks and injuries just to experience the amazing dangerous things that you can do with a horse. Two of the most famous of these were The Duke of Albuquerque who I sadly never met and Chris Collins who I met several times when competing in the Melton Hunt Club Ride. The Duke was a Spanish aristocrat who rode in the Grand National for many years until 1976. During this time, he suffered seven broken ribs, fractured vertebrae, a broken thigh, collar bone, major concussions, and on one occasion was in a coma for two days. He once competed in the National whilst wearing a plaster cast and finished eighth behind Red Rum. He even had sixteen screws removed from his broken leg so that he could ride in a race. Finally, in 1976 after he fell in a race and was badly trampled by other horses, he was so severely injured that he was in a coma for several days. When he awoke, he told the nurse who was attending him that he planned to take part in the race the next year. The racing authorities however had other ideas and took it upon themselves to revoke his license preventing him competing in the 1977 National. As if to stick two fingers up at the health and safety whimps he returned home to Spain and continued to compete in races until the age of sixty-seven. He died in 1994 aged 76.

The other hero of mine, Chris Collins, who not only rode as an amateur steeplechase jockey, competed in several Melton Hunt club rides and was also a successful three-day event rider competing at Badminton, Burghley and representing Great Britain at the World Equestrian Games. His greatest triumph however was competing in and winning the Velka Pardubice in what was then communist Czechoslovakia. Not only did he have the formidable fences of what is recognised as the hardest cross-country race in the world to contend with, but mountains of red tape for his horse and himself to be allowed into the then, staunchly communist country. I will talk more about this terrifying course later.

Dick had that same true grit and determination coupled with a humility of understanding the risks. There was nothing gung-ho about his character. If there had been, I would not have taken on the quest of teaching a forty-three-year-old novice to race ride.

We started that very day to make plans, draw up goals and a time frame. Dick was a great guy and I wanted him to know exactly what he was letting himself in for.

The biggest priority was a budget to buy a suitable racehorse and once Dick had given us that we could start putting feelers out for an experienced racehorse that jumped well and was a gentleman to handle.

Our first port of call was the sales at Newmarket which took place just a few weeks after our initial conversation. Although Dick was keen to buy as soon as possible this trip was more a recognisance trip to get a feel of the market and what we were likely to get for our money. However, we did pencil in two horses that might fill the bill.

My wife and my two brothers all love horse sales but I have always loathed them as I can't bear waiting around for the lot, I am interested in. I suppose it goes back to when Dad used to take me to the hunter sales at Leicester Repository. This was situated in the centre of Leicester city. It was the grandest horse auction house I have ever attended. The whole place was tiled and scrupulously clean, horses were trotted up on bed of gleaming yellow straw with buyers seated either side and the auctioneer at the head of the trot up. Even the indoor standings for horses had polished brass ends and the straw was neatly plaited across the end of each standing. The Repository even had its own hotel so that wealthy buyers could stay over for the multi-day sales. This shows how important fox hunting was to Leicestershire in the 1930s. Glorious as it was, as a small boy it was hellishly boring and I hated going although it was the highlight of my Dad's year.

At the sales we traipsed around endless stables looking for the two horses that we thought might suit. The one that had the best form was soon dismissed by Dick. As we went into the box to have a better look at the horse it ran at us with its ears flat back and teeth bared, we all nearly fell over each other as we scrambled back through the half open door and slammed it shut. As we dusted ourselves down Dick declared "We can cross that one off the list, I don't care how bloody good it is. If I cannot go into the box to pat him, give him some treats, and have a nice chat, I'm not interested."

The other horse was sold for several thousand over our budget. Everyone thought it was a great day out, that is except me!

Although Dick rode a couple of times every week his work was very sedentary, as it required a lot of reading to prepare for cases, and then a lot of sitting around in court not to mention some good lunches. His weight however was not a problem, as he was not tall and light framed, in fact you could say he was built to be a jockey. My main concern was a dodgy knee that he had; it was the legacy of playing cricket in his younger days. In race riding your knees are vital and they have to take immense stress during a race and in training. I discussed this with him and we decided to graduate the fitness training and see how it stood up. Although it was a little sore to start with but as the leg muscles strengthened it improved greatly. Dick's cob Garth was entirely unsuitable for getting fit to race ride but luckily Dick's wife Sue had a little thoroughbred that was ideal to make a start on while the search for a suitable racehorse continued. I explained to Dick that he needed a strict training regime and it had to be on done on a daily basis that would get longer and harder as his fitness improved. I had less than a year to find him a horse, qualify it, and get Dick fit to ride in his race.

The race in question was the Pegasus Saddle Club Members Race. The club was open to any member of an Inn of Court. The race was run at Little Horwood near Milton Keynes and has been run nearly every year since 1895 except for the two world wars. The race has now moved to the VWH point to point meeting at Siddington near Cirencester due to the closure of the Little Horwood Track.

I have always done my training of both me and my horse first thing in the morning as I found, that if I tried to do it later, the events of the day got in the way and the training was either missed or done in a stressed, tense, and tired way, which was not good for the horse or rider.
Dick's work suited this timetable perfectly as he didn't have to be at court until mid-morning. He would arrive at the stables just before 7am, catch his wife's horse and ride-out, performing the exercises that I had set out for him. We started in early June and during the summer he trained most of the time on his own with me giving him a lesson about once a week. I tended not to ride during the summer except for Jousting as it was a busy time hay making, straw carting and of course much touring with the jousting show. I would start getting myself and my horses fit towards the end of August ready for the Autumn Teamchase season and the hunting season which also meant qualifying the pointers.

We finally located a horse for Dick through a horse dealer in north Nottinghamshire called Jack Todd. He was a real old-fashioned dealer who knew a lot about horses. I had already bought a particularly good horse off him a year or so before, so when he rang me, we went straight up to view his horse. He was by a well-known stallion called Cantab. Mr Todd's daughter had been hunting the horse and had also ridden him in eight point to points. His jumping record was superb and had never fallen in his career. His racing form however was very mediocre to say the least hence his sale at a reasonable price. Mr Todd also told us that he was a genuinely nice friendly horse. My foremost concern was for Dick's safety so in my mind his safe jumping far outweighed his form. By the time we went to view him Dick had researched the horse's whole life history through endless form books (no internet in those days).
Dad, Lou, and I went to look at him and for once we all agreed that this was the horse for Dick. We brought him there and then. Mr Todd's daughter informed us that his stable name was Oggie. It seemed to be a strange name and when we asked her about it, she explained that the name came from the Coronation Street character Stan Ogden who was one of his daughter's favourite characters in the TV series. It was an easy name that rolled off the tongue so we decided to keep it. Personally, I always like to keep a previous stable name as I feel it provides a little continuity for the horse when moving yards and ownership.

Oggie had been turned out to pasture since the end of the racing season and had lost all of his muscle, so when we brought him home, he looked a bit of a scruffy thing. I think most of the people at the stables wondered what on earth we had seen in this horse and I think this included Dick, but he was much too polite to say anything. Although Dad and I did not see eye to eye on many things, he had a great gift of being able to see the potential in a horse that was unkempt, covered in mud and looking very scrawny. This what had made him money and provided his customers with good value horses.

Within a few days the caked mud was brushed out of his coat and his mane and tail carefully pulled, (none of this abhorrent cutting of manes and tails that seems to be the in fashion or perhaps I should say bloody lazy, lacking in knowledge way of the day). Anyway, little rant out of the way and feeling much better, just like Oggie did after his pampering. Another thing that Dad and I agreed on was that having a supple horse was imperative no matter what sport you were going to use your horse for. Oggie was as stiff as a board especially on his left rein so as part of his gently getting back to fitness routine Lou started to do some dressage work with him to get him more supple. Oggie turned out to be a lovely ride and I think Lou along with our head girl Jackie were the first to fall under Oggie's spell. Dick however was a little confused that his racehorse had started doing dressage instead of hurtling up some gallops but being a man of high intellect bowed to our superior knowledge in horse matters. In fact, he was not allowed to sit on his new purchase until Lou deemed it safe to do so.

Through the summer and into Autumn we gradually got the would-be jockey and his mount fitter and fitter. It was a slow process, especially with the jockey who had a liking of cigars, red wine and the odd malt whiskey or cognac. By the time of the opening meet of the Quorn Hunt at the beginning of November, Oggie was fit and ready to go hunting and get his qualification to race in point to points.

The plan was the same as it had been with all my other horses which was to get him qualified by the first of January. This sounds an easy thing to do but it is only eight weeks and you could easily lose several days to snow or frost as November and December were much colder months before global warming started to kick in. Add this to the good chance that the horse might also pick up an injury whilst out hunting it was not an easy target to achieve.

Many point to pointers would try to avoid actually hunting and just follow the hunt along roads for fear of injuring their mount. Some hunt master's frowned on this practice and it was not uncommon for these riders to get a humiliating, loud bollocking in front of the whole field and a threat to not sign their qualification certificate.
Personally, I loved my hunting and believed that if a horse's legs could not stand up to half a day's hunting it should not be on a racecourse. I also believe that hunting teaches a horse to be clever - natural fences are much more difficult than race fences. I genuinely believe that the low number of falls during my racing career was largely down to having hunted properly.
When I started racing, I used to qualify with the South Notts on a Monday which was very tame and had field numbers of about thirty and there was very little jumping if any. When I changed to the Quorn as our finances improved, the field numbers were regularly one hundred and thirty and sometimes even more. It was a mêlée trying to find enough space to jump and both horse and rider had to cope with both aggressive and bad riding. It was no place for gentlemanly conduct.

With the Quorn the number of fences and the height of those fences dramatically increased. With the South Notts on the Monday's you were lucky if you jumped a couple of fences, whereas with the Quorn it was usually around about fifty before change of horses meaning the horse and rider were so much fitter at the end of qualification and you could easily get your horse fit enough to race for the opening of the pointing season which in those days was February the first.

At this point I would like to point out that the South Notts have some great country for their Thursday meets, especially up in high Derbyshire where I have had some of my most enjoyable days hunting ever, but more about that later.

Our plan was to have both horse and jockey fit by the beginning of February ready for the start of the season. This was earlier than usual as I usually started around the beginning of March when the ground was not so wet and there was less chance of meetings being cancelled. Dick's big race was on April the fourth so we did not have much time to get both of them into prime form for the big day. I rode Oggie in his first race a bit like a test pilot to see how he went and if he had any quirks. The race was at the Brocklesby Point to Point held at Brocklesby Park near Grimsby. It was a long way to go and not on my usual list of tracks to compete at. However, it was on well drained land and on old turf so tended to be good going whatever the weather. The course was a flat fast galloping track not suited to Oggie according to past form books but an ideal uncomplicated course to test him out on and give us both a good pipe opener.

The race was run at a cracking pace. Oggie jumped superbly, I cannot recall making any mistakes at all during the race. We were up with the leaders right up to the penultimate fence when his lack of pace showed. We finished a close seventh and I was delighted with the outcome. I knew we had bought the ideal horse for Dick. I did however have one scary moment coming around the final bend. I write about this as a warning to anyone riding with short stirrups. I normally tied a knot in the end of my reins as did all jockeys. I was told that it was a safety precaution which I assumed was to stop the reins becoming unbuckled. For some reason I forgot to put a knot in my reins that day, whether it was because I had been out late the night before at a dinner or just forgetfulness at the start of the season I do not know. There was a lot of pushing and shoving around this last bend and as I went to elbow the rider on my outside who was leaning on me, my arm suddenly stopped as if it were snagged on something. After a couple of more unsuccessful attempts to elbow my opponent's ribs I traced the problem to my foot. Looking down I saw that the loop of rein from my hands to the buckle end had hooked over my foot and worst still hooked behind my stirrup. The last thing you wanted in the middle of an "argee-bargee" at full gallop is to be looking down at your foot. Despite several attempts of fiddling with the reins it remained firmly stuck. This was serious because I could not give the horse any extra rein over the jump. This meant that as the horse stretched his neck it would lift my leg up and flick me off the horse or worst still bring the horse down. I realised I would have to take my foot out of the stirrup to free the rein. Now this is the last thing a jockey wants to do as it is devilish hard to get your foot back in as the light alloy stirrup bounces about all over the place. The Gods were with me that day, it was a long run to the next fence I whipped my foot out freed the rein and somehow managed to get my foot back in the stirrup first try. I never ever forgot to tie a knot in my reins ever again whenever I rode with short stirrups. The race also yielded one of my favourite photographs of me jumping a fence at speed. A most enjoyable start to the season.

The following week having race tested our new purchase, it was time to race test the jockey. I knew from my own experience, that no matter how hard you train nothing can prepare you for the real thing. I had trained Dick mercilessly and his usual polite manners disintegrated into him questioning my parentage and calling me names that are best not put onto paper. It was during one of these tirades at the start of the gallops at the local racing stables just down the hill from us that I was so distracted by his complaints, that my horse reared up and broke my nose. Both horses knew what they were doing and just wanted to get on with it, a moment's hesitation while Dick sorted out his reins out was all it took for my horse to rear, plunge, and then throw its head back into my face and break my nose. As we thundered up the track the wind spread blood all over my face in long streaks. When we pulled up and Dick saw my face he went as white as a sheet. I think this was a defining moment in his training as he realised the consequences of a split second of hesitation. The other consequence was that his blasphemy towards me changed to abject apologies which continued all the long ride home. I still cannot decide which was worse.

Dick's first race was similar to mine, total shock. He finished over a fence behind the rest of the field but sadly didn't have my luck of all but one falling in his race. He was in total shock when he dismounted. After he had dismounted, he just stood in absolute silence, which was an exceedingly rare thing for him, hands on his hips, just staring at all around him. It was as if he had just fallen out of the sky and landed in a strange place. I had been like that many times during my riding career so after the initial slaps on the backs and congratulations, I ordered everyone back to the cars to celebrate so that Dick could contemplate what he had just done. I kept an eye on him from a discrete distance and after about fifteen minutes collected him up and took him back to the cars to celebrate. I on the other hand had to go and get changed as I had a ride in the maiden race. By the time I had ridden in the last race of the day the party was over and everyone was packing up to go home but Dick, being Dick, had squirrelled away some sandwiches and a bottle of champagne which we quietly drank together while discussing our respective races. One of the sandwiches that had been saved was cold, black pudding and mustard and I commented on how nice it was. In fact, any food was nice at four thirty in the afternoon when you hadn't eaten since the previous evening.

The following week it was Garthorpe and I was back in the saddle to give Oggie a good run out and up his fitness. Dick and I both agreed that Garthorpe was a difficult track and the risk of him taking a fall before his big day was not worth it. We had entered the adjacent hunts race and there were seventeen runners. The race was a really hot one from start to finish. Oggie was very keen and took a strong hold, in fact we were in the lead for the first three fences although his jumping was not so fluid in the early stages of the race. I think he was a little confused about the differing riding styles of his two jockeys. We finished seventh in what turned out to be the fastest race of the day, pleasing all connections.

It was now just two weeks before the big race and Dick had his final prep-race at Carholme, Lincoln. The racecourse was formerly a national flat racecourse and home to the famous Lincoln Handicap, a one-mile race run in a straight line. Consequently, the point-to-point track had a long straight finish. The plusses for this track was it was on flat meadows below the escarpment on which Lincoln is built, and as you looked up from the course, the castle and cathedral towered imposingly above you. The other great thing about this track was

that the old brick changing rooms were still in good order so you had the luxury of getting changed in the warm and dry instead of a tent.
I missed this race due to other commitments and was gutted when I heard Dick had finished fourth and had the privilege of being led into the winners enclosure and having to weigh-in, even though he had been some way behind the winner. But as I said earlier the name of the game is jumping and if you cannot get over those fences you are not a contender. I was so pleased with that result and I felt that all our training was on course and that we were peaking at the right time. Oggie was one paced but his jumping was flawless and Dick, although he lacked style had worked like an Olympic athlete to get racing fit. I felt that barring a complete disaster they would complete the Pegasus race and fulfil his dream.

Victory

It was April the fourth and the day of Dick's big race. The race was held at Little Horwood which is situated to the west of Milton Keynes and not far from the town of Buckingham. It was bucketing it down with rain and we phoned the race secretary to see if the meeting was still on but there was no answer, so we set off in trepidation and praying that it had not been cancelled. It was a long slow trip down to the course with heavy rain and swirling wet mist that reduced visibility to less than fifty yards.
When we finally found the venue, it was down a narrow country lane and there was a long queue to be towed onto the field by a tractor. Having been towed to a parking place we trudged through soggy grass and mud to the secretary's tent. That tent and the changing tent were both sodden and limp. The white canvas looking more like a grubby grey. The site was devoid of people unless they actually had to be out in this atrocious weather for some important reason. The course was on the side of a steep hill, two thirds of the course was on the side of the hill and the final third that included the finish was on the flat meadow at the base of the hill. The flat meadow was also home for the administration tents, parade ring, winners enclosure and car parks.

After the usual formalities of stowing racing kit in the changing room and making a formal declaration to run in the race, we set off to walk the course. The course was a really old fashioned one with no running rails except at the finish. A couple of round bales with red flags tied to them marked turning points and apart from them it was all open county between the fences. It was a right-handed track hence the red flag. If it had been a left-handed track the flags would have been white. It is amazing how many people do not know the equestrian rule that you pass a red flag to the right of you and a white flag to the left of you.
As we trudged up the steep hill through the sodden turf I wondered if Dick would have any energy left to ride his race. When we had completed our walk, we stood near the finish line and I reminded him not to be on the inside when approaching the marker bales as it would be easy for his opponents to push him into them and tip him up or have to go to the inside of it and get himself disqualified. Although Dick had ridden in two previous races he had always been at the back and had not posed a serious challenge to the race contenders.

Consequently, he had never experienced any of the underhand tactics that he might face in this race.

Dick was aghast that he might be exposed to such underhand tactics from members of the Bar. When I pointed out, that was what I thought Barristers did to each other every day in court in order to win a case, he laughed and said" Golly, never thought of it that way" and burst out laughing. His laughter eased some of the tension that was obviously building inside of him. I suggested that I run through how I would ride the race fence by fence to which he readily agreed. It was a fairly straightforward course and my main concern was the heavy going, it was something that Dick had never experienced. I told him to stay in touch with the others if he could but not to push hard up the steep hill and to try and make up ground on the downhill and flat sections. I also warned him that about three quarters of the way around, fatigue could hit you. My exact words were, "Along the top, just before you turn to go down the hill that is about where you start to feel it." Dick's reply came almost immediately "Oh my gosh! How on earth do you find the time to do such a thing during a race. I must say Mr Humphrey I am amazed at your ability to multitask during a race". I had forgotten the barrister's razor-sharp attention to what is said and to twist it. I stammered as I realised how easily you could be misconstrued. We both burst out laughing and another bit of tension was released.

Dick was a bundle of nerves and was getting worse as the time got closer to go and get changed. It was at this point that I issued the command that Dick never let me forget. We were at the horsebox and I turned to Lou and said, "Right Lou would you walk the horse around to relax him and I will walk the Jockey around".

The race which was the fourth of the day was run at a steady pace, as the going by this time was what riders describe as bottomless. Dick settled in third place but as they went up the hill, he lost ground and seemed to be taking my advice of not pushing on up the hill a little too seriously. Oggie's jumping was superb despite the atrocious ground conditions. Three fences from home it was the open ditch, the leading horses were struggling and jumped it very messily but still had a commanding lead of about fifty lengths and Dick hope of being placed was looking very doubtful. Over the previous two fences I had been willing Dick to push on and try to close the distance between him and the leading bunch. Oggie sailed over the open ditch and then it seemed that Dick was shaken out of a dream and he started to kick on. The enthusiastic riders in front had burned their horses out racing against each other. It was as if a pause button had been pressed on all the runners except Oggie who now flew down the hill eating up their lead. He jumped the last fence well and won by twenty length's an astonishing achievement. Dick had the ride of his life and dined out on it until the day he died. Sadly, only a handful of people were there to cheer him over the line as most had opted to view the race from the dry comfort of their car.

Dick was presented with a large and old solid silver perpetual challenge cup. The presentation was watched by team Bunny Hill, the race officials and a couple of brave spectators as the heavens still continued to pour water on us. It was such an achievement and should have been accompanied by rousing cheers.

We quickly shared a bottle of champagne in the back of the horsebox with Oggie looking on and then headed home wet, soggy but incredibly happy.

Next day was celebration day at the stables the weather was much better. Dick was the hero of the hour and his achievement inspired several other customers to take up competing and fulfil their own dreams. It was a long and lively Sunday lunchtime in the bar. A great way to really celebrate Dick's great achievement.

The Road to Cheltenham

Oggie was already entered for Lincoln the following Saturday and after his success at Little Horwood Dick opted to ride again. It was a race with some scary moments. Dick was now much fitter and had gained confidence from his win. He started very positively and was right up with the leaders but unfortunately mixing it with the big boys has its risked and I think Dick probably got half-lengthed at the third fence, Oggie hit the fence hard sending Dick up his neck. Dick clearly remembered having his chin between Oggie's ears buy somehow Dick managed to recover and continue the race. A few fences later a horse just in front of him ran out at the fence and crashed straight through the rails. The going was heavy again and consequently there were many fallers and much carnage. Dick finished a very credible third. Although he was absolutely delighted with the result, he wore an expression that he was very thankful to have finished in one piece.

Things may have seemed to be going really well but there was a worrying problem that had arisen during my races on Oggie and that when I put him under extreme pressure, he was making a noise in his breathing. We had had him examined by the vet who diagnosed that one side of his larynx was paralysed and would need a Hobday operation. It was a fairly common operation but required quite a long recuperation afterwards. The vet said it was not urgent although, it was obviously affecting his performance. He suggested that we have it done as soon as the racing season finished as it was only slightly affecting his performance and did not present a risk to Oggie's health.

We had three more races already planned and the ground had suddenly changed from bottomless to rock hard which did not suit us at all. After a counsel of war, we decided that his last race of the season would be at Cheltenham where he was already entered in the three-mile two-furlong Hunterchase. It had always been my dream to ride at Cheltenham but I never believed that it would happen. Dick had always followed National Hunt Racing even before he took up point to pointing and had a pipe dream of having a runner at what is considered to be the home of jump racing and the premiere course in the world. Come hell or high-water Dick and I were not going to miss out on this once of a lifetime chance.

The next race was the Woodland Pytchley Adjacent Hunts Race at Dingley and I was back in the saddle. It was another extremely fast race recording the second fastest time of the day only bettered by the ladies race who I think in those days carried a stone or maybe a stone and a half less weight. Whenever I took over from Dick, it always took Oggie a bit of time to adjust to my more aggressive style of riding. Next to Garthorpe, Dingley was my favourite course to ride and the only point to point course that I ever rode that included a water jump. We finished seventh but he gave me a great ride and I loved every minute of it.

Two days later Dick rode Oggie at the South Notts. Hunt point to point on Easter Monday. Dick was in the men's open race. You may wonder why Dick always rode in the open race which is always the top race of the day. The reason is that it tends to attract top horses and jockeys. Because of this the races tend to be more tactical and run at a slower pace until near the end of the race when they dramatically speed up. This meant that there was a lot less rough and tumble, and usually a lot less runners, making them a safer place to learn your trade, as long as you stayed at the back and kept out of the way of the big boys. Because they were so hotly contested a lot of horses fell at the last few fences or pulled up if they thought they could not win to save their horse for another day. If you jumped clear there was always a chance you could pick up a minor placing. This is what happened to Dick at Lincoln and now at Thorpe again coming third. However, I should point out that both Dick and Oggie had both improved a lot. To put it in perspective in his first race at Thorpe he was two fences behind the winner and now in a much faster race was only twenty lengths behind the winner and he beat a horse that had convincingly beaten him in his first race. I was a proud trainer. Three days later we were racing at Cheltenham!

Tuesday morning, I nervously felt Oggie's legs for heat. Two days racing in three days on rattling hard ground is always a worry. Thankfully, his legs were stone cold and it was all systems go for the granddaddy of them all, Cheltenham. Both Dick and I were extremely excited and nervous as were the rest of the team. There was truly little to do to Oggie, except walk him out on Tuesday, then gentle exercise on Wednesday.

The big day arrived; it was an early start as we wanted to make the most of our day at Cheltenham. Our race was at 2.35 and it was about a three-and-a-half-hour drive down to the racecourse, I had added extra time for unexpected delays as we would be starting our trip during the rush hour. Things were a bit slow around Birmingham but were making good time as we trundled down the M5 in our Bedford TK.

We had decided to travel down in convoy and I was constantly checking my wing mirror to check that Dick was still with me in the car. Yes, I was driving the lorry myself to ride in a race at Cheltenham. We were approaching Tewksbury when there was an almighty loud bang that shook the lorry and frightened my passengers to death. I braked as hard as I dared without upsetting Oggie and pulled over onto the hard shoulder. It took a few moments before there was a gap in the traffic that made it safe enough to get out of the cab. By the time I got to the rear of the lorry Dick was already pacing back and forwards at double time looking very agitated. He greeted my with "Why the bloody hell have you stopped on the side of a busy motorway like this?" "Blowout" I replied. Dick became even more agitated and stammered "What, what do you mean by blowout! Blowout what?" "One of the back tyres has exploded, it's called a blowout. I need to get underneath the back axle and find out which one has gone. It has to be one of the inside tyres as the outside tyres look fine" I replied. This was all routine for me as we regularly had blowouts on the horsebox. A couple of years before, we had built a new horsebox body with the help of my good friend Alan Lane. We were immensely proud of our new horsebox which had been built to carry the jousting horses. Soon after we put the new lorry body on the old lorry, we noticed that we seemed to be getting more blowouts. We put it down to the extra number of miles we were doing as it was boom-time for our jousting business. We used to buy second-hand wheels with tyres already on them as spare wheels and we just thought that may have been another contributory factor. The following year the lorry was weighed as we went onto a ferry for Belgium. It's total weight was eleven and a half tonnes. That was four tonnes over its maximum permitted weight. We had built an incredibly good strong new body but it was way too heavy for the chassis. On returning home we bought a lorry capable of carrying the heavy body we had built and after that the blowouts stopped.

Luckily when I wriggled under the back of the lorry, I discovered that it was the near side inside rear tyre. This made changing the tyre much safer as I would not be working on the traffic side which is quite terrifying. It was obviously out of the question to unload Oggie on the motorway so I risked jacking up the lorry with him still on board. Luckily, he was a placid traveller and didn't move around much, in fact it was big lorries passing us at speed that rocked the lorry more than the horse inside. Jacking up the lorry was a very unpleasant experience as I was lying underneath the lorry that was balancing on the four-inch square base of a jack that was being constantly buffeted by passing big articulated lorries. I set out all the tools and spare wheel ready for a super-fast change and explained to everyone what I was going to do and the help that I was going to need to make this happen super quick. Every second that the lorry balanced and wobbled on that jack was a disaster waiting to happen. When I pulled the two back tyres off the hub it was like a formula-one tyre change, the spare wheel was ready and waiting. Wiggling it onto the hub studs was scary but it went on without too much trouble although the body did rock, then the second wheel went on. Eager helpers passed me the wheel nuts and wheel wrench, I popped two nuts on opposite sides of the hub and quickly tightened them. Once I had two tight wheel nuts, I knew we were safe and that I could fit the other nuts at a more relaxed pace. I lowered the jack and wriggled it out from under the axle while horse pee dripped all over me. Dear Oggie had decided the break in travel was a good time to relieve himself. I had to retighten all the wheel nuts using a bar and scaffolding pipe until each nut made a cracking noise. It took just under thirty minutes to complete the wheel change. Dick was ecstatic and could not believe what we had just done. So, we set off again to the premier racecourse in country covered in oil, grime and smelling very strongly of horse pee. Oh, the glamorous life of a jump jockey!

Luckily, I had brought a change of clothes with me so I was able to wash and change before presenting myself to the clerk of the course and then proceed into the changing room.
The whole of Cheltenham racecourse had recently undergone a multi-million-pound redevelopment which included a new stand, parade ring/winners enclosure and new jockey facilities such as weighing in room, changing room and medical facilities. Compared with the other changing rooms these were ultra-modern, very bright with just about everything a jockey could desire including sweat boxes to shed off those naughty extra pounds that always plagued a jockey. The valets were still the same super-efficient bunch but now had a much larger working area and super-efficient washing and drying facilities. Best of all it was really warm and comfortable. I was given a changing area next to a professional jockey who kindly chatted to me and gave me some tips on riding the course. The one thing I still remember him saying was watch out for the open ditch at the top of the hill it can easily catch you out.

Having checked in myself, all my kit deposited with my valet, I went to meet-up with Dick and Lou who had sorted out the declaration to run and all the other paperwork. We then set off to walk the course. To say that I had butterflies would be an understatement, I just couldn't wait to step out onto this hallowed turf. It was like an amateur cricketer or footballer stepping out onto the field at Lords or Wembley. What had always attracted me to Cheltenham was seeing those solid black fences so beautifully prepared, the top of the fences looked like you could put a spirit level on top of every one of them and they would all be perfectly level. There are two steeplechase courses at Cheltenham, the old course, and the new course. That day we were riding the new course. As I walked up to the first fence it didn't disappoint me, big, thick, tightly packed birch manicured to perfection, it was a work of art to my eyes. The going was good to firm so I did not need to examine the ground in any great detail as it was not going to suit Oggie. Walking a steeplechase course isn't technical like walking an event course, most of the fences are the same but the lay of the land can throw a spanner in the works if you haven't given it worthy consideration. For me, the climb up the hill was much longer and steeper than it looked on television, as was the downhill section. Along the top section after the water jump the ground runs gently downhill before rising quite sharply before the open ditch. Again, this looks a lot less pronounced on television and I could now understand the warning from the jockey who sat next to me in changing room. Except for the fairly sharp bend at the bottom and the water jump everything was pretty straightforward, thankfully I was riding an excellent jumper.

I returned to the changing room and changed into my riding clothes and weighed out. The weighing room even had flowers in it, something I had never seen before. After weighing out I returned to my allocated peg and sat staring at the floor contemplating anything and everything. My trance was broken by the bowler hat official shouting "Right! Jockeys out". We all immediately rose to our feet and marched out into the parade ring to meet our connections. It was a lovely sunny day and it felt good to be alive.
As usual all strength in my body ebbed away as I cantered down to the start but returned as the familiar routine of checking girths, names and numbers prior to the start was carried out.
Finally, the starter climbed his rostrum and raised his yellow flag. Wave after wave of adrenaline rushed into my veins, the starter's flag dropped and he called out "Alright jockeys off you go". The tight bunch of horses rumbled forward towards the first fence picking up speed as they went. A calm descended on me, this was it, the highlight of my racing career.

The race itself was run at a steady pace for the first circuit and jumping the water was a real thrill. We were still all closely bunched as we approached the open ditch for the second time. The pace had quickened substantially on the downhill approach but then changed as the ground rose again. As my new jockey friend had warned me in the changing room, we met the big open ditch on a flat stride and we went through the top of the fence. We didn't fall thankfully but it knocked the stuffing out of both of us for a couple of strides and cost us a couple of lengths. The race was now firmly on and we flew down the hill and I was thankful that I had ridden down the Garthorpe hill so many times otherwise it would have been a terrifying experience. It was an amazing thrill, foot flat to the floor, going as fast as your horse could go, knowing the slightest mistake would mean a terrible wipe-out. The only other time I get this feeling is skiing when you schuss down a long steep section of a mountain and you know you are out of control but are going too fast to do anything about it and just have to hold your nerve and hopefully ride it out to the end.
Our mistake at the open ditch had woken us both up and we flew the tricky downhill fence in great style as we made our way towards the home straight. Two fences from home the leading two horses found another gear and pulled away, I was now lying fourth, Gee Armytage riding Celtic Beauty was about five lengths in front of me and I became hopeful of catching her and nicking third place but the long uphill run up to the finish emptied Oggie's final bit of stamina and gradually Celtic Beauty started to gain ground and I realised it was fourth for us. I glanced over my shoulder to check on my nearest rival but he was a safe distance behind us and looking very tired so I eased up and cantered the last few strides over the line.

Riding into the winners enclosure led in by Jackie Clarke was like a fantasy dream coming true. The winners enclosure is next to the parade ring which at Cheltenham is like an amphitheatre, always beautifully bedecked with baskets of flowers. To see the beaming smiles on the faces of the small team that had made the long journey down to support us made me even happier.

Events in racing move on at a rapid pace and as soon as the weighing-in was completed the tannoy announced "Horses away" which was the cue to take the horses back to the stables and for connections to vacate the parade ring before the horses and owners for the next race came in. I think the term moment of glory is very apt.

As with Dick's big race the celebrations were short lived, black pudding sandwiches and couple of bottles of champagne shared between the group. Nevertheless, a glorious end to the 1987 season.

Shortly afterwards Oggie had his Hobday operation and was confined to his box for six weeks. Hopes now moved forward to the next season.

Although the operation was a success Oggie was dogged by minor leg problems and unfortunately Dick was unable to defend his Pegasus trophy due to Oggie's lameness. We did however run him in several Hunter chases and although he was never in contention to win, his immaculate jumping saw him placed virtually every time out. The prize money was much higher than in point to points and Oggie certainly earned his keep that year.

A Little Foreign Adventure

I am trying to write this book in sections to give it some sort of clarity and structure. However, certainly from my mid-twenties until my sixties I was taking part in several disciplines simultaneously and certain events have a foot in more than one camp. I feel that this story belongs in the racing section because it involves both Dick Benson and Oggie

The story is about the Velka Pardubická race in the Czech Republic which was held in Czechoslovakia at the time I write about. My interest in this race began by chance. I was watching the news one day in 1973 when a short report came up in the sports section about a guy called Chris Collins taking his horse over to the communist state of Czechoslovakia to compete in the world's toughest steeplechase. People compared the race with the Grand National but was described as being much tougher and far more dangerous. It was said that it was usually won by a jockey that had only had to remount twice during the race. I was intrigued! I started to research what I could about the race but I could find nothing.

Some years later I met Chris Collins while hacking down to the start of the Melton Hunt Club Ride and he briefly mentioned the Pardubická during a long chat about nerves which was our problem in common that day as we rode the two miles down to the start, where we would be doing battle with over one hundred other riders in one of the toughest cross-country races in the equestrian world.

It was not until many years later when some of my teamchase mates decided to have a crack at the race that my interest was re-awoken. By this time, we had computers and basic internet so it was much easier to find more information about the race.

However, I was not in a position financially to take a horse halfway across Europe and so even though I now knew a lot about this terrifying race it remained a pipe dream. It was not until after Dick's first season with Oggie did I start to think that Oggie might be the one that could cope with the fences. Dick was enthusiastic about everything after his fairy tale first season. Also because of the British Teamchase contingents regular visits, the race was now getting a lot more television coverage. Channel four featured the whole race on the channel four racing programme. I wrote to them explaining that I was interested in competing and asked if I could have a copy of the race video. They very kindly sent me a copy and asked me to let them know if I decided to enter the race. The video raised more questions than answers, so I started to look into the possibility of going to watch the race live and hopefully meet up with the organisers to find out about how to enter, stabling, qualifications etc.

Unfortunately, Dick and I decided not to risk Oggie. I had a conversation with Gerald Morgan one of the teamchase riders who went to ride in the race and he had sadly lost his horse in the race. His horse had broken its back jumping one of the canals. Gerald was a farrier and very down to earth, he warned me not to take a horse that you are close to as the risks were too great. As soon as I heard these words, I decided I could not take Oggie, he meant so much to Dick, Jackie his groom and me and my family.

However, I still hankered to ride in the race.

It just so happened that our twenty fifth wedding anniversary was close to the date of the race so Lou and I decided to make a long weekend trip as a way of celebration.
Research told me that the city of Pardubice was only 60 miles from Prague. Prague was just starting to open up for tourists and there were now regular flights there from Heathrow. As the planning progressed Lou's best friend Vanda and her partner Ian showed an interest in joining us. We then mentioned it to our new friends in Ireland Jim and Patricia Brennan who were keen racing enthusiasts. They immediately said that they wanted to go as well.

The race is always run on the second Sunday in October, so we decided to stay in Prague for a few days before the race and do some sightseeing, along with the obligatory eating and drinking before spending a couple of days in Pardubice. Our reunion in Windsor the day prior to catching an early morning flight from Heathrow got very out of hand and we all boarded the flight with mega hangovers.
Prague was an unbelievably beautiful city and so cheap. We had a great time and lived like kings for just a few pounds. The day before the race we hired a minibus, Lou and Vanda took on the responsibility of driving. We left Prague about 11am expecting to be at our hotel just after midday, after all it was only 60 miles away. It took us over an hour to find our way out of Prague and then, when we finally got onto the correct road to Pardubice it was single carriageway and made of cobble stones. The cobblestones caused a loud drumming noise that vibrated through the old minibus. To make matters worse sections of the rode had sunk causing the old minibus to rock and roll. It was like being on a fairground ride that threw you around while the seat vibrated shaking every bone in your body. Forty miles per hour was about the maximum speed that we could tolerate and even at that speed we had to make

several stops to give our bodies a rest. The planned one-hour journey ended up being near three hours.

How to describe the city was a conundrum. As we approached the city it appeared to be an industrial city but then as we got closer, we could see a medieval castle high on a hill that dominated the city. But this was no Prague, as we neared the centre the architecture was all a cheap 1960s concrete jungle.

Our trip back to the pop art sixties continued when we checked in to our hotel. The curtains in our bedroom were brown with large yellow and cream circles. On our bedside table was a large telephone and a huge radio with a big dial on the front for tuning into different stations. It was like going back to my childhood. Unlike Prague very little English was spoken and we had to revert to sign language to try and be understood. Walking down into the town there was a distinct smell of burning oil caused by hundreds of little two- stroke Trabant cars pouring out white oil smoke from their noisy little engines.

We found a busy café serving wholesome food. The menu was only written in Czech and no helpful pictures. Luckily, it took some time for the waitress to return to take our orders and we were able to observe what others were eating on tables close by and ordered by pointing at the various plates of food that were being eaten in our vicinity. Thankfully, the common understanding of the word beer made ordering our drinks much simpler. This was definitely not a tourist destination. When the bill arrived, we opened it with trepidation as we had eaten and drunk very well. We were more than pleasantly surprised. Prague was much cheaper than the UK but in Pardubice prices were about half of those in Prague. We were not going to live like kings for the next couple of days but like emperor's.

As we were leaving the restaurant a couple stood up and introduced themselves. They were also from the UK and had heard us speaking English and like us were over to see the race. We learned from this conversation that there was quite a group of English race goers over to watch or take part in in the race and that most were staying in our hotel. Most importantly they told us about a particularly good restaurant where all the English contingent dined every evening, apparently great food, and wine, all cheap as chips.

The recommended restaurant took some finding but when we finally got there it was just as our informant described. The restaurant was already buzzing with noisy groups of Irish and British racegoers making good use of the good value wine and beer. All equestrian sports carry risks and steeplechasing is right at the top of that list, with great highs and unimaginable lows. To cope with this everyone knows how to party, whether it is celebrating victory or drowning their sorrows. Jim Brennan was the keen racegoer of our group and was soon picking out well known people from the racing world sitting at various tables and announced with a smile "I think we are in for SOME! weekend" which meant that there was going to be some serious drinking and partying. Chance encounters revealed that there were three British runners in the main race and two more in other races at the meeting. The three jockeys riding them were all highly ranked in the UK. Richard Dunwoody, Ruby Walsh, and Paul Carberry. The trainers of their mounts were also blue bloods of the steeplechasing world at the time being, Mark Pitman son the famous female trainer Jenny Pitman, Ferdy Murphy and Enda Bolger whose wife Sarah had travelled over with the horses, Charlie Mann also travelled with the horsebox group. Charlie who had been a jockey was the last English jockey to win the race back in 1995 riding the Irish Horse "It's a Snip" and was the first English jockey to win the race since Chris Collins in 1973. In true steeplechasing tradition, Charlie had been banned from riding in races by the Jockey Club after breaking his neck in a race at Warwick, he however managed to convince the Czech authorities that he had a current license to ride. He was later fined £1,000 by the Jockey Club, as a thank you for being only the second English jockey in that century to win the race. God save the good old Jockey Club!

After a fine meal we restricted ourselves to only a couple of nightcaps in the hotel bar as we wanted to be in good form for the drive to the racecourse and see the big race. I especially needed a clear head as I was hoping to meet some officials to find out all the ins and out of entering the race, and to walk the course to inspect the awesome obstacles.

Next morning after a very substantial breakfast we made our way to the hotel reception to get directions to the racecourse. The only map that we had was a basic paper map that covered the whole of Czechoslovakia on one page and a map of Prague on the reverse. Thankfully, Pardubice was not a large city and the racecourse was right on the edge of town. After ten minutes of instructions repeated several times in broken English, we were reasonably confident that we could find the racecourse. We left the hotel early and after minor wrong turns arrived at the racecourse two hours before the start of the races. Our first shock of the day was about two hundred animal rights demonstrators at the entrance to the car park. They were all dressed in black boiler suits and white ghost masks covering their faces making them look very macabre. Many carried banners written in Czech. It was all very unsettling! The racecourse was very quaint surrounded by tall poplar trees whose leaves were simmering in the gentle breeze and the autumn sunshine. However, dark clouds were building in the distance, threatening rain later. There was also a definite autumnal nip in the air.

As we entered the racecourse, we were shocked how basic and small the racecourse was for such a famous race. It was more like a big Point to Point than a National Hunt Racecourse. There was a family selling huge sausages that were being cooked by the heat and smoke coming out of the chimney of a small wood burning stove, their serving counter was a battered-up old trestle table but boy they were delicious, who needs modern catering equipment.

An ex-army tent hosted the bar that offered two options, beer or schnapps, toilets were in another tent. There was a small open-air grandstand that had been white once upon a time but now most of the paint had flaked off giving it a mottled appearance. You had to be brave to use the grandstand as much of the wood was rotten, there were gaping holes in the floor everywhere. None of it was cordoned off, you used it at your own risk.

I left the rest of our party and went in search of the administration block to find out about entering the race. I only got as far as the entrance where I was stopped by armed police who didn't speak a word of English and looked very menacing. After a bit of sign language, I got the message no badge no entry, how you got a badge to gain entry remains a mystery to this day. Things were not looking good for my reconnaissance trip. Next project was to walk the course. I knew the rest of the party also wanted to do this so I decided to find the entrance onto the course and then go back and collect the others, who I had left testing out the bar. Access to the course was not easy, a strong spiked metal fence separated the course from the public areas. I eventually found a gate onto the course but like the admin block it was guarded by two similarly clad policemen and same rules applied, no pass no access. I was devastated, my whole purpose for making this trip had failed miserably. I trudged back towards the beer tent to tell the rest of the party my bad news, as I passed the gents toilet I decided to pop in and empty my bladder before I started on the beer. There were no urinals just a gutter long enough for six to eight people to stand in line, all very social! Halfway through relieving myself I was jostled as a new person pushed into the line. He was an immaculately dressed gentlemen in a tweed coat and brown trilby hat, the unmistakable uniform of an English racehorse trainer. I chanced a few words "English I presume, over-here for the big race?" I enquired. As we left the tent, he introduced himself as Ferdy Murphy and told me that he was the trainer of Irish Stamp. Two years before Irish Stamp was narrowly beaten here in the big race and now Ferdy and his connections had returned determined to go one better.

Out of politeness he enquired about my purpose for being at the race. So, I told him of my plans to ride in the race and my tale of woe trying to get access to walk the course. Quick as a flash he replied I can solve that problem for you, I am about to take a group of connections for a course walk. If you want to tag along, meet at the course entrance in twenty minutes.
 I immediately agreed to his offer and thanked him profusely and then at the last minute chipped in that I had also had a party of five others over with me including a couple from Ireland and was there any possibility that they could tag along as well. With an instant broad grin, he replied "Of course the more the merrier. See you all in a few minutes". With a quick wave of the hand, he bade me goodbye and strode off purposely into the crowd. Now all I had to do was to find the rest of our party in time for the course walk, I tried my mobile phone but there was no signal so I made a bold guess and headed for the bar. It wasn't yet noon but our group had already started to party along with most of the other racegoers.
At the security gate a group of about twenty people gathered around Ferdy Murphy, a mixture of English and Irish accents perfumed the air. I introduced my party and Ferdy told us he was just waiting for one more group and then we were good to go. He also told us as soon as we were passed security we could stay with his group or do our own thing as long as we were off the course before the start of the first race. What a super man!

We all walked together to the race start line where we were greeted by a large number of crosses that remembered the jockeys that had lost their lives in this race. A regular visitor to the race in the group informed us that just before the race starts, all the runners and riders are called together to say a prayer with a priest for those that lost their lives in the race. The priest then gives all the horses and riders a blessing just before they start the race. What an unnerving way to start a race! As we walked around the course, we came across further crosses that marked the place where a particular a jockey had lost his life, the little cross bearing and remembering the name of the unfortunate jockey. It was all very sobering. As we walked on the size and complexity of the obstacles became mind blowing. Our Irish friends announced, "yer must be fecking mad to want to ride in diss race".
We reached fence number six and noticed a cluster of crosses. It was easy to see why, a large plain fence with a ninety degree turn to the right. The infamous Canal Turn in our Grand National is similar. However, there are two big differences, in the National the horses turn left and, in this race, it is a right turn, but the real difference is the width of the track on landing. In the National the track has been widened to allow the horses to be able to swing out and reduce the severity of the turn, whereas in the Pardubická you are faced with a

twelve-foot-high black wall of hedge and trees, only the width of the course away from landing, forcing the riders to turn sharply on landing. Another problem is a large mature tree on the right-hand side of the fence that obscures the view of where the course goes next. To the horse it appears that the next fence is the wall of hedge and trees and this is a big problem especially for the leading horses.

Little did we know what carnage would take place at this fence in just a few hours' time and tarnish the great weekend.

About twenty-five percent of the course was light plough which severely tested the stamina of the horses. The race was also run on a figure of eight which was unheard of in English racing with added twists a turns making it more akin to the Melton Ride or a Teamchase. Certain parts of the course are wide and it is not unknown for some riders to leave the main body of the runners and take their own line.

Every fence on the course was a challenge but for me there were seven jumps that stood out as serious tests. There was the infamous Taxis fence, this fence had claimed the lives of 28 horses in the past and had been modified that year to make the fence safer after repeated animal rights protests. Originally the obstacle was a 1.50 metre hedge that was also 1.50 metres wide with a 5m wide ditch that was 2m deep on the landing side. The hedge was still the same height and width but the ditch was now, only 4 metres wide and the ditch only 1 metre deep. It was still an awesome fence.

Then there was the French jump, two large hedges with a ditch separating them, both hedges were each 1.50 metres wide as was the ditch, the first hedge was 1.20 metres high and the second 1.30 metres. This beast of a fence was jumped as one fence.

There were several water ditches that could be better described as canals. These stretches of water had no fence in front of them to help get the horse to take-off. Fixing a good take-off point into these obstacles would be exceedingly difficult.

The small gardens fence was more akin to something that you would find in the Eventing world. It was a square box hedge 1.25m high with a white a pole the diameter of a telegraph pole in front as a guard rail followed rapidly by an identical fence that was 1. 30m.high. I think it would be best described as a narrow lane crossing with barely one non-jumping stride and probably a bounce when taken at speed.

In a section of the course that had been ploughed was an Irish Bank. A large mound of earth about 3 metres high with a deep wide ditch on both sides. The walls are not quite vertical probably about 60 degrees. The horse has to jump the ditch, land on the steep face, and then scrabble up to the top, it then has one stride to compose itself before slithering down the other side and making a leap off about halfway down to negotiate the second ditch.

These are just a sample of the 31 fences that have to be jumped during this ten-minute race equivalent of riding the National Teamchase Championship course twice nonstop. Wow! You needed a clever quick-thinking horse for this race.

The race itself was a bit of an anti-climax as the viewing of the course from the grandstand was not great and parts of the course were obscured by trees and the fences themselves. The commentary was in Czech so we didn't have any idea what was happening.

What we did know was that it was not the English Favourite, "Risk of Thunder" that crossed the finish line first place or any of the other English horses. We learned later, that in fact none of the English horses finished the race.

A massive pile-up at fence six, the sharp right-hand turn, had taken out Ruby Walsh on Superior Finish and Paul Carberry riding Irish Stamp. Richard Dunwoody who was riding Risk of Thunder was in the lead at the time missed the carnage but was left alone with no company in the lead, two fences later at the in and out Garden Fence his horse ducked out at the second element depositing Dunwoody into the hedge. That's jump racing, you never know what will happen!

On our tour around the course, we chatted amiably to members of the group and one couple asked Jim Brennan if we were going up to the castle that evening for the reception. Apparently, all the people associated with the three English horses had been invited. On our way home Jim told us about the reception and suggested that we have a crack at gate crashing it. We all agreed it was a good plan.

That evening dressed in our best clothes we made our way up to the castle. The main gate was open but there was not a sole in sight and it was pitch black. Perhaps we had made a mistake, I was ready for turning back but the majority were in favour of pressing on to explore the castle. I had visions of somebody locking the gates and leaving us locked in for the night. We walked slowly forward up the wet cobbled road that glistened in the moonlight. Fifty yards in we saw a dim light off to our right up a narrow-cobbled path. Nervously we picked our way up the narrow path, a vertical black wall rose skywards on the right-hand side of the path. Should we turn back? Was the castle reception a bad joke, surely such an important event would be well lit. Three times we considered turning back. A murmur of voices grew slowly louder as we neared the light that lit a pointed medieval door, a rosy glow emanated from deep within. As we entered the door our way was barred by a well-dressed man who gabbled something in Czech. At a loss for words, we all blurted out the word "English" almost simultaneously. How arrogant to think that saying English would grant you access to anywhere or anything. We stood close together awaiting a response with trepidation. The man slowly repeated the word English and then a broad grin spread across his face saying, "Ah English come, come, welcome, welcome". We were escorted into a room of well-dressed people in suits and ties and cocktail dresses and were presented to a man wearing a heavy gold chain bearing a badge of office, presumably the Mayor. He smiled and shook our hands profusely uttering the only English word that anyone in the room seemed to know, "Welcome". He waved his hands towards waiters bearing trays of drinks and a table full of delicious looking food repeating the word Welcome.

We sipped our drinks and cast our eyes around the room, a group of trumpeters sat in one corner dressed in seventeen century Cavalier costumes that were black and heavily brocaded with gold, they wore broad brimmed hats, dressed with an ostrich feather. The big question on all our minds was where were the English contingent? We listened hard but could not hear a word of English being spoken anywhere in the room.

We felt a little uneasy that we were all dressed casually in jackets and open necked shirts, our partners fared better as they had all packed smart dresses just in case of such an eventuality. Finally, another English couple appeared on the scene and the riddle on the missing English revealed.

Apparently, the big pileup at fence six had taken out all of the well backed Czech horses, this was being blamed on the English jockeys who had taken an unorthodox route to the fence and that had caused a lot of bad feeling. Most of the English contingent including the jockeys had decided that it was safer not to attend what we now found out was the official prize-giving. We now felt vindicated in gate-crashing the ceremony as we felt that it would have been a great insult to our hosts if no English had attended, a sentiment shared by the other couple from the English camp.

After the presentation of prizes, we were asked to have our photographs taken with the Mayor and then again with the Fanfare trumpeters. I still have the photographs to this day and they are a great memento of this fabulous, surprising weekend. The other English couple told us that the rest of the group were having a kind of wake to drown their sorrows in our hotel. We couldn't converse with anyone at the party so along the other couple decided to slip away quietly after the presentation and return to the hotel.

When we arrived back at the hotel the noise from the bar hit you. If you didn't know the story you would definitely have thought that the English or Irish had won the Velká Pardubická. As we entered the bar the party swallowed us up bouncing us this way and that as we made our way to the bar, greeting new friends all the way. The common denominator was horses, not only racing but hunting, show jumping and eventing. It was a great evening, everyone was open to conversation. Everybody was having a great time and for most it was their last night in Czechoslovakia, and as so often happens when drinking in a highly sociable atmosphere time flew by. Just as the buzz of the party was reaching its crescendo the bar suddenly closed without warning. As you can probably imagine this caused a near riot, things were starting to get a little ugly as the revellers demanded more drinks only to be stalwartly refused by the bar staff. We happened to be close to the entrance when the manager arrived to calm things down. In broken English he explained that this bar was only licensed until 11pm but if we wanted to continue drinking there was a club downstairs that stayed open all night and pointed towards the stairs. His parting words were "You must go now! Police come!" He then moved on to the next group to repeat his message. As we descended into the basement, we all laughed at the name of the nightclub, "Club Erotica." As we were all couples and having been directed there by the manager, we gave no further thought!

The first room was quite small with a bar in the corner, to the right of the bar at the back of the room was a dimly lit curtained off area, opposite the bar on the right-hand side was an archway, from which dance music and flashing lights emanated. We purchased a round of drinks that were much more expensive than the bar upstairs and looked around for somewhere to sit. We were the only people in the bar but there was not a table or chair in sight. The young girl who served us and looked about sixteen years old and spoke more English than anyone else we had met in Pardubice realised our predicament and pointed towards the archway saying "Sit through there. Show starting in minute." We moved tentatively though the archway into another small room that had been made to look like a cave. The flashing lights constantly changed the colour of the room and reminded me of the first disco's in the early sixties, extremely basic! A sculptured faux stone bench went around two thirds of the room forming a horseshoe seating area. The music was pop dance music with undertones of Moroccan music used for belly dancing. There was one other man sitting on the other side of the room. We had only just sat down when the music stopped and a naked girl appeared who looked about the same age as our fifteen-year-old daughter. She performed a small bow; the music restarted as she started to leap around the room and perform all sorts of interesting poses around a pole in the centre of the room. All our party were feeling extremely uncomfortable and were squirming in their seats. We would have got up and left but the small intimate nature of the room meant that we would have to all walk through the girl's performance to get out of the room. We decided that there was no other option but wait until the end of the performance before we made our exit from the room. It was then that things got even worse. The girl danced across the room to the man on his own and started to gyrate in front of him and then to sit astride him stroking his face and body before moving back to dance in the room. Our party immediately shuffled as close together as possible; the men grabbed their partners hand. The men had a look of terror on their faces, the women on the other had were in hysterics. Lou elbowed me in the ribs and whispered in my ear. "What are you going to do if she does that to you" "Not a f***ing clue." I replied. "Well, I'm going to die laughing at you. You are going to be so embarrassed." This seemed to be the general consensus of opinion of all the female members of our party as they waited eagerly for the public embarrassment of their partners. Thankfully, the girl saved us by ending the dance a couple of minutes later, two of the longest two minutes in my life.

We all needed a strong drink. The bar was now quickly filling up with rowdy racegoers and we now had to fight our way to the bar. By the time we had fought our way to the bar, the dancer had dressed and was serving behind the bar. Our request for a local spirit at the bar was fulfilled by something called Becherovka a powerful alcoholic shot that tasted of the worst cough medicine you could ever imagine. We couldn't pronounce the name so we called it "Buggeroffsky". The fact that we were all in a brothel didn't seem to bother anyone and being squeezed into a small space like sardines in a can, only increased the atmosphere. Every time you fought your way to the bar you lost the person that you had been talking to, sometimes you never reached the bar, people at the bar would just shout back and ask you what you wanted. Every time we tried to repay somebody always said, "no worries it's on the big fella." I never found out who the big fella was until I researched the Velka Pardubická to cross check a few things for the book, but now I finally know his name. His name was Paddy O' Donnell owner of Irish Stamp. He had declared that the trip was his party and generously paid for a lot of things, asked later how much the trip had cost, he estimated somewhere between £8,000 and £10,000. A very generous man.

During my many casual chats to complete strangers, I met a smartly dressed young man looking as if he was enjoying himself but at the same time looking a little uneasy about his surroundings. He seemed to know a lot about what had happened to the English horses in the race. Eventually, I discovered that I was talking to Mark Pitman who had just taken over from his famous mother, Jenny Pitman. When I mentioned I lived in Leicestershire he told me that he was the trainer of Superior Finish and asked me if I knew his owners Richard and Elaine Robinson. Richard was a motor trader in Leicester. I had to confess that I didn't know them and that I hardly ever visited the city. As our conversation continued, he explained what had happened at fence number six. Unbeknown to each other both Richard Dunwoody and Ruby Walsh had decided to miss out the plough leading to fence six and veer off to the narrow headland at the side of the field. Twenty-two others immediately changed their plans and followed suit. The narrow strip caused a lot of congestion. As they approached the sixth fence Superior Finish was bowled over sideways through the hedge by a horse taking a different line into the right turn. A Czech horse was brought down by Superior Finish and then Irish Stamp cannoned into the Czech and fell, after that it was just mayhem, like a motorway pile-up. I commented what a great atmosphere there was despite our unusual surroundings. Mark's reply was "yes, it's been a great weekend despite the drama. I hope this doesn't get back to my mum, if she knew I was drinking in a brothel she would kill me!"

Morning came with a mega hangover thanks to a few too many "buggeroffkys". At the airport the party was still in full swing and it seemed impolite not to join them, hair of the dog and all that!

I never did find a horse that would take me back to compete in the Velka Pardubická.

That was the end of my racing career, the prices of horses had gone through the roof taking it way out of my modest means. I was also now one of the eldest members in the jockeys changing room. I never set foot on a racecourse for the next fifteen years and then it was only because a friend had sponsored a fence at the Belvoir Hunt Point to Point.

Great while it lasted!

Chapter Seven
Drag Hunting and Bloodhounds

The Readyfield Bloodhounds

My first taste of trail hunting was with the Readyfield Bloodhounds. We met at Osberton Park in north Nottinghamshire just off the A1 or the great north road as it used to be called. It was in the early eighties and I had never had any experience with trail hunting before this. It was while out hunting with the South Notts that Gwen Streets told me about the Readyfield Bloodhounds and what fun it was. The hounds were owned and hunted by Peter Boddy who lived at Readyfield farm just outside of the village of Caunton in North Nottinghamshire. The Osberton Estate was also home to a British Horse Trials course which later became known as British Eventing. This was another horse sport that in the early eighties I had no real knowledge of except from visiting Burghley Horse Trials which was an annual family pilgrimage.

The marvellous thing about the blood hounds was that they met on a Sunday which was a very no, no day as far as fox hunting was concerned. I can never understand religion. In England at that time everything closed on Sundays, no sporting events, even the pubs had very restricted hours, whereas in Ireland, a much more religious country, everything happens on a Sunday even hunting. In the sixties and seventies, a lot of people would dash off to Ireland for Sunday hunting so that they could hunt seven days a week. To hunt seven days in a week was always a pipe dream but the reality of, money, time, and horseflesh sadly confined it to staying a pipe dream.

For those of you that are not acquainted with bloodhounds, they hunt the scent of a man, known as hunting the clean boot, all they need is something that the runner has touched like a piece of cloth they have handled. They have a fantastic nose and make a deep baritone sound when they speak on a scent.

At Osberton there were drinks at the meet just like fox hunting, and after the first hunt we stopped and had a rest with food and drink being brought around by members of the hunt. All very agreeable.

What a day we had, Dad had come with me and it was a revelation to us both. Peter Boddy was a bold man across country and gave us a great lead. The standout things I remember about that day were jumping a pair of big hedges onto and off a road. We also crossed a canal which was great fun jumping into the deepest water that I had ever encountered at that moment in my life. I was very well mounted on a mare called Cariad and after the canal I spotted a stone wall capped with timber. It was one of the event fences. Adrenaline coursing through my veins made me bold and cheeky so I hung back after the canal. The hounds went into a big wood and so did the big wall, I let the field go and then put Cariad at the wall, we met it well and sailed over it and into the wood. There was a clear track ahead which was the route for the event course, I followed it up hill and jumped a log pile on the way to the top where I could hear the hounds. By the time I reached the top the hounds had moved on and were now below me. I looked for a way to get down to the lower part of the wood and saw a track heading down in the direction that I needed to go. About one hundred yards down the track was an upright brush event fence. This was great fun I was on my own in a wood full of fences the like of which I had never seen before. I kicked on boldly at the large brush. Again, Cariad put in a huge leap then shit happened! On the other side on the fence were a series of big steps. We were going far too fast and she was a big rangy mare. We hurtled down them, I think she jumped clean over one of the steps, I thought we were both going to die. Somehow, we made it down the steps in one piece and I was just thinking, my god we've made it, when another large fence sprang out of the ground in front of me. I now know it is called a pheasant feeder, but back then it just looked plain weird. My reins were at the buckle end and there was no time to shorten them so I just sat back, kicked, and hoped! We made it! I don't how. Eventually I managed to get her back to a halt. I was shaking like a leaf. When I had regained my composure, I decided now would be a good time to end my little adventure and re-join the hunt. I now realise that I managed to jump an advanced event brush, a set of three steps and a pheasant feeder, all back to front and I survived.   Quite an achievement on a young horse.

When I re-joined the hunt, Dad said, "where the hell have you been?
" I told him I took a wrong turn in the woods and got lost. I didn't dare tell him I had just nearly killed myself and his new horse which he had high hopes of selling in the very near future, once I had showed it off in the hunting field.

I had many great days out with the Readyfield and Peter Boddy. Peter would plan the hunt so that we would jump the very biggest and best hedges. He always gave a welcome speech at the meet which he always ended by saying, "I have some big hedges and ditches in store for you today so make sure you kick on hard or you won't make it." My favourite areas were Osberton and Great Dalby. After Peter retired my friend Richard Brooks became Master and we had some great days around Willoughby and in the Vale of Belvoir.

Once some years later Dad and I returned to Osberton and during the hunt I saw Dad pull up just before a gate that we were jumping off a road. Dad was a fierce man across country and something pretty awful must have happened for him to pull up. I quickly reined up and went back to see if he was alright. He could hardly speak, he looked extremely distressed and was very red in the face. We rarely hunted together as we shared a day with the Quorn. I realised that it was his heart, I knew that he had angina and had seen how cold wind could stop him dead in his tracks but hadn't realised it affected him so badly at other times. It was a real shock to me and made me incredibly sad, as like every son or daughter you hope that your parents will live forever. It brought it home to me that Dad was a lot more poorly than he had led everybody to believe. I stayed with him for a few minutes but he said that he was ok and that it was not the first time it had happened. He would follow on as soon as he got his breath back and insisted that I leave him and enjoy the fun. Just as he had said, he caught us up about ten minutes later, but for me it was a long ten minutes with me constantly looking over my shoulder for him wondering if he was really ok.

Our family had a long association with the Readyfield and my daughter Emma did a season as whipper-in to the bloodhounds. She was just sixteen years old and even with all her successes eventing she still has a picture on the wall of her riding her little horse Cassy in the maroon bloodhound livery. They were jumping off a farm road over a big ditch and hedge just outside Widmerpool on Geoff Brooks's farm. She had to go off on her own chasing wayward hounds and she would have to jump whatever got in her way to catch them and send them back to the huntsman. She came home one day and I asked her about her day. "Pretty scary" came the reply, and she went on to tell me that she had jumped three footpath gates along the banks of the River Trent which at the time was in full flood.
Yes, that is pretty scary!

Drag Hunting

The Cambridge Universities Drag Hounds

Oh Wow! Did this hit the right buttons. Although the bloodhounds were great fun and there was some exceptionally good jumping in the early days, it wasn't as fast as a good day with the Quorn bitch pack on a Monday. With the bloodhounds the field was not strung out, everyone stayed together, whereas with the Quorn if you got a good run and you were well mounted you were soon a couple of fields away from the main bunch of the field, and not hampered by horses stopping, running out or their riders falling off. The speed sorted out the wheat from the chaff very quickly and you could get down to the cut and thrust of trying to be first home at the end of the hunt, always trying to second guess where the hounds would go and taking the shortest line to beat your rivals.

Drag hunting had that same speed if not a little more. The only downside to drag hunting was that you knew it would end at a predetermined spot, whereas with fox hunting you never knew where or when it might end, you were always hoping that it might be one of the classic hunts that can go on for many miles. There is an account of the Quorn hounds once running for eighteen miles and remarkably they passed Bunny Hill about halfway through the hunt, but that was probably one hundred years ago, but we can always hope!
The great thing about the bloodhounds and the drag hounds was that they were a quarter of the price of fox hunting, you could do it on a Sunday, and you were guaranteed a blistering day of speed and jumping that was over and done within a couple of hours. Perfect for busy people.

The first pack of drag hounds that I encountered was the Cambridge University, a famous hunt that dates back to the 1800's. The Masters of the hunt are always students at the university and I have been privileged to have known several of them. I am not sure how it happened but we were asked if we could kennel their hounds overnight at the stables. As a thank you, we were invited to hunt with them at Old Dalby which is in Quorn Friday Country.

After the meet we hacked up the road and across some fields to warm up the horses and then we hit the first drag line. The hounds flew away at an unbelievable speed, there was no time to think we just had to kick on as hard as we could. Normally I can remember every fence I jump out hunting and can count them up when I get home. This run was so fast and intense I can only vaguely recall steep hills, big hedges and huge drops on the other side and jumping a brook just for good measure. The field that followed the two dynamic girl masters, both named Polly, and both vet students were the best of the best cross-country riders of their day. It was electrifying and exhilarating and I could fill a page full of other adjectives to describe how I felt that day. As fast as it started it was all over, it seemed to be just a blink of the eye but we had covered about two miles and jumped twenty or more fences. When the hunt finished, we were able to see the man that had laid the trail, he had run the two miles dragging a rabbit skin soaked in a scent that the hounds were trained to follow. While we all regained our breath, the intrepid runner was whisked away on a quad bike to start his next drag line from another secret location. I became to really admire these super fit long-distance runners who laid the trails. We had a few minutes break, some good guzzles on our hip flasks, and we were off in search of the next trail. When we had hacked for about ten minutes we dropped onto the next line and did it all over again but this time we went a bit further. Two hours and it was all over, horses and riders absolutely exhausted. I had many great days with the Cambridge all extremely enjoyable but not something I would want to do on a regular basis. Why?

Firstly, it is like a mass teamchase, a great adrenaline rush but no time to savour the experience. The difference was a bit like having a couple of quiet pints in the pub with friends or going to a party and drinking a bottle of spirits. Nice very occasionally but not on a regular basis.

Secondly it can blow horses' minds. I had a great day on an exceptionally good hunter but the experience ruined the horse. After that day, the horse just flung itself at fences, it broke my heart and even after re-schooling she was still never the same. An old horseman summed it up when he said that drag hunting was great for livening up stuffy cob type horses but you had to be incredibly careful with thoroughbreds as you can easily send them wappy. Wise words.

The Mid Surrey Farmers Drag Hounds

My visit to this famous pack came about through my teamchasing. We were short of a team member for a teamchase being held at Tingewick just outside the town of Buckingham. Being short of riders was a regular occurrence teamchasing as both horses and riders got injured on a regular basis. Usually, you can find a horse and rider quite easily, as many teams would not be able to raise the minimum number to start which was three. This left two others looking for places in other teams and it was quite common for the open riders to ride in other teams if their team couldn't run. However, on this occasion we had drawn a blank. Our team sponsor Mike Elvin said he knew of somebody who wanted to start teamchasing. He lived a long way away down in Surrey but was desperate to get into a team and was prepared to travel the long distance.

His name was Richard Cook. He travelled all the way from Cobham near Guildford in Surrey to ride with us.

When Richard arrived, he was introduced to us and he immediately shook our hands and said in a cockney accent, "pleased to facking meet you lads, thanks for letting me come and ride with you".

To have someone ride with you at the top level who had never ridden in a teamchase is worrying to say the least and could be extremely dangerous, but he had made a long journey to ride with us and he seemed an extremely genuine and sensible guy.

We had a blistering round and I think we won. After we finished Richard came up to us and again shook our hands again saying, "facking great lads, facking great, you lads are the business. I'll follow you lads anywhere any day of the week. Facking marvellous just facking marvellous". It was the start of a long and great friendship.

It was just before Christmas when we got a call from Richard inviting us down to his house for the weekend and a day's drag hunting with the Mid Surrey Farmers Drag Hunt. Bring some smart clothes he added we are going to a bit of a do the night before. This was by far the longest trip that we had ever embarked on with our own horses in the pursuit of equestrian fun.

Richard was a self-made man and proud of his routes which were a terraced house in the east end of London. He told me the story of how he left school and had no job. After two weeks of not working, his father sat him down and told him that if he didn't bring some money into the house by the end of the week he didn't eat. That focused his mind about earning money. He now had an import business and owned houses in Florida and the Far East as well as a house in an expensive part of Surrey. He had told us nothing about himself at this point in time, everything I have just written just popped out during conversations over a period of time. Every time we had met him, he was always dressed in tatty old jeans and a faded polo shirt. We knew nothing about his house or the village of Cobham.

When we arrived at his house, we stopped in front of a large gate that barred the driveway to the house. He had told us to call at the house and he would show us the way to the stable yard. I jumped out of the lorry and went up to the house to announce our arrival as this was pre mobile phone era. A lady came to the door and I introduced myself thinking that I was talking to Richard's wife. She politely explained that she was not Richard's wife but his housekeeper and that he did not live here, his house was further up the driveway. She told me Richard had told her to expect us and give us directions to the stable yard and his groom was waiting to greet us and he was on his way home and should be back shortly.

The stable area was beautiful with paddocks and ample horse box parking, the stables and barns were classic for the locality made from waney edged timber boards painted black. Large mature trees gave it an air of an old country estate.

It was about 4pm on Friday afternoon and we had just finished stabling the horses when Richard arrived in a Mercedes G Wagen. "Sling your kit in the back, we've just got time for a quick drink before we go out. Hope you brought your best bib and tucker with you, we are going somewhere posh" he said with a cheeky grin but offered no more information.

His house was grand and after being introduced to his wife and having a drink we went up to shower and get ready for our surprise evening. When I told him that I thought the house by the gate was his house he roared with laughter saying, "Yes well it is my house but that's where the housekeeper lives, her husband is the gardener". It was about five o' clock when we left the house with his wife reminding him to be back for dinner at eight and no later. Our drive took just under an hour and still nothing was mentioned about or destination. As we reached a village called Frogmore Richard passed us two invitation cards, they were for a cocktail party and auction at the Royal Military Academy Sandhurst, a fund raiser for the Staff College Drag Hunt. We arrived a couple of minutes later. To say that I was bowled over by the venue was an understatement. Uniformed cadets welcomed us and checked the invitations as we walked up the steps to the portico supported by huge Greco-Roman pillars. Inside took my breath away, words just cannot do it justice. I would not have missed it for the world and it was a great honour to be there.

Sadly, it was like being invited to a wedding and only knowing the bride and groom. After I had a couple of drinks I slipped off and explored the area's available to view, my love of history was well catered for that evening and I loved every second of it.

At 7.15 we left Sandhurst to drive back for dinner and arrived safely back just before the deadline. Like many of the phenomenally successful people I have met over the years, Richard had immense energy and packed a lot into every day.

Our evening meal was a long and sumptuous one with exceedingly good wines, port and finally brandy. When I refused another brandy at gone midnight pleading an important day on the morrow he grinned saying "I know, that's why I'm trying to get you buggers pissed to peg you back a bit tomorrow so that you don't show me up at the hunt" I retorted that we were already well pissed and pretty sure that we would have good hangovers in the morning.

We staggered upstairs to our beds with a warning of not to come downstairs until after eight in the morning as the downstairs was alarmed.

Morning came with a headache and a large breakfast and instructions to eat plenty, as there would not be time for lunch. After breakfast Richard announced he had some work to do and slung the keys of his G Wagon at me saying, "go and have a play around the farm, don't be frightened of getting it dirty it will go anywhere". For those of you that are not acquainted with the G Wagon it looks ugly and like a big army Jeep and is extremely basic inside yet it costs more than a Range Rover. It was an extremely expensive toy. I had great fun putting it through its paces through streams, climbing steep banks and descents.

At midday we put on our hunting clothes and packed our bags because we were driving home after the hunt. It was a good hours drive to the meet which was of course at a pub. In the pub I met up with David Robinson, a teamchase friend, who beckoned me over to his table and welcomed me. During our chat he asked if anyone had explained to me about the tissue paper. I was confused, I had heard scary tales of the mighty Mid-Surrey hedges and ditches   did the hunt issue toilet paper in case you shit yourself? Thankfully, he went on to explain that the hunt put tissue paper in the hedges to mark where it was safe to jump and backed this up with a stern warning. Do not under any circumstances take your own line or jump outside the tissues because you will kill yourself. This came from one of the craziest teamchase riders I have ever met. He went on to further warn me that if there wasn't a ditch in front of a fence there would surely be one on the landing. He qualified this by saying that the ditches were so big and deep that they had a mobile crane on standby to lift horses out if they fell into them. I decided it was time for a stiff drink before I mounted. We were all summoned to leave the pub and mount our steeds as the time to start approached. At the meet the Master, no other than the fabled owner and creator of Hickstead, the inventor of teamchasing, also a multi-millionaire, Douglas Bunn, welcomed us and gave the same warnings again about the tissue paper. Talking of millionaires, I think that a good number of the mounted followers were in that category.

There was little warm up before the hounds screamed away. Both Dad and I were well mounted that day. Dad on his best hunter Frenchie and me on Mike Elvin's horse Red, who was my regular teamchase horse of the time. The first fence was causing a lot of refusals as the horses were not really warmed-up enough. It was a good set of post and rails but not impossible. I knew Red would be quite capable of jumping them, visions of me giving all these famous people a lead over this first fence crept into my brain. Oh, the glory! Then David's warning came back. If there isn't a ditch in front there will be surely one behind. I crept forward and took a sneaky peak. Hidden by the grass growing at the base of the rails was the biggest mother f***er, of a newly dug ditch, over six feet wide and just as deep, all black and dark like a grave. My grave, as my plan had been to hook my horse back and show jump the big rails, not a sensible approach with a ditch of that magnitude on landing. I went back to Dad who asked what was causing the problem. "A huge f**ing ditch is the problem" I replied. By this time, some people were jumping it and we both launched ourselves at the rails at a worryingly fast speed for a set of big upright rails. Thankfully, both of us cleared it and we were off with bucket loads of adrenaline coursing through our veins. After the messy start everyone settled down to the task of conquering the massive hedges and ditches. There were no easy fences. You and your horse had to dig deep for everyone. Finally, it was over, hounds, horses and humans all steaming in the cold winter air. There was so much steam it blocked out the whole paddock that we had halted in. Everyone had huge grins on their faces as they gasped in the cold air demanded by over worked lungs. No wonder these guys were so good at teamchasing, they were jumping bigger fences than the best open courses every week of the winter.

I cast my eye around the field and it was like the Who's Who of open teamchasing. George Goring came over and thrust a large hip flask towards me. I declined saying "Thanks George but I won't. I think I need a clear head for these fences." He replied with a shocked look saying "Good Lord, you don't mean to say you are jumping these fences sober. Bloody hell, I could never do that! I am amazed!". George was one of the nicest guys on the teamchase circuit and a true gentleman. He often ran several teams and was a great benefactor to the sport sponsoring the National Championships for many years. If you beat his team, he would be the first to congratulate you.

On the other side of me was Robert Crosby the journeyman teamchase rider who rode for several different teams at every event. Robert lived near Spalding in Lincolnshire. He and his family were horse dealers supplying many of the top teams with their horses. He gave a knowing grin of a fellow conspirator and said "Alright boy, not bad bit of fun eh" in his broad Lincolnshire accent.

We moved off again following the hounds at a gentle hack across beautiful countryside allowing our horses and ourselves to recover before the next onslaught. When it came the next line was just like the first, big fences all the way, I only have two clear recollections of that last run as my mind was working too hard to record memories. I remember seeing a horse in a ditch so deep that the only part visible was the tips of its ears. Both horse and rider looked ok, so I put all my efforts into keeping my horse straight and not allowing him to become distracted by the horse in the ditch. Luckily for me Red was a very honest and sensible horse, he kept straight and got on with his job.

Towards the end of the run there was a sudden check, Douglas Bunn raised his hand, the universal sign to "Hold hard" or to stop immediately. Douglas turned and faced the field. We were on top of a high hill and the light was just beginning to fade. Before us stood the biggest holly hedge, I have ever seen. All the hedges we had jumped that day had been in that class but this out classed the others in both height and width. He explained that there was a massive drop on landing. He said that there was a way around if you felt that either you or your horse was not up to it. We were told to only jump it one at a time, if a horse or rider fell and wait until you were sure that it was safe to jump.

With these last words he turned and attacked the holly hedge. Now Douglas was a big man well over six-foot-tall and solidly built, his horse was close to eighteen hands high. They sailed into the air taking out the top eighteen inches of the hedge and then he disappeared, the last thing we heard was two grunts one from a man the other from a horse. Then there was just the sound of wind in our ears. Everyone was transfixed did he make it or not? A long minute passed and a cry went up, "He made it! He is down in the valley!" They shouted in relief. Now it was our turn to do battle with the giant holly hedge. When it came to my turn I kicked and hoped I knew Red was an exceptional jumper and would do his best for me. What we would meet the other side was anyone's guess!

As we went through the top of the fence, I stuck my legs forward slipped my reins to the buckle end and headed for earth. The ground fell away sharply nearer to 60 degrees than 45 degrees. To some that would be terrifying but having jumped many big drops up in Derbyshire I knew the gradient would help take the sting out of the landing because the horses feet would slip forward a bit like skiing. We touched down with a huge bump but safely. I let out a huge scream of delight as I galloped down the hill waving my hunting whip over the top of my head. It was the last fence of the day the huntsman and his hounds were waiting for us in the farmyard below. As I got to the bottom of the hill something cold hit my face. It had started to snow, a magical way to end the day just a few days before Christmas.

We were invited back for drinks and food at the pub but we had to decline as we had a four-hour drive home ahead of us. We thanked everyone and anyone for our fabulous day, it still remains the best day I ever had cross country. As we made our way back towards the M25 we passed through a small town that looked like it was straight out of a Dickens story, shops with Georgian bay windows all beautifully dressed for Christmas and colourfully lit Christmas trees all along the pavements, snow was falling and there was a light covering over the road and pavements. I imagined that colourful character Jorrocks created by R.S. Surtees hacking back through this town in the 1830s after a good day's hunting, dreaming of a roaring fire and a table full of food and drink. It was gone five o' clock on the Saturday before Christmas and the streets were empty. Except for the eclectic lights little had changed in the last 150 years and what had changed was hidden by the gently swirling snow.

We stopped on the motorway to buy sandwiches and coffee, the snow had stopped as soon as we left the South Downs and we had a good run home arriving in the yard just before nine but it was nearer ten by the time, we had put the horses to bed. We were both exhausted but in a glorious way that only thrills and adrenalin can produce.

What a way to start Christmas, thanks Richard Cook

The Welsh Borders Drag Hunt

I met Johnathan Lee and Tracy Mc. Taggart originally teamchasing. Their team The Jolly Green Giants was one of the best open teams in the country. I got to know them even better when they started competing in the Melton Rides. Like me they loved anything to do with challenging cross-country riding. Our lives seemed to follow a parallel course because we then both became involved in drag hunting. They invited me to visit their pack and I jumped at the chance, although it was a long drive to get to their hunting country which was along the Welsh Border roughly between Whitchurch and Shrewsbury.

I was riding a horse called Santini that belonged to Caroline Howitt. He was my regular teamchase horse of the time and I was also using him to field master on with the Trent Valley Drag. I asked Caroline if I could take him to visit Johnathan and Tracy for a day's drag hunting. She came to watch the teamchasing on a regular basis with her husband Mark so she knew the pair well and very kindly gave her permission.

I cannot remember the exact location as it was out in the wilds but it was near Market Drayton and like my visit to the Mid Surrey it was around Christmas time. In the horsebox it was about a three-hour drive. This time I was all on my own and as I write this again, I am reminded by how attitudes have changed. Yes, I know there are still some of you who still go out on your own to do dangerous riding, and hats off to you, but these days you are a small minority. In the early eighties it was quite normal and most of us didn't have any public liability insurance or personal accident insurance. You trusted fellow riders to look after you and your horse if something untoward happened. So, I set out in an old TK Bedford that was over twenty years old and had probably clocked up over two hundred thousand miles to drive three hours into the foothills of Wales in mid-winter to follow a pack of drag hounds all on my lonesome.

Crazy eh!

Luckily, I had my trusty Phillips Navigator map book with me. This great map book is ordnance survey standard and shows every tiny track, road and even names of farms. An essential bit of kit for a roaming equestrian pre sat nav era. After many stops to consult the map, I finally found the farm where the meet was taking place. The weather was typical December weather, dull, cloudy, and cold.

When I arrived, I received the warmest welcome I have ever had hunting. I was invited into the farmhouse as an honoured guest and offered sandwiches, tea, and coffee, I ate light and had half a cup of tea as you never know what life will throw at you. The countryside was stunning but not at all what I expected. Knowing Johnathan and Tracy I had expected lots of grass and hedges a bit like Quorn Monday Country however this was very different. There was a lot of forestry in fact vast tracts of it. What was not forested was mainly grassland for a mixture of sheep and cattle on small but rugged hills at a deceptive high altitude. It was what I would describe as well sheltered cuddly country.

After the meet we set off and very quickly had a short run over some post and rails and a couple of hedges before entering the forest. Once in the forest, hounds picked up several short trails and we were galloping to and fro along the forestry's roads and tracks. This was reminiscent of my hunting in Charnwood Forest with the Quorn and in North Nottinghamshire with the South Notts. I was impressed, this was just like fox hunting. Being a sort of guest of honour I spent most of the day up at the front with Johnathan and I complimented him on making it so like the real thing. It turned out that he also had reservations about the two or three quick blasts employed by a lot of drag hunts. We both felt that it was not good for horses to do that type of hunting on a regular basis. This type of drag hunting was exactly the same as my brother Phil and I were trying to create and it gave me a great moral boost to witness somebody of Johnathan's standing doing the same style.

Every now and then we would burst out of the forestry and have a scamper around a few fields before looping back into the woods which so often happened with fox hunting. A lot of care and thought had gone into the laying of the trails. As we neared the end of the day Johnathan took me to one side and asked if I fancied following the huntsman on the last line as there were some really good hedges. He was going to take the field on a longer but easier route. Santini was a great jumper and I readily accepted his offer. This had obviously been arranged beforehand as the huntsman greeted me by saying, "Ah you must be Sam, I hope your horse is a good jumper? Just hang back a bit and give me a bit of space with the hounds. He was as a great horseman and extremely well mounted. I could tell by the twinkle in his eye and an almost imperceptible grin that I was being challenged. He dropped the hounds on the line and off we went. There were a couple of post and rails first and then the hedges started. They were just natural and untrimmed; the first couple were quite big but not thick in the top and easy to brush through. However, as we progressed, they became bigger, blacker, and really took some jumping. I was very aware that I was being tested but also painfully aware that I was riding someone else's horse. Every time I landed over a fence the huntsman would look back to see if I was still there and then pick out a larger bit of the next hedge. We were definitely not taking the easiest route at each fence, thankfully Santini rose to the occasion at every fence. Towards the end of the run, we had an audience who were all cheering on the huntsman. I suddenly realised that this could be a tricky situation, the huntsman was obviously a local hero. The last hedge was into the home paddock of the farm where we had met. I pulled up before the last hedge and took my hat off and saluted the huntsman. He had given me a great ride and he ended the day with his honour still very much intact. When I entered the paddock, I went over and shook his hand and thanked him for such a great lead. He looked me in the eye and with a knowing look said, "And thank you!"

We all saw to our horses and I checked Santini's legs for any cuts or thorns and thankfully everything looked fine. It is a great responsibility that you carry when you are riding someone else's horse and I knew Caroline loved him to death.

Everybody was invited back into the house for a sumptuous hunt tea, hot soup, sandwiches, pies, and cakes. I hadn't eaten anything substantial since breakfast and I was ravenous. Just as I was feeling very well repleted, someone announced it was snowing very heavily. I was just about to accept a bottle of beer when the announcement was made and I immediately declined. People suddenly lost their appetites and prepared to depart. The last few miles up to the farm was down lanes that you really would not want to drive a horsebox down in snowy conditions. The owner of the farm asked me where I had come from and what route I had taken. I had come via Derby, Uttoxeter, and Stoke on Trent and after much pondering and asking other locals they suggested that I head the opposite way and go south instead of north. This was uncharted territory for me but they said that the A roads south were much better than going north. I was to head for somewhere called Telford as a new motorway had just opened. It was called the M54 and from there it was motorway all the way home. They all agreed if it was snowing the motorways would be the safest option.

It was about five o' clock when I prepared to leave the farm and I was glad that it was not a minute later as snow was starting to settle on the road and it was coming down so heavily that it was hard to see where you were going. Travelling down to Telford the snow was having a mesmerising effect as it swirled around in the headlight beams, and with all the adrenaline I had pumped into my body I was starting to feel very drowsy. The drive down to Telford was a nightmare, the snow had not been forecast and the roads were terrible. How I wished I had a pal in the cab to talk to. I crawled along at less than twenty miles an hour fighting sleep all the way. At last, I reached the M54 and what a relief the motorway was, lit and been salted, I was able to get moving at last. The trip from the meet to the motorway should have taken thirty minutes but had ended up taking over one hour. It was still snowing but now I could maintain a good constant speed. I was still feeling drowsy and had to keep winding the cab window down and give myself a blast of freezing air to keep myself awake. The snow was so heavy that it was hard to see the road signs and suddenly a gap in the snow opened up just as I passed the exit road to change onto the M69 which I should have taken but it was too late. However, I did glimpse that it showed the M1 straight on so I drove doggedly on. Missing the M69 had just added another twenty very unwanted miles to my journey home. When I reached the M1 I nearly went down the A14 to Ipswich but thankfully realised my mistake at the last minute. Now that would have been a disaster ending up in Ipswich.

I finally pulled into the yard just before 10pm. There was a good two inches of snow on the stable yard. I was totally exhausted and so thankful to have made it home safely.

Did I wish that I never made that trip? Not on your life it was a day to remember!

There is one more Drag hunt to write about but I am saving that for later!

Chapter Eight
Ireland

I had never had a desire to visit Ireland because of many warped reasons. The main one was that we were being bombarded on television with news and documentaries about the bombings in Northern Ireland. The IRA were also conducting a successful bombing campaign here in the UK with many lives being lost. So, I considered it to be a dark place that hated and wanted to kill anyone who was British. My second reason was that I believed that it was a cold wet place full of bogs and it never stopped raining. This is totally illogical but I can only suggest in my defence that it was formed from programmes that I had watched on television and other people's opinions. The final reason was that Dad liked to go there and anything that Dad liked I hated because that was our relationship and it was mutual. However, it was more complicated than that, every time he went over there, we ended up with a lorry load of extremely poor horses, skin, and bone hat racks. To be fair to Dad he had a good eye for a horse and could see that when they had been well fed and muscled up, they would be good quality horses. They also brought disease, most were full of worms and had ringworm. The ringworm came from the horse transport, as did to some extent their poor condition. There were no health or hygiene regulations in those days and horses would be packed into lorries like sardines. The ferries in those days were not stabilised and so if it was a rough crossing, they could quickly lose condition. The ringworm I am sure came from the lorries. Thankfully, this was a long-time in the past and things have been much better for many decades.

At this point you must be wondering about my sanity but I can assure you that I am very ashamed and embarrassed to have held those views which I now know were totally wrong. After my first visit I came home with several books about Irish history that I read avidly and then continued research on the internet. After some years reading, I have a broad view of Irish history from 1200 to modern day. For an Englishman it is sobering reading and I have a feeling of shame the way the Irish were treated by England.

I first arrived on Irish soil at Rosslare in June 1992. I had brought the jousting horses over on the ferry from Fishguard in South Wales. It was 6am and I was dog tired as we had been travelling through the night and not slept for twenty-four hours.

The first thing I noticed was that the weather was much warmer than in the UK and they had palm trees growing along the roadside. It felt more like Jersey than Ireland. We were waved across to a parking place in front of an isolated building away from the main ferry terminal. I gathered my paperwork together and entered the building with trepidation, I was by now a seasoned transporter of horses having done many shows abroad. I say with trepidation.

because we only did about one show a year abroad and they were constantly changing the regulations and I had spent many frustrating hours stuck at the docks because something was not quite right with my paperwork.

As I opened the door into the building a cheerful voice greeted me saying

"Morning, a fine day we have today, the vet is running a bit late but we were expecting you. Leave your papers with me and I'll get them seen to. Why don't you wander over to the café and get yerselves a cuppa and I'll come and find yer when the vet gets here".

I could not believe my ears, a friendly customs officer. The one I had dealt with in Fishguard had trained hard to be the most miserable man in the world and also seemed to be trying to impersonate a Gestapo officer.

True to his word the customs officer came over and told us the vet had arrived. Another cheery fellow apologised for being late and said, "Right I'll just have a quick look at your paperwork and your horses, I'll have you on your way quick as I can". Ten minutes later we were on our way. My views on Ireland were already changing.

Things were a bit confusing travelling up to Kilkenny as the distance to our destination changed dramatically from signpost to signpost. We finally worked out that they were in the process of changing from miles to kilometres, about ten percent of the signs were in kilometres and ninety percent still in miles. We arrived at lovely stables in what was called the deer park just on the outskirts of Kilkenny and received a warm welcome from the organisers, nothing was too much trouble. We were accommodated at the Glendine Inn owned by Michael Brannigan. Much to my brother Stuart's delight, Michael was a great horse racing fan as were the majority of the pub's clientele. There was even a small room off the main bar that showed live racing from all over Ireland and you could place your bets with the landlord, which over the years I have discovered is common in Southern Ireland but I am not too sure about its legality.

Everyone was so friendly why hadn't I been over here before? To quantify how impressed we all were by their hospitality, the majority of that original crew have revisited Kilkenny many times since and are still going back there after twenty-eight years. Jouster Pete Webster was married in Kilkenny in 2019, many of that original cast were there, and it was one of nicest weddings I have ever attended.

To say we had a good time in Kilkenny would be an understatement, the crowds were huge for our shows, press estimates were ten thousand at just one show. Our shows created a lot of press and television interest and after the reviews aired on television and in the newspapers, we became celebrities, everyone wanted to buy us drinks and both of the two nightclubs in town gave free admission to anyone wearing a jousting sweatshirt. Along with the success came interest from other venues in Ireland. Two of these inquiries asked me to come over and meet with them. A living history site in Waterford, and Blarney Castle home of the famous Blarney Stone which is just north of Cork in the south of Ireland. We had a terrible overnight crossing, I went down with a feverish cold and felt dreadful during the two business meetings. I had decided that I would mix business with pleasure and take a short break with Louise (Lou) my wife and John Cook my racing mentor. Lou was desperate to see Kilkenny after all my tales from the jousting tour and we were all keen to sample some of the fabled Irish hunting. I was so ill that I thought that I would not be fit enough to ride. After my second meeting of the day at Blarney Castle, we stayed overnight in Blarney village pub. I desperately needed paracetamol but when I enquired if there was anywhere, I could buy some, I was told that it was too late, all the shops were closed. The barman recommended a hot toddy in front of the fire instead. I ended up having five or six and had to be helped upstairs to my bed. I awoke in the middle of the night drenched in sweat and by morning my fever had gone, I was weak but feeling much better. A huge Irish breakfast made me feel even better. We left early as it was a three hour drive up to Kilkenny and the meet was at eleven. We were staying again with Michael Brannigan at the Glendine Inn and arrived just in time to check in at get changed into our hunting kit before being whisked off to the meet. Michael had organised everything for us and we were hunting with the Kilkenny's. Although I was still a bit wobbly from my virus, I declared myself fit for hunting. Unlike English hunts which tend to meet at a pub or large house many Irish hunts meet at crossroads in the middle of nowhere. We finally found the crossroads after a couple of wrong turns. I found it a little disconcerting that a local could get lost so many times but, in the end, we found the right crossroads. It was mayhem in the middle of nowhere. There were trailers towed by cars and cattle wagons towed by tractors that served as horse boxes. All the horse trailers seemed to be of the same design and constructed from corrugated galvanised roofing sheets. After driving up and down through the mayhem a couple of times Michael located the man that was supplying our horses. After giving us a quick look up and down the man allocated our mounts for the day. There was no stirrup cup everyone just milled around blocking all four roads chatting away happily in an excited manner. There were no cars traveling along these back roads or for that matter any other sign of life at the crossroads so it wasn't a problem. We were literally in the middle of nowhere.

The huntsman blew his horn and we moved off. Suddenly as we hacked down the road the hounds struck up and we were off, we hadn't even drawn a cover and we were hunting. The first obstacle was a six-foot-high bank off the road that had had recently had a mature hedge chopped down almost to ground level leaving pointed bits of growing thorn all over the bank. I was on a strange horse that didn't belong to me and a fence that looked more like medieval defensive structure. To both sides of me horses were scrabbling up the bank and leaping into the field. I truly had no idea how to tackle the obstacle without injuring the horse, I turned toward the bank and in the blink of an eye I was on top of the bank and sailing off it into the field. We landed and followed the field of about thirty at a smart but urgent canter, the country certainly didn't lend itself to galloping. We had only gone a few hundred yards when we were greeted by a mounted follower screaming at us saying "Headlands lads, keep to the fecking headlands. Fer feks safe keep to the fooking headlands yer idiots" - the man turned out to be the hunt Secretary who relieved us of our cap money when the hounds checked in a dense thicket after just a few fields. As sooner as he had secured the cash, he asked to be excused for a moment saying he had forgot to bring his stick and needed to cut a new one out of the hedge. Hunting was certainly different in Ireland and we had only been going ten minutes if that. Seconds later there were screams of "Whoa, Whoa, you stupid fecking animal, Whoa". I looked across to the thicket to see the huntsman being slowly pulled off his horse by a thick dog rose briar that was hooked across his neck, the vicious barbed thorns were tearing into his neck and blood was starting to turn his white stock red. It was a grim and gory sight and nobody could help him as he had burrowed his horse into the dense thicket with no room either side of his horse to get to him. Thankfully after what seemed like forever but in reality, was probably not much more than a minute, he got his horse to rein back and stop the briar garrotting him. Thankfully, the cuts were only superficial and most of his neck had been protected by his hunting stock. If the carotid artery had been ripped, he could have died. This was a sobering start to our first day's hunting in Ireland. The fox had run to ground and there was a long delay while the fox was dug out and shot. This was something that was not allowed in England, sporting chance and all that. In Ireland, the only good fox was a dead one in the eyes of the small farmers who suffered from this extremely pretty but ruthless predator.

The hunt resumed and we soon came to a small earth bank less than three feet high and only two feet in width which was causing great problems with all the horses refusing to jump it. It was nothing at all to jump but the horses were saying a definite no. I was about to show them how it was done when Dad's words of warning came back to me about hunting in Ireland. "Don't take your own line, look before you leap, always follow someone and see how they cope with it". I wandered over to the mud wall and looked over and saw my first Irish drain! Ten to twelve feet wide and deep enough to bury a horse and rider, oh my god this was serious stuff, I was exhilarated, a new riding challenge! We fought our way across the country, this was totally different from English hunting and I was constantly learning new skills. Our horses didn't look much but they performed brilliantly and really knew their job. There is an old horseman's saying, "Handsome is as handsome does". This was certainly true of our three mounts, we jumped so many obstacles that I thought were not jumpable and my opinion of what a horse was capable of changed immensely that day. It was nearly dark when we finished hunting, all three of us along with the majority of the field had blood on their faces from pushing through thorn bushes. It was my first time hiring a horse to go hunting on and when I handed my horse over, I offered to take the saddle off and put a rug on my horse. The offer was gracefully declined and the horse was loaded straight onto the lorry still tacked up and with no rug. This was the first inkling I got that horses were treated very differently in Ireland.

We returned to the Glendine Inn and devoured a hearty meal and many pints of Guinness with the extremely friendly locals. It had been truly an exceptional day although exhausted, my illness had vanished and I was back on top form. Hot toddies were definitely going to be part of my remedies from now on and still are to this day.

It was a great trip and I was falling in love with this great little country and kicking myself for not coming sooner. As we drove down John's Street over the river Nore, Kilkenny Castle loomed high above the town to our left, I felt a great sadness to be leaving this lovely place.

We returned the following year to repeat our jousting show at the Castle and this time we did our Robin Hood Show that we performed every year at Nottingham Castle. We were stabled at a farm with racing connections near the town of Gowran some way out of the city. Again, my brother Stuart and I travelled over via Rosslare two days before the main crew arrived. We always had to do this when performing abroad to ensure that the horses got there in time for the shows, because the ferries are not allowed to take horses if the wind exceeds a certain level. Because this was our second trip, we made better time and arrived in a village near to our destination just before 8am, we had estimated that we would arrive at 9.30, so decided to stop and try and find a café for some breakfast. The only place open when we arrived was a newsagent, so we went in and enquired if there was somewhere nearby, we could get some food and drink. Although we all spoke English there are subtle differences in the meanings of certain words. In Ireland drink tends to refer to alcohol. The newsagent looked a bit uneasy and said it was a bit early to get a drink but if we were desperate, we could try the back door of the pub just down the road and if we were lucky the cleaner might just let us have a pint. It was then that the penny dropped and after rephrasing our enquiry found out there was nowhere in the vicinity that did breakfast so we settled for two cans of warm coke and a packet of crisps. I'm sure the newsagent went around telling all his mates about the two Englishmen who were desperate for a beer at 7.30 in the morning.

We arrived at our destination at 9am a bit earlier than expected, everything was ready and waiting for the horses. Our host was away when we arrived but was due back any minute. We had just finished seeing to the horses when a cloud of dust appeared at the end of the long drive and proceeded to come towards us at high speed. If my memory serves me well it was a short wheelbase Mitsubishi shogun and behind it was an Irish corrugated iron horse trailer bouncing around behind it. I assumed that it was empty but when it pulled up it contained a fine thoroughbred fully tacked up with a racing saddle. It had no head collar on just its bridle with the reins twisted up. It was completely loose in the back of the trailer which was devoid of any partition. When he unloaded the horse, I noticed that it had no boots or bandages for travelling. It was our host returning from an early morning gallop and after shaking hands and being introduced to him by my brother Stuart, who already knew him from last year's visit. I enquired about his horse as horse people do. Was it a youngster I asked? The reply that it had run at Cheltenham the previous year came as a shock. That put the value of this horse at several tens of thousands of pounds and he had been bouncing around in the back of an old trailer completely loose, tacked up with no leg protection. In England it would have been wrapped up in cotton wool.

My two children Mark and Emma joined me on this trip, they were both in their mid-teens and I was keen for them to experience the wonders of Ireland at an early age and not miss out like I had done. It was through my children that I came to know the Brennan family Jim, Patricia and their two children Ian and Michelle. The children were of similar ages to my two. Jim owned a hotel in the centre of Kilkenny and Patricia was master of the Kilmaganny hunt which had been started by her father Charlie Blacque, owned, and run by him since the 1930s. He had recently retired and the Hunt was now being run by a committee. We became exceptionally good friends with Jim and Patricia and have travelled the world together having many adventures for almost 30 years but it was Patricia's involvement in hunting that has the most significance for this book. Jim was involved in the organisation of our second visit and was a close friend of Michael Brannigan who owned the Glendine Inn where we were all staying. Jim's hotel called the Club House Hotel was one of the hotels in the city that gave us an evening meal as part of our performance deal. The hotel had historic connections with hunting and horses dating back to the mid-1800s. Over the week we saw each other often and when Jim found out my children were with me immediately got his children to show Mark and Emma around the city. They became great friends to this day.

The incident that really cemented our friendship was strange. It all started during our final show at the castle. The castle grounds were vast and for our second visit the organisers had moved the arena much closer to the castle which made logistics much better although we lost the hill which made a superb natural grandstand. Throughout our two days performing we were plagued by tinkers' children around the horsebox and coach. They were scruffy cheeky little irks who were trying to steal anything that they could lay their hands on. We were always chasing them away and had to mount a guard on the vehicles during our performances. The castle security knew them well and helped us keep chasing them away. We performed our final show, packed up and sent the horses back to the stables which was about a twenty-minute drive away. After we had packed up, we went off for our evening meal at Kytelers, an old inn the dates back to the 13th century, we delayed our meal waiting for Jim McCartan our driver and the horse crew to return. They were extremely late and, in the end, we had to sit and eat as the tables were all booked for later in the evening. The waiter kept asking when the others would be arriving and all I could say was any minute, I hope! We had just finished our meal when the waiter came to me and said that there was a telephone call for me. This was pre-mobile phone era and the news was bad, our lorry had broken down on the way back to Kilkenny about half a mile from the stables. We had no car with us but transport was quickly arranged and I was driven out to collect the lads. Luckily, it had broken down on a quiet side road just before getting onto the busy Carlow road. By the time we arrived at the stables to rescue the lads the light was fading and I had no option but to leave the lorry until morning. Luckily, we were not travelling home the next day.

Early next morning while everyone else slept off their hangovers, Mark and I set off to try and mend the horsebox. After an hour I had determined that it was a fuel problem. I always carried a full tool kit and many spare parts including fuel filters and by lunchtime we had changed the fuel filters but were still having trouble getting the fuel to flow.   Eventually I came to the horrible realisation that the problem was in the fuel tank. Jim Brennan had organised a trip out in our coach to do a pub crawl of some of the unique out of town country pubs. Mark had two mates over with him and although only sixteen he was desperate to go out with them. He had worked extremely hard all morning with me so I took him back to the hotel so he could go out with the lads. I was at my wit's end how was I going to get the horses home. I would have to re-book the ferry as we had shows both days over the next weekend. I was exhausted and seriously frightened about the consequences of being stranded in Ireland and the costs involved.

I dropped Mark off at the hotel grabbed a pint of Guinness and returned to the lorry with trepidation. It was a major job to get the fuel tank off and the rusty tank straps didn't fill me with optimism. Thankfully, we had not refuelled so the tank was not too heavy I finally got it off and the owner of the stables collected it in his pickup and took it back to the farm so I could decant the fuel into some empty oil drums. When I poured the diesel out, I

immediately saw the problem. The tank was full of old dead leaves. It was an old Gypsy trick and I had a good idea who had done this terrible thing. The tinkers' kids!
It was 4 pm by the time I had replaced the fuel tank and bled the system through. The lorry was running sweet as a nut. I left the lorry at the stables and returned to the hotel hot, sweaty, covered in diesel and very hungry. I had showered and changed into clean clothes ready to go into the town for a late lunch. Foolishly, I decided to have a pint in the bar before ordering a taxi. I was halfway down my drink when Michael Brannigan came into the bar and said "Sam. I'm to take you to a pub in Kells. Your lads are too drunk to drive the coach home." I was not amused they had a dedicated driver who had come on the trip with the sole purpose of driving us around so we didn't have to drink and drive. I had never heard of Kells but it took almost 30 minutes to drive there. To say everyone was drunk was an understatement and this included my son and the other two young lads Tom Arris and Jamie Tom. Robin Hoods Minstrels who had come over with us as part of our show had now morphed into their other act of a fifties skiffle band known as Kick and Rush and dressed in their costumes of top hat and tails with Union Jack waist coats were thumping out well known folk songs with a sprinkling of singalong pop classics. In Ireland, the bush telegraph works like magic if craic is occurring. People had flocked to see this weird English group playing. There were two guitarists and a tea chest double base. The pub was called Shirley's and was so full we had to park a hundred yards down the road but even at that distance the singing could be clearly heard. By the time I entered the pub I was ready to explode in anger but soon realised that causing a scene was going to be counterproductive. Mark my son was the first to greet me. He had a silly grin on his face shouted, "Hi Dad", and promptly fell off his barstool into a heap on the floor. Everyone was trying to apologise and buy me drinks. All I wanted to do was to get them onto the coach and get them back to Kilkenny so I could finally get something to eat but that clearly was not going to happen.

It was then that Jim Brennan approached me and said it was all his fault. He had just wanted to show his appreciation to all of us for the great shows we had done and the huge amount of good-will we had created in the town. I told him the story of the leaves in the fuel tank and that I hadn't eaten since breakfast. He calmed me down and said what a credit all the lads were to me and that they deserved to be allowed to let their hair down. He also said how sorry he was that I had missed such a wonderful afternoon. Then with a sting in the tail, he said if I could just drive them to one more special pub before returning to Kilkenny, he would take me back to his hotel for a meal and as much as I could drink. I took him up on his offer and this was when I really got to know his hotel and his family before leaving the next day. My children and his had become friends and I left with an invite to hunt with the Kilmaganny Hunt.

On our second trip to Ireland not only did we do our shows but we were also involved with a parade through the city of Kilkenny. We followed the Irish military pipe band at the head of the parade. I never realised until that day that bagpipes were as much of a part of Irish culture as they are of Scottish culture. The big difference was that the Irish wore plain orange kilts instead of tartan. The parade attracted huge crowds and was an exciting start to our long weekend. We were also asked to parade the mounted knights at Goran Park Races that were taking place that weekend. The six of us with banners trotted passed the grandstand side by side in a crisp line as good as any cavalry parade. It made a fine sight with all our banners blowing in the wind. The crowd were extremely appreciative and gave a rousing cheer as we passed the grandstand. Flushed by our reception we decided to give them a gallop past on our return past the grandstand. The horses were really on their toes. A couple of them had raced in their earlier lives and thought they were racing again. We performed an impressive wheel manoeuvre a few hundred yards past the end of the grandstand and then started our canter past. The horse jumped off as if they were coming out of flat racing starting stalls instantly at full gallop. Someone shouted, "What the f**k let's just go for it" and so we did! We held our line for a couple of hundred yards and then it was every man for himself because the horses were as we say in the horse world, seriously pissing off with us. The funniest moment was the rider of one of the ex-racehorses desperately trying to hold onto his extra-large banner as he steamed ahead of us. We could see that the pull from the huge banner was starting to pull him back off his horse. His face was contorted trying to keep hold of his banner which we found highly amusing. Fight as he did, he finally relinquish his hold and let the banner go. It was some way past the finishing post before we managed to pull up but we drew a huge roar from the crowd and plenty of free drinks at the bar during the evening. I was just hoping we still had six sound horses for the next day's show and we hadn't knackered any tendons.

The organisers had asked if we could do something different for our second visit and I tentatively suggested our Robin Hood show that we had developed for the shows we were performing at Nottingham Castle as part of the Robin Hood Festival. They thought it was a great idea but both me and some of the troupe had misgivings about how an Irish audience would react to an English hero. We need not have worried, it went down a storm and if anything, they were more enthusiastic about Robin Hood than the people of Nottingham.

My traumatic time on this trip had not ended, high winds and industrial action by one of the ferry companies delayed our departure. After lots of telephoning on our behalf the organisers and myself managed to get us on a ferry out of Dublin to Holyhead in Anglesey but only when the gales subsided. We were to go to the Dublin show ground where stabling was arranged and wait on standby.

Stuart and I drove up to Dublin and found the RDS show ground quite easily as it was not far from the ferry terminal. We were a bit worried about stabling at such a prestigious location but we need not have worried, it was used by the ferry companies on a regular basis as horses were often delayed due to rough seas. We stabled the horses and then had a coffee with the manager. He had transported expensive horse all over the world and his stories were illuminating. You never stop learning about horses and during our conversation he commented about the fact that we bandaged our horses for travelling. Both Stuart and I agreed that it was a fiddly time-consuming business but a necessary evil. Our new friend disagreed and told us that he had found that horses travelled much quieter without anything on their legs because bandages make the legs sweat and can make them kick trying to relieve the itching. We both looked surprised and told him that we had a mare that kicked the side of the lorry constantly. Try her with no bandages he suggested. We did and she stopped kicking. He also said they often used bandages to load and unload young stock as that was when most injuries occurred. We decided not to bandage for the trip home as an experiment. It saved us half an hour at each end of the journey and no injuries or kicking. We never bandaged again.

After our coffee and educational chat, he suggested that we take a taxi into Dublin city centre and see the sights. All we had to do was ring in every hour for a weather update. The taxi driver said.

"Where to lads"

we didn't have a clue so he dropped us off at Grafton Street which was a busy shopping street. It didn't take us long to find a pub and get ourselves a good meal as we had a feeling that it was going to be a long day.

A friendly local recommended walking down to Temple Bar as it was full of trendy bars and restaurants. Having got directions, we were about to head off when we remembered about phoning into the ferry company. To our shock and dismay our new friend at the stables said "Good news lads, get yerselves back here as quick as you can. The wind is dropping and you are on the next ferry". So, our night in Dublin never happened but at least we had spent enough time there to get to know our way around. It's a lovely city and I have been back many times since.

It was a rough slow crossing, we landed at a wet and windy Holyhead around midnight. We still had a long drive of about four hours ahead of us. As we snaked off the boat, we were pulled over by special branch officers, questioned and our lorry thoroughly searched for guns and explosives. The last thing we wanted for ourselves or the horses was another delay but hey-ho we were at war with the IRA, it just added another forty-five minutes onto our trip. During my two visits to Ireland, I had fallen in love with Irish music especially sung by female artists whose haunting melodies really pulled at your heart strings. Thankfully, I had purchased three cassettes by top Irish artists. They were Mary Black, Mary Coughlan, and Delores Keane and by the end of our trip I knew all the words to all of the songs on those three cassettes. Another twenty-one-hour day and the start of a busy day catching up after being away for nearly a week.

A client once said to me, you live a lovely life, riding your horse around the fields all day in the sunshine. If only he knew just the half of it.

Some years later and what seemed like fate I was walking past the Royal Concert Hall in Nottingham on one of my exceedingly rare trips into the city and I saw a poster for a concert by Mary Black. I immediately bought tickets and it was one of the most emotional concerts that I have ever attended, absolutely beautiful!

That autumn of 1993 I started to fly over to Ireland for hunting trips from Birmingham. The cost of air travel had significantly lowered and for one person travelling it was much quicker and cheaper than taking the ferry. Dublin Airport in those days was tiny, very relaxed, and friendly. It was a joy to travel there. My favourite time to travel was just before Christmas because the Irish celebrate the festival much more than we do in England. At Christmas time Dublin Airport was just full of trees and decorations. It was just beautiful and really put you in the mood for the forthcoming festivities. Usually, Jim Brennan picked me up from the airport or I would hire a car which again was easy, quick, and relatively cheap. The only downside to flying was that the airport was on the wrong side of Dublin which made the journey about two hours to Kilkenny.

I often took pork pie and Stilton cheese over as presents and this caused a few funny incidents. I always went hand luggage as after the first few trips I left a hunt jacket over in Kilkenny. Once my plane was delayed on the outward trip to Dublin. We had already been called to the departure lounge which was hot and overcrowded. I managed to find a seat but I noticed that the seat next to me kept changing occupants on a regular basis. As soon as a person left the seat it was grabbed by another. It wasn't until I opened my hand luggage to get out a snack that I realised the reason people were not staying next to me. The stench of warm blue Stilton cheese hit me as soon as I opened my bag. The people who sat next to me must have thought I had terrible B.O. or just farted. On another occasion a few years later, I was at East Midland Airport when I was stopped at security. My bag came out of the scanner and was taken to one side, when I went to collect it the official asked if this was my bag and had I packed it. Having answered in the affirmative he asked me to open it, but not until he told me to do so. It was then that I noticed everyone had been cleared away from where I was standing. I was told from a distance to slowly open my bag and takeout its contents one piece at a time, first to come out was the Stilton followed by my electric shaver. I was required to identify each item as it came out. When I called out Stilton cheese all the officials seemed to breathe a sigh of relief, after the electric razor came out the official returned to the case, checked Stilton, razor, and then apologised for the drama. He explained that the scanner had identified a large organic mass with an electrical device attached to it. All the hallmarks of a homemade bomb. I can laugh about it now but it was very frightening at the time.

I was so lucky to be able to experience the old Ireland for a few years. On my first trip over I remember standing outside the Glendine inn waiting for a taxi. The inn is on one of the main roads out of Kilkenny, I was waiting for ten minutes and only one car came past me. These days the roads are clogged with cars. In the first half of the nineties things were just starting to change and every year I noticed more change. EU money was starting to have an effect. On my first trip in 1992 there were few cars on the roads and the majority of those were old Morris and Austin cars dating back to the late sixties and early seventies.
There were no drink drive laws and it was not unknown for the police to drive drunken drivers home. All of the above changed drastically over the next few years.

My tales of hunting in Ireland and the partying in pubs afterwards soon had friends wanting to come over with me and sample the fun. Jim and Patricia Brennan had shown me and my family great hospitality so it was nice to bring a party of us over to stay at their hotel. On our first group trip Patricia had arranged for us to all hunt with the Kilmaganny's, she also arranged all our hirelings. In those early days I think the cost of hiring a horse was about fifty punts which was usually ten percent lower than pounds. And the cap about thirty punts. For those that don't know, the punt was an Irish pound which has now been replaced by the Euro. They were full on weekends with hunting, visits to quaint out of town pubs and sumptuous meals at varying venues around Kilkenny. There was not a single day that we woke up with a clear head. On our first group trip Jim as usual had arranged something special at the meet bringing drinks and sandwiches to the meet which was not the norm for Irish hunting although it was warmly received. His piece-de-resistance was a large flask of hot poteen, the Irish moonshine made from potatoes, and devastatingly strong. One large measure of this had me floating as we trotted down the road and I nearly fell of cantering around the corner of the first field. Thanks to god, as the Irish say, my head started to clear after galloping around a few fields. As we chatted to the locals at the meet one friendly fellow commented about the stirrup cup. He went on to say that he had heard that the English even had pre dinner drinks commenting, "Jesus, if we did that over here, we would never get around to the eating". The big thing I was learning about Irish hunting was that each pack's country is vastly different with both horse and rider needing to cope with each country's unique challenges. The question people always ask me is, did you take your own horses over to ride, I just laugh when this comes up. If you tried to ride an English horse you and your horse both would be lucky to survive the first obstacle. I say obstacle because you don't gallop across the country leaping hedges, post and rails or stone walls, you fight your way across an almost impenetrable country. Each hunt has its own horse hirer and their horses are trained specifically for the local obstacles you might meet. I am not saying that you cannot hunt a good horse in several different hunt countries but it does increase the risk.

I only hunted with a few packs and the type of obstacles you came across varied greatly. The common denominator was that nothing was straightforward, every obstacle was littered with brambles, bushes, and trees, both on take-off and landing. Both you and your horse had to weigh up all the problems before you committed to jumping. People talk about jumping banks and I imagined them like a wider version of a stone wall that you would find in high Derbyshire. In the Scarteen country you can find banks that are more akin to a railway embankment but with deep wide drains on both sides. They are covered with brambles, bushes and trees thrown in for good measure. The Kilmaganny's had deep narrow drains but the banks were sometimes more like a stone wall or even narrower, very often there was another drain on the other side so the horse would land on barely a-foot-wide piece of earth and instantly skip off to clear the other drain. I witnessed a horse and rider get stuck in one of these narrow drains. The horse was about 17hh and its withers were below ground level. It had slipped back off the bank and was sideways to the bank in the ditch. It was flailing about in the ditch trying to get out, the poor rider's legs were wedged against the walls of the ditch and every lurch the horse made crushed his legs. He was a big, strong man but I can still hear his screams of agony as I write this passage. It really brought it home to me that even the little narrow drains could be deadly if your horse missed a footing. I have witnessed a lot of horrendous falls in my time but this shook me up more than any other.

The nicest banks to jump were about five feet high and five feet wide you could hop up unto them and then pop off them, they were like an upside-down bounce and great fun as long as you managed to miss the trees growing on top of bank or the low branches. I twice knocked myself senseless after misjudging how low a branch was and ruined my best velvet Hunt cap, although it did save me from a fractured skull. Lou suffered a broken nose in a similar mishap and had to attend all the social gatherings including a hunt ball looking like a boxer that had just taken a severe battering. As most of the people were hunting people that we were meeting she didn't feel so self-conscious about two black eyes and a fat nose as other ladies recounted their encounters with low branches and trees. It was more a badge of honour. I could write a whole chapter about banks and trees but it might deterred readers following in my footsteps.

I have mentioned a bit about drains or ditches and dykes as we refer to them on this side of the pond. They also come in all shapes and sizes with one common denominator they are all extremely deep and are often full of water. Drowning is a serious possibility! The widest drain that I ever jumped was on Patricia's mother's horse, it was out with the Kilkenny's and it was more like a river with at least twelve feet of water to clear and steep banks on take-off and landing. I quickly learnt that it was better to be near the front and jump early, as the landing side of drains quickly get very slippery from water being splashed up from the back legs of horses that don't quite make the other side. Once the landing bank becomes slippery the carnage starts. Thankfully on that day my horse gently slid down the take-off side and then made a fabulous leap across the water clearing it with ease, it was one of the most exhilarating jumps I have ever done. To clear such a distance from a standstill was like being fired from a catapult. If only I had a photograph of it, it would have pride of place on my office wall.

Water has always been a fear of mine so whenever I came across a drain that was full to the brim my stomach always somersaulted. I had taken a party over from Nottingham and we were having a day with the Kilmaganny's. We were having a good hunt and having a lot of fun until we came to a fairly wide drain with a generous amount of water in it. However, we were well mounted and it was a clean jump with no brambles or trees to contend with. However, it was causing some problems, I jumped it fairly early and already the landing side of the bank was becoming very slippery from horses' back legs dropping in the water. The other problem was that the horses were turning sharp right on landing as we had strict instructions from the master to keep to the headlands (the edge of the field). This was causing the horses to jump at an angle to follow the horse in front. Just before taking off, I saw what was happening so I tugged my left rein and slapped my hunt whip down it's right shoulder. This just about kept it straight but it felt like a giant magnet was trying to pull us to the right. I shouted back to the rest of the party to keep straight but it was easier said than done. Lou's horse pecked on landing, her fall was soft but her horse slipped back into the ditch and disappeared under the water. Lou was riding Patricia's mother's horse and she still tells the story of how she desperately tried to keep its head above the water to stop it drowning while all the time thinking how I can go back and tell Francoise that she had let her horse drown. Thankfully, after what seemed like an age the horse scrambled out of the drain dripping with water and mud which is a common sight when hunting in Ireland. Unfortunately, the drain claimed one of our friends who broke her wrist in the fall. I tried to get her to remount as we were in very boggy country and I had no idea how far the nearest road was or where the meet had been held but she refused because of the pain. After cloying her way through the bog for about a hundred yards she decided that that the pain of remounting was better than trying to cross the bog on foot.

Talking of bogs brings me nicely onto the next great hazard of Irish hunting - the fabled Irish bog. When out hunting with Patricia she would often point out dangerous areas of bog and warn me to follow very carefully in the footsteps of the horse in front of me ending the warning with, "If you stray to the side of the track, you'll be gone and we will never see you again".

On one occasion, Kim Turner the long serving master of the Quorn Tuesday country came over with us to hunt. As we crossed what looked like a normal scrub field Patricia gave me the warning which I passed back to Kim who was following me. Kim laughed and told me to stop making up tales to frighten her. I insisted that I was just passing on a message from Patricia. Kim was having none of it, we were long standing friends and knew my mischievous sense of humour. As soon as the hounds checked Kim sought out Patricia and spoke. "Mr Humphrey here is trying to terrify me saying that field we just crossed had a bog that could swallow me up if I didn't follow exactly the horse in front of me".

"That's true somebody went in a couple of years ago and it took two hours to pull them out with a tractor" she replied.

Kim went noticeably quiet but still not sure if we were winding her up. During the next hour she questioned several other people who confirmed how dangerous the bog was. Kim's final words on the matter were.

"You are all bloody mad".

On another occasion Lou and I took a pupil of mine over to sample the delights of Ireland. I had coached her for several years from a child to a teenager and at the time of the trip she was about eighteen and was regularly riding in my Teamchase team. She and her mother were both keen Foxhunters and members of the Atherstone Hunt. Her name was Ginny Sherwin. Ginny loved jumping and the thrill of the chase. She had originally wanted to event but the nice thoroughbred she bought had other ideas. Like many talented horses I have known they do not always excel in the job that we buy them for. This was the case with Ginny's horse who excelled at teamchasing and in the hunting field, as did his owner. During our day out with Patricia and the Kilmaganny's I was constantly giving Ginny tips on how to tackle the wide range of new obstacles that confronted her. Like Kim Turner she was convinced that I was trying to wind her up and scare her to death. It was late in the afternoon Patricia suddenly said,
"Orr no, I think he's going to take us through the horrible bog".

Patricia went on to explain that it was a large area of flooded bog land. There was a track across the bog known by the hunt and locals. However, you could not see the path because the water was jet black and the surface was covered with a green algae. As we entered the bog the water came up to the horses bellies and Patricia reaffirmed her warning of following exactly where the horse in front went or else, we would disappear into to bog. Ginny laughed and was convinced we were just trying to frighten her. At that very moment, a horse that was about six horses ahead of us started to flounder and then both horse and rider disappeared under the black brackish water. The bog was like something that you would see in a horror film. It was littered with black dead tree stumps which protruded out of the bog all ragged and spiky from where the dead upper part of the tree had snapped off. A swear word slipped from both my mouth and Ginny's. All that was visible of the horse and rider was a well battered velvet hunt cap floating on the surface of the bog. For what seemed an age both horse and rider were gone, but it was probably only a second or so and then there was an explosion of water as the horse and then the rider broke the surface. This panicked the other horses and everyone was fighting to keep their horses still so as not to suffer the same fate. Thankfully, they both found the submerged track and with help got remounted. Ginny had gone very pale and whispered, "I thought you were just trying to frighten me and wind me up. My God it was all true"! We continued on and experienced several more incidents of horses slipping off the unseen path and flailing around in the water but all the riders stayed on board and quickly found the track again. I held my breath every step of the way, I am not a strong swimmer and I am terrified of water. The poor girl that went under had to go home as quick as possible before hyperthermia set in.

Something that I thought was a joke on my first hunting trip with Patricia was her asking where my change of clothes were as we were about to set off to the meet. Every time I told friends who came over hunting with me to bring a change of clothes, they all laughed and were convinced it was a prank. The times I have come back from hunting in Ireland soaked through to the skin and been glad of a change of clothes are too many to recount. On one occasion down with the Scarteen better known as the "Tan's" my thick, wool hunt coat was so sodden with rain it was so heavy that I could hardly pick it up. On another trip to the Tan's, we had a quiet day and struggled to find a fox. There was a lot of standing around and hacking but no good runs to warm you up. The weather worsened and a bitter wind steadily strengthened as the day wore on, by mid-afternoon small specks of icy snow were cutting into my face. My body was getting colder and colder as the wind-driven snow streaked across the wild open hill tops. I had hired a horse so I had to stay out to the bitter end clinging on to the hope of finding a four o' clock fox. Unfortunately, all foxes were sensibly tucked up in their nice warm earths. When Patricia picked me up at the end of day, I could hardly feel my legs. Although I was wearing hunting breeches, they were the nylon-based ones and not the thick woollen ones worn by hunt staff. I staggered to her Land Rover Discovery which was another Irish anomaly in that it had no rear windows or seats. This allowed it to be classed as a commercial vehicle and avoided a higher car tax. Once I got into the car, I thought that I would soon warm up but instead I started to shiver and shake, I just could not seem to get warm despite having the heater on full bore and drinking a large flask of hot chicken bouillon that Patricia always brought with her for the end of the day along with generous portions of ham sandwiches. It was a long drive back and I still could not feel my knees when I arrived back at Jim and Patricia's house. It took well over an hour in the bath to get my knees warm again, all the time topping the bath up with more scalding hot water. I also warmed my inside with a generous measure of Irish Whiskey which probably not what a doctor would prescribe for hypothermia but it seemed a good idea at the time.

I paint rather a dower picture of hunting in Ireland but it is anything but that. It is far more fun to me than English hunting, a bit like the difference between soccer and rugby. In England we are far more formal and everyone defers to the master. The master leads the field and nobody passes the master. In Ireland it is more the huntsman that leads the field but not always. Many hunts have done away with red coats so it is not easy to spot the master and often he will not necessarily be at the front of the field. When a fox is found the field go into a frenzy to get with the hounds. It is like some alien has just injected everyone with 10,000 volts of electricity, - everyone seems to be buzzing. Although there are some regular routes, the nature of the land requires more of a treasure hunt approach with searchers fanning out seeking a suitable exit from each field. The longer it takes to find a way through, the more manic the mood becomes as the once deafening sound of the hounds screaming on the scent gets quieter as they pull further away from the followers. The resolve of the field to overcome the barriers that they face in crossing the country has never ceased to amaze me.

I once watched as the field was faced with an impenetrable wall of thorns and brambles, riders rode up and down trying to find a weak spot. I would have given up hope but they kept looking as it was the only hope of getting to the hounds, the neighbouring farm was a no-go area. When somebody suggested going that way the answers was, "Go yer self if yer want to get shot". Finally, someone found what might be a weak spot. It looked very impenetrable to me! A child on a small pony was called up and told to push into the thorns. The child lay flat on the pony's neck and with lots of encouragement from two dismounted riders from behind, the child and pony started to make progress into the thicket. Once the hindquarters of the pony had disappeared into the thicket, a slightly larger pony followed and then a small horse. Suddenly a shout of jubilation came from the far side, they were through! As I went through the hole, thorns and brambles clawed at my clothing and unprotected face. Low branches scraped along my back as I leant forward trying to get as low as possible. I was met on the other side by jubilant bloody faces grinning as the blood continued to trickle down from the scratches on their faces. It was not over, even as the last person exited the hole two men had dismounted and were preparing to block the gap and make the field stock proof once again. This was locals hunting and caring for the land they were hunting. Unlike the shires of England where visitors outnumber the locals and don't give a hoot about the damage, that they do to farmers land.

Hunting is a true day out in Ireland and before the strict, drink drive laws came into force the day of pleasure would be extended to the pub or very often several pubs.

The first party I brought over for hunting were treated to a day that they would never forget.

It started with an early drink in the bar just after an early breakfast before setting off to the meet and our unknown mounts for the day. I think that the meet was at Windgap which was about a 40-minute drive from the Club House Hotel. We had a minibus to take us and then bring us back after the hunt. Our day's hunting was not the best but that is hunting and we all had a thoroughly good time especially as none of the party had been to Ireland except for Lou and me.

At the end of day, we were retired to the local pub which even surprised me. Not only was it a pub but also the local food shop and also a hardware store. It was a gorgeous pub and like so many other pubs in Ireland they look small and quaint from the outside but once you get inside, they have other large rooms a bit like Dr Who's Tardis. We settled down to several pints with our fellow hunting compatriots and were expecting it all to come to an end as soon as our minibus arrived to collect us. We were having a great time and I think all of us were hoping that the bus might be delayed.

Much to our surprise Jim Brennan arrived with a large, insulated container full of Irish stew. After a long days hunting and a few drinks, it was just what the doctor ordered for we all had a bad case of the munchies. After an hour of eating and of course more drinking an Irish band turned up and the party really started, dancing, singing, and drinking - it was a good craic as the Irish would say. It all wound up about 11.30 and as we all staggered out to our minibus drunk as lords, I noticed that all the horse trailers complete with horses still onboard, were still in the car park. That was something you would never see in England even in Derbyshire.

By the time we got back to the hotel it was gone midnight but the forty-minute drive back had renewed our thirst and conveniently the hotel bar was still open. Whenever I am drinking, I get ravenously hungry so to end the day, I along with several others found ourselves in Super-macs eating a burger at 2am, still in our hunting clothes, covered in mud, and dried blood on our faces. Not your normal hunting day in England.

I had been out hunting with the Scarteen and had a great day tackling some huge banks and big drains. Patricia Brennan had taken me down to the meet which was well over an hour's travel from Kilkenny. As always, she had packed a basket full of sandwiches and a large flask of chicken bouillon. I had brought with me the obligatory change of clothes in a supermarket bag and both the food and clothes had been deposited in the cab of the horse hirer's lorry for later. The other thing she always did when I was off on my own was to arrange a buddy for me in case of an accident and to advise me on the country. On this occasion it was the local doctor from Fethard which is also the home of the famous hunting, racing pub and restaurant McCarthy's Bar, but that's another story. Dr Mat had been my buddy on several occasions and we got on famously discussing a range of topics in great depth during lulls in the hunting. Food and drink were our most common topic of conservation and I had first met him in The Ship Inn restaurant in Dunmore East. The Ship was an exceptionally good fish restaurant and Lou and I were holidaying at this quaint little seaside village just south of Waterford with Jim and Patricia. Dr Mat was an old family friend of the Brennan family and seeing them in the same restaurant had popped over to our table to pay his respects.

Out hunting on the day in question during a conversation about food he suddenly told me that he knew of a particularly good restaurant not far away from where we were at the moment. He also knew the farmer next door to the restaurant and was sure we could stable our horses for a couple of hours while we had a good meal. I was flabbergasted, food definitely did not rank higher than hunting for me and having just paid out about three hundred euros for my horse and cap, I had no intention of missing two hours' worth of hunting to eat a meal.

On another occasion I was telling him about my experiences of riding the back country in New Zealand and he confessed that it was one of his ambitions to explore the world on horseback following it up with a profound statement that I will never forget. He said, "I keep telling my patients that this life is not a rehearsal it's the real thing, you only have one chance so make the most of it". That was one of the best statement I have ever heard especially as we were galloping over a field at the time. Those words still influence my life to this day.

At the end of the day horseboxes were waiting to collect horses and hounds at yet another obscure road junction with no signposts. The diehards of the hunt spent the next fifteen minutes reliving the day sharing drinks and sandwiches before heading home. I kept looking for Patricia's discovery to appear around the bend at any moment as one by one the horseboxes left. Finally, it was just me in the middle of nowhere sitting on a stonewall with just my change of clothes and a wicker picnic basket for company. Time ticked by and I was expecting Patricia to appear at any moment. I nibbled away at the sandwiches and poured small cups of bouillon to pass the time. As the sun disappeared the temperature started to fall and despite my thick woollen hunt coat, I was starting to get cold. The light was fading and I was hoping to see the lights of a village but I could see no sign of civilisation. I started to march back and forwards to keep warm trying to work out what to do. I had been on my

own now for over thirty minutes, eaten all my sandwiches and drunk all my chicken bouillon plus my hip flask, and I was getting very cold. The big dilemma was to stay where I was or risk trying to find a village and ring Jim or Patricia. There was no signal for my mobile where I was but the next village could be miles away - I had absolutely no idea where I was. I decided to give it another ten minutes then I would have to make a move as it was nearly fully dark. Just a few minutes later car headlights appeared and my hopes soared. Finally, the headlights came around the bend. The approaching car was clearly not a discovery, my heart sank. Then I noticed that it was slowing down. Were they going to offer me a lift, my mind was racing trying to think how to respond? The car slowed to a halt alongside me and the window wound down. To my surprise it was Jim Brennan in his jaguar. "Thank God, I've found you, I've been driving around for ages looking for you, I don't know this area at all well" he said. I was in the car in a flash and said, "Can you turn the heater up, I need to thaw out". Jim explained that Patricia had been held up and had asked him to go down and collect me but not knowing the area had known idea how to find me. It was the early days of mobile phones and getting a signal in remote locations was nigh impossible.
It was certainly a memorable hunting day.

The other pack that I hunted with was the Tipperary or "The Tipps" as they are commonly known as. The Tipps country bordered the Kilmaganny's country but they were like chalk and cheese both with their country and their size. They were like the Quorn of Ireland wearing scarlet and having much a larger number of followers. Their country was much more open with larger fields and a more galloping type of country. I met many famous people out with the Tipps and had some great but vastly different kind of fun but never the life-threatening kind as with the other hunts. I always had a warm welcome and there was certainly no shortage of foxes.

As I have already mentioned I have a fear of deep water and one day out with the Kilmaganny's we were having a fierce hunt. I was riding woody one of Patricia's horses. I had ridden him several times and we just gelled together. I trusted him and we had shared many hairy moments together and I trusted him implicitly. The hounds were screaming and the drains were flying by and I was soon with the lucky few to still have sight of the hounds and huntsman. Eventually we came to a narrow road which had a stone bridge that went over a small river. The huntsman tried desperately to find a way onto the road as his hounds screamed on towards a covert on the other side of the road. The gate onto the road was padlocked and barbed wire was tangled around the top bar of the gate making it impossible to jump. The hedge along the roadside was also high, solid and well wired, so no way out onto the road. The searchers spread out like a fan looking for a way out and quickly a cry went up.

"Over here by the bridge!"

The huntsman was there in a flash, his horse paused and then after much kicking and shouting the horse leapt forward and disappeared in a plume of water. Oh shit! I thought we are jumping into a river and a deep one at that. The field had to push through a hedge and then creep along the bank towards the bridge to where a stone wall had been built to stabilise the bank and the bridge. Here there was just enough room to shuffle the horse around and make the leap off the wall into the river. The drop was six to eight feet and the water was coming over the top of the saddle on landing. None of the horses were keen to make the leap and neither were the riders, especially me. Worse still was it was slow going to the jump off point. Plenty of time to contemplate all the things that could go wrong. The only good thing I could see was that the river was narrow at this point hence the very deep water, two bounding lurches from the horse after landing in the water carried you to the other bank that was soil and easy to get up.

Finally, it was my turn, I pushed Woody forward, he hesitated and had a good look around sizing up the task in front of him. All good Irish hunters do this and it is important not to push them to jump until you feel that they have got it all worked out in their head. It only takes a few seconds but rush it at your own peril. I grasped the pommel of the saddle, kicked, hoped, and prayed, although I am not religious. Wow! What a buzz! Woody bless him was foot perfect and it was all over in a couple of seconds. Wet up to my crutch but thankfully no swimming. The hunt proceeded at great pace after our hold up at the river but it was difficult going as the other side of the river was very wet, marshy ground. Our progress was again delayed by the river which we had to cross yet again. The crossing looked much easier than the first one with shallow fast flowing water over a shingle bed to the centre of the river and then deeper water on the far side with a soil bank about a metre high. The huntsman made light work of it but it was hard for the horse getting out of the deep water and up the bank. Everyone was keen to get across and catch up with the hounds. The next rider crossed with no problems but the third horse suddenly flipped over backwards as it got to the far bank and disappeared under the water with its rider. As I stared in horror, I saw the rider's hard hat floating away down the river followed by a shout from the unfortunate rider as he surfaced saying.

"Quick someone catch my hat before it floats away".

The same thing happened to the next two riders and then one made it unscathed. I studied the crossing very carefully and noted that those riders getting into difficulties were aiming for the easier exit where the riverbank was slightly lower. To say it was carnage was an understatement as more horses disappeared into what must have been a very deep hole in the riverbed. I hung back and studied the mayhem until I was sure about the extent of the hole. The lower bank was drawing the horses to it like a magnet and so into the hole. Woody was a great horse and I had every confidence that he could cope with the larger bank and hold the line that I asked of him. I took a large deep breath and set off across the river hoping and praying that I had got it right and expecting to go under at any moment. We held our line and except for a scrabbling exit up the steep bank, the crossing was uneventful and I joined the ranks of the jubilant few who had made the crossing successfully.

We spent the next twenty minutes in a very boggy wood hunting our quarry hopping over endless small drainage ditches before the hounds pushed the fox out into marshland. As we left the dark, wet woodland that was rather foreboding, we burst out into bright warm sunlight. Good for drying wet clothes but bad for scenting conditions and the hounds soon lost their fox. The day stayed unseasonably warm and a bit of an anti-climax after all the river drama.

Moral of the story is - Never forget your change of clothes when hunting in Ireland!

These days I think we often over dominate our horses and don't let the horse think for itself. In many cases it is not intentional, it is the technical nature of the popular horse sports these days that require the rider to be more in control. Hunting in Ireland and riding strange horses that I had never sat on before reminded me of the joy of working in a true equal partnership with the horse. It is that waiting for the horse to work out how it is going to tackle a complicated manoeuvre and sensing when the horse has worked it all out and then giving a kick to say ok let's do it. I found this awfully hard to do in the beginning as I was one for dominating my horse until then. In Ireland I kept coming across obstacles that I had no idea how to tackle. When I asked for advice, the answer was always the same. Leave it to the horse, give him time to work it out and he will look after you!

I remember once hunting with Patricia Brennan, I think it was near Stoneyford and it was with the Kilmaganny's. Hounds had run into the ruins of a large Church or Abbey. Just the odd wall and a gable end protruded out of the brambles that had taken over the site, we slowly moved through the site until we were in what had probably been the main building. It was late in the day and there was only a handful of us left, slowly following the progress of the hounds as they hunted through the thick undergrowth. We came to what had probably been a large window but was now just a gaping hole in the wall. The lead rider jumped through the hole and disappeared. Patricia and I were next. "You go first" she kindly said to me. When I got to the edge, I could not believe what we were jumping into. It was a good six to eight-foot drop into a mixture of brambles and huge chunks of fallen stone some up to three feet square all tangled up in brambles. These were leg breakers and I was riding my friend's best horse. I turned to Patricia and said. "We can't jump here; the horses will break their legs".

"They will be fine, just give him plenty of time to look and work it all out" came the reply.

After what seemed like an age my horse crouched down and then very gently plopped off the edge landed on one leg between two large stones and manoeuvred his legs over several more stones as if he were playing hopscotch. I never did a thing except sit as light as possible and try and stay in balance with him. That horse knew exactly what he was doing and had worked it all out before he made a move. If I had tried to make him do that jump it would have ended in disaster. It was one of the most incredible things I have seen a horse do and I will never forget that moment.

Hunting in Ireland opened my eyes to many more of the abilities that a horse possesses and riding and meeting horse people from around the world have opened my eyes to even more. All I ever hear today in England is that this horse is a dressage horse or show jumper, the list is endless. They talk as if the horse is only capable of doing that discipline, this is not true. I have worked with many horses that have excelled at more than one discipline. Sure, if you concentrate on just a microcosm of that ability it will excel in that, but so much is wasted. Geeks have their place in this world and produce great things but give me a person that has travelled and done lots of things any day. Years ago, a man would spend more time with his horse than he did with his wife. I personally think we have lost more knowledge about horses than we have gained.

I was lucky enough to be over in Kilkenny for the opening meet of the Kilmaganny's one year. Again, I was borrowing one of the Brennan family horses. It was unseasonably warm that day and there seemed no hurry to start as old friendships were rekindled in the pub. Eventually there was a loud banging of a pint glass on the bar and someone shouted.

"Right lads best drink up and get mounted. The priest is here ready and waiting".
Glasses were quickly drained and the bar quickly emptied leaving just two old boys wearing cloth caps and smoking in the corner.
Outside the hounds were waiting in the car park. A shout came for us all to gather round and the Priest came out of the pub dressed in his finery. A prayer was said that included a request to the man upstairs for a good hunting season. Then to my astonishment he proceeded to walk through the hounds sprinkling them with holy water and blessing them. That was it the horn blew and the familiar cry of

"Hounds please".

And we were off! The weather was much too warm for hunting and hounds never found. However, we were high up and the views over the valleys and hills with the mountains in the distance made it all worthwhile. When hunting in Ireland so often you are hemmed in with high hedges that obscure your view but then you breakout onto the top of a high hill and you are treated to stunning views for miles around. It is quite magical!

My biggest regret is I did not go hunting in Ireland enough, more over that I never got to visit the Galway Blazers over in the west and sample their formidable stonewalls!

Most horse events and especially the high-risk ones go hand in hand with drinking and partying and this is the case for both England and Ireland. However, I think the Irish have the upper hand when it comes to enjoying themselves.
On both sides of the water this has been severely subdued in recent years with the much stricter drink drive laws. Since these laws have come in, many rural pubs have reduced hours or closed completely, which is incredibly sad as they provided a social lifeline to many small rural communities, often acting as a local shop and post office as well as serving food and drink. I was privileged to visit some of these pubs thanks to the hunts and Jim Brennan. They were tiny pubs often in very remote locations that you would never find without local knowledge and certainly not on any tourist route. I have forgotten most of their names and would never know how to find them on their own.

Two pubs stand out as truly from a by gone age and both have now sadly closed. O'Gorman's was a tiny one room pub not far from Kells. It was run by a very elderly couple who were also farmers. Their farmhouse was a small cottage with two small rooms, one was their living room and the other was the bar. You could only enter the bar if you were known to them and even then, you still had to ask permission to enter unless you were one of the local regulars. Outsiders like me had to be vouched for and were treated with great suspicion. The bar itself was very plain, a couple of old chairs and a plank of wood supported by two rusting five-gallon oil drums. The walls had chipped plaster and were last painted well over thirty years ago. A high plain shelf ran around the seating area and had a variety of cigarettes and canned food on it. Some of the cans showed signs of rust. The couple were in their late seventies or maybe even in their eighties. Toilets for the men were anywhere in the crew-yard along with the cattle. The ladies toilet was in a small outhouse and consisted of yet another five-gallon oil drum with the top cut out and a toilet seat balanced precariously on top. Whenever a female asked for the toilet, the landlady would accompany her and stand guard outside the toilet door as the door didn't have a lock. I might add that I only know the detailed description of this toilet thanks to the vivid tales provided by Lou and her friends. The thing that caused the most amusement with the ladies was the loud drumming noise when they passed water into the thin tin oil drum.

Another old pub we visited had actually closed down but reopened for the hunt meet. It was like going into a derelict house. The plaster was falling off the walls and ceilings, the bar was tiny and well worn. There was no draught beer only bottles and the crown bottle tops were rusty. Most people were electing to drink hot port or a hot toddy as the safer option. The water for these was being boiled in an old aluminium kettle circa the nineteen thirties with a very frayed power lead. The kettle was being boiled in a separate room which I glimpsed into when the landlord opened the door to get the kettle. The room was full of steam as the kettle did not have an automatic cut off switch for when the water was boiling. Readers of my age will remember walking into a steam filled room as a child when someone had forgotten to switch the kettle off. Not only was this room full of steam but there was a pile of rubble in the centre of the room where the ceiling had collapsed. When the ladies went to the toilet it was so disgusting, they decided to stand guard for each other and squat on a piece of secluded grass as it was the safer option.

There was a tiny bar not far from the Club House Hotel called Little Andy's. How he made it pay I will never know it was so tiny. Andy was a musician and the walls were covered with musical memorabilia. A lovely dark intimate bar, sadly like the others no more!

Another lovely bar but much larger was Shirley's Bar in Kells which was often a stop off after hunting. Always a big roaring fire and full of characters. We once met a man in dinner dress who was quite drunk. It was about five-thirty in the evening. It was the day after the hunt ball and he obviously still had not been home. On seeing us dressed in our hunting clothes, he shouted across the bar room.

"Been after foxes have you! I have a fox if you want it!"

We took no notice of him and he got up and staggered out of the room. A few moments later he returned dragging a very smelly dead fox which he ceremonially laid out in front of the fire. For those of you that know the smell of a fox you can imagine how quickly it stank out the bar aided by the hot fire. The Landlady reacted swiftly ejecting both the man and his fox swiftly, but even with windows and doors open the smell clung in the bar. Certainly, a night to remember. Sadly, also now closed down along with so many others that were national treasures.

Ireland a place of so many happy memories!

Chapter Nine
Riding Abroad

Every time I have ridden abroad, I have gained more equine knowledge and an understanding of why people in different countries have different styles of riding. Also, the different ways that they look after their horses.

My first experience of riding abroad was on my honeymoon, it was my first trip to a foreign country unless you count a couple of holidays in North Wales. The honeymoon was in Cala Llonga in Ibiza. If I remember correctly, it cost £29 for ten days full board in a recently built sixties style concrete hotel. It was also my first flight in an aeroplane which I have to admit I found a bit scary. Even to this day with dozens of flights under my belt and a love of visiting foreign lands I still find them a necessary evil. Of course, we were conned into the obligatory day trip which unbeknown to me included a ride to the top of a mountain on a donkey. Lou still talks about it to this day; she still thinks it was one of the funniest moments of our forty-seven years of marriage. I tend to think of it as the most degrading moment. At first, I down right refused to get on and told her to go up by herself. I would wait under a tree until she returned but then she played the honeymoon card and much to my embarrassment mounted the animal. Even worse was that I was given instructions by a Fawlty Towers Manuel character on how to ride the bloody thing in broken English. Sitting on a cushion strapped onto the back of a donkey that had only one gear, and that gear was walk, it was not the highlight of my equine career and I have nothing more to say on the subject except that I have never repeated the experience.

What my trip to Ibiza did do was to spark a desire to visit foreign lands and cultures and writing this in 2020 the year of Coronavirus this will be the first year that I haven't travelled abroad since our honeymoon in 1973. A couple of years later our good friend and fellow jouster Clive Broadbent was offered a job in America. It was an exceptionally good job and he decided to emigrate and make a new life in West Virginia. Once settled he invited us to visit and so we made the momentous decision to fly the Atlantic and visit him, thanks to the new no frills budget airline Laker Airways.
It was a fraught journey; we missed our connection in New York and had to stay overnight in the city. Watching American films, I thought we spoke the same language but we had to constantly ask people to repeat things several times before we could understand what they were saying. They spoke so fast and with such a strange accent. We were so naïve we didn't even know that we had to change airports for our next leg to Pittsburgh. Luckily, the airline put us up in a hotel overnight and arranged for taxis to pick us up next morning and take us to the other airport which was called LaGuardia. Our second leg of our journey took us to Pittsburgh. It was autumn or fall as the Americans call it and as we descended into Pittsburgh the colours of the forests were utterly amazing. Flying internally in the USA was very relaxed with no security. It was like catching a bus and our next and final leg that took us to Parkersburg was so laid back it was unbelievable. We were travelling on a Boeing 737 which was a relatively new plane in the early seventies. No sooner had we taken off than we were starting our descent into a small airport. We landed, dropped a few people off and some more boarded, then in a matter of minutes we were on our way again. The engines never stopped, they just dropped the steps down for people to get on and off. I will always remember the pilot saying over the intercom.
"Ok folks hold tight. I'm just goanna crank the engines up to full power and we will be on our way in just a few minutes. Next stop will be Parkersburg".
Oh, if air travel was still like that today. What joy!

In Parkersburg, Clive had lined up a busy couple of weeks for us including a visit to a horse college which was truly something else. It was and still is called Meredith Manor and was the brainchild of Dr Ron Meredith and his wife Faith. I should have realised that this was the future but was too blind to see it. We were warmly welcomed and Ron took a lot of time out to spend with us. The complex was massive, well over one hundred and fifty horses all stabled. The accounts for student fees were computerised, something that was unheard of in England at that time, there were three indoor schools all flood-lit and the teachers used microphones when teaching. The new indoor school that they had just finished was so big they could hold multiple classes simultaneously. He had on site vets, and a laboratory for doing regular worm counts on all the horses.

Ron was a specialist in western riding and it was the no frills attached kind, straight and true. He taught me a lot in just a few days and I will be forever grateful. It made Lou and I think a lot about our business and how we needed to modernise if we were to progress, we put a lot of the things we had seen and learnt into practice in the coming years. In a few days I learnt about whip breaking a horse, barrel racing, firing a gun on a horse and how to do worm counts from horse droppings.

The whip breaking sounds very cruel but when Ron Explained it to me it made sense. Cowboys riding the range often many miles from any form of civilisation relied on their horses for survival. If your horse was killed or severely injured, you needed a replacement quickly to survive. If you could drive a wild horse into a box canyon to contain it and then hold it there by cracking your bullwhip every time it moved, it would eventually stand still. At this point, the horse was broken in and the cowboy could tack it up and ride it away. Not the most humane way of breaking a horse and I am not suggesting it be used today, but a lifesaving piece of knowledge from 150 years ago and an interesting window into how a horse's mind works.

In Europe we think of barrel racing as a kid's gymkhana game but in America and Canada it is a serious sport with high prize money. Ron told me how he had left his Zippo cigarette lighter in his shirt breast pocket when doing some barrel racing and the G-force of the turn had torn the pocket. That is serious stuff.

Firing a handgun or a rifle from the back of a horse usually didn't bother horses because it was so quick. However, he told me some highly strung horses never took to it. You start by firing the gun on the ground until the horse is ok with it before firing it mounted and never close to its head and especially its ears. As with all good horse trainers his mantra was the same.

"Slowly, slowly. Repetition, repetition".

Doing worm counts was easy for me to learn with my background of working in the research laboratories at British Gypsum some years earlier. When I returned home, I managed to acquire the chemicals required and started to do worm counts on our horses but to get a really accurate result I needed a much higher quality microscope than I could not afford. Having said that, it did show me which horses had no worms and which had a high infestation so we could target our worming programme.

Our visit to Meredith Manor led to Dad being invited to go over and lecture at the university and also, they sent some students over for training at our school.

My next foreign riding experience was again in America but this time in the far south of that vast country in the sunshine state of Florida. I have covered much of that trip in the Film and Television chapter however the stables that hired me the horse for the photo shoot was a place of great interest for me. I saw my first American horse barn and liked the concept. These days they are very common here in England but at the beginning of the eighties I had never come across one. The daughter of the stables owner had a retired Olympic Dressage horse but strangely she knew nothing about Dressage. At that time, I used to ride dad's stallion quite a lot and although I never had an interest in dressage, I did know how to press the right buttons to show off the horse's ability. Everyone at the stables was fascinated by my English style of riding which they found so different to the western way of riding. As a thank you to Ed the owner, I gave his daughter a couple of lessons on her dressage horse. She was a good rider and quickly adapted the English style and by the time I left, she was already sampling some the delights of this well-trained horse.

In 1985 we were asked to perform a jousting show in Cyprus as part of the opening ceremony for a new luxury hotel in the town of Paphos called the Cyprius Marris Hotel. It was too expensive to fly our horses out there and it looked like we would have to turn this very lucrative job down. Thankfully at the last minute the organisers managed to persuade the British Army to lend us their polo ponies. The horse world is a small one, and when I asked, how on earth they had managed to persuade the army to do such a thing, the answer came back that the officer in charge of the polo ponies knew us very well and had no hesitation in allowing us to use them. The officer turned out to be Tim Hercock, his father was a joint master of the Quorn and Tim also went on to become a master of the Quorn after leaving the army. My brothers and me had hunted with Tim and his sister for many years but I had no idea that he had joined the Army and was posted to Cyprus.

The polo ponies were a delight to ride, quick and nimble. They were also used to galloping at each other and having sticks waved around their heads, almost ready trained jousting horses. We had great fun in Cyprus, it was a lovely hotel and we were part of a large group of film and television celebrities who were also there for the opening ceremonies. The jousting took place on the beach and was the highlight of the of the opening. Even the president of Cyprus was there.

We also spent a lot of time at the army recreational base known as Happy Valley training the horses where again we were very well looked after. We lived the life of true celebrities that week, with free food, drink, and entertainment. Nice for a few days but not all the time.

We did many jousting shows in Belgium and stabled our horses in many different yards in various locations around the country. I did not have the opportunity to ride other horses in Belgium, it was always full-on whenever we were over there. Most of our shows were in city centres and our stabling was usually quite a way out of the cities making logistics a nightmare. To make matters worse the old cities were like a rabbit warren with narrow streets and extremely complicated one-way systems. Trying to navigate a six-horse lorry through these streets was a nightmare and very time consuming.

Whenever we visited this lovely little country, we always received a very warm welcome. Giving food and drink is part of their culture, beer is a religion and taken very seriously. The kind people who let us use their stables became friends. Our first visit was to Horst castle about a thirty-minute drive from the city of Leuven. After leaving the motorway, our last fifteen minutes were down narrow lanes that our lorry almost completely filled, to add to our stress Belgium still had the priority from the right driving rule which meant that any tiny lane to the right had priority onto a major road, crazy but it was the law. We survived several near misses on that last fifteen minutes, and when we arrived at our stables glad to be alive, we were met by a family who hugged and kissed us three times and then thrust a bottle of cold beer into our hands. After a twelve-hour drive, we really wanted to get the horses off the lorry and into the stables. Even as we were leading the horses down the ramp, they were trying to give us another bottle of beer. Now, I and all the jousters like a beer or two but there is a time and place for that. By the time we had put the horses to bed, food and more beer was being offered. An hour and a half later we were picked up by the organisers and taken to our hotel in Leuven full of food and drink. The family have remained friends with us to this day which is over thirty years ago.

The variety of yards we stayed at was impressive. At Knokke-Heist we were at a show jumping yard and it was there that I saw my first electric horsebox ramp. Knokke is a seaside town close to the Dutch border and relied on incredibly deep dykes to keep the land drained. The roads were again extremely narrow and negotiating some of the road junctions with our large lorry with these huge dykes either side was a nightmare. Again, we kept in touch with the owners for many years.

In Bruges we were stabled at a trotting racing yard, it was amazing to see the speed at which these horses could go pulling a sulky in trot. There is so much we miss if we just keep our heads down in one chosen discipline. Again, on our last day there we were asked to join them for a meal and something to drink. The meal was held under a large lean to on the side of their house. These are very common in Belgium; they love alfresco dining but have similar weather to the UK most of the tables under these shelters seat ten to twenty people at one huge table. It is so lovely to sit down with fellow horse people over a meal and just chat about your equine experiences, you always learn something new.

For one of our shows at Leuven we were stabled in a lovely old barn that was two stories high and must have been a couple of hundred years old. It was here that I witnessed a Flemish Farrier at work. It was vastly different from our highly skilled farriers in the UK. The farrier had an assistant who lifted and held the horses leg for the farrier to dress the foot and nail the shoe on. It seemed an incredibly dangerous way to put on a shoe especially with the hind feet as the farrier's face was close to the foot when he was working. If the horse kicked, the farrier was reliant on the strength of his assistant to save him from what would be a potentially life-threatening injury. The farrier also extensively used an electric angle grinder to dress the hoof and also to grind the shoe away to fit the horse's foot. We had several farriers in the jousting troupe and they could not believe what they were seeing. I now understand why our farriers are considered to be the best in the world.

In the late eighties and nineties, we did a lot of jousting in Portugal. Because of the distance, we were supplied with local horses. These were all Lusitano bullfighting horses, which are closely related to the Spanish Andalusian horses. Our horses were all about fifteen hands, so ideal for falling off. Their training was similar to the way we trained our horses. They have an extremely short stride which made it look as if they were going extremely fast and very manoeuvrable, ideal for jousting. We loved these horses and they added flash to our shows. One piece of our tack fascinated the owners of these magnificent animals and that was the standing martingale. We always use them when jousting to stop the horse throwing its head up and accidentally hitting the knight's lance. They just didn't use them in Portugal.

The horses we used were in the main grey, but Stuart my brother and me, rode two magnificent black ones when doing some film work out there. We felt like Clint Eastwood and Lee Van Cleef in the film The Good the Bad and The Ugly.

From 1998 until 2012, we went over to America and Canada to take part in Tournaments against teams of knights from those countries. This was real jousting, for prize money against people that we didn't know. Although the initial approach came to me, I felt that it was far too dangerous for the limited company to be involved with. We were already having trouble getting public liability insurance for our UK shows following the Lloyds insurance crash, and despite endless days of trying hundreds of brokers no company would insure us for foreign shows, let alone prize jousting.

The jousting lads were all up for it so I suggested that they do it as individuals. My brother Phil took on the organising and they went over as The British Jousting Team. First to Estes Park high up in the

Rocky Mountains about two hour's drive from Denver City in Colorado, and then to London in Canada which was not far from Toronto. By this time, I was well past jousting and definitely not up for jousting for real. However, the British Jousting Team was much loved in both countries and after two years I was invited to commentate, both in Canada and in Colorado.

We came across a wide variety of both horses and people during our years visiting North America and again learned a lot. The lads hired their horses from a trail riding centre in the town. The owners were marvellous, they let them try as many horses as they liked before choosing the ones to train for jousting. They had forty- eight hours to select and train their horses to compete against horses that had been jousting for years, and still we beat them.

The horses came in all shapes and sizes. The Canadians and some of the Americans were big lads weighing in at over twenty stone plus. They all rode huge, heavy horses. Apparently in Canada the heavy horses are plentiful and cheap to buy. Mare's milk contains oestrogen and is used for making HRT. The by-product of this industry is a glut of unwanted, heavy horse foals. In contrast there was a lad from East Texas who rode lightweight horses known as the East Texas Horse breed. Apparently, they were direct descendants of the horses brought over by the Spanish conquistadors in the fifteen hundreds. They might be small but they were extremely tough.

There was also a group from California, they came from real cowboy backgrounds. One guy who was a mountain rancher told us he always carried a few sticks of dynamite in his saddlebags to clear trails of fallen trees and land slips. He lived near a place called Lake Tahoe. He was a great guy and we got on really well with him and his team. All the teams except the English had driven to Colorado with their horses. The distances were mind boggling, the Californians travelled about 1,000 miles, the Canadians over 1,500 miles and the East Texans about 950 miles. They all transported their horses in huge trailers towed by super large pickup trucks and were coupled to the pick-up with by what is known as a fifth wheel coupling, the same as our articulated lorries.

The Californians suffered a broken trailer axle at Flagstaff in Arizona. It was midnight when it happened and they said it was the most god-forsaken place in the world to break down. Next morning, they hired tools, a welder and found a scrapyard that had a suitable axle. They salvaged the axle from the old vehicle. They then removed their broken axle and replaced it with the salvaged one. This took them nearly a day and a half to complete. They then set out with another 700 miles to go and drove 13hrs nonstop except for fuel and sandwiches. Now that's true cowboy spirit.

We are given to believe that Americans are bar loving drinkers from the films that Hollywood makes but in reality, many are teetotal. I don't know how it is today but in the mid-seventies West Virginia had a maximum beer alcohol limit of 2.5% and North Carolina was teetotal. Most of the jousting competitors didn't drink and they found it strange that we could while away several hours in the bar every night after jousting and still beat them the next day. I will let you draw your own conclusions to that.

Usually, I try never to have anything to do with horses when I go on holiday. I like to rest the mind, body, and soul. But after Lou had a hysterectomy, we decided that she could choose a holiday of a lifetime and she chose a horse-riding holiday in New Zealand. My mother had a penfriend in New Zealand from an early age and they wrote to each other from 1940 until she died. Mum visited her in New Zealand and her penfriend came over and visited her when they were both in their sixties. Her description of a land that was similar to Britain in the 1950s intrigued me, so when Lou told me that she wanted to go there I was all for it. Although I was somewhat lukewarm about the horse-riding part. As it turned out, that is what made the trip to this unique country.

We flew via Japan with a couple of hours stopover in Osaka before the second leg down to New Zealand, which was the longest most painful flight that I have ever experienced. Despite trying all sorts of strong sleeping pills, I have never managed more than a catnap on any long-haul flight. My body wants to go to sleep but just won't do it, and it makes me feel awful. The flight from Osaka to Christchurch was the longest and most painful I have ever endured. It was already over 24 hrs without sleep and I felt dreadful. The only thing that cheered me up was the drinks trolley on the plane. Instead of dubious wine served in diddy little plastic bottles they had proper full-sized glass bottles of good quality wine and hand poured your drinks. When breakfast was served, we decided to push the boat out and have a glass of fizz with it. When the trolley came around again, we asked for a refill. The stewardess handed us the bottle saying, "You might as well have the bottle, nobody else is drinking it". Good old New Zealand Airlines thank you very much.

We finally checked into our hotel totally numb and exhausted. In the bar we ordered a bowl of yesterday's soup as the menu stated that soup always tasted better the next day. The next thing I remember was being gently woken by the waiter saying our soup had arrived. Lou and I were both sound asleep at the table.

We went to New Zealand with no plans except the riding holiday and we had hoped to visit Queenstown in the far south of the South Island but it was under eight feet of water due to torrential rain that was still affecting the South Island. We were picked up from the hotel by the riding centre late the next day and taken to a farm which was going to be our starting point for the ten-day trek into the wild back country. It was dark by the time we arrived and after a light meal we went straight to bed, as the jet lag was really kicking in.

I woke to a loud drumming sound early next morning, still extremely muzzy from a deep sleep and I struggled to work out what could be making such a weird noise. As my head cleared it came to me like a bolt of lightning, it was torrential rain hammering down on the corrugated tin roof of the farmhouse. I recalled mum telling me that nearly all the houses in New Zealand had tin roofs. Lou stirred not long after me. Still feeling somewhat numb from jetlag we lay for over an hour starring at the roof just listening to the rain noisily hammering down onto the tin. It was strangely very soothing.

After breakfast, the rain stopped and I had a poke around the farmyard to see how it compared with British farms and not surprisingly it was remarkably similar. I then took a stroll down the lane which was totally devoid of any traffic. It was hilly countryside and reminded me of Derbyshire. At the bottom of the hill a brook ran under the road. I stopped on the bridge and observed the water gushing along with enormous force, this was more like the Lake District where the becks can change from a trickling stream into a broiling torrent when it has rained heavily up in the mountains. I leant on the bridge wall, transfixed by the power of the water, and my jet lag. We had spent our first night in Christchurch but now out here in the hills I could take in the awesome beauty of this country. We had a taste of it's beauty from the Christchurch Gondola that takes you up Mount Cavendish and gives you a panoramic view of the city and of Lyttelton bay. Foolishly, we decided to take the option of a one-way ticket up and a mountain bike ride down. It was years since we had ridden a bike but, hey ho, they say you never forget how to ride a bike. We now know when relearning to ride a bike after thirty years, it is not a good idea to start with a 3,000-foot descent down rough and extremely steep tracks. We finally reached the bottom, battered, bruised and our brake hand numb from desperately trying to slow the bikes down. It was a fantastic experience and we were glad to be alive when the road finally levelled out. I came to the sad realisation for the first time in my life that perhaps I was getting a little too old for the wilder side of life, but I would not have missed it for the world.

The next day we were collected by the trek organisers and taken to the ranch, where we were asked to ride before being allocated our horses. While we were tacking our horses up, Rob the organiser of the trek came around to the English members of the trek and explained that in New Zealand, they set their saddles on much further back from the withers than in the UK. He could not give me a reason why but that was the way it had always been done over there. Our next shock of the day came as we were issued with a long-waxed mac and a wide brimmed waxed hat and a thick canvas bed roll. The bed roll was very heavy and into it we were allowed to put our wash bags and a basic change of clothes. Each of the rolls were then weighed. There was a strict and meagre weight limit and many of the riders became inconsolably upset when ordered to ditch some of their so-called essentials but the weight limit was mandatory and not negotiable. Some of the members failed several times before the weight limit was reached and a few tears were shed. It was hard even for Lou and me and we were used to travelling light but being horse people, we could understand the need to keep the weight down when you were riding for twelve plus hours a day. We also had two saddle bags in front of the saddle for our daily ration of food water and a camera. We were shown how to fix the small saddle bags and the bed roll with great emphasis being placed on getting the weight evenly balance across the horse's back. After much argument from some of the members, all bedrolls, and saddlebags weighed-in at the correct weight and we were ready to go. Only we were not going anywhere! The heavy unseasonable rains had caused the river levels to rise dramatically and rivers that were normally fordable were now raging torrents.

Rob our leader and owner of the trekking operation explained that at the present time we could not go anywhere as all the rivers we needed to cross were in serious flood. We were going to be taken to a sheep farm with our horses and wait for the weather to improve and he was going to try and find a way to get into the back country by circumnavigating the worst affected rivers. Our accommodation was to be the old sheep shearer's bunkhouse which dated back to the early nineteen hundreds. It was a wooden bunk house not designed for more than one sex to share. It was very cramped and absolutely no privacy. Again, there was uproar from some members of the trip followed by shock when Rob explained that this was luxury compared with what we were going to face during the next ten days. I realised that this was exactly how the trip had been described, a true taste of riding the back country! The toilet was the classic long drop, a small wooden hut set away from the other buildings just like you see in the Cowboy Western films.

The rain continued to pour down and we were stuck in this tiny cabin for two exceedingly long days. The only good thing about it was that we got to know our fellow riders very well. Most were from the UK but two were from America. At the end of the second day Rob appeared and announced that he had found a passable route and that we would be leaving early next day and, that we needed to get up early and be packed and ready to go by 8am. This proved an ambitious time as some of the party had little experience of tacking up and horse management. It was closer to eleven by the time everything was packed to Rob's satisfaction. The rain was still pouring down and I was glad to have the long-waxed Mac and broad brimmed waxed hat. We set out in single file at a steady walk across lush green fields slowly heading for the mountains that were for the most, obscured by the lashing rain. An hour later we were climbing up a steep rocky track, the rain continued to lash down and the higher we went the colder the rain. Two more hours and we were into the snow fields and it was snowing so hard that you could barely see the rider two lengths in front of you. My hands were starting to throb with the cold and it was hard to hold the reins. We plodded on relentlessly into the driving snow and after another half-hour the ground levelled out. We were at the top of the mountain and starting to descend, after a few hundred yards the wind slackened and I started to feel much warmer, another half hour took us to the edge of the snow field. Shortly after Rob stopped and ordered us to dismount and eat some of our food. During our break Rob explained that for the next hour or so we would be walking in front of our horses leading them at the buckle end so that we were well in front of our horses. This was in case if a horse spooked, they would not knock you off the track and down the mountain. Sometimes the track was barely a metre wide and a shear drop of several hundreds of metres. Scary stuff!

We continued to walk down the steep trail for over an hour. On the lee side of the mountain there was no wind and it was considerably much warmer. Every time we stopped for a rest, garments were removed and by the time we reached the bottom we all in tee shirts and sweating. In two hours, we had gone from snow to twenty-eight degrees centigrade it was unbelievable. It was early evening when we reached our first stopping point which was an incredibly old log cabin literally in the middle of nowhere. Rob explained that it had been built in the early nineteen hundreds for drovers to sleep in when rounding up the sheep. It slept about fourteen and had a water tank that was fed by a spring. We hobbled the horses (new experience) and let them loose on the range. I have to admit I had my doubts whether we would find them next day. Once the horses had been seen to, we were all designated jobs. Mine was to find firewood. Rob explained that the hut was maintained to provide refuge for anyone roaming the hills and the rule was that if you used the hut, you always left kindling, dry wood, some matches, and a candle for the next visitors. That's the same all over the world but sadly he told me that city people in four-wheel drive trucks and motorbikes were coming out to these refuges and were being used as party places. They used all the wood, didn't replace it, never left matches, and left beer cans and other rubbish that attracted rodents. He was very bitter about these ignorant people and I would not like to think what he would do to them if he ever happened onto a group.

He told me that his other form of income during the winter months was wild boar hunting. He would be dropped by helicopter deep in the backcountry with his dogs and a pal, taking supplies for several weeks. Although they carried rifles, he preferred to let the dogs hunt the boar until it was cornered and then go in on foot and cut it's throat with his Bowie style knife. Doing it this way avoided bullet damage to the meat and assured a clean kill. Wild boar are extremely dangerous and I have seen the effects of the horrific wounds that their tusks can wreak on the human body when my father had his leg sliced down to the bone by our domestic boar. Anyone brave and strong enough to face and kill a wild boar with a knife is definitely not a man to mess with. The wild boar are actually feral pigs that escaped from the settlers' farms in the eighteen hundreds and are now a real pest in the backcountry. He killed so many that most weeks he would have to call the helicopter in to collect the carcasses. I spent a lot of time talking to this knowledgeable man during our trek and we got on extremely well. I was fascinated by the pack horses as they were something that I had never come across in my life of working with horses. This was no executive trek where you ride to a luxurious campsite and have chef prepared dinners, with all your clothes transported to the campsites. This was just as the drovers did it over one hundred years ago. The pack horses carried everything we needed, food, tents, first aid and a hundred and one other items. It took over two hours to pack everything onto the horses. Everything was weighed and carefully balanced on the horse' backs, wrapped, and sealed against water, it was slow monotonous work but our lives depended on it. Two of the more unusual items we carried on the pack horses was an emergency radio beacon that when activated would summon a helicopter to air lift a casualty to hospital. The other was an old Winchester style rifle. When I asked why we needed to carry a rifle he looked around to make sure nobody was in earshot and quietly said

"I can tell you but keep it to yourself, it's the first aid for the horses if they injure themselves. You understand you're a horseman but the others haven't got a clue".

After a night sleeping on un-sprung, stuffed mattresses that looked and smelled like they too were a hundred years old. Thankfully, our thick canvass outer sleeping bags protected us from the nasties that called the mattresses their homes.
I woke early next morning, left the others sleeping soundly in the cabin and went to see if we still had horses. To my great relief, I found them happily grazing in a little natural meadow just a few hundred yards from the cabin. I wandered around soaking up the sounds and smells of this wilderness that always seem to be at their best in the dawn air just before the sun rises into view. My wanders took me to the water tank and intrigued by the modern blue plastic water pipe that fed the tank. I followed it up the hill for about two hundred yards, it ended at a natural spring that fed a

small stream. The pipe had been weighted down under the water by some heavy rocks at the source of the stream. Gravity did the rest, total simplicity that gave running water in the cabin, to me it was wonderful.

Our second day brought our first river crossing. I have already mentioned my fear of water and lack of swimming prowess but this really challenged my mental strength. The river was wide and fast flowing due to the heavy rain, probably a bit wider than the river Trent between Nottingham and Newark. Rob called me over and asked me if I would follow him over. He wanted somebody with horse experience with him on the far bank just in case anyone got into difficulties. He admitted that he had never crossed a river with such a strong current, I admitted that I had never crossed a river or swam a horse in my life. The plan was that he would go first and gauge the strength of the current and then I would follow, while Tom his assistant would stay with the others and send them over one at a time. It seemed to take Rob forever to get across and the current swept him some way down stream of where he said he was headed to. My instructions were to look straight ahead and not look down but most importantly keep kicking at all costs and as hard as I could. He explained that if I stopped kicking, the horse would stop swimming and we would be swept away downstream. His final warning was not to look down at the water because the current will mesmerise you, make you dizzy and disoriented. Once on the other side Rob shouted over to me and told where to aim for. This was about fifty yards further upstream than my destination point.

I set off, oh boy did I kick my horse, the current was unbelievably strong and I could feel us being dragged down stream. Every now and then, I could hear faint shouts from Rob urging me to keep kicking. By the time I reached the middle of the river my best friend adrenaline had kicked in, and I was actually starting to enjoy myself. I had my new Canon SLR digital camera in the front saddle bag and I was worried that it might be getting wet, as my bottom was already soaked. I looked down and immediately a vertigo sensation rolled through my body, causing me to grab the pommel of the saddle to stop me falling off, a cold sweat instantly drenched my body and I immediately looked up and focused on the far bank. That few moments of hesitation had carried me several yards further downstream than intended but I made a safe landing on the far bank and was greeted by a well done from Rob who informed me that he was going further downstream to be ready to rescue anyone who was swept away. His final words were "Keep shouting at them to keep kicking and to look at you".

Lou came over next grinning like a child opening Christmas presents and greeted me with a "Wow that was exciting". It reminded me of the look on her face that I had noticed when she had her first gallop around Bunny Park on a Shetland pony called Clem, it was on one of my dad's Sunday morning rides in the early sixties and thinking there is someone who really gets a thrill out of riding!

Several more of the group came over one at a time but struggled to keep kicking all the way over and they were swept much further downstream before reaching the other side. Last to come over were Tom and the packhorses, to my horror once they were in the water, Tom let go of the lead rope and the packhorses were swept away spinning around and around as they disappeared around a bend in the river. We stood in silence as the gravity of the situation dawned on us, all our food, cooking equipment and tents had just floated away down the river and we were a day and a half away from any civilisation, even our emergency beacon had gone with the packhorses. It was several minutes before Tom reached our bank.

"That's a bugger! You lot stay put here. I'm going to go down stream to help Rob get the packhorses ", he said as he clambered up onto the bank and cantered off along the shoreline to find his boss.

We just stood around speechless each lost in our own thoughts. Eventually Rob and Tom returned but without the packhorses and our mood deepened. Rob announced we were leaving without the pack horses and led our gobsmacked group forward. I dropped back and asked Tom how we were going to survive without our supplies and he just laughed saying,

"Don't you worry about those old pack horses; they will find somewhere to get out of the river and then come and find us".

I was not convinced and worried for the next hour or so until the drumming of hooves brought me sharply out of my, what if, daydream. The packhorses had returned and they automatically slotted back into their places in the group as if nothing had happened. Wow, another thing that I did not know about horses, they continue to surprise me.

When we reached our next campsite, we found that some water had found its way into the packs but it was very little thanks to Tom's very careful packing and we soon had things dried out around our first campfire. It was just like the western films - an iron tripod over the fire with a cast iron cauldron hanging over the fire. We had camped by a lovely, lively stream and we all went over to refill our water bottles from the stream, only to be sternly told by Rob to never drink from streams unless we were so high up in the mountains that we were above the height that stock would graze. He made the point that there could be a dead sheep further upstream decomposing in the water or animal faeces polluting the water.

The terrain was very mountainous and covered with wild rose bushes and broom. Both of these species like so many other plants and animals had been brought over by the European settlers and they wiped out native species, it was a big problem being fought on a national scale. By all accounts it was a losing battle and much of the sheep grazing had been lost to these invasive plants. In the main it was very safe, peaceful riding but every now and then a wild pig would burst out of the dense scrub squealing its head off, frightening the life out of both the horses and riders. We swam four large, fast flowing rivers during our trek and I really enjoyed it despite my fear of water. To sit on a horse and feel it swimming is a marvellous sensation and I am so lucky to have been able to have the opportunity.

In the mountains the tracks were narrow and rugged with cliff edges that dropped hundreds of feet and much of our time was spent walking leading our horses because it was too dangerous to ride, the heavy rains had also caused land slips which compounded the dangers. On our sixth day we came to a halt in a lovely wild meadow scattered with shady trees. Rob announced that we would be having a longer than usual lunch break as he and Tom were going to scout on ahead to check the trail over the next mountain as it was notorious for land slips. Tom was going to check a longer route that circumnavigated the mountain but hadn't been used that year. Glad of the rest and shade, we ate and dozed under the trees and waited. Two hours later they were back. Rob had discovered a land slip on the mountain trail but it was passable with care, he had already ridden passed to check it was safe to ride around. However, it was dangerous and not suitable for the pack horses or the more novice riders, they would go with Tom and take the longer route and so we divided and went our separate ways. We set off at a leisurely walk while the other party set off at a jog trot. Our party led by Rob started to steadily climb up the mountain trail which didn't present any problems and the views got more stunning by the minute, perhaps Rob had exaggerated the problem. An hour later we were high up the mountain and the ground fell away to our left almost vertically for hundreds of feet to the river down in the valley that was winding its way around through the mountains. The view was exceptional but my stomach flipped if I glanced down. We rounded a bend and there was our land slip, it had taken out a section of the trail completely. It was as if a monster had taken a large bite out of the trail leaving a horseshoe shaped hole that measured fifteen yards across and around the edge was deep wet mud, the drop was shear right down to the river below, all you could make out of the river below was flashes of sunlight reflecting up from the fast-flowing water. "Shit" I muttered, and the rest of the group also said the same or other expletives. Rob immediately saw the panic in the group and assured us that he had already circumnavigated the hole earlier and pointed to the hoof prints in the mud. Rob led the way then it was my turn, my instructions from Rob were don't look down under any circumstances, sit quiet and don't rush the horse, let it pick its way through the mud. It took less than a minute to walk around that hole but it was one of the longest minutes of my life. My admiration for those horses and Rob for his confidence in their ability cannot be put into words. Even today writing this many years later I still find it hard to come to terms with the fact that Rob let us do it because you either got it right or you and your horse were dead.

It was a fabulous holiday where I learnt so many new things about horsemanship that were once common knowledge but now are almost lost in the specialised riding that most people do today. When I rode out of the mountains and saw a tarmac road, a wave of sadness swept over me and tears filled my eyes as I realised that civilisation was just up the road and that we were leaving a very special place!

Chapter Ten
Team Chasing

Team chasing has always been my favourite equine sport. I started team chasing, a year after it was conceived by Douglas Bunn, the owner of Hickstead Show jumping arena, and Alan Mouncer, a sports producer for the BBC. The BBC televised the Hickstead Derby and had extremely high viewing figures. Like all media people he was looking for something different to attract even more viewers. It was after a long leisurely lunch and several glasses of port that Duggie Bunn proposed a new competition. It was a cross-country race for invited teams over the formidable natural fences of the Hickstead Estate. Teams would represent many equestrian disciplines such as racing, eventing, show jumping, and hunting. Twenty teams of five were invited with the fastest four in each team to count. This was because given the severity of the course, a considerable number of fallers were anticipated. There would be thirty fences and the course would be approximately one and a half miles long. The rules for the race were minimal and it is rumoured that they were hastily scribbled on the back of the lunch menu. To give you an idea of the severity of the course, fence number two was a hedge with a ten foot drop on landing, quickly followed by two sets of very solid, five-foot-high rails at the railway crossing (For the younger readers who only understand metric, five feet is one metre fifty-two and when you take into account that the maximum height for 5star eventing such as Burghley and Badminton is one metre thirty, you start to understand it was an extremely elite competition.

 The sport quickly developed with hunts recognising it as another income stream like their point-to-point races. Within a couple of years most hunts were running Team chases and gradually the sport split into two seasons. The spring season started at the end of the hunting season, roughly at the beginning of March and ending in mid-April, and then the autumn season started in mid-September and finished around the time of the hunts having their opening meets which is usually in early November.

For cross-country addicts like myself this was great as it added another three months of adrenaline pumping fun to the calendar. For me it was a dilemma because the spring season ran at the same time as the point-to-point season. In the main, point to points ran on Saturdays and team chases on Sundays so it was not a time issue but more a money issue of competing two horses at the same time. Also, as the sport evolved, teams started to be sponsored, a sponsor was not going to be happy if you rang up the night before a competition to tell them that you were injured from a fall steeplechasing. Likewise, racehorse owners did not like jockeys that risked injuring themselves team chasing. Consequently, I did extraordinarily little spring team chasing during my racing career. Another factor was that the jousting season started at Easter, and that was another worry as that was one of my sources of income. I spent many hours lying in bed at night trying to work out how I would explain to people that I could not ride because I had injured myself doing another dangerous sport.

My first team chase was the Quorn Hunt Team Chase, held at Muxloe Hill and was sponsored by The Bunny Club of Great Britain. The flamboyant CEO of the Bunny Club was Victor Lownes and he had his own sponsors' tent, complete with Bunny Girls dressed in their Bunny costumes. It was rumoured that the champagne for the invited elite was flowing like water. Our good farmer friend, Geoff Brooks, approached dad to see if he could find riders to make up a team for one of the Quorn's distinguished subscribers who wanted to have a team take part in the competition. Dad suggested himself and his three sons. Our sponsor was David Wilson, who owned a large building company Wilson Homes. Our team name was Wilson's Wasps, we made no preparation for our new adventure except a couple of gallops up Bunny hill in the field where I trained my pointers. I only had one pointer at that time which was Dadda Boy so my horse was much fitter than the rest of the team. I ran him on Easter Monday and won the members and then team chased him six days later. There were two classes, the open and the novice, we were in the novice class as we did not have the horsepower for the open which in those early days was truly terrifying. The novice was no walk in the park with fixed fences of three feet six inches and hedges a good eighteen inches higher than that. There was a prize for the fastest individual rider and I really fancied my chance of winning it with my racehorse and pointing experience. I flew around the course at racing pace and was well ahead of the rest of the team when I finished. I was sure I had the fastest time in the bag but when I looked at the scoreboard, I was second, beaten by a friend, Geoff Perfect who was riding a solid hunter type. I asked him if he thought the times were correct as I just could not see how his horse could be faster than my racehorse. His answer was a revelation and I learnt my first lesson about team chasing.

He smiled and said "Yes you were much faster than me but you went nearly twice the distance. While you were galloping huge wide turns, I was jumping at angles and never wasting a yard, this game is not all about speed but not wasting a yard anywhere on the course". He was dead right; I felt such a fool for not seeing that. It was a thoroughly enjoyable day and we were all up for doing some more events in the autumn if there were anymore not too far away. Autumn suited us all much better and it tied in nicely with getting horses fit for hunting.

Our next outing was at the Meynell hunt and at that time I had never hunted with them so we were going into unknown territory. It was another stiff course and rather hard to find your way around, as we were searching for an elusive next fence, we bumped into a jolly bunch of chaps who were having the same problem. We struck up a casual conversation and were immediately confronted by two almost identical men wanting to shake our hands and announcing themselves as the Boring Gorings. They were the Goring TWINS, George and Richard and you would be hard pushed to find two nicer chaps to meet anywhere in the world. At that point we had never heard of them but they quickly established themselves as household names in the ever-blossoming team chase community.

For me, the joys of team chasing were many, within in a few years the sport developed rapidly with fox hunts quickly jumping on the bandwagon and using it as a new stream of income. I think the reason it developed through the hunts was that you needed a lot of grassland and you needed a fence building team and both were readily available at most hunts. To set up a private team chase would have been awfully expensive if you had to employ fence builders. However, two of my favourite team chases were not connected directly to fox hunts. They were the injured jockeys fund team chase and another that only ran once I think and again, I think it had something to do with another fearless rider Geoff Lockwood but more about those later.

Unlike point to points that were sighted more for the paying viewing public, team chases tended to be sighted in some of the best of the hunts' country and that was a revelation to me. Few team chases charged spectators and those that did come tended to wander from jump to jump or stay in the bar which always tended to be in a good viewing position.

Locally the Belvoir team chase was by far the best, it was held on Richard Chandler's farm close to the village of Long Clawson in the Vale of Belvoir. The Vale of Belvoir is a big milking area thanks to the local Stilton cheese dairies and has been able to retain some fine patches of grassland to hunt over. Richard was a dairy farmer, keen fox hunter and team chaser. Richard's original course was the longest and stiffest course I have ever come across, it included two water obstacles and a lane crossing which was two hedges that had an extremely awkward jumping distance requiring the rider to kick-on and hope for the best, or hook back and try to fit in an extraordinary set of short strides. As with most jumping problems in team chasing the majority always favoured the bold approach.

The biggest course I have ever jumped was the one that I think was organised by Geoff Lockwood. I have never jumped so many enormous hedges in my life. I remember walking the course with Mike Elvin who is over six feet tall and he was wearing a brown racing trilby hat, he stood in front of the first fence and had his photograph taken. The fence was an upright hedge, railed in front to about 1m 20cm, in the photo you could see a good amount of hedge above his head and to make matters worse it had a downhill approach. Later on, in the course, two massive wide hedges were both jumped twice in a tight zig-zag loop. I was riding Bumper who was only 15.3hh but he was a superb jumper. The first fence jumped a lot better than expected, we all survived and went off out into the country for about half a mile jumping a mixture of hedges and stout post and rails before returning to near the start for the four gigantic hedges. A large crowd had gathered around each of the fences and this just added to the pressure. The first fence jumped well, it was big and wide but we all negotiated it safely, the next hedge was jumped twice as you looped back over it the other way fifty yards further up. As we approached it, I became aware that Bumper was smaller than the hedge and I was giving a big ask to a little chap but I also knew that he had a big heart. I sat back and kicked as hard as I could and then something strange happened, it was a once in a lifetime experience. Bumper shortened his stride and I thought that he was going to stop with me, his front end came up in a kind of a rear, his hocks must have almost touched the ground, and for a moment time stood still, then we rocketed into the air. For those of you acquainted with high school dressage it was a classic capriole done naturally, the hedge was so wide you could have parked a car on it. I thought that we would never make it, but we did and only brushed through the top few inches. The landing was harsh and nearly unseated me but there was no time for celebration, I had a tight left-hand turn to make, and at the end of the turn there was the previous hedges' twin, that waited to be assaulted. The previous jump must have taken a lot out of Bumper as we went fairly deep through the top foot of this whopping great hedge but we managed to stay on our feet. The paddock that we landed in was narrow and we arrived at the next hedge in less than fifteen strides, again another big hedge maybe not quite as high but definitely just as wide and imposing. Thankfully, we met it well but again we went through a little lower than I would have liked but to be fair to my horse, each of the previous jumping efforts must have taken a lot out of him and they came so quick and fast he had no time to get his breath before the next one was upon us. Our next fence was much smaller, it was the box fence, designed to allow the horses to get their breath back mid-course. Hated by most team chasers you had to have three members in the box before you could jump out and these boxes were very tight, only about the length of four horses nose to tail. They were the nemesis of many a good team and caused great amusement for the spectators. We got it wrong that day and it cost us a couple of seconds which does not sound much but when events are won or lost by one hundred's of a second, it was an age. The rest of the course was challenging to the end, I think we came sixth that day, but nobody cared, we had all had one of the best rides of our lives. Having said that, although I have always emptied my bladder before any cross-country event, having walked this course I felt the need to empty my bowels as well, and that is the one and only time this has ever happened.

These days people are obsessed by winning, but in cross country events, winning is always nice but having an exhilarating ride comes extremely close. Loosen up riders, enjoy the ride, prize money is crap and a rosette is just a piece of coloured cloth. Nothing beats the joy of flying over natural fences in complete symmetry with your horse.

After our first outing at the Quorn Team Chase, we did very little for the next few years but always managed to do a few in the Autumn as a family team which always meant arguments. On one occasion the arguments were so veracious, that complaints were made by spectators about our swearing. Dad was called up in front of the judge and was told that our team must moderate our language if we wanted to continue to team chase. We were all aware of the volatile nature of our family team and even named our team The Humphrey Hot Heads. There has always been a tongue in cheek approach to team names often aimed at causing the commentator some verbal grief. Some of the famous names that come to mind were The Pheasant Pluckers, The Cunning Stunts, Bollocks to Blair when the hunting ban was introduced and also Fight the Ban another politically motivated team name. Both these team names were extremely popular with both the competitors and the spectators. Sadly, Bollocks to Blair was eventually banned, much to the dismay of the team chase community. I think the banning of that name was the sad end to the glory days when you had a cavalier attitude to the risks that you take and it was up to the individual to make up their own mind to what, if any safety precautions you wanted to take rather than be forced by a governing body. Like so many sports that start so carefree, certain individuals feel that they need a governing body to develop the sport and the first thing that they feel that they have to do is produce a set of unified rules for the sport. One of the joys of team chasing was that there were very few rules and very often some rules varied from one event to the other. Imagine making a rule in the wine industry that all wine should be made and taste the same, what a bland world that would be. As soon as we had a governing body you had to wear a body protector, you could not remount if you had a fall and the list goes on, all done in the name of growing the sport. It was a great sport when Duggie Bunn invented it. It was a sport for elite cross-country riders not the nanny state masses. I choose to wear a hard hat when I ride but it is not the law. It cheers me so much when I see the Queen riding in her nineties, just wearing a head scarf. We all talk about freedom but we have lost so much to laws, rules, and lawyers encouraging everyone to sue for compensation which is at the heart of the problem.

One of the great joys of team chasing for me has been to ride with my father, two brothers Phil and Stu, my daughter Emma, and my wife, Louise. There has always been intense equestrian rivalry between us and many raging arguments between us about things equestrian but we have always been a close family and would always be there for each other if the chips were down. As a family we all chose different equestrian disciplines but team chasing was the only sport that brought us all together.

Team chasing had a friendly atmosphere about it, we were all there for each other, bitter rivals one week and riding in the same team the next. Team chasing was hard on horses and their riders making it hard to maintain a topflight team. When Mike Elvin was sponsoring the team Elvin and Co., we started the season with three teams which rapidly dropped to two teams and by the end of the eight to ten-week season we were struggling to field a home-grown team and desperately looking for spare riders. When the Quorn stopped having their team chase our only local competition was the Belvoir at Long Clawson. As I have already said it was always one of my favourite courses and I had many fantastic rides around both the novice and open courses. On one occasion we were short of riders for the open and could only field two home grown riders but in the week prior to the event we had managed to secure another well-known rider to join us. You have to have three in a team to start and near the end of the season it was quite common to see teams of three. On the day we had a novice and an open team running and did not seek out our third member until we had finished riding in the novice team. When we found our extra team member, he unapologetically told us that he had changed his mind and was riding for another team. We were fuming, we had paid the substantial entry fee on the understanding that we had a team of three. Desperate to jump the famous big hedges we searched for another rider but to no avail. We had fielded a family team in the novice and it was dad's last ride in a team chase for he was well into his sixties by then. We came up with a cunning plan and after much persuasion we got dad who had ridden one of our riding school horses called Drummer around in the novice. The great thing about team chasing was the lack of rules and there was no rule about competing a horse twice in one day. I forget who my partner in the scheme was, but I am fairly sure it was one of my brothers. The first three fences were of a reasonable size so the plan was for dad to jump those three then pull up, and for me and my co-conspirator to kick-on and have a jolly to get our money's worth. All went to plan, Dad pulled up after the third fence for no apparent reason which confused the commentary, but we were off and running. For some strange reason, the stewards tried to stop us, presumably because we could not record a time, the commentator was calling for us to pull-up and stewards were leaping out at us waving their hands but we played deaf and blind and almost ran down a couple of stewards. The course was huge and I lost my mate about three quarters of the way round but I was having one of the rides of my life; big hedge after big hedge but they finally stopped me three fences from home which was a Trakehner type fence with a huge drop and wide ditch on the landing side. The steward held his ground waving his arms furiously. I did consider trying to ride around him but it was a serious fence and I had no wish to harm him or my horse Red who was not mine and belonged to Mike Elvin. He was one of the great horses in my life and he gave me many wonderful rides. I received a mild reprimand and they accepted that I was too focused on the fences to see or hear people trying to stop me. I am sure they knew I was lying but this was teamchasing and it was all about the fun.

Another of my great joys later in my team chase period was riding with my daughter Emma. I think she was fourteen when she started riding with us and it was at the Belvoir Team chase that I did something that she has never let me forget. At the time, we had an extremely competitive novice team. In novice events although the fences are smaller you have to go like a bat out of hell if you are going to get placed, it is foot to the floor from start to finish, you jump every fence at the most acute angles and make ridiculous high-speed turns. It is the equivalent of hurdle racing in national Hunt racing. Like hurdling if you get it wrong, the falls of both horse and rider can be spectacular. It is not a sport for the faint hearted. After each run, we would immediately de-brief, analysing every turn and angle to see where we could have saved an extra one hundredth of a second, because it was often a hundredth of a second between first and second place.

During our run at the Belvoir, Emma had taken some wider than usual turns in the closing stages. Our family de-briefs were volatile to say the least and I berated Emma about her turns. When I had stopped screaming and shouting, she said that she had hurt her finger landing over the drop fence and couldn't hold her reins properly. This set me off again saying, "hurt your finger, what sort of an excuse is that you are going to have to get tougher if you want to ride with us". Her reply made me cringe "But daddy look, it doesn't work and it has gone all floppy". I looked at her finger and realised it was completely broken and dangling awkwardly at a strange angle. I felt so bad for shouting at her, she must have been in so much pain over those last few fences. To make matters worse, Lou gave me a good bollocking for being such a cruel, uncaring father.

Team chasing like racing is a tough sport and although many of the top teams were sponsored, it usually only amounted to paying the team entry fee, help with the fuel costs and providing a set of team colours, although some like Mike Elvin did much more. Mike learnt to ride at Bunny and was always a flamboyant character. He soon mastered the basics and purchased his first horse. He asked me one day about which riding sport I thought he should take up. At that time, I was primarily doing point to points and national hunt racing which is extremely tightly governed due to the betting element of the game. Everything was profoundly serious and done by the book and by the minute and definitely not for Mike. Dressage was way too tame as he loved speed and jumping. Show jumping involved hours of waiting around doing nothing, again not the sort of thing for Mike. That left team chasing, no rules, full of wealthy flamboyant characters who just wanted to have adrenaline pumping fun, perfect for Mike. To say he flung himself into his new sport was an understatement and he soon had his own team. Not long after that, he was sponsoring a fence at local team chases and was completely integrated into the team chasing community. At the height of his involvement, he ran three teams Elvin & Co, Elvin & Co 2 and Elvin & co 3. We had some great years together and keeping all his horses fit and organising entries was almost a full-time job.

One of the horses he bought was from Jack Todd the dealer who Dick Benson bought Gladstonian from. All Jack's horses were top quality and the one Mike bought was no exception. His name was Red and he was a big strong gelding with a huge jump in him. When we went to try him, he put in a huge jump that totally caught me by surprise and I was nearly jumped off, much to my embarrassment. I rode him in many open team chases and he always gave me a great ride and in all the times I rode him he never fell or unseated me. Red is definitely up there as one of my favourite horses that I have ridden.

Elvin & Co were definitely my glory years of team chasing and I had the honour to ride with some great riders and fantastic people. In the early days, our team was Mike with three members of my family, Dad, me or my two brothers Phil and Stu. We alternated depending on who was available and had a sound horse because as the years went by and the more events we did, we needed a bigger pool of horses and riders to keep the main team running week on week during the season. During those years we were joined by some really brave and gutsy female riders and their talented little horses that often-jumped fences that were so big they could not see over them. My daughter Emma started when she was fourteen and soon moved up to open classes although she was under the minimum age of sixteen to ride in open classes. Not normally a person to encourage young girls to wear makeup I suggested that if she wore a bit of eye makeup and lippy nobody would be any the wiser. I think she also used this advice when she joined young farmers and started to go to the pub with them before she was the legal drinking age. Emma's horse at the time was a horse called Cassy. He was bought for Emma from a stud that specialised in breeding dressage horses to compete in Dressage competitions and came with the posh official name of Knabhall Cascade. Although talented in dressage he soon showed us that he much preferred jumping. Dressage was Lou's idea as like most mothers she was trying to steer her daughter away from the riskier jumping sports that the male members of the Humphrey family favoured. This was strange as Lou was a keen team chase rider before she had children. My son's daughter Katherine has also favoured the thrill of jumping and is now following in aunty Emma's footsteps eventing, much to the detriment of mummy's nerves.

Sue Coverley was a local rider who joined us on a small but very brave little horse. I still have a DVD of both Emma and Sue riding together at the Grafton Team Chase, jumping the huge wide hedges that are a feature of that course. On that same day, a young man called William Foxpit was riding in an opposing team. He was already making a name for himself in the eventing world and arrived with a film crew in tow, much to the delight of the two girls in our team. William was destined to become one of eventing's greats, winning three Olympic medals and just about every other major eventing competition on the planet, often many times over. I have to say I couldn't fault the girls for spotting a bit of equestrian talent.

From the Belvoir country we had Clare Carter, always feeling sick before the start but once the flag dropped, she was a tiger and never let us down.

Vicky Deakin only sixteen and like Emma had a small but talented little horse that was bold as brass. Her parents came and videoed her proud moment but were shocked at some of the expletives that were uttered by her as she flew over the big fences at speed, when they played the tape back.

Toni Bailey who was always rushing around finishing jobs off when we picked her up and telling us the long list that she had to do when she got home but again never let us down and loved every minute of it.

Elaine Bywater, cool calm and determined, took a ride on a horse she had never seen. It bolted and somersaulted at one of the early fences. She was lucky to be alive but after her stay in hospital was soon back in the saddle.

Yvonne Goss, who said she only had a four-year-old left to ride but would ride that young novice horse if it helped us out. When I popped around to her trailer to give her the team colours her dad was bottle feeding her young baby. Another cool calm consummate rider.

I am sure that I have probably missed people out and I do apologise if I have. However, it was a manic time and much was done on the hoof as we managed one rider crisis after another.

Geoff Perfect and his daughter Belinda, came as a double act. Geoff always had a cigarette in his mouth even when riding. Geoff was the guy who beat me into second place for the fastest time at my first team chase. The first time we linked up was probably ten years later, it was at the Whaddon team chase. It was the last Whaddon Hunt event as they amalgamated with the Bicester Hunt the following season which was a great shame as it was a lovely course. The start was on top of a small hill and Nobby, as Geoff was known to his mates set off at a blistering pace, and took the lead, I was riding Santini, a lovely thoroughbred owned by Caroline Howitt, who along with her husband Mark were great team chase fans. We swept downhill over the next four fences down to level ground and to a big hedge with a substantial ditch in front of it. Belinda and I were hot on Geoff's heels as we approached the hedge, you could have thrown a blanket over the three of us. We were a stride out when Nobby's horse suddenly tried to duck out to the left. The next second or maybe more like a thousandth of a second, just as Santini was about to take off, Nobby and his horse crashed into the ditch. Nobby was injected into the bottom of the hedge and his horse flipped over and became cast upside down in the ditch. Its four legs were flailing madly in the air, doubling the width of the hedge. Neither Belinda or I had any chance of stopping so we kicked hard, hoped, and prayed. Miraculously both of our horses put in stupendous jumps and we cleared Nobby, horse and hedge. There was a brief moment of elation before both of our horses crumpled on landing and slid along the ground on their sides with Belinda and I doing the same. It was like synchronised falling; I remember glancing across at Belinda and she like me was laughing, why, I can't truly say, but I think it was just a weird reaction of survival, I think we were expecting to wake up in hospital and here we were sliding along the ground together in total unison. It never ceases to amaze me how your mind speeds up in times of crisis and records massive amounts of information that occur in the blink of an eye. Both Belinda and I along with our horses had soft falls as we say in the business. Mike Elvin, who was tail end Charlie had vital extra seconds to steer out of trouble and jump the fence safely on the far right. I have always told the number four in the team to try and stay a few lengths back from the others just in case a catastrophe like this happened. We caught our horses as they jumped up and with the help of some spectators we were quickly legged back up into the saddle and we were on our way as a team of three, with a niggling worry in the back of our minds hoping that Nobby was ok. The amazing thing was that as it was one of the biggest fences on the course, the event photographer was at that fence and captured Belinda and I with our horses sliding along the ground. I still have the photo and it remains one of my favourite to this day.

We continued around the course without mishap but vital seconds were lost so we were well out of the money. To make matters worse, I lost my special whip that I had carried around Cheltenham the previous year. It was at a large elephant trap fence near the end of the course, Santini put in a big jump and it got flicked out of my hand.

Our first thoughts were for Nobby as we crossed the line, thankfully, except for looking like he had been attacked by a tiger from all the thorn scratches, he was ok. The funny thing that made us laugh was that when the ambulance crew finally pulled Nobby out of the hedge he still had his fag in his mouth and it was still burning.

Another great day out team chasing!

Many bizarre things happened team chasing. At the Hatton Team Chase which was not a hunt team chase but raised money for the injured jockeys fund, a charity that was remarkably close to my heart. It was renowned for its challenging fences but the most worrying thing about this course was a canal. You didn't have to jump it just avoid it because you had to make a sharp turn in front of the canal after jumping an exceedingly wide set of rails. To give you a bit of confidence they had a crane on standby to winch any unfortunate horse and rider out of the canal if you didn't make the turn.

During our round, a loose Staffordshire Bull Terrier chased us around the course, it was snapping at my daughter Emma's horse's heels for several fences and forced her horse out over five strands of barbed wire. Luckily, Emma was riding Cassy and his fantastic jumping skills saved the day but it could have been horrendous. Please if you must bring your dog to an equine event, make sure that you have it securely under control and have a lead that it can't slip out of. Also consider if it is likely to yap or bark because sudden noises can panic horses as well.

On another occasion we had a horse stop unexpectedly at the first fence and the rider was ejected clean over the fence taking the bridle with him. A steward managed to catch the horse, the bridle was put back on and the rider remounted and completed the course.

In team chasing you are pushing everything to its maximum and things can go spectacularly wrong. At the Badsworth Hunt teamchase up in Yorkshire I was having a great ride until we came to a hedge that you jumped and then looped back immediately to jump it the other way. We were going really well and I knew we were in contention for a place. I tried to make my turn as tight as possible and shave another second off our time. As I made my turn my horse slipped and lost his back end. These hedges were big and the second hedge had a substantial ditch in front of it. It was obviously a place where there would be lots of thrills and spills and the organisers, had cunningly placed the beer tent directly in front of the second hedge.

When my horse slipped, he must have pulled a muscle in his back because he became disunited and there was a distinctive lack of power, I had given myself three non-jumping strides with full power out of the turn which was taking a gamble, so I knew I was in trouble. It was what we call a stiff hedge which means that there was a lot of well grown timber in it that could not be brushed through. We hit it hard and at considerable speed, I was catapulted forward into the top of the horse's head, that was flying back at me and into my face. It was like being hit by a large block of solid concrete. I remember pain, mane-hair and then the trilogy well known to cross country riders, ground, sky, ground, as I somersaulted into the ground. The next thing I remember was someone asking me what my name was. I started to say "Never mind my name get me back on my horse" but I drifted away before I could finish my sentence. I kept coming around but then drifting off to sleep again. The guy kept asking me my name every time I regained consciousness. Gradually my consciousness got longer and they told me my team had successfully completed the course. After the third attempt I managed to stand and was helped off the course; much to the relief of the commentator who was waiting to start the next team. I assured the ambulance crew I was fine and wandered off in a drunken manner to find my horsebox and horse. My horse had been caught and had no serious injuries and had been taken care of by Lou who had brought our Irish friends Jim and Patricia Brennan to witness an English team chase. I assured Lou I was fine and so she left with our friends and went home to prepare supper. The truth was that I was not ok at all. I wandered around for about an hour telling everyone I met that I was ok, trying to clear my head before driving home. I forget who came to groom for me that day but they probably saved my life on that horrendous drive home. Me and concussion have been good friends since my teens, thanks to the many risk sports I have been involved in. I know the symptoms well and an aversion to bright lights is high up there. The problem with concussions is that you say things you don't mean and as I drove our eleven-metre-long twenty tonne lorry out of the horsebox park I was already regretting turning down Lou's offer to drive it home. It was getting dusk when we finally left and my eyes felt like they had been joined together with an elastic band that pulled them opposite ways, every thought or eye movement was painful. It is not until you have had concussion that you truly realise how many times you move your eyes every second. Sounds are magnified and make you jump. As the light faded it started to rain and some of it was falling as sleet which seem to be magnified on the windscreen so that it was like looking through a kaleidoscope. The wet roads flared up at me like burning fires in the light from the oncoming headlights.

I was sweating and worried, I kept my speed down to about thirty miles per hour and told my groom to keep talking to me and to hit me if I went quiet. It felt like the longest drive of my life but finally we made it home. It was not until my head cleared several days later that I realised what I had done and how dangerous it was and it gave me an insight as to why the rule of not remounting after a fall was being brought into cross-country events. However, I still think that there should be some discretion as many falls are unbelievably soft and do no harm at all. Out hunting it is normal to remount several times a day after falls.

Another bad day at the office was when I took a ride with the then top team of the time The Green Giants, I think they started out as The Jolly Green Giants but in the team chase community their name had been shortened until they were known as the Giants. It was at the inaugural running of the Quorn team chase at its new venue. I have already mentioned the two core members of this team, Johnathan Lee and Tracy Mc Taggart in drag hunting. The Quorn Teamchase moved from Muxloe Hill to a new venue after many successful years at Muxloe but I think it only ran one year at its new venue and certainly didn't have the razzmatazz of the old venue. People go to these events and think it just happens with a bit of tidying up of the fences and flagging the course but it is a massive year-round operation to keep a top team chase course up to standard year after year. When I heard that the Belvoir team chase was moving from Richard Chandlers farm in Long Clawson to Garthorpe racecourse I was mortified and asked Richard why it was moving. When he told me about the weeks of strimming the grass in front of the fences, putting fences around all the jumps so that they are not jumped during the hunting season, and protecting the take off and landings from getting poached by the cattle. Then taking them all down again the next year, not to mention a hundred and one other unnoticed jobs. It is not hard to understand that fatigue and dissolution can set in after many years when trying to run a busy farm.

When Tracy phoned me, I was elated to be asked to ride. The only problem was that I had just bought a new horse and hadn't competed him. I had bought him off a friend, the horse's name was Hoots of Laughter and I knew his abilities as a good jumper. Unsure how he might react to team chasing I sought advice from his previous owner about what bit to put him in. She suggested a Dutch Gag and although not a fan of this or the American version I took her advice. It was all last-minute stuff and I never had chance to ride him in the bit before the competition.

On the day he warmed up well, I was to be tail end Charlie and felt so proud to be wearing their famous colours. We set off like the bat out of hell which I expected and raced down to the first fence which we hurdled rather than jumped, a little alarming but not unusual, at the next we went through a hedge very low and I was getting too close to the number three in front of me and the last thing I wanted to do was upset the three main team members as I knew my job and that was to stay back and only move if one of the others fell, so I took a pull on the reins. That was when the alarm bells rang, the more I checked the faster he went. I tried every trick I knew but to no avail. I knew his brain had gone and I had to pull up or else it was going to end very badly for one or both of us. I knew my only chance of stopping him was to circle but unfortunately the early part of the course was narrow and roped off giving me no opportunity to make the big circle I needed, I was just going to have to sit this one out until we got into some open fields before I could take evasive action. I have a memory that is still clear in my mind and still haunts me to this day. We were galloping down a steep hill and at the bottom of the hill, was a solid timber tiger-trap fence built over the natural ditch, in the valley bottom. On the far side of the fence was an ambulance with its back doors open wide and the driver sitting in a canvas director's chair watching the action. I could see the stretcher and bed neatly made up in the back and thinking, I'm going to be in there in a few seconds and probably wake up in hospital.

How it happened I do not know but we managed to get over the fence in one piece. I was hoping that the hill up the other side of the valley would slow him down but I was wrong. It was a sharp left-hand turn at the top of the hill to a hedge which we smashed through but again amazingly we survived and we were out into open grass fields which gave me the opportunity to try to pull him up by turning ever decreasing circles. I managed one circle and thought I had got him but he took an almighty snatch and he was off again trying to catch the others. We went through the next hedge even lower and harder. This fence knocked some of the stuffing out of him and we floundered on landing, that gave me a vital split second to take control and start circling again but this time I had him on a much tighter circle to start with. It was still a hell of a battle that could have gone either way but eventually we came to a halt. Exhausted and mortified my chance of glory gone and all my savings gone into a crazy useless horse.

Yes, a very, very, bad day at the office!

This story actually has a happy ending, it turned out that Hoots had never been ridden in a Dutch gag but his previous owner only thought that he might go well in one. Unfortunately, she forgot to mention that at the time. As with everything thing to do with horses it is mainly guess work and I think it was the action of the bit that upset him but probably throwing him in at the deep end with a top team could also have blown his mind. People think that going number four in a teamchase is easy but it is not. Yes, you get an amazing lead round but you need a good level-headed horse that is happy to follow and not panic. The key to any successful team is getting a good balanced team that can maintain safe distances and keep a good rhythm even when going flat out.

I tried many bits on Hoots and finally came up with something that the purists would say is totally wrong. My answer to that is, if it works use it.

Hoots obviously had a soft mouth and if you hurt him, he just lost the plot. My solution like so many important discoveries came about by pure accident. I did most of my teaching in those days mounted as I had a lot of horses to ride every day and this allowed me to exercise some of them while teaching. I would tell who ever was working in the yard what horses I want at what time and what tack I wanted on each of them. The horses were brought out to me every hour at the end of a lesson. I was going through a phase of riding Hoots in a different bit every day. This day it was to be a vulcanite Pelham with roundings. As soon as I got on him and took up the reins and he felt the curb I knew it was wrong and felt sure he would rear if I asked him to go forwards. I had a large class and another one after that, so didn't have time to change bits. I took the reins off the roundings and put the reins on the top ring of the bit so it worked like a straight bar snaffle. When I tried to remove the curb chain, I found it had been permanently fixed on one side so I just loosened it off and hoped that Hoots would be ok with it. To my amazement he ticked like a clock in it but was still a bit keen when jumping. Next day I had more time to play around and I managed to get the curb chain off with the help of a pair of pliers. He was too strong without a curb chain and too sensitive if the curb was too tight. Lou suggested I try her leather curb chain and bingo, it worked, all the books said it shouldn't, but it did and he became a delight to ride, jump and even team chase.

He was a lovely horse but extremely sensitive and quirky. He hated vets with a vengeance and could smell one as soon as they came in the yard. His previous owner worked for us part time, teaching, and working in the yard. When the vet arrived to give him an injection, his previous owner, renowned for her straight talking gave the vet, who had not visited us before and I think had only just qualified, some advice. "I'll just warn you mester, he hates bloody injections and he hates vets even more. You've got to be bloody quick or he'll have you". Like so many newly qualified he was full of confidence and self-importance and retorted that he knew exactly what he was doing and did not need any advice from a yard girl. "Suit thee sen", came the droll reply. Syringe raised, the vet boldly entered the stable, followed by scraping hooves and a lot of banging and crashing, a very pale bedraggled vet staggered out of the stable, the syringe still unused in his hand. Hoots's former owner, snatched the syringe from the Vet's hand and dashed into the stable with the syringe held high like an attacking Ninja warrior, a second later she returned with an empty syringe. She gave the dishevelled vet a look of distain and handed him the empty syringe saying "Toad yu, yu had to be quick, but you wouldn't listen, wud yu?" and with those parting words she strode off to get on with her work.

Hoots went on to be a great team chase lead horse but not a second, third or fourth horse and I had some great years with this lovely horse before I sold him into semi-retirement. He was well loved in his new home and I received many communications as to his exploits from his new owner.

Throughout my time working with horses, I have slowly come to believe that there are very few bad horses but a lot of misunderstood horses and most of those are being asked to do a job they don't like. Some horses are extremely amenable and will be happy to do whatever job they are asked to do. Others show strong opinions when asked to do something they don't like. Almost all of our jousting horses were outcasts from the equine mainstream but blossomed in the world of show business. The same was with team chase horses, they needed to like the game. I have seen a lot of horses minds blown by team chasing and I have witnessed many so-called bad horses become stars team chasing. An old horseman told me when I was a child that every horse and dog needed a job. However, finding the right job for them was the hard bit.

How true his words were!

My father gave me one of his best hunter's foals. She was named French Gauntlet and her stable name was Mitten. Her mother was French Mistress and her sire was John of Gaunt who was a Grade A. show jumper. She was a great hunter and was my field master's horse at both the South Notts and the Atherstone hunts. It is easy to look back and see your mistakes after they happen but, in the moment, you have to make snap decisions and one of these nearly cost me and my horse's lives. Mitten was a fantastic jumper. An obvious choice for team chasing as although she was not a thoroughbred, she had a ground eating stride that put many a thoroughbred to shame but more about that later. I had team chased her several times always in the lead and she was proving to be extremely good. Things were going well and we were getting excited about the potential of our new team but it had been a year of injuries and the more injuries you get, the more it upsets the balance of your team and that increases the risk of more injuries. Like junkies desperate for their next fix, we had found the only team chase running this particular weekend. It was the Old Berkshire and out of our normal distance to travel as it took place at Faringdon south west of Oxford. Our normal rule was no more than two hours travel but this one was nearer to three hours. We were down to two team members, my brother Stuart and myself, but a call to the secretary found us two other riders who we were assured were of a similar standard to ourselves. When we arrived, we met up with our two new members and true to the secretary's word they were top class riders. When we walked the course, we were dismayed by the size of the fences as they were much smaller than we were expecting, more a novice course rather than an open. This meant it was going to be a flat-out galloping course, lickety-split all the way. We got on great with our new teammates until it came to what order we were going to ride in because they like us went one and two. None of us were happy and as they were local, they were desperate to lead. In the end I made the fatal mistake of saying that I would go last. These were the two places that I liked to ride in first or last because you had the freedom to ride your own race whereas two and three you were in the middle of a sandwich with nowhere to go.

We set off at a blistering pace but after fence two Mitten was taking a fearsome hold, I was riding her in a double bridle which is a strong bit but that was what I always rode her in. Any team chaser's reading this will probably think me mad to ride with two reins but I hunted her that way and it had worked well until that day. Very quickly the gap which I had given myself from the number three rider disappeared and I was struggling not to jump onto the back of him. When we came to the road crossing which were two tree logs only about one metre five but they were solid as a rock and would not take any prisoners. I had paced them out ten yards which equated to one long non-jumping stride but this was fine when galloping on. When we got there, Mitten put in a huge ground covering jump and I thought "Oh shit! We are going to be too close for take-off at the second log". A nanosecond later we were soaring through the air and skimming over the second log, I couldn't comprehend what had happened until we had landed over the second log and then it hit me, "Holy shit! She has just bounced a ten-yard double (for non-horsey people the distance for a bounce jump usually ranges from three and a half yards to four and half yards and ten yards is suicidal madness but does show the massive scope this mare had). I had no time to ponder on this as we were now well and truly out of control and heading for an extremely steep bank that dropped down onto a narrow track some fifty feet below with a sharp left-hand turn into a wood. How we got down that bank in one piece I will never know but once into the wood it was single track only and I was way too close to the horse in front of me and Mitten's mind had gone, there was no reasoning with her. It was dark in the wood and the log pile was black. To this day I don't know exactly what happened, I don't think she saw the fence until the last second and I think that she went to take off and then put down, perhaps the bounce at the previous fence had caused her to lose her confidence, all I know is that there was a terrible crash and I hit the ground hard. I remember a sort of splat noise and a groan as Mitten landed just inches away from me, how she missed me I will never know because it was such a narrow track with trees either side.

I lay on the ash track like a fish out of water trying to breathe, badly winded. I don't know what happened to Mitten, the two fence judges stood over me and asked me if I was alright and could I get up. I was totally winded and could not speak so I slowly moved my mouth in a no gesture. It seemed an age until I got my breath back and could whisper a few words. I could hear the walkie-talkie radio; the commentary box was urging the fence judges to move me off the course so that they could start the next team the two fence judges were urging me to try and sit up but I could not move despite great mental effort. It was horrible listening to the organisers not wanting to despatch the ambulance to me because the other ambulance had already left the course, and if their only ambulance had to leave the grounds, they would have to suspend starting teams until the other ambulance returned from Oxford some thirty minutes away. Finally, the fence judges convinced the control to dispatch the ambulance. I have never been so pleased to see a doctor in my life. He took charge and I heard a sharp exchange with the control when they asked if he could get me moved off the track so that they could restart. Eventually after much questioning they very carefully put me on a spinal board, strapped me tightly onto it and started the long-complicated journey through the trees and down a steep bank to the ambulance where they fixed a needle into the back of my hand. They must have pierced a nerve because I had no feeling in one finger for nearly a year. After a long painful journey along winding roads, a nurse asking constant questions to keep me awake interspaced with doses of gas and air I finally arrived at Oxford hospital where it looked like world war three had started with bodies on trolleys parked everywhere. They parked me in a draughty corridor and said someone would be along as soon as possible to have a look at me. I had a feeling I was in for a long wait. About two hours later I was assessed and sent to X-ray for another long wait. During my wait I managed to wriggle my toes which was a great relief. After X-ray, a cheerful doctor informed me, I hadn't broken anything and could I please sit up for him. I tried really hard but just could not sit up. I was then wired up and given an ECG which again proved my ticker was working fine. Again, I was asked to sit up but still couldn't and when they tried to assist me, I screamed with pain. The doctor assured me that my spine was fine and that I must have torn my back muscles and that he was going to give me a couple of morphine pills to see if that helped. Ten minutes later I sat up with a smile on my face and walked out to be greeted by Stuart who had arranged for the horses to be driven home and had come to pick me up. I felt the odd twinge of pain but the little pink pills had done wonders. I felt normal, but Stuart said I was high as a kite. Later that night and after another dose of pink pills, Horse and Hound magazine phoned to see how I was. I cheerfully told them I was a bit bruised and sore but other than that, I was fine. I slept like a log that night but in the morning and no more pink pills I was in agony. It was a week before I could get out of bed and I had been double dosing on Ibuprofen all week. I did not realise that there were two different strengths.

Dad had sent some of his tablets that he got on prescription and you should only take one 500mg every four hours. However, the doctor said that was preferable to him prescribing morphine. When I went for my check-up, I decided to walk up to the doctors which was about a quarter of a mile away in the centre of the village. Halfway there, my legs gave way and I went all woozy. I slid down a wall and ended up sitting on the pavement opposite the Bulls Head Pub. People gave me a wide berth; I think they thought I was drunk and had just staggered out of the pub. My back was black and then gradually turned yellow it was a long slow road to recovery and no more teamchasing for me that season.

Mitten surprisingly came out of the fall without a scratch but sadly never recovered mentally but more about that later.

In all risk sports you pick up many stupid superstitions and a common one is wearing the same clothes every time you compete, especially sock and pants. It is amazing how many top riders have a pair of lucky socks or pants and I have seen really tough nuts go to pieces if they forgot to pack their lucky socks or pants. An extension of this is never wearing new clothes or using new tack that hasn't been worn previously. Mike Elvin thought it would be a nice surprise to present us each with a new set of team colours. To his dismay everyone refused to wear them until they had taken them home and ridden in them before competing in them. When I became a field master, I rode out through Bunny woods in my new, red masters coat before wearing it out hunting. I got some strange looks from walkers and the woodsman who is a big anti hunt man. It was especially confusing as it was on a Sunday, traditionally not a hunting day. I chuckled for days at the look of annoyance on his face as I galloped past him, and him looking desperately around for hounds and followers.

Another amusing incident occurred at a team chase near Scarborough. It was in the early days of Elvin and co and I can't recall the name of the team chase but I think that it was at Carnaby on the A614 a few miles before you get to Bridlington. My brother Stuart was being asked to ride in several teams at this time with his horses being supplied by the team sponsor. Besides riding for Elvin & Co he had a ride with the Boring Gorings and much to the surprise of Stuart, George Goring informed him that he had entered all of his team in an on foot cross country race over the team chase course including the fences. With two rides around the course and a two-mile cross-country run, Stu was somewhat knackered by the end of the day.

In the early days, the Atherstone team chase heralded the beginning of the autumn season but as the number of events grew other venues had earlier dates and now there is even an event in late August. The Atherstone have had three different venues for their team chases and all of them have been exceptionally well built with lovely inviting hedges. When I heard that the first venue was closing, I was mortified at the loss of such a great course but the next one, and the one after that, have all been excellent courses with lots of big but jumpable hedges, hats off to the Atherstone!

Another thing I loved about the Atherstone was that they gave you a mug with their Hunt logo on it if you were in the placings. If you haven't seen it, the logo is a large red capital A and the cross bar of the A is a running fox one of the best logos I have ever seen. I collected quite a few over the years and enjoyed my early morning cuppa out of them as looking at that logo always invoked fabulous memories. An excellent way to start the day!

Team Chasing started in 1974 and went from strength to strength and like many other sports in the eighties they started to tap into the growing number of new horse owners that just kept on growing as the economy boomed. These newcomers were not elite riders but they were keen for some fun and had money to spend. British show jumping brought in new classes of sub one metre and they were packed. British Eventing quickly followed suit. These competitions of seventy, eighty- and ninety-centimetre classes were all packed and great money earners for the event organisers and their governing bodies.

Team chases could not offer the same range of low-level classes but they did respond with the addition of a smaller class of below one metre. Team chasing at this time was still fairly independent and had no hard and fast rules governing the maximum height or names of classes. This was a dangerous time for the newcomer looking for some low-level fun as various names were given to the new classes. Some called them the fun class, others called them the novice class and changed the novice to intermediate. This is where a national body had its merits because things became a bit confusing for the newcomer to the sport. It led to many novice riders getting the bug over one of the smaller new courses called a novice and entering another novice competition only to find they were facing a substantially larger course which was way out of their depths and extremely dangerous. As a rule, most events never published any maximum or minimum heights for their classes and I found it was best to ring the secretary and find out what sort of fences you would be facing in each class. It did the sport no good to see, extremely novice horses and riders trying to tackle an old-fashioned novice course of one metre fixed poles and hedges that were considerably higher when 80cm was their max competent height. Sadly, it so often ended with early elimination or injuries.

I enjoyed sixteen great years team chasing until in nineteen ninety the money sloshing economy crashed. Until that time people were spending money like water without a care in the world. Interest rates shot up and so did mortgage payments. The higher mortgage repayments took spending money out of peoples' pockets and many people lost their homes. It hit our business awfully hard and within weeks of the interest rate rises we lost ninety percent of our children's riding business and adult riding lessons dropped significantly as well. To make matters worse our business loans were costing more and banks were asking for overdrafts to be repaid or significantly reduced. Luckily, Lou and I had never overstretched ourselves by borrowing money, but these were tough times. As the recession got worse our livery business started to struggle and clients were having to sell their horses to cut their outgoings as their businesses struggled or they were made redundant.

The party was over we had to cut our staff and work harder ourselves. Team chasing was put on the back burner. For much of my time team chasing, I had ridden other people's horses with all expenses paid and to keep going meant a significant capital outlay on a horse plus the on-going costs of keeping a horse and not to mention the risk of injury to me or the horse.

To make matters worse our jousting business was also changing. Bookings started to drop in the UK as the recession deepened but a favourable exchange rate was boosting our overseas bookings and many of these were in the spring or autumn right in the middle of the team chase seasons. Another nail in the coffin for my team chasing career was film and television work. This part of our business was thankfully booming and bringing in much needed income but it required you to be available for months at a time, as filming schedules were ever changing and you had to always be available at a drop of a hat.

I kept team chasing but only occasionally at a lower level for a bit of fun and to encourage newcomers into the sport. At the stables there was a group of up-and-coming riders all keen to have a go at the lower levels. I started two teams based primarily at the stables. The Bunny Hoppers for the newcomers and The Bunny Hill Toppers for more advanced riders. Both of my brothers and daughter rode in this team along with some clients and a host of friends. We mainly competed in the new intermediate class or the old-fashioned novice classes but also in open classes if we had the horsepower. My horse at the time was Bumper and he was a great lead horse but did not cover a lot of ground whereas my daughter's little horse Cassy ate up the ground with a slow effortless stride. I would start in the lead and then about halfway round, Emma would come cruising past me and lead us home.

I remember warming up at the Cottesmore and flicking effortlessly over the large warm up fence and feeling a great sense of pride in my horse. We set off at a blistering pace and early on in the course I made an extremely sharp turn into a simple log combination and Bumper stopped. It was a complete shock, as it was the only time, he ever stopped with me. Emma took up the lead with Stuart hard on her tail. I was soon over the log and expected to catch up quickly but Bumper was not his exuberant self, I dug in hard to get him over the fences and stay with Stu and Emma. We won the class but it was at a high cost as Bumper pulled up slightly lame. I felt so bad about pushing him around the course but he didn't feel lame at the time just lacking in energy. Next day I expected to find a hot swollen leg, the sign of an injured tendon but there was nothing to show, so I hoped and waited. After a week I called the vet because he was still lame. John Coope a senior partner at Chine House Veterinary Practice came to examine him. John was a brilliant horse vet and rode himself. His first words to me were, "this must be something difficult if you haven't been able to diagnose this yourself" and I agreed as Bumper was still lame but there was no heat or swelling. Nowadays vets have all manner of technology to help with diagnosis but this was just before scanners came into general veterinary use.

After much twisting and squeezing, the diagnosis was a pulled check ligament on his near fore. John told me it was a common team chase injury because you idiots are always making such tight turns at high speed. His cheerful prognosis was that he should make a full recovery but if he were me, he would not do anymore team chasing with him as there was a high risk of it going again. I had originally bought Bumper as a four-year-old for Dick Benson as a replacement for Gladstonian but he had done a tendon as a five-year-old whilst getting him fit for his first race. That, like the check ligament required six months of box rest. These days the treatment is vastly different as the healing process can be monitored by scanning and horses are got moving much sooner. This was however the end of Bumper's team chasing career. We never insured any of our horses for vets fees or loss of use because of the numbers we owned. Nowadays vet bill insurance is normal but I have mixed feelings about this. Years ago, being a vet was a vocation and you served the local community providing the lowest cost treatment possible for all kinds of animals. Nowadays vets specialise much more and many practices have spent millions on veterinary equipment and hospitals and need to earn much more to pay for all the investments. Years ago, you had the same vet for most of your life. Today you are lucky if you have the same vet for six months.
You will hear more about Bumper later on.

After losing Bumper I continued to do the odd low-level local team chase but my heart had gone out of the sport after Bumper broke down and I was also in my fifties. I know a lot of people of my age were still competing at the very top of the sport but they had the money to buy top class horses and I didn't have that money to buy those sort of horses.

I had been thinking about giving up for some time and had made the decision but not really told anybody although I had no plans to ride that season. I had gone to watch the Atherstone and hopefully meet up with some old team chase pals for a beer. The other reason I went, was to watch a young client of mine ride in her first team chase. Her name was Ginny Sherwin and I had coached her and her mother Suzanne for several years. Ginny and her mother were keen mounted followers of the Atherstone Hunt and Ginny had teamed up with three of her hunting pals to ride in the fun event. People often do this thinking that it will be great fun, but so often it ends in tears. The word team means that you have to work as a team and with great discipline and have a clear plan of action. Ginny's team gave the impression of four people intent on killing each other, cutting each other up in front of fences and riding erratic lines causing chaos and confusion. Consequently, there were several falls and many more near misses. I watched in horror as I watched all my confidence building with Ginny destroyed in minutes. When I saw her mother later in the day, I rashly offered to put a safe beginners team together and show Ginny how to team chase safely. Suzanne, still in shock at what she had witnessed earlier, gratefully accepted my offer. I thought it was going to be a one off and then back to retirement but oh how wrong I was!

I hadn't got a horse of my own at that time so I borrowed Lou's horse Blossom for this one-off jolly. I recruited another client of mine Phillippa Slater and I believe we rode as a three-member team. I started to take the Slater family when they were in Pony Club. Their mother Jane trained with my Dad for her BHS Teaching Exams. Jane has five children and I still coach four of them to this day and they are my oldest and most loyal clients that I have had spanning probably twenty-five or maybe thirty years.

On that fateful day I drilled them about keeping their distance, always being slightly offset to the rider in front of you, keeping a good rhythm and not to stop if one of us fell. We had a great round and all finished on a high. It was an optimum time and we were too fast so I was delighted. I always tell teams to ride at the speed that they feel happy with, because trying to hit a secret optimum time messes with your team's natural rhythm and keeping that is far more important than winning a rosette.

As with every good ride in a team chase, we finished on a high and when you still have the adrenaline flowing through your body you say things on the spur of the moment. For me what I said next was like a smoker who has given up smoking just having one cigarette or an alcoholic just having one drink and falling off the wagon. I said, "that was fantastic you were both great, we could do it again if you want sometime".

I think we did it again the very next week, and so for me it started all over again, no ambitions just a bit of fun. The fun events were soon a thing of the past and we moved on to novice and we became a solid team to be reckoned with, honing our skills all the time. Ginny and Phillippa were solidly reliable, both turning up week after week and sticking to the game plan. We were a noticeably quiet team and took each competition as a bonus, never making long term plans just enjoying good thrilling rounds. I will always remember our starts quietly circling as the starter counted us down, white faced, deep in contemplation about the course we were about to attack, asking both of them if they were ok and ready and as the starter got down to two seconds, saying, "ok let's do it", and kicking on to cross the start line at the gallop.

We had our mishaps but all teams do, because it's an extremely high-risk sport but we had so much fun, both the girls were well mounted, Ginny's horse was an eventer and that was what she planned to do with him but he had been pushed on too much in his early days and could not cope going into the start box. As I have said before, many horses fail in the job that they were bought for but shine doing another. Ginny's horse Sojar was one of these as he became an excellent hunter and team chaser.

Phillippa's horse Theo was also a retired eventer which she had purchased from my daughter Emma. He was bold and an impeccable jumper that held a tight line however the tightness of the angle. I had started out riding Lou's horse Blossom that had been brought for dressage, but these were hard times and we could not afford another horse at that time. Blossom proved to be a good jumper and gave me some superb rides.

By complete accident I bought a horse in Ireland on a day visit and what a day that was. It all started in a supermarket in Loughborough. Lou and I had dashed in after work to replenish our depleted larder when the phone rang. It was Jim Brennan inviting us to come over to Kilkenny for a day at Goran Park races where he had sponsored a race. Goran park was just a few miles outside of Kilkenny. This sounded like a great idea, the only problem was that it meant flying out the very next day. Nothing like a bit of advance warning Jim! I was sure we couldn't make it but I said I would call him back in about an hour when I had checked if it was possible but my gut instinct told me it was stupid to even consider. Lou and I raced through our shopping and discussed the possibility of going on the way home. We had been working incredibly hard since the recession and things were slowly getting better and we both thought we had earned a break. Incredibly we managed to find a flight from East Midlands Airport to Dublin the next evening and so the trip was on.

Jim and Patricia invited us to join them at a restaurant in Thomas Town which is about ten miles south of Kilkenny where they were meeting Patricia's sister and her husband who were over on a visit from Spain where they now lived. We should have arrived in plenty of time for the meal but delays hiring a car and getting around Dublin delayed us for over an hour. We just made it before the kitchen closed, totally exhausted after a remarkably busy day sorting cover for our trip. After an exceedingly good meal washed down by excellent wine, we left the restaurant not long before midnight. It was a twenty-minute drive back to Kilkenny but when we left the restaurant a dense fog had descended. I had only been to Thomas Town once before as a passenger so was unsure of the route back.

Follow me said Jim, we will cut through Mount Juliet Estate and take the back roads home to avoid the Garda (Police). We had hired a cheap Nissan Micra and Jim was in his Jaguar. I hung onto his taillights for as long as I could but as he zoomed off at a tee junction his taillights were swallowed up by the thick swirling mist, never to be seen again. We chugged along at a snail's pace, the back roads were narrow, full of sharp bends and high banks either side of the road. Eventually we came to another junction and a sign pointed to Kilkenny. The new road was wider and the fog became less dense and we were able to drive a little faster. When we arrived at Kilkenny our next challenge was to find their house. I had stayed there several times but never driven there myself. When I am a passenger, I tend not to log the route into my brain. Finally, we saw Jim's Jaguar parked outside the house. We gratefully accepted a night cap to calm the tingling nerves. It was way past midnight and we were very tired so when Patricia said we should all go to bed it was a great relief but her next words were not what I wanted to hear. "Lou, you can have a lay in but Sam you need to be dressed and ready to go by five in the morning because the hounds are meeting a long way from Kilkenny tomorrow. It was September, we were cub hunting and the meet was at six thirty that morning. As efficient as ever Patricia had food and drink packed in a wicker basket so I just had time for a quick cup of tea before heading off to the stables to collect the horses.

It was a gorgeous morning and we were high up in the hills, the air was crisp and the sun was already creeping up over the top of the hills. People think of hunting as all galloping and jumping but what is so often overlooked is meeting new people, making new friends, and having access to wonderful countryside not normally available to the general public. Sitting on the back of a horse gives you a grandstand view of all of those spectacular views. This is what I was doing that morning, we were high up on the hills which fell away into wide valleys far below, the chill breeze slowly blowing away the mild hangover from last night's meal and lack of sleep as the hounds and huntsman methodically drew the patches of gorse that flourished on the hill tops. My daydreaming came to a sudden halt when unbelievably my mobile phone rang. I quickly answered it fearing a problem at home. Mobile phones were still relatively new and network coverage was notoriously patchy in rural areas both in Ireland and the UK. You can imagine my surprise when I discovered that it was the BBC costume department wanting to know what size gloves I wore; it was barely eight o' clock and I never imagined anyone at the beeb starting work before ten. I told her that I had no idea probably large "no no no I need an exact size they are sized one to ten, perhaps you could find a pair and look inside for a size. It is very urgent" she said. This really put my back up. I had never heard of glove size numbers, only a Londoner or city person would buy gloves by numbers, in the countryside world it was small, medium, or large. I informed the pushy young lady at the other end of the phone that it was out of the question. Knowing how most of the beeb's employees were, left wing, anti-blood sports, anti-meat and anti-just about everything else, it gave me great pleasure to inform her that I was sitting on a horse on top of a mountain in Ireland hunting foxes and that was far more important than glove sizes.

By nine thirty it was too warm and there was no scent so the huntsman blew for home and we retired back to the trailer to finish off the coffee and sandwiches before making our way home to change our clothes and grab some lunch before going off to the races at Goran Park. On the way we popped in to view Jim and Patricia's new home to be. It was a Georgian house set in its own parkland but in need of massive restoration. Unknown to us at the time, Lou and I would spend many happy times there over the coming years.

As we turned off the Carlow road towards the racecourse Patricia suddenly announced that a horse dealer friend of hers had a horse, that he thought I may be interested in and to call into his pub after the races to have a look and try the horse as it was going cheap. The dealer's name was Pat Loughlin and a well-known local character, not only did he deal in horses and hire out hunters, but he also owned the pub in the village of Gowran strangely enough called Loughlins and was the local undertaker.

We spent a jolly but unprofitable afternoon at the races. Jim had laid on a lavish buffet as part of his sponsorship accompanied by equally lavish liquid refreshment. It was almost dark by the time we reached Pat's pub and neither Lou or I were not really in the best of states to assess and buy a horse. We looked the horse over, he was a well put together hunter type, about 16.2hh. They trotted him up and down the village Main Street in the twilight and then they legged me up and I rode him up and down the Main Street in my best clothes. We did the deal over a pint of Guinness stood on the pavement outside of the pub. The most embarrassing thing was that I didn't have any money to pay for the horse as it was a cash only deal, however Jim had already whispered in my ear that he would pay for the horse and I could pay him next time we met.

Now that is a true friend and how I came to by my last team chase horse. His name was Connelly.

It was also the most I have ever packed into one day and a day I will never forget. More drink had to be taken to celebrate the deal and then back to Kilkenny for a meal in a restaurant and then onto the famous Langton's pub, restaurant, and night club. We left the nightclub at 2am and the Brennan house at 5am to catch the early flight back to East Midlands Airport. I had big work plans for that day but as soon as we got home, we went straight to bed and slept until late afternoon. What a 24 hours!

The intermediate team chases required quick, small horses that could whizz around the course making tight turns and jumping at tight angles and although Connelly was a capable jumper you could not swing him around like a motorbike through the bends and so after a season, I ask the girls what they thought about having a go at an open class. I knew that they and their horses were capable of jumping the big fences but were they ready themselves to make that quantum leap to open classes. They did not reply immediately and I think the colour drained from their faces. They looked at each other and seemed to come to an agreement without actually speaking and then said, "Well if you think we are ready we can always have a go and see how it goes". We had climbed all the rungs of the ladder from Fun, Novice, to Intermediate and finally The Open. However, fate had an unexpected surprise waiting for us further down the road.

It was not an easy promotion to the open classes and we had bumps and tumbles. Up until then we had not had any falls or mishaps but it is only when you start to hit the deck do you really know the calibre of the people you ride with. I have said many times that the team chase community is small and you soon get to know the other people on the circuit. The regular open teams numbered only six or seven with the odd few local teams that only ran at a single event. None of our team realised at the time how the other teams and supporters viewed us until we went to the Atherstone which was Ginny's home hunt.

Since our fall at the Badsworth and me being knocked out, my horse Connelly was not the same horse as he had injured his back when he slipped on the turn before the crashing fall. He seemed to have lost his nerve at big wide ditches and looking back I can now see that he had a reluctance to extend and stretch his back over the wider fences. As we walked the Atherstone course fence five was a big hedge with a substantial ditch in front. Ginny had already shown that she could lead when she took over and completed the course at the Badsworth, I suggested that I lead over the first four fences and then Ginny took the lead for the open ditch. All was going swimmingly well, we turned around a marker and headed for the open ditch, Ginny swept smoothly past me and I tucked in behind her and after a few strides I noticed that the pace had slackened just a bit and I was struggling to hold my horse back at a safe distance. I assumed it was because Ginny was preparing herself and horse for the ditch; four strides out and we were all kicking like hell for the big one when Ginny's horse slapped the breaks on. It all happened so quick, I cannoned into the back of Ginny and knocked her clean through the hedge, momentum carried me through as well and we both ended up in a tangled mess on the floor. Phillippa riding as number three had that split second to take avoiding action and cleared the fence safely but pulled up as she had nobody to ride with. Thankfully, Ginny and I were ok and our horses were quickly caught and we remounted and completed the course without further problems. As we passed the spectator area three fences from home, we were surprised to receive a standing ovation of cheering and clapping with even a few hollers thrown in. It was a special moment, I thought it was probably down to Ginny being an Atherstone girl and never realised that we had a fan club that knew that we had started, right at the bottom and slowly worked our way up to the topflight of the sport.

It was late in the season and I think it was at the Cottesmore, all the hedges were railed in front with tightly spaced rails making them extremely unforgiving when jumping them. It was a very testing course as you started at the top of a hill and then swept down into the valley over a series of drop fences and a pair of new five-bar gates thrown in for good measure, on a small area of flat land halfway down the hill, followed by a sharp right turn to a big hedge with a huge drop on it. These two fences were our biggest concern and I remember hearing squeals of joy from the girls as they safely negotiated the two bogey fences. Once into the valley floor it was exceptionally deep, wet going, and we had some worrying moments as the horse strained to get their feet out of the deep mud to jump the fences and we rattled nearly every fence along the valley floor. As we left the valley another right turn presented our tiring horses with a massive steep hill with two solid timber fences one near the bottom and the other at the top of the hill and we watched in horror as top team after top team were wiped out as their exhausted horses were brought down by these two unforgiving fences. I looked over at Phillippa and Ginny and noticed they their faces were even whiter than usual. I pointed out to them that the other teams were burning their horses out in the mud along the valley floor and told them we would nurse our horses through that stretch and hopefully have some fuel left in the tank for the big hill. It paid off, we all slithered over the fence at the top of the hill but all the horses scrabbled up onto their feet, bless them they were so tired. We trotted a few strides to let them get their breath back before picking them up for the final hedge which was again an uphill fence. Thankfully, it was a soft sloping fence flauched in front with Christmas tree branches. Our horses made one last great effort for us and we were home safely. Not many teams finished that day and we were elated to have had such a good round. Again, I was surprised at the exuberance of the crowd as we crossed the finish line. We were all grinning like Cheshire cats and hugging our horses. The deathly pallor of Phillippa and Ginny's faces had gone and we all chattered happily recalling hairy moments that we had survived; we were all on a massive adrenaline high as we wandered off to walk our horses around to cool them off in the horsebox field. I think we were the last team of the day to go and we were not listening to the tannoy announcements as we were so wrapped up in our little bubble. It was only when someone who had come with us, came running over to us waving their hands that we snapped out of our bubble. We immediately thought we had done something wrong maybe missed a flag or a fence. We racked our brains trying to think of anything whilst the waving figure got ever closer. When they arrived out of breath and barely able to speak, they told us were in the placings, which was a first for us, up until then we had been happy just to finish. More elation but it was short lived when we got the next bit of news! We had secured the last qualification place for the Team Chase Championships. There was a stunned silence, the colour drained from the girls faces much to the bemusement of our messenger. We had just completed a tough course that had wiped out several top teams and I think we all felt that we had all used up our nine lives in that afternoon. It was fabulous to have qualified and the girls had earned every bit of that qualification but the championships were something else! We had so little experience in open classes and to be honest we really needed another year of doing opens before tackling the championship but with horses and risk sports you have to seize every chance that is offered to you.

We returned to the horseboxes with a jumble of emotions bubbling in our minds. The prize giving was fantastic, we won money and lots of goodies. As part of the qualification for the championship the lead horse received a day rug with the words Team Hero emblazoned on it. I was so proud of it for Connelly's sake. He was a horse that had cost extraordinarily little, had his problems but had really done me proud that day. We went to the beer tent for a celebratory drink and were touched by other open team riders congratulations, but that is team chasing, such a of super bunch of people.

Connelly was not right after that team chase and after a week he was not quite sound so I took him up to Phil Arthur's to have his back checked out. Phil had been master of the Meynell hunt and lived up in high Derbyshire and was a renowned back man. It is amazing how things have changed in the last twenty years regarding people that treat horses' backs. Nowadays there are a plethora of sports massagers, physiotherapists, chiropractors, and osteopaths that treat horses on a regular basis but at the time I am talking about, which is not so long ago, the vets claimed to be the only people that could treat horses' backs or do any dentistry despite people out there having far more knowledge than them. Having your horse treated by a back-man or a dentist could end up with a prosecution by vets. It was like a black art and always done on the quiet. In the horse world people are not stupid and the use of these people by horse professionals had been common all my life. Thankfully, the vets have relented on their restrictive practices and these exceptionally talented people can now practice without fear of prosecution.

Back to Connelly, Phil confirmed my fears and told me that all his back muscles were tied up down one side of his spine. He freed them off and showed me how to massage them to keep them loose. This was on the Monday before the championships which were taking place on the Sunday. This was not really enough time for Connelly to be match fit but this was the chance of a lifetime for Phillippa and Ginny. We also needed a fourth member as we all appreciated the fact that we might have casualties on the way around. We were incredibly lucky that local farrier Andy Brown, a long-time friend and regular team chase rider agreed to ride with us. Andy didn't have an experienced horse but he said it was a good bold jumper and was quite sure it was capable of getting round. I remember giving Connelly 's back a good massage before putting his saddle on, hoping, and praying that his back would hold out for our big day.

We warmed up and our spirits were high, we were not serious contenders by any stretch of the imagination and so there was much less pressure. My team talk was let's just enjoy the day. The course was a championship course beautifully presented, big, bold, and very jumpable. You started over an easy fence and was then presented with a serpentine of three big hedges all in the same hedge line. We made super work of these, riding extremely tight lines on the turns. The horses were eating them, with big bold jumps that knocked the wind out of you as you landed over them, several more fences took you to the top of the hill where there was a big hedge with a good drop on it, this led us back down the steep hill, at the bottom of the hill was a large solid black palisade, next a sharp turn to the pen where you had to have three members in before you could jump out. Our discipline was spot-on and we were in and out without a pause and then across the valley over some nice hedges before a small combination of logs with a sharp turn on undulating ground probably the smallest fences on the course. I pulled Connelly round on a tight turn to save ground as he was blowing hard after his layoff and like Bumper some years before he stopped. I circled him around and jumped it but now the team was well ahead of me and he hesitated at the next fence which was the water jump and I lost the ground I had just made up. His enthusiasm had gone, I was losing ground all the time. I wasn't sure if it was his back again or lack of fitness. I could see the others were going well and slowed down to hunt him home well behind the others. Again, we received an enthusiastic response from the crowd as we crossed the finish line and again, we received many a slap on the back, followed by well-done from competitors and spectators alike.

That was mine and Connelly's last team chase, sadly no fairy tale ending, but this is fact not fiction. Despite going off to university, Ginny carried on riding in opens with several of the top teams, Phillippa and her sister Hannah formed a new team.

For me, other challenges were on the horizon. I had twenty years of the most unimaginable fun and fear and it was the longest time I spent in one equine sport. It is the fun and fear that produces the adrenaline that gives us the buzz.

Thank you, Mr Bunn, for inventing this magical sport.

Chapter Eleven
Field Master

Being a field master was something I always dreamed of, but never thought that I would ever do. I would have loved to have been a full master of fox hounds, if I had been much wealthier but sadly, I never won the lottery. What is the difference between a field master and a full master you may ask? This is a question that is hard to answer as it varies from hunt to hunt. I answer this purely from my own experiences and it is definitely not a definitive answer. In a nutshell a full master pays a fee for the privilege of the title and esteem that it brings. Often, they will sometimes provide a horse for the hunt staff when first joining and are responsible for making good for any shortfalls in the hunt's income. They have responsibility for the day to day running of the hunt and seeing that they operate within the law and are responsible for any damages. They are also responsible for clearing the country which means that they visit farmers and landowners to gain permission to ride over their land.

During the 1800s and up until the end of the First World War, hunts tended to have one master and they would be people of wealth and high standing in the local area. After the First World War, the aristocracy lost a lot of its' wealth and influence and many of the big estates had to be sold off. Being a master of hounds was a luxury that many could not afford on their own and to make matters worse, the cost of running a hunt was rising. It is around this time that we start to see some joint masterships and also shorter masterships. Pre 1914 many packs of hounds belonged to wealthy families with the Mastership being passed from father to son. The Beaufort hunt is one of the few that still survives to this day, with the Duke as master of the hunt, having only recently retired after holding the position for sixty years. Many other hunts still bear the names of their former owners such as the Berkeley, the Fitz William and the Sir Watkin Williams-Wynns (known as the Wynnstay). The Second World War brought more problems for hunts, and joint masterships became even more common despite the hunts attracting large fields, sometimes as large as two hundred mounted followers. Every recession brought more pain to the hunts as many people struggled with the rising cost of keeping horses. A big blow to the hunts was the collapse of Lloyds in the early nineties when many names suffered horrendous losses. That and the following recession spelt the end of the big hunt subscribers that hunted four or more days a week. Some even popped over to Southern Ireland to do the full seven days. I always dreamed of doing that but never managed it.

So, end of history lesson; back to the Field Masters responsibilities. As it became harder to find master's that could boldly lead the field across country and have the time and money to run the hunt, a new type of master emerged, often a wealthy follower that was wealthy enough to invest in the hunt for the title of master but didn't want to; or have the time to spend visiting farmers, or lead The Field, and so The Field Master was born.

When I was Field Master, I attended the master's meetings and even some Hunt Committee meetings. Just to clarify what the hunt committee is; it is the body that appoints the masters and oversees all the aspects of the hunt including the finances, the subscription rates, and future policies of the hunt, much like a board of directors.

My responsibilities were to clear the country for each of my days in charge, organise meets and liaise with the huntsman as to the order of draws for the day and inform him of any no go areas. Lead the field wherever the hounds took us which meant that I had to know the country like the back of my hand. After each day's hunting I had to report back to the joint masters about any problems that might have occurred. I also had to check with the countryman about unlocking and re-locking of gates on each days hunting and ensure any damage to farmers' fences had been made stock proof and repaired to a high standard. My final task next day was to visit all the farmers whose land we had crossed, to thank them and make sure any damage had been repaired to their satisfaction. Damage to the fields by horses crossing them often required a bottle of whiskey and an abject apology to calm them down. This was the one task I always started with some trepidation, as you never knew what stupid act somebody had done at the back of the field out of your sight.

The Trent Valley Drag Hounds

It was my brother Phil who gave me my first opportunity to act as a field master and I shall be forever grateful to him for that opportunity. As the recession of the nineties started to bite, many people were looking for cheaper ways to enjoy the thrill of riding to hounds. People were having to work much harder to make ends meet or to hold onto their job. Taking days off mid-week was not an option anymore. In those days, a good day with the shire packs would set you back over £100 and a lesser day around £50 to £60. The Readyfield Blood Hounds or the Cambridge Drag Hounds were charging £25 and both mainly hunted on a Sunday. Finally, if you went hunting just for the galloping and jumping, you were guaranteed a good day every time with Drag or Blood hounds

Phil loved working with the hounds and watching them work. His work as a farrier took him to many farms and he was well liked within the farming community. Not all farmers welcomed the fox hunts, and the damage done by the large fields of the seventies and eighties had prompted many to say no to the hunts crossing their land. The move towards more arable farming was another major factor. To be able to say to farmers that you could guarantee where the hounds and field would go was a deal breaker for many anti hunt farmers, and Phil opened up a lot of ground for us that was not available to fox hunts. The fact the field numbers were much lower and it was primarily local people crossing their land was another major factor in the granting of access to their land. Finally, because it was primarily for locals you didn't get the London Hooray Henry's coming out. During my meetings with farmers when trying to gain access to their land when I was field master of fox hunts, I regularly came across families that would not let hunts across their land because a wealthy "Toff" had spoken down to their grandfather or even their great grandfather decades ago.

When Phil asked me to be field master of The Trent Valley Drag Hounds, I asked him why he chose that name, he replied that it gave him the opportunity to hunt from Staffordshire to the Humber estuary, which he thought was plenty to go at. I was lulled into a false sense of what the job was all about, as he did all the clearing of the country, and organised all of the meets, as well as keeping the hounds in his back garden and of course hunt them. There were two more joint masters, Judge Dick Benson and Isobel Crosby. Luckily for me I had access to some top-class horses at the time and all I had to do was try and follow Phil and his hounds, which if you know Phil, was no small task. I never walked any of the country as we hunted over a wide area and it was much more fun not knowing where you were going or what obstacles you were about to meet.

From the outset we tried to make our drag hunting as much like fox hunting as possible. Most drag hunts had two or three big runs which sometimes blew horses minds. We tried to have five or six smaller runs and plenty of hacking in between to keep all the horses sane and sensible. We also started the multi-master idea with a master to take followers on a route that avoided the big fences and boy did we have some big ones. This approach went down well with locals and farmers as it eliminated people getting lost and going across land that we were not allowed to cross. Word soon got out that we were a friendly and safe hunt to go out with. The sport that we were providing suited both thrusters and your everyday horse owner. From day one we started to regularly attract fields of between thirty to fifty people.

Phil gained us access to some stunning hunting country thanks to his energy and enthusiasm for hunting hounds. It ruffled a few feathers in the fox hunting community in the beginning but it also benefited them in the long term as a lot of land that Phil opened up had been closed to fox hunts, sometimes for generations. The fox hunts had let a lot of land go stagnant because nobody had bothered to try and rebuild bridges and Phil proved that if you took the time, doors that had been closed for a long time could be re-opened with careful diplomacy. We always called around to thank the farmers after we had finished and gave them a bottle of wine as a thank you, which was always appreciated.

The Drag hunt had its own livery which was worn by the hunt staff. It was a dark green jacket with a black collar. It was one of my proudest days of my life when I stepped out in that livery at our first meet which fittingly was at Bunny Hill.

In the beginning, Phil was living on the edge of Costock village in a semi-detached house, he kept his pack of hounds at the bottom of his garden which adjoined a grass paddock. Phil had managed to get permission from the owner of the field to use it to exercise his hounds. We lived in East Leake at the time and my son Mark and his friend Tom Arris who lived in Costock both cycled up to Phil's every morning to help look after the hounds before going to school.

I think the hounds must have been the only pack of hounds in the whole of England to be kept in a back garden. The hounds were donated by various hunts that Phil knew.

One of the most important things that we had to do was to get public liability insurance for the hunt and the only way to be able to get this was to join The Masters of Drag Hounds Association which is the sport's governing body. All the meetings were in London and I took on the job of representing The Trent Valley Drag Hounds. The meetings were quite dreary, settling boundary disputes and dealing with legal matters, but it was good to meet up with likeminded people, hear their problems, and how to solve them. I knew a few of the other masters as the cross-country community was small and we all tended to teamchase, point to point, and hunt in all of its' various forms. George Goring and David Robinson from the Mid-Surrey Drag were two masters that I knew well and they invited me to have lunch with them after my first meeting which was far more fun and informative than the meeting itself. One thing I did love about the association was receiving letters from them; the address was written in proper blue ink with a broad nib pen in exquisite flowing script. The top line of the script was.

Mr Sam Humphrey Esq. MDH. Which always sent goose bumps down my back when I read it.

We had so much fun with the drag hounds and made many new friends. The generosity of the farmers who allowed us access to their land and the people who invited us to meet at their houses, never ceased to amaze me, not to mention the lavish hunt teas that they provided for us at the end of the day. I think the post hunt tea is a fabulous institution and it is sad fox hunts don't do it very much anymore. It allows all the participants to interact with their hosts and the farmers who have so generously allowed us to cross their land and thank them personally. It is hard to remember all the days that we had but a few still stick in my memory.

On our inaugural meet at Bunny Hill, we took the bridle path through Bunny Old Wood onto Windmill Hill on the Wysall lane. Although I had hunted this area as a child and teenager with The Quorn, they had not hunted it for over thirty years. Again, Phil's art of persuasion resulted in us having access to land that was no longer available to The Quorn. I was awfully glad to be well mounted that day as Phil took us over some massive hedges, many of which had never ever been jumped to my knowledge.

The Brooks and Woodhouse families of Widmerpool both gave us superb meets and access to some of The Quorn's best Monday country.

In the Quorn Friday country, Sue Henson invited us to Ingarsby near Houghton on the Hill where we were treated to a sumptuous meet before tackling the tightly railed hedges of this picturesque hilly sheep country.

Also, in the Quorn Friday country we had a joint meet with the Cambridge University Drag Hounds at Quenby Hall and this meet threw up some memorable moments most of which were not entirely pleasurable. Quenby Hall Estate is a hunting Mecca, the Quorn has built many hunt jumps and it is a joy to cross on horseback. A storm was forecast for the day of the meet but it was dry and calm as we left home to visit this beautiful wild part of Leicestershire. The roads are narrow and signposts are few and far between. It is a land of grand sporting estates and Quenby sits in the middle surrounded by Baggrave, Ingarsby, and Lowesby Halls.

I knew the estate and its owner, Squire De Lisle, as he had asked us to stage a jousting tournament there some years before. When I arrived at the Hall, I was surprised to see how many horseboxes were in the parking field considering the weather forecast. This was definitely the biggest field and most hard riding field that I had been associated with. After a generous meet the joint packs of hounds set off to find the first line. It was a fabulous sight to see so many hounds together and it is a memory I will never forget. The plan was to keep the field back a little further than normal to give the two packs time to settle in. I had joint charge of the field with the master of the Cambridge, all went well as we hacked away from the hall down the narrow estate road, as the field were contained behind us. I don't think either of us had been in charge of such a big field before. As if a warning of trouble to come, the wind started to pick up and the first flecks of rain started to sting our faces. As we left the road into a field, the followers started to swarm around us and shouts to stay back were totally ignored. Two horns of riders started to grow either side of us as riders pushed forward. Everyone was in a state of high excitement and our screams to stay back were just blown away in the ever-strengthening wind.

The hounds picked up on the first line and their music sent a shiver down my spine. As field masters we had no control whatsoever as the field swept forward with absolutely no regard for hunt etiquette, it was mob rule. There had been a lot of wet weather before the meet, the clay land was heavy going, and the gung-ho brigade soon came to grief as the clay sucked at the horses feet, resulting a significant number of fallers on the first drag line. By the time we finished the first line the full force of the storm had hit us and along with many of the fallers a substantial number of followers decided to call it a day.

The second line was difficult for Phil and the hounds, as the strong winds blew the scent all over the place making it difficult for the hounds to follow the trail. Likewise, for myself and the followers, maintaining a grip on the reins or seeing where you were going was a challenge. The second line became more like a steady fox hunt than the usual racing drag hunt. We continued on to the bitter end and I remember crossing a brook near the end of the day that was fordable earlier in the day but had turned into a raging torrent, it was so deep the water came over the top of my boots and I was on a 16.1hh horse. When we returned to the Hall, cold and well and truly soaked, there was just the hunt staff and a handful of brave followers. It is on days like that, an extremely expensive wool hunt coat proves to be good value. Our host Squire De Lisle had laid on a sumptuous hunt tea for us which we devoured. The warm room along with food, alcohol, and lashings of hot tea, slowly revived us ready for the journey home.

It was dark when we left with our clothes still wet. I was driving an old Bedford TK and I was not looking forward to the drive home as the cab heater took forever to warm up. We had only been going about ten minutes and the cold was starting to seep back into my body. I kept putting my hand down to the heater hoping that I might feel warm air starting to come through but it was wishful thinking. It was then that I saw the dim twinkle of lights up ahead, I remembered that there was a steep hill down to a narrow bridge, before climbing up the other side to the village. I let my speed pick up a bit to give me some momentum to get up the hill on the other side of the bridge. Car and lorry lights have come a long way these days but the lights on the old Bedford only gave an orange glow that lit the road for about twenty yards ahead. As I neared the bottom of the hill I was suddenly thrown forward and it was only the large steering wheel that stopped me going through the windscreen. I could not understand what had happened! It happened so quickly and violently. As I have said before in this book, in times of crisis, time seems to slow down and you manage to do a lot of things in a few milliseconds. That happened in this incident, even as I was pushing myself back into the driver's seat, I noted my head lights had gone out and then the engine had stalled, a few more milliseconds and I registered the sound of splashing water, almost like small waves breaking on the beach. It was then that I realised that I had driven into deep water at speed and that the bridge was underwater. Momentum carried me through the water and as we met the rise of the road to the other side of the bridge, I slammed the lorry into second gear, we dramatically slowed down but the revs of the engine screamed and with a cough and splutter to my great relief the engine came back to life as the water was pushed out of the exhaust pipe. Oh, what ecstasy, the thought of being stranded in the middle of nowhere, damp, cold and with a tired horse on board did not bear thinking about.

It sure was an eventful day, not what I had been expecting, but exceedingly exhilarating!

Sibling rivalry was never far away and Phil found many testing lines hoping to catch me out, however it was a tiny fence that caused me the most embarrassment. We were hunting around Wymeswold and had just arrived at John Mill's farm for the start of a line across his land, a large crowd of supporters had gathered at the end of the farm drive to welcome us and cheer us on. John had kindly taken the top two rails off a set of post and rails, to make it easy to jump off the tarmac drive, which was slippery for the horses. The jump if you could call it that, was no more than 70cm high. I was riding Bumper who though an extremely talented jumper, he was also a supremely talented dickhead. John was standing next to the fence and I took my hat off held it high to salute him and shouted my thanks for allowing us to cross his land. Bumper always ready to spring a surprise felt me take my leg off. I plonked my hat back on my head and casually asked him to pop the inconsequential rail. To my horror and embarrassment, he stopped dead and then ran back into the followers behind me, much to the delight of the onlookers who gave a cheer and burst out laughing. It was one of the most embarrassing moments of my life. I think Bumper was incredibly pleased with himself that day.

That day was a day for Sam being had, because not twenty minutes later while I was still seething over Bumper's little trick, Phil got me as well. We had crossed the Rempstone road next to the Wymeswold Cemetery and were heading towards the aerodrome. It was a patch of land that I had never crossed before. Determined to make amends for my earlier mistake I was riding Bumper with great determination and sitting in Phil's back pocket all the way. A large uncut hedge loomed up in front of us and Phil kicked on with great determination and not to be out done I followed suit. To my amazement at the last-minute Phil seemed to have second thoughts about the hedge and pulled out. God had sent me a chance to redeem myself from the earlier embarrassment and I kicked

Bumper on with a do or die determination, on the stride before take-off I glimpsed across at Phil and saw a smug smile of satisfaction on his face. Shit! I knew I had been done over. Bumper gave me a perfect jump and I had to forgive him for his earlier misdemeanour. As so often riding cross country ecstasy can quickly change to horror as I saw the reason for Phil's smugness. A huge depression in the ground lay on the far side of the hedge. To this day I do not know if it was a dry pond or maybe the remnants of a bomb crater from the Second World War when the airfield was an active RAF base. Whatever it was it was several feet deep and sort of circular. The hedge was high and it made a mighty drop on landing, thankfully Bumper was an extremely agile horse and always seemed to have a fifth leg in times of crisis, we crumpled on landing but he scrabbled up over the rim of the depression and we were soon galloping away after the hounds.

What a Buzz!

We had so many good days with the Trent Valley, in fact I do not think that we ever had a bad one. I think we had three seasons but it may have been four. Phil moved to a new house that needed a large amount of work. Sadly, Phil decided to disband the hunt at the height of its popularity but I understand the reasons why. It was very much Phil's Hunt and he did all the work to make it such a success. All I had to do was rock up and follow him.
Thank You Phil!

The Atherstone Hunt

Some years later lulled into a false sense of what the duties of a field master actually were, I became a field master of the Atherstone hunt. I had a group of clients from the Atherstone country for many years. I do not recall how it started but their numbers grew steadily and we had some great times. Their common denominator was that they had a great thirst for equine knowledge. Suzanne Sherwin and her daughter Ginny were the earliest of this group. At this time, I did regular cross-country clinics, these were especially popular with hunting folk during the autumn for getting both horses and riders fit for the forthcoming season, I think this is how the association with the Atherstone Hunt came about. Helen Milner a joint master of the Atherstone came along to some of these clinics and she asked me if I could teach her husband Mark to ride so that he could join her out hunting. The time scale that Helen and Mark gave me was daunting to say the least. If I recall correctly, it was about six weeks. I had taught several actors and would be stunt people to ride in short time frames and always enjoyed the challenge but to go hunting and deal with the melee of a hunt galloping and jumping was another matter.

Mark was tough, super fit and very dedicated. A perfect pupil. To say I put him through the mincer was an understatement. Unfortunately, being super fit, riding mind boggling miles on a racing bike and spending hours in a gymnasium does not make learning to ride a walk in the park. I learnt many years ago that every sport has its own specific fitness requirements. For riding it is flexible yet strong muscles, not the tight bunched up muscles that you produce running or in the gym. Mark had great determination and was confidently doing the rising trot after two sessions and canter came quickly after that. We became good friends and had great fun. I think we missed the deadline by about a week or so but it was a phenomenal achievement. I offered to chaperone Mark on his first day's hunting and that was how I first became involved with the Atherstone Hunt.

Helen and I talked a lot about hunting during our schooling sessions with her new hunt horses and top of the list was the many challenges that hunting was facing going forward into the new millennium. Top of the list was the relationship between the hunt and farmers, especially as more and more farmers were becoming totally arable and grass was becoming ever scarcer. The other topic was the funding of the hunts. The number of Subscribers continued to fall and finding masters that had the equestrian skills to lead a hunt and have the time and money to run the hunt was becoming a major challenge. To add to these woes, it was starting to look like the government was going to ban hunting in the not-too-distant future. I didn't realise at the time but I was talking myself into being a candidate for a field master.

When I joined the Atherstone it was a big change from the drag hounds in that I had to get to know the country from ground zero. With drag hunting you knew exactly where the hounds and field would be going. Fox hunting was vastly different as you had to be prepared for endless possibilities. Many farmers would allow hounds and the hunt staff to go anywhere but not allow the followers or restrict them to defined corridors. Much of these restrictions were down to grants for farm stewardship from the EU. and the way different ministry inspectors interpreted the rules. One farmer told me that he stood to lose £30,000 in grants if the inspector found hoof prints on the grass margins around his fields and would prefer me to take the followers up a tramline across his cornfield. However, a couple of miles down the road another inspector took a completely different view and we could gallop on the beautiful ten metre grass margins but with the caveat that if he found as much as one hoof print on his cornfield, he would never allow us across his land again. Little wonder that the followers were confused by my orders to ride on one bit of grass and then ten minutes later issue orders not to set foot on another piece of grass.

My appointment came in late summer, a week or so before the start of the season. I had been a controversial choice as the Atherstone had traditionally had masters that lived in their country and I was the first that lived outside the country. I had little time to get to know the country and had to learn on the job. Thankfully both the retiring master Richard Phizacklea and the hunt countryman Pete Clarke held my hand and gave me invaluable help and advice during those early days of autumn hunting.

Sitting in the centre of my area was a massive problem. It was the Thorpe Estate. Many decades before, the family had been masters of the Atherstone and keen supporters of Fox Hunting but now it was a no-go area. Unfortunately, nearly every meet in my country held the possibility of hounds running onto the Estate.

My first Autumn Hunting meet was on the land of the Gilman Family who were great supporters of the hunt. They owned two large farms and we had permission to go wherever we wanted. It was a great place to start to cut my teeth into what I was beginning to realise was a much more complicated job than I had anticipated. We met at 6.30 am and everything went like clockwork. There was only a small field out and I was able to take some time to get to know some of the regular followers of the hunt. Our morning was almost over, things had gone swimmingly well, it was just past eight o' clock, the sun had risen and it was pleasantly warm as we rode along the top of a hill across some stubble fields. Here and there I would deviate and jump small bits of hedge much to the glee of the followers. I was happily chatting to newfound friends and feeling incredibly pleased with myself when suddenly the hounds stumbled on a fox laid up in a hedge and flew off down the hill. We didn't follow as this was autumn hunting and the horses were not fit and that is not what you do. We watched mesmerised as the hounds screamed after the fox and the hunt staff desperately trying to stop them. I suddenly realised that I hadn't walked the land that the hounds were heading for, so I casually asked a follower who owned the land on the other side of the valley, "Oh that's the Thorpe Estate" came back the reply. My first outing as field master and I was already in trouble! I shall always remember sitting in the office staring at the phone trying to decide what I was going to say as an apology. It might have been my first but it certainly wasn't my last!

My section of the Atherstone country had many pro farmers, I made some great friends and they welcomed the hunt. Others had bad experiences and along my border with the Meynell Hunt around

Lullington and it was not necessarily the Atherstone that had caused the problem. Even if farmers did not want the hunt across their land, I tried to build relationships with them and would always visit them and apologise for hounds going onto their land. Most understood that with the best will in the world hounds will get away from the huntsman and accidents will happen. Others held deep seated grudges and would never budge.

My country had three major problems that constantly gave me nightmares and there was no way of solving these problems. The first was a high-speed railway line. A couple of seasons before I took over, hounds had run onto the line and some were killed. The previous master had been warned that legal action would be taken against the master and the hunt if it ever happened again. The next major problem was the M42 and the carnage that could result in the hounds running out onto the motorway just does not bear thinking about. The nearest we held a meet to the M42 was the village of Seckington. We always met at a farm on the edge of the village and hunted away from the motorway for safety. As we moved off from the meet, hacking towards our first covert which was several fields away, the hounds picked up a scent and flew away at an amazing speed, straight towards the motorway. For a few seconds I was not worried as I had every confidence that the hunt staff would quickly get them back and under control. Unfortunately, as we had no intention of going anywhere near the motorway, I had not cleared the country although it was all owned by friendly farmers. As the hunt staff valiantly galloped off in pursuit, they came across unexpectedly locked gates due to surge in rural crime. It rapidly became clear that the hounds were putting more and more distance between themselves and the pursuing hunt staff. I started to feel sick as the hounds raced towards the motorway and I could see that the hunt staff were having to use the roads to try and catch up with the hounds which I knew was hopeless. Gradually the sound of the hounds speaking faded away until there was just an eerie silence. I led the field to the nearest road and then hacked on with them after the hunt staff, dreading what I might have to deal with. After about a mile to my great relief, I saw John the huntsman leading his hounds back up the road towards us. The hounds had checked in a covert just two fields from the motorway.

That was a very close-run thing!

My first year with the Atherstone was extremely enjoyable, we were having to change the way we did things due to the hunting with dogs act that banned traditional hunting, but several exemptions such as flushing to a bird of prey and trail hunting were permitted. The exemptions were just starting to be challenged by the league against blood sports and new directives were being made by the Masters of Foxhounds Association so that hunts could prove that they were hunting within the law. This included filing routes that we were going to take marked on large scale maps and writing reports of any accidents of foxes being found unintentionally by hounds that were trail hunting. I also videoed the trail layers starting their trail laying and date and time stamped the video. As added proof I carried a spare bottle of the scent we used, plus spare rags and strings for the trail layers in a pouch on the front of the saddle. The trail was laid by runners and riders dragging a scented rag behind them. The scent was the vilest smelling stuff I have ever encountered and I was always worried about having a bad fall and bursting the bottle because if you got it on your clothes no amount of washing would get rid of the smell. I particularly enjoyed the days when we had a falconer out with us as I have always loved large birds of prey.

I got on extremely well with the farmers and became good friends with many of them and still stay in touch with some of them to this day. They welcomed me into their homes fed me with tea, cake, and biscuits. I talked to them about their crops and was genuinely interested in their lives. I tried to keep abreast of market prices for livestock and cereals and new innovations within the industry. Having spent many lonely hours driving tractors and lost hay crops to bad weather, I could understand their problems. I got to know what crops were going to be planted and where they were happy for me to go and places, they wanted me to avoid. If things went wrong, I explained why and in the main were very understanding.

My first season went well but looking back I now see that things were changing; two long standing masters left the Mastership. One left the year that I joined and the other the following year. That first year, masters' meetings were chaired by the seasoned senior master and everything was harmonious. The next year the financial problems of the hunt were the main topic of the meetings with revenues going down and expenditure going up. It was the beginning of the worldwide financial crisis. Everyone in the hunt was singing from different song sheets, especially the masters and the hunt committee. An extremely wet season just poured more petrol onto the fire. The full masters were responsible for the hunt finances and I think the field masters started to be viewed as free loaders by some of the masters. As we neared the end of the season the full masters were grappling with the finances and the field masters were not invited to all the meetings. Decisions that affected my ability to run my hunting days smoothly and to the standard that I had promised the farmers were made without any consultation. The end of that season ended on a sour note with the powers that be. I almost resigned then but at the beginning of the next season things came to a head when Pete the country man who unlocked all the gates that needed unlocking for a day's hunting, relocked them after hunting was finished, also he took wire down at jumping places, again replacing it at the end of the day, had his hours severely reduced. The full masters retained most of his time whilst I only got a small fraction of his time. Living so far away from the country I could not perform these tasks myself and act as field master. This was done without any consultation and I only found out when Pete phoned me to say he would no longer be available to help me set up days. I resigned with a heavy heart as I was really settling into my position during the summer at the end of the second season, I hosted a thank you party for the farmers in my hunting area. One of the landowners Richard Blunt owned Clifton Campville Hall, which he had lovingly restored to its former glory and had scoured the country for period furniture to furnish it. It truly was a magnificent achievement. During my visits to arrange to cross his land and hold a meet in front of his house we became good friends. Clifton Campville sat in a central position for my country and so when I was thinking of having the farmers' party, I chanced my arm and asked him if I could use his house as a venue. To my delight he agreed. Having the bar at our stables meant we were used to hosting parties. I organised the drinks side, and Lou sorted out a buffet of home cooked delights. It was a lovely summer's evening and everybody that I invited turned up. The night was a huge success and so appreciated by the farmers. I cannot thank Richard and his wife enough for that night and I went home with offers of building new fences and ideas of opening up new bits of country for us to hunt. Things were on the up, two years of hard work were now bearing fruit in abundance. Everything pointed to an exciting new season. How wrong can you be, perhaps I ruffled some feathers with the success of my party, I do not know but my relationship with the hunt took a dive after the party and I resigned at the beginning of the next season.

I never saw that coming on that balmy summer's evening, as those lovely farmers shook my hand and warmly thanked me for a wonderful evening.

The South Notts. Hunt

I was extremely demoralised with hunting when I left the Atherstone, it is amazing that for all my years hunting, I had never considered the complex operational side of the sport. I had always been surprised how so many master's never hunted again when they finished their Masterships. I now knew the reason why. I think that except for a few days hunting in Ireland I didn't hunt at all the following season. However, there was a bitter feeling that I had not fulfilled my potential after that successful farmers party.

I was over in Ireland with a coach load of pals for a surprise birthday party for my brother Phil's fiftieth. It was a mixture of hunting and jousting friends and we were going to spend a long weekend in Kilkenny based at the Club House Hotel. One of the members of the party was an old hunting friend, his name was Carl Haspel who was the Hon secretary of the South Notts Hunt.

It was mid-morning and we were nursing hangovers in the hotel bar with yet another pint of the black stuff. Carl had just been out to look at a large horsebox that was for sale with the view of buying it on behalf of the South Notts Hunt. He joined me in a quieter corner of the bar and I asked him about the horsebox. After discussing the pros and cons of the horsebox we drifted onto how the South Notts were coping with the hunting ban. Although technically we lived in the Quorn country, the South Notts country started just a few miles down the road and I had many old friends from my gymkhana and show jumping days who still hunted with them. That moved onto my time with the Atherstone and another pint of Guinness and eventually he mentioned that they were desperately looking for a master for the following season and might I be interested. I was, but I needed to think about it, and talk it over with Lou when I got back, because the economy was slowing down and that always hit our business hard. After a lot of thought and the promise to Lou that I would only do it for a year I phoned Carl and told him I was interested. I felt it was like helping an old friend, such was my affection for this hunt. An interview with Carl and one of the masters over a beer in a pub and we were good to go. Such a breath of fresh air after the formalities of the Atherstone.

My only problem was that it was August, and that gave me precious little time to get to know the farmers before the new season. Thankfully, the retiring master was an incredibly old pal and we went right back to pony club days. His name was David Manning, he gave me endless help and advice, including the loan of an OS map of my country with every field marked up with the owner's name, and those marked in red were no go areas. Along with the map was a list of names and addresses of all the landowners. Without all of this meticulous information I would have struggled to get off the ground. All I had to do now was to get to know the country. I had last hunted this area many years previously when qualifying my first point to pointer Dadda Boy. It had been extremely boring and was more of a glorified hack than a hunt. I spent two days a week going around meeting farmers, landowners and walking the country. An unexpected surprise was that despite the area being mainly arable, the country was wilder than expected. During my days walking the country I discovered many hidden gems of remote countryside. My walks became the most enjoyable days of the week. A real voyage of discovery. My next surprise was how many people knew me. Many people who lived in this area had been former clients of our riding school, going all the way back to my dad's day. This made my job so much easier because this area was obviously a close-knit community, and even people that I had never met, seemed to know a lot about me when I first introduced myself. I was desperately trying to meet up with a farmer who farmed a large area in the centre of the country. I had called many times but could never find anyone at home. This was worrying me as the season was about to begin. The outbuildings of the farm had been converted into residential houses and one afternoon as I was about to leave, a car pulled up in front of one of them. I decided to introduce myself and ask when a good time was to catch the farmer at home. As the lady got out of her car, she greeted me before I had time to open my mouth, saying, "oh hi Sam I was wondering when I would bump into you. I heard you were going to be the new master". That really kicked my feet from underneath me as I had no idea who she was, but she obviously knew me. My mind raced trying to think of a polite reply but in the end, I opted for the direct approach by saying I was sorry but I didn't know who she was. She replied, "Oh sorry it is a long time ago but I thought you would recognise dad's old number plate" As I don't even know my own car number plate there was little likelihood of that However, further conversation revealed that her father was our family doctor in Ruddington, and she had kept her horse at livery with us during the sixties, well over forty years ago. Having sorted out identities I discovered that the farmer and his wife were on a long holiday in the Far East or Australia and would not be home for another week.

One of my great joys was meeting up with my old racing pal Brian Crawford who had a farm on the edge of my country. We never went on his land as it bordered a railway line but I always enjoyed popping in and chewing the fat with him over a cup of tea. I could write a whole chapter about long-lost acquaintances that were renewed but that would serve no purpose. One final surprise came when I visited a former master of my area. I was greeted by a former employee of my father called Jane Abbot who was looking after the former master's horses.

The South Notts was going through a series of changes as all hunts do and not only had part of the Mastership left, so had the huntsman. The new huntsman was the former whipper-in Ollie Finnegan who has later hunted the Atherstone and is now huntsman of the Quorn. Ollie was young and fearless across country and was a hard man to follow. I once witnessed him and his whipper-in jump a huge hedge, it was out of deep plough with a rotten steel gate embedded in the hedge - it was an utterly amazing feat from both horses and riders. The whip's horse came down on landing and gave it's rider a crashing fall, Ollie's horse pecked on landing and broke its bridle. The horse then proceeded to bolt with Ollie still on his back but with no means of control. We were close to the point-to-point course at Thorpe and this area is like Fenland with huge deep drainage dykes that are up to fifteen foot deep and considerably wider. Ollie galloped about a furlong and a half before he threw himself off at the gallop into one of the deep dykes and disappeared from sight. A moment later we arrived at the motionless body of the whip laying on the grass headland but thankfully by the time we had dismounted he was starting to stir. I dispatched a couple of followers to look for Ollie, my big worry for Ollie was that these dykes often carried several feet of water in them and certainly enough to drown an injured person. Thankfully, the next time I glanced over to where Ollie had disappeared, he was leaping into the saddle of one of the helper's horses and galloping off after his hounds. The whip was not so good and I sent another pair of riders back to the farm where we had met to get a truck to collect the injured whip. When we asked the Whip if we could do anything else to make him comfortable, he whispered that he was dying for a fag. By the time the pickup truck arrived he was sitting up chuffing away on his cigarette. It was like one of those war movies with the wounded soldier having a cigarette hanging out of his mouth. This all happened at the end of the day just after Christmas, the meet had been delayed until twelve o' clock because of frost. All the other local hunts had cancelled but we had a lot of flat headlands with good grass cover so I took a chance and it paid off, the sun came out and the going was good. Half an hour had slipped by since the incident and it was now pitch black and bitterly cold. Thankfully, the ambulance was waiting at the farm and a generous Hunt Tea awaited us in the cosy farmhouse of the Hardstaff family.

I had invited Helen Milner and her husband Mark out that day as my guests. Helen was still a master of the Atherstone and I think that great day's sport was the inspiration for Ollie to be offered the post of huntsman for the Atherstone.

Unlike the Atherstone I was left to get on with my job. It was Ollie and I who set up the days hunting, and like me Ollie got on extremely well with the farmers. I really looked forward to those days. Ollie worked hard at the kennels and I often popped in for a chat along with my granddaughter Katherine who was about four year's old at the time, she loved going in with the hounds and being licked all over by them. The kennels were also home to the local Beagle pack. Beagles are extremely pretty hounds and I always could not resist popping over to their kennels to say hello.
In my year at the South Notts I only went to two meetings, the AGM and an extraordinary committee meeting to consider if the hunt should continue, due its lack of funds. As ever the ever-resourceful South Notts found a way to continue because they are a big family and have been associated with the hunt for generations. The only other meeting I had was with two other masters

in a pub for lunch to rearrange some meets due to bad weather. We had some great fun that season. The followers were a nice bunch of happy go lucky people who really enjoyed their day out. My only problem was I had too many offers to host meets and could not fit them all in in just one year. I worked hard to try and reopen some country that had been lost due to past misdemeanours. I didn't manage to reopen much country in my year, but looking at the meet cards for following years, many of the seeds that I had sown, seem to have borne fruit.

The South Notts restored my faith in people. I met many farmers doing innovative things to diversify and continue farming. Their warm welcome made it a pleasure to do my job and I would have loved to have stayed on. In fact, I was asked if I would do another year. However, many factors were working against me, I had promised Lou I would only do it for a year and me being away from the business placed a lot more work on her shoulders. The financial crisis was really starting to bite. We had cut staff and were doing more work ourselves. The final nail in the coffin was that my horse Mitten had come to the end of her hunting days. I had bought a replacement, called Marnie who was a good hunter but he was a follower not a leader, in fact he was a nightmare as a master's horse stopping dead as soon as he was in front. I just didn't have the time or money to buy and train another.

Thank you South Notts for a great and memorable year!

Chapter Twelve
Teaching

Teaching has been a big part of my life since I took my first lesson when I was ten or maybe eleven years old. Dad had been "delayed" and there was nobody else at the stables in those days but our family. Mum was heavily pregnant and that left just me and my younger sister Dawn, who was several years younger than me. The clients were a wealthy young couple who wanted to learn to ride. It was their second lesson. There was no such thing as a manège in those days, but we did have a round pen made out of trees cut from the woods next door. The round pen was in fact oval as dad liked to modify or improve nearly everything he constructed. Our riding school was the only one of it's kind in the area that focused on adults. There were several stables that did riding for children and teenagers but adults wanting to learn to ride was a new phenomenon. Remarkably, the two adults did not seem to mind a child telling them what to do, which at the beginning of the sixties was an extremely rare thing, given the attitudes of the time concerning children. I continued teaching them the rising trot which they had informed me was what, dad had started to teach them. There were no disasters and the couple seemed happy with my lesson and much to my surprise they gave me a tip. I never saw my tip as it went into family funds which was a common occurrence during my early life, much promised but nothing ever received.

You could rightly expect this to be one of the longest chapters in the book as my teaching is about to reach its sixtieth year but it will actually probably be the shortest. My teaching has always been unorthodox in that I have always treated riders and horses as unique individuals and have sort to find a rapport with them. I grew up in the era of army style instruction where orders were barked out without explanation and you were publicly belittled if you did not get it right first time. It was focused on group learning and private lessons were a rarity.

As a child this style of instruction turned me away from riding and I only rode under duress. Dad was born in the mid-nineteen-twenties into a large family that struggled to make ends meet, especially during the Second World War. He left school at fourteen and was also fostered out during his younger years with his Uncle Tom who was a stud groom. Tom and his wife were childless, they lived in Long Bennington some seventy odd miles from the home village of Ravensthorpe in Northamptonshire. It was a massive distance in those days with few opportunities to visit the rest of the family. I know dad worked on a farm back in Ravensthorpe during the war and also at a racing stables where the trainer would literally kick the grooms up the backside all the way up the stable yard if they did not come up to standard. From what I can gather, this was a pretty normal way of going on in those times. Dad told the story of a young boy's first day at the yard. The trainer gave him a large basket and told him to go into the field and fill it with dandelion leaves. The naïve lad made the mistake of answering back saying "What's them for mester; do you keep rabbits"? Dad said the trainer went purple in the face and kicked him not only all the way up the yard, but into the paddock as well.

The style of riding has changed greatly since my childhood and so has what we do with our horses. Before the Second World War, horses were the main form of transport all around the world and for power in agriculture as well. The war speeded up mechanisation and by the nineteen-fifties, horses were obsolete for work and transport. The horse was now a pleasure tool for mainly the rich. Hunting, polo and showjumping were its' new uses. When I started to ride, I was taught to sit on my buttocks at the back of the saddle with my legs stuck forward and we did something called the rising canter, now rarely seen except in the hunting field. Show jumping was the up-and-coming sport and much more accessible to the less well heeled. With it came the forward seat and a lighter, balanced way of riding. Sadly, nobody explained to me why I suddenly had to drastically change everything I had been taught to do, which was extremely confusing for a child. It was during those years of change that the seeds were sown of how I would teach if I ever had to do it. I would explain why we had to sit in a certain way and what the benefits, for the horse and rider were.

For many instructors and trainers, teaching children is a No-No! My experiences as a child made me want to give up riding. Thankfully, I was forced to continue although I certainly was not thankful at the time. If I had given up, I would have missed everything that I have just written about and that is quite terrifying.

Children are our future and that is why I have supported the Pony Club, making our facilities available and teaching at discounted prices. If they can have good encouraging instruction at an early age, they will hopefully continue and some might become the stars of tomorrow. It has given me great pleasure to see the seeds of knowledge that I have sown blossom. One of my great pleasures is receiving news of pupils, past and present, that have achieved success.

I never had any ambition to teach riding or run a riding school. It was jousting and getting married that brought me back to the family business. Like so many young people in the countryside, I was drawn to better wages and the shorter, set hours of industry. I returned from Wales in September 1972 an older and wiser person. The six months in Wales involved managing twenty people and ten horses, dealing with the castle management and a thousand and one other things that cropped up on a daily basis. A good apprenticeship, you might say, for running a riding school. Previously I had done two years business studies at college when working for British Gypsum. Lou had just completed her secretarial course at college. My plan was to make a living from jousting and dealing in medieval arms and armour for the rapidly expanding re-enactment groups that were springing up everywhere after the massive publicity that jousting had received over the last three years. What dropped a bombshell on these plans was VAT. It was part of the cost of joining the EEC, which later morphed into the European Union. VAT was a complicated tax that required meticulous record keeping. Dad had never kept any records at all except, for throwing receipts into a cardboard box. Mum did the banking and our accountant did the rest. Mum and dad were in their late forties and it was all too much for them to cope with. They were seriously thinking of giving it all up which meant the end of jousting as well and the end of my plans. Lou and I decided to try and sort things out for them and after many meetings with the accountant, we formed a limited company to protect the family house and land. The four of us became directors of the new company with Lou as the company secretary and keeper of the accounts, I was to be the Managing Director. Dad and his partner Major Ritchie had changed the name of the Business from Bunny Hill Riding School to the grand title of The School of National Equitation but that is another long story. For the sake of continuity, we just added the Ltd to the name.

Dad was a good trainer but of the old school, plenty of bollockings if you did something wrong. Strangely he was revered by many and had a large loyal following. Dad and I saw riding from different ends of a telescope. We were both saying the same things, but in an entirely different way. It was not until many years later, when I took my diploma in sports psychology did I understand about the different ways we favour receiving information. That is, that some people like to be shown what to do (seeing, e.g. I see what you mean), others prefer to be told what to do (hearing, e.g. I hear what you are saying.) alternatively others like to feel things. (feeling
I get the feel of what you mean). It upset me greatly that Dad and I had so many arguments over riding. It was not until I started to attend the lectures and demonstrations, from some of the leading riders and trainers from around the world did I start to realise, that it was not just me that saw

things in a different ways. The arguments I witnessed between, Charles Harris who was the first Englishman to graduate from the Spanish Riding School of Vienna and Nuno Oliveira the Portuguese Riding Master, about what you should feel when riding high school movements, did I start to realise that even the world's greatest, viewed and felt things differently. Although I greatly admired Nuno Oliveira and his quest for lightness, I found Charles Harris's descriptions more closely aligned to what I felt and still use many of his descriptions in my teaching to this day. Dad was a BHSI and became friends with many of the great trainers of their time in England, such as Brian Young, Geoffrey Hatton, Molly Sivewright and many more. Several of these trainers visited Bunny and gave lectures and demonstrations to our enthusiastic riding club. This was a broad church and it allowed me to understand that riding is an art not a precise science. Some people love to ride one way, whilst others might hate it, just the same as looking at a painting. There was also John Lassiter, who was based at Goodwood, a top dressage rider and international trainer with a great sense of theatrical humour, who performed sketches making fun of his sport at the horse of the year show. He gave a lecture-demonstration in our indoor school. My cousin Maria was guinea pig. She was incredibly nervous and after she had warmed up, he called her in to him and said in a loud voice, "now I have a very important question for you". Poor Maria blanched at being questioned in front of such a large audience. "So! What I want you to tell me" he said, then paused for dramatic effect, poor Maria's mind must have been racing, trying to guess what this important question might be. Finally, he asked his question, "does your horse", he paused again holding everyone on a knife edge before quickly saying, "prefer sugar lumps or polo mints?". Everyone including Maria burst out laughing. Maria relaxed, he gave her horse the preferred polo mint and both horse and rider were relaxed for the start of the demonstration. I learnt a lot of simple things from that demonstration. From all the great trainers I had the privilege to watch, they all had a common thread.

KEEP IT SIMPLE!

I have always preferred to teach one to one. However, it is not a sustainable way to run a business that has massive overheads. Class lessons are what you need to make ends meet, as they boost your hourly rate by at least five-fold and provide affordable lessons for a much wider range of clients.
The classes I took were for the more advanced riders and there were often up to fifteen in some of the classes because they were so popular. To successfully take classes of that size you had to be extremely quick thinking and ensure that everyone got a fairly equal amount of instruction. The other thing was to work them hard and I mean really hard. In the wintertime I would have two short breaks to shed layers of clothes. These classes were so intense, I had clients riding in tee shirts when it was minus ten. The way I ensured everyone got an equal amount of instruction was to start at the front of the ride, assess the rider, make a comment for improvement, and quickly move onto the next rider until I reached the back of the ride and then go back to the front and repeat the process over and over again. It was quick fire stuff and I also had to fit in instructions for the various movements we were performing. Inevitably working so fast you said things you didn't mean to say or could be construed the wrong way. This was all part of the relaxed nature of these adult classes and they loved it when I made mistakes. At the time we had a large number of legal clients, barristers and solicitors. They just loved to seize on these moments and the ride loved their interpretation of my comments. My good friend Dick Benson, who was a barrister at the time, often reminded me of the time, when Mike Elvin a solicitor was riding in front of him. Mike was slouching slightly at the sitting trot, as was Dick, who was directly behind him. This is where working at speed can catch you out, my comment was meant for the two of them. Dick pounced on them, as if he were in court. My words which he has regularly reminded me of at many a dinner party were, "Mike sit up! Stick your chest out, and Dick too"! I think Dick's instant retort was, "I say Mr Humphrey, that's really not on! There are ladies present". This caused the whole ride to dissolve into raucous laughter and the orderly ride to end up looking like a multiple pile-up on the M25.

At it's height in the nineteen eighties, we were running approximately twelve to fifteen of these classes per week with many of our liveries on three to four lessons per week. I didn't take all of these but I did do the lion's share. I often did two classes back-to-back and that left me physically and mentally exhausted. I was like doing a one-man theatre show on stage for two hours. I have never liked performing in front of people and it was extremely difficult for me to go out and teach these large classes. I was always ok once I got out there and started teaching, but it was hell for Lou as I was always bad tempered and irritable the hour before I started to teach as I fought my inner demons.

It was in the mid-eighties that my worst nightmare came true and I had been dreading it ever since we started to do our jousting shows in the early seventies. We had under-studies for every character in the show with the exception of the Knight Marshal whose job was to run the tournament but also act as commentator. To the public, it was the high-profile knights that were the stars of the show but in reality, the show's success or failure was entirely down to the commentary. The Knight Marshal was the vital unsung hero of the show and I knew that one day for whatever reason I would have to stand in for Brian who was without doubt an outstanding, brilliant commentator. The thought of walking out in front of thousands of people on my own was terrifying. Far more frightening than all the racing, team chasing and jousting. My first commentary was in Cyprus, Brian Hinksman our regular jousting commentator had used all his holiday entitlement up during the busy summer months of jousting, so wasn't available. I did not want to turn the show down as it was a massive opportunity, so I accepted the inevitable and did the commentary. It was my experience teaching and the fact it was thousands of miles away where nobody would know me that gave me the confidence to do the commentary. What I did not know until I arrived in Cyprus was that my audience included the president of Cyprus and a host of film and television stars also that I was expected to commentate on several other acts as well. The temperature was 30 degrees when I stepped into the arena and by the end of my first sentence, I was drenched in an ice cold sweat. It was the hardest thing I had ever had to do in my life and without my teaching experience I would never had got through it. I actually got some compliments from the stars that day but I couldn't wait to get away to my hotel room close the curtains and lay on the bed shaking from inside to out.

From my demons to joy.

Teaching has also given me great pleasure. I much prefer to give private lessons rather than the much more profitable class lessons. I hate having to raise my voice, sadly I have not been blessed with one of those deep booming voice that easily carries over distance. I believe private means private and I don't like people sitting in with me unless the client has specifically asked if someone listen. Sometimes people will sneak into the gallery to watch. Rather than cause a scene I move my lesson to the far end of the school where only the client can hear me. I like to discuss things quietly at halt where I have the client's full attention because raising your voice so the client can hear you distracts them from their riding and also the ability to digest completely what is being conveyed to them.

I teach what I feel when I ride, how my skeleton is moved by my muscles and which specific muscles I use to move different parts of my skeleton. Lou and my dad always felt things in an extremely specific disciplined way, perhaps that was because they were both born under the sign of Aquarius. I have always just had a feeling to do things when it felt right. They were both drawn more towards dressage whereas me and my brothers all favoured the jumping game which relies on making quick instinctive decisions a long way from the point of take-off. Whenever I have logically thought about a stride into a fence bad things have always happened. Studying sports psychology has helped me understand this when I learnt about the left and right brain. People are either left or right brain dominant, put in its simplest terms, the right brain is instinctive, whereas the left brain is logical. When you use your logical brain vital milli seconds are lost processing and sending messages to your muscles whereas the instinctive brain does it instantly. The majority of my adult customers came from academic backgrounds and use their logical brain most of the time as they deal with facts and figures. They find riding a real challenge because they are not used to using the instinctive brain. The fact that they are sitting on an animal that has a brain and will of its own is a real challenge to them mentally and they love it. It takes them a long time to let go of their tried and trusted logical brain and accept that a horse will throw random unexpected spanners into their carefully laid plans. Over the years I have developed, with the aid of what I learned studying sports psychology, endless distraction techniques to trick them into using their instinctive brain.

Occasionally I get people that come for a one-off lesson. They hope that I can wave a magic wand and turn them into an excellent rider in forty-five minutes. Yes, I can correct some bad habits and point them in the right direction but to really improve you have to think in months and years. Knowledge is useless unless both you and your horse have the suppleness and muscular fitness to make use of any knowledge. Suppleness and fitness take a long time to develop and as you move forward to the next level you have to bring both your own and your horse's fitness up to a new higher level. It is the same for all sports, only riders have the added burden of having to get our horses fit as well.

These days when I take on a new client, I tell them that they are embarking on a long endless journey, how far they travel on that journey is up to them. Like all journeys there will be times when you take a wrong turn for a while but that is part of the fun especially when you finally get back on the right road and start to make good progress towards your goal again.

Teaching has given me as much satisfaction as all the adrenaline pumping, that I have done. However, it is the passing of knowledge onto future generations, for them to enjoy some of what I have experienced, that leaves the warmest glow.

Chapter Thirteen

The Melton Hunt Club

The Melton Hunt Club was a great part of my life from the late seventies until the early nineties and provided me with some of the most thrilling and memorable experiences of my life.
There has been a Melton Hunt Club in Melton Mowbray during the eighteen hundreds and maybe into the early twentieth century. Whether or not it was an official club, or a name given to a group of hard riding, hard partying, group of wealthy people who based themselves at Melton Mowbray during the hunting season, I do not know.

Melton was like the hub of a wheel from which radiated the three famous hunting countries of the Belvoir, the Cottesmore and the Quorn. This allowed a group of hell raising aristocrats to hunt six days a week for the whole hunting season. I have a set of paintings that depict some of their famous antics. Some of you will have heard of but probably do not know how they became part of our language. The saying "Paint the town red" is said to have originated from an incident that happened in Melton Mowbray in 1837 when The Marquis of Waterford and a group of drunken friends decided to paint the toll bar and other buildings in the town with red paint. The exact reasons for this are not known, but they were also reported to have painted two, night watchmen red as well. Another of their acts that has made it's way into our language is the "Midnight Steeple Chase". Again, this actually took place near Melton when a group of riders rode in a race at midnight across country, dressed in their night shirts and jumped hedges illuminated by servants holding lanterns to mark the course. Now that is something that I would have loved to have done. I did jump a hedge at night, it was illuminated by car headlights as a stunt for the TV series Boon, the big difference was that I had to jump the hedge bare back! That gave me a great buzz, but a race in the dark, wow! they were some wild boys. The final antic that is well documented but is mainly only known to hunting people is the jumping of a five-bar gate in the dining room of Lowesby Hall for a bet. On horseback of course!

The modern Melton Hunt Club was formed in 1955 with the aim to raise money for the improvement of the Leicestershire side of the Belvoir Hunt. It's first chairman was Colonel James Hanbury who was at that time Master of the Belvoir and the Hon Secretary was Lance Newton who by all accounts was the driving force in it's formation. The inaugural committee was made up of some of the most well-known members of the hunting fraternity. 1955 was a special year for me. I was four years old that year and it was the year we moved from West Bridgford, a suburb of Nottingham to Bunny Hill Top, where I still reside to this day. Most of the names of that original committee mean nothing to me but I remember Tim Molony's name cropping up in Dad's conversation on a regular basis during my childhood and another member, Dr Tom Connors was still going strong when I started hunting regularly on Monday's with the Quorn in the seventies. Lance Newton's vision was to make it possible for people especially the younger ones, from different hunts outside Leicestershire to sample the delights of hunting in the county. The following year 1956 at the AGM, the Cottesmore and the Quorn were invited to join the scheme with the proviso that any money donated to them was used directly for the improvement of the country and not to go into general hunt funds.

By joining the club whose membership was extremely modest, I think when I joined in the seventies it was just five pounds if you paid by yearly standing order. As a member of the club, you could buy a ticket to hunt with any one of the three packs. The tickets were approximately half the price of the normal cap rate so it was a real bargain and made the cost of joining negligible. In later years, the Meynell and South Staffs also joined the scheme. However, it was not the hunting that originally drew me to becoming a member, but the point to pointing side of the membership. At the end of my first season pointing, I was hooked and any chance of one more ride over fences could not be missed. The Melton Hunt Club Point to Point is traditionally held at the end of May, for most it signals the end of the season although Wales and the South West there is the odd one in the first week of June. To most of the pointing fraternity it was like an unofficial championship because horses came from all over the country and you were racing against the best in each class. I loved this meeting; it was held at Garthorpe my favourite course and to many was considered to be the Cheltenham of point to point. Held at the end of May it was nearly always top of the ground going which never suited many of my horses but the joy of skipping around that course in the company of top-class horses was irresistible. It makes such a difference riding in warm conditions with your muscles warm and loose, it was the for the horses too as they all seemed to perform that little bit better. The race times confirmed this with considerably quicker times for all races. I never won a race at the Melton Hunt club meetings as the fast ground never suited my horses although I did pick up some placings which considering the class of horses I was competing against, was no mean feat.

Having joined the MHC I received their newsletter that told me the cost of buying their hunting tickets and about their annual hunt "Ride". It was called a ride not a race because the jockey club does not allow jockeys or owners to take part in races that are not sanctioned by and run under their rules. The penalties for doing so are severe including being barred from racing and I believe that also involves entry to a racecourse. So, to get around this it is called a ride and prizes have to be of modest value and in kind. As soon as entries opened, I sent my entry in, only to be told that the race was already oversubscribed and that I was on the waiting list. Unbeknown to me at the time, the maximum number of runners allowed was a staggering one hundred. Shortly after I was out with the Quorn and found myself hacking along next to Urky Newton who was now the secretary of the MHC. As I mentioned earlier, she had always been truly kind and helpful to me. As we hacked along, I told her that I had joined the club and how disappointed I was that it was already oversubscribed. She turned to me with a little smile and said, "don't you worry, you are on the waiting list, a lot of people dropout, I assure you that you will get your ride" and with that she kicked on to catch-up with her friend Migs Greenall.

My first Melton ride was a bit like my first race, I was poorly prepared and out of my depth. It was being held in the Cottesmore country that year between Somerby and Knossington. Prior to the race you got a photocopied map of the course with the instructions of pass red marker boards on the right, marker boards white on the left. There was an X on the map with start written next to it and another X with finish written next to it. No other instructions!

I had expected the course to be clearly marked and the fences all flagged like a cross-country course or hunter trials. I started to walk the course a few days before and I am glad that I did. The first fence was a newly laid hedge staked and bound, about sixty yards wide, nice, and straight forward but then it got confusing as the map was very much out of date because not all the fields corresponded to those on the map. After bumping into several other people that were as lost as I was it started to dawn on me that it was just like hunting, you could go and jump wherever you wanted as long as you passed the turning boards on the correct side. I think there were three turning boards two red and one white. The permutations of where you went from the start to finish were endless. The distance was between four to four and a half miles and unfortunately the start and finish were not in the same place so you had a long walk back to the car. All in all, it was a good half day or more when you added in the drive there and back from home. I only walked the course once because of the time involved and had no clear plan of where I was going. There was one bit fairly early on in the course that seemed to have options but to jump a five-bar gate going uphill with some very bumpy ground on the approach but other than that most of it was straight forward. The start was a revelation as one hundred horses lined up, up until then I thought a big field pointing was over twenty runners. I was riding a horse called Solomon that belonged to Dad. He was a good jumper and Dad thought it would be a good selling point that he had done the Melton Ride. As the flag fell a large rumble like thunder grew as the ranks of horses galloped down to the first fence. It looked deceptively small as we galloped down to it because it was newly cut and laid but it was probably still about one metre forty high. However, the danger came from the tightly twisted hazel binding along the top that was woven around small stakes. It is like a thick rope ready to trip you up. As always in races people tend to go too fast into the first fence when there is a large field, and the thunder of hooves was interspaced by cracks like a rifle shots as the horses' hooves rattled the hazel bindings. Several horses and riders crashed to the ground, you never looked back to see if someone was ok, you just thanked you lucky stars it was not you and focused on the job in hand which was to avoid loose horses and get a clean line into the next fence. As I left the carnage behind, I was surprised to see the field veer off to the right in a totally different direction to what I had planned. I made a snap decision and decided to follow them. It was not long before I recognised the undulating ground that led to the five-bar gate, I took a check and prepared for the big gate just around the bend. I need not have worried, there was nothing left of the gate - it had been smashed to pieces. I drew a sigh of relief and kicked on up the hill. We were getting spread out now, it was fairly misty that morning and every now and then a loose horse or a dazed, staggering rider would loom out of the mist. Except for dramatic incidents I have few memories of individual races, it was just relentless damage limitation and no time to log everything into the brain as the brain was far too busy on more important matters. After about three miles I realised that we had seriously underestimated the fitness level required for both horse and rider, and I knew if I tried to keep up with the leading bunch it was going to end in tears, also if I injured Dad's horse it could be the end of hunting and racing for the Humphrey family, such was the precarious state of our finances. I dropped my pace from racing to hunting and picked off one fence at a time until the finish came into sight. As I cantered across the penultimate fence my horse was wandering from side to side with exhaustion. Just one more fence and I was home but I knew my horse could not jump another hedge. I pulled up to a trot and was about the call it a day when I spied a hole in the fence. There was still a large ditch and the tangled remnants of the hedge to contend with but having got this far I had to roll the dice one last time. I pulled Solomon together and trotted towards the gap in the hedge. I shouted and tapped him with the whip behind the saddle. He jumped the ditch but his feet got caught in the remnants of the hedge and he went down on his knees. I thought how cruel it was to have got to within yards of the finish line and not make it. I threw myself back pulled his head up and gave him one last kick. To my surprise he scrambled to his feet and we trotted over the line to loud cheers. I was the last to finish and a little down hearted, I had sorely underestimated the quality of horses and riders that took part in this so-called ride. I had thoroughly enjoyed it and was stunned to find out that I was about the fifteenth to finish. That put it into prospective I had beaten eighty-five! Things were not so bad after all!

Sadly, I cannot even remember some of the horses that I rode in those rides. I think I did eleven rides and I never fell but pulled up twice and that was on two young horses. Each ride had its scary bits and I still remember many of those. The worst was in one of the Quorn country rides. We started at High Holborn Farm near Hickling Pastures and headed for Muxloe Hill which involved jumping across the A606 Nottingham to Melton road between Hickling Pastures and Upper Broughton. Thankfully, they closed the road briefly for the crossing and sanded the road to take some of the slipperiness off the tarmac. The crossing had three problems to overcome. The first was a huge wide hedge with a big wide deep ditch on the landing side. It was about the fifth fence so we were still bunched up, some never checked and galloped bravely but madly at the hedge probably wanting to make sure that they cleared the big ditch on landing. I like many others took a more cautious approach realising that the road was just as dangerous as the ditch because when metal horseshoes come into contact with tarmac at speed you might as well be riding on ice. Normally a Melton ride is a noisy affair with riders shouting at other riders or their mounts. As we approached the road people suddenly became silent and all you could hear was the drum of galloping hooves on the wet turf. It was eerie and I felt my stomach churn. My plan was to back off the pace, collect my horse and jump it on more of an eventing pace than racing pace, that would allow me to clear the ditch but still land on the grass verge and get a check in to rebalance my horse before hitting the tarmac. Thankfully, I got a good stride into the hedge. I was riding Mike Elvin's horse Red who was my regular teamchase mount at the time. Red was a phenomenal jumper and we negotiated the hedge and ditch without a problem, but what I had not planned for was the carnage that lay before me on the road. It was like the end of the charge of the Light Brigade, horses, and bleeding bodies everywhere. It was at this moment I was so glad to be on a well-trained balanced horse, in two strides after landing I was back to trot, we slipped a bit on the road, but managed to weave in and out of the bodies on the road to the next obstacle. On the other side of the road the ground fell away sharply into what is the beginning of the Vale of Belvoir. The hedge on this side of the road was several feet lower than the road. And a strange obstacle to jump as you were sort of on top of the hedge before you took off. The drop was immense but you were landing on ground that fell away from you. On landing we slid for about eight feet but it took the impact out of the landing. As we dropped down into the vale under Muxloe Hill it was like being on home turf having hunted across this land so many times I knew where to jump and where to avoid. I came 6th that day and narrowly missed out on being the first Quorn subscriber to finish beaten by friend Richard Morley.

I could write about endless scary moments that I had on my Melton rides but I will leave you with one moment that I am particularly proud of. The ride that year was in the Belvoir country near Eastwell. Like many of the rides you came across a fence towards the end of the ride that was a do or die fence, usually a big ditch with an enormous hedge in front or behind. On a fresh horse out hunting, a daunting challenge, but after four miles you needed a supreme Grand National type of horse to attempt it. There were always two or three of those professionally trained horses in the ride such was the prestige of winning the ride and claiming that bottle of whiskey. Usually there was always a longer way around but this year I could not find one despite much searching. Most of my rides were on other peoples' horses and the last thing I wanted to do was to seriously injure their horse. So, with much melancholy I decided that this was where my ride must end. The fence in question was a true old-fashioned oxer, the name now given to a parallel show jump. In its true form it was a hedge and a ditch that had a back fence of a rail to protect the ditch from damage by livestock. You often see them in old hunting prints and as you can imagine they were a formidable challenge to jump.

This oxer was slightly different because instead of a rail protecting the ditch it was a small hedge about 80cm high, as I have already said a nice but challenging fence to meet on a fresh horse but after four miles of heavy, deep going, it was a risk that I was not prepared to take so I decided to walk the rest of the course and see what I was missing. When I got to a gate in the hedge line, I noticed that there was a large pipe under the gateway that allowed the water to flow free along the ditch. This is common practice but luckily for me the pipe was about half a metre longer than the width of the gate. The extra bit had also been covered in hardcore and a short post and rail filled the gap between the gate post and the hedge. It was very tricky with no room for error but I often jumped my horses over 1.m 20cm out of trot so I decided that was the route I would take. You can take whatever line you like in the race so I was not breaking any rules.

It was a gruelling race that year due to the heavy going but I got safely to the big fence, I pulled up to a trot shook my horse up it to get its attention, got my horse straight and trotted into the narrow rails hoping and praying that I got a good clean jump because clipping those rails or slipping into that deep ditch did not bear thinking about, it was a big ask on a tired horse but that was what the ride was all about. I got the clean jump and again it was a top ten finish.

A big gamble but well worth it when you pull it off!

It was the tradition in those days that the hounds would meet after the prize giving. As the Rides took place in the best part of the host Hunt's country the meet was always a two-horse day. I always liked to stay and see the hounds meet after a ride. The Belvoir hounds are a much darker colour than the Quorn hounds and the huntsman of the time had a unique talent of getting all of his hounds to sit around his horse. It really was a sight to behold. As I watched those hounds, I wished I could be following them. My adrenaline was going down and I wanted more. I noticed that a few of the competitors had changed into hunting clothes and were at the meet. A seed was sown, a new challenge, complete the ride and then hunt two horses afterwards. At the time I was at my peak of fitness as I was hunting Monday's with the Quorn, racing both in point to points and doing National Hunt, Hunter-chases plus open Teamchases. I was riding for several people at that time and it was Mike Elvin and Dick Benson that allowed me to achieve this ambition. It was the following year that it all came together at the Quorn Ride. It was the one that I have described with the road crossing at Hickling pastures. I rode Mike's horse Red in the race and hunted Dick Benson's horse Gladstonian and one of Dad's horses for the rest of the day. It was dark when Lou picked me up hacking home. It had been a blistering day and we jumped well over eighty more fences. As I hacked home, I felt content with the world, it was that time when the light fades, the countryside slowly becomes silent. It is my favourite time of the day. As the sun goes down on a cold winter's evening I often standstill for a moment in silence and just take it all in.

When I jumped off my horse on the dark, back lane where Lou had found me, I crumpled into to the road as my legs gave way due to partly from exhaustion and partly from the cold, as the temperature had plummeted and the cold had eaten into my tired legs making them completely numb. However, it was nothing a hot bath and a large whiskey would not cure as I reflected on a perfect day.

Another tick for the Bucket List!

The Melton Hunt Club's discounted hunting tickets also allowed me to sample the delights of the Belvoir, Cottesmore, and Meynell hunts whose normal fees were well out of my reach financially, you have already read about those earlier so I will not bore you with the details.

The Club is still going strong, so if my tales have inspired you, give it a try. It helps local hunts keep going in these difficult times and opens the doors to some fantastic fun.

Finally, it gave me great pleasure to watch my niece Pippa Bracewell formerly Pippa Humphrey, my brother Phil's daughter, ride in and complete the Melton ride a couple of years ago when it was held between Hose and Long Clawson.

Well done Pip extremely proud of you!

End of Book Reflections

So, the end of three books about my life. The Bunny Hill Chronicles. What made me put that in the in the box that said, "Name of series" when filling in the endless pages of questions that you have to fill in to enable you to publish a book on Amazon I do not know? I only ever intended to write about our crazy life jousting. Some may say it is a lot to write about one life. It certainly makes you reflect on it. Wow! What a journey, it has taken me back to some great places, or should I say memories. I come, warts and all, so this trip has taken me to some dark places. Some I have shared and some too dark to share. I think everyone has experiences in their lives that have been buried and need to stay buried. I hope my books have felt honest and not too frivolous, yes, I had some great experiences but I have had many battles on the way. I am sure everyone who has read my books have led equally interesting lives if they only took the time to sit down and really think about it. I have spent seven years thinking and writing about mine. I never intended to go this far; it was only your fantastic comments that encouraged me to go past book one.

People often ask me if I have any regrets? Yes, that is a no brainer, I wish I had done a lot more. I have met so many interesting people during my riding career and continue to do so. Another big regret is that I did not take more time to talk to some of the old horse people my dad introduced me to. It was a lost opportunity to gain old knowledge before it was lost forever. Unfortunately, I was young and in those days the rule was young people should be seen but not heard. Also, I have been incredibly shy all my life. You may think that is nonsense teaching, jousting, and commentating in front of huge audiences, not to mention all the film and television work.

There are two sides to me. One side is saying you need to have a go at that, the other side kicks in when I have got the job and I wonder what on earth possessed me to take on such madness and all self-confidence drains away. Perhaps it is because I was born a Gemini under the sign of the twins. Two opposing personalities both fighting for dominance. I am sure many readers suffer the same lack of confidence; all I can say is you must fight it to achieve your ambitions.

I have taken enormous risks and without my wife Louise to support me I wonder how much of all this might not have happened.

One thing that stands out to me more than anything else is that horses have opened nearly all the doors for me during my life. That is why I have been so passionate about encouraging children to take up riding. I left school at sixteen with seven O Levels. I did not go to college until some years later and successfully increased my formal knowledge but I never had a degree in anything but life. However, being a horseman has allowed me to talk to a prince, a president, film stars and captains of industry.

The old saying of "It's not what you know but who you know that counts" still stands today. Riding horses teaches you many more life skills than a degree and often opens a lot more doors.

Today is February the Eighteenth 2021. This book is all but finished. I am knocking on the door of my seventieth birthday, my glory days riding are over. Lou and I still ride out twice a week and I am still teaching. My son Mark now lives and works from the family home on Bunny Hill. He is a successful farrier with several apprentices and works closely with local veterinary surgeons. Mark rides very little these days although in his younger days he whipped in for the Trent Valley Drag and the Rockwood Harriers. However, he is still Jousting. Mark is married to Vicky who competes at advanced level dressage. My daughter, Emma, is now married and lives in Warwickshire. She is now Emma Forsyth and has pursued a successful eventing career competing at home and abroad. One of my proudest moments was watching her complete a clear cross-country round at Burghley Horse Trials. She is still competing, bringing on youngsters and teaching, despite having two very energetic, young daughters. I have three grandchildren. Katherine who is Mark's daughter is fourteen and another eventer competing at BE100. She hopes to move up to novice but COVID has thrown a spanner in the works at the moment. She is also showing promise in pure dressage showing off flying changes on mummy's dressage horse on Facebook recently. Florence, Emma's eldest, is four and Georgina the youngest, is two and a half. They both ride regularly and love it. Who knows what next!

Keep on riding and follow your heart!

Thank you and What's Next!

A big thank you for reading my book and I hope you enjoyed it. Writing this book certainly helped me cope with the lockdowns and all the uncertainties that the virus has brought to the world. What next? Writing has become part of my life even though my typing and spelling has not improved. I am still typing with one finger on my iPad but I have managed to speed up a bit. I have decided to have a crack at a fictional thriller as my next project. It has horses at its roots and spans many countries and several decades. The Title of the book is The Raggedy Bush Girl and begins in Southern Ireland in the mid-nineteen-fifties. Although the book is fiction the Raggedy Bush is real and has intrigued me since I was first shown it in the early nineteen nineties.

The central character is Maeve and charts her life as it twists and turns over four decades from the nineteen fifties until the eighties. A period known as "The Troubles" in Ireland. Although it has horses at its heart, it charts a web of love, deceit, and espionage in a dangerous time when bombs and assassinations were the order of the day.
Below is the beginning of the tale. I hope you enjoy it.

The Raggedy Bush Girl

Maeve

A shawled hunched figure trudged slowly along the winding windswept road that ran from Kells towards Kilkenny. Kells was now just a village but once home to one of the largest priories in Ireland. It was starting to rain, not heavy but driven by the cold harsh wind, the raindrops stung the woman's face causing her to look down and give her the appearance of a hunched older woman, although in reality she was barely thirty. She was hunched because she was carrying a small child and was desperately trying to shield her from the bitter wind and rain. The child was crying, interspaced with bouts of coughing. Her name was Maeve, her mother's name was Ciara Henderson. Ciara was married to Dermot Henderson; they had a small farm north of Kells which barely gave them a living. Ciara had given birth to three other children but none had past their second birthday, she was desperate to see her fourth survive. She had prayed to the Virgin Mary and been a good Catholic all to no avail, one by one she had lost her beloved children. The same words, of god moving in mysterious ways and not to worry you can always have more children, uttered by the priest had given her little solace. The same old words churned out over and over again.
As Maeve's cough had worsened over the past week Ciara had become resolved in what she was going to do. It was a big risk and the possibility that her actions might destroy her marriage weighed heavily on her thoughts. She had planned this day with great care so that her husband would not discover what she was about to do.
It was market day in Kilkenny and Dermot had left early loaded up with eggs and potatoes to sell in the market and then use the money he had made to buy essential supplies from the other traders in the market. Maybe if it had been a good day, he would have enough to buy a pint of Guinness and spend some time chatting to the other farmers before heading home. He was a good husband never exceeding his one pint, but it was a long day and he would not be home before dark. That left the feeding of the animals to Ciara, this always made him feel guilty.

Ciara was always up early on market day but today it was just a little bit earlier to give her a head start on the day. When Dermot came down his breakfast was ready and when he acted surprised, Ciara covered it by saying Maeve had woken her early and after feeding her it wasn't worth going back to bed.

"You will be able to get off a bit earlier and hopefully get one of the prime spots for selling before the others get there", she said.

Dermot gave her a smile and speeded up eating his breakfast, thinking how lucky he was to have such a forward-thinking wife who was always trying to better their life even though it was hard to make ends meet. Even through the tragedies of losing the babies she had never stop thinking forward for better times.

"Right, I'm away now".

He kissed her and moved quickly towards the door.

"Good luck and get that good spot and sell all our goods. If you do well, bring back a bottle of Guinness and we will share it over supper.

With a wave he was gone.

Ciara went into top gear; baby was already fed and had gone back to sleep, so she went out into the yard to feed the animals. Spring was on the way but the fields were still too wet to have stock on them so everything was in the barn or the stone-built sheds that was the farmyard at the back of the cottage. The mud clawed at her wellingtons sometimes bringing her to an abrupt halt when the deep mud refused to let go of her boot leaving her desperately balancing on one foot trying to get her foot back into the stuck Wellington. As she wriggled the boot out of the mud, which was made up of roughly equal parts of soil and animal excrement, she pondered how nice it would be to have a solid concrete yard like some of the larger farms. Fat hope of that she mused, we have hardly enough money to put food on the table. She struggled across the yard to feed the pigs who were squealing for their food.

At last, everything was fed and watered, she would get around to bedding down when she returned from her travels. It was time she was on her way. It was about five miles to Bamford from the farm and her destination was just before you reached the village. It had been dark when Dermot left the farm but now dawn breaking and it was almost morning, the sun would soon be rising but if it was going to be visible was another matter. The low dark grey clouds covered the sky and gave the landscape an eerie dull grey colour wash. Was this a bad omen?

Well wrapped up against the elements she set out on her mission. If all went well, she would be home about lunch time and that would give her plenty of time to bed all the stock down and give them their evening feeds. Hopefully, Dermot would think that she had been at the farm all day on her own just the same as any market day. The wind was behind her as she made her way up the road towards Kilkenny where Dermot would now be setting up his stall. She was about halfway to her destination when it started to spit with rain and the wind became blustery. She trudged on only pausing to step off the road when a very occasional car came up behind her. She would turn her head away from the road and pull the shawl across her face to hide her face in case the driver might recognise her and mention it to Dermot.

She had been walking for nearly two hours when she rounded a bend in the road, and there it was before her, one of the sacred trees of old Ireland. It was an ancient hawthorn bedecked with strips of different coloured cloth flapping in the gusting wind. A shiver ran down her back as she stared at the ancient magical tree. What she was about to perform was a ritual that went back into the mists of time, long before Christianity came to Ireland. She was staring at the Raggedy bush or the Raggedy tree as some people called it. The tree was one of the great mystical trees of ancient Ireland known as St. Patrick's Tree, close to it was a holy well and an ancient stone with strange holes in it and a simple Latin cross scratched on it. Custom had it that magical fairies (The Sidhe) lived around the base of the tree.

Ciara fumbled under her layers of clothing until she found the strip of cloth torn from one of Maeve's night gowns and touched to Maeve's lips just to make sure the Sidhe or as many called them, the little people, knew whose rag this belonged to.

She carefully tied the strip of material to the tree not too tight so that she didn't harm the sacred tree. As she tied the strip on, she muttered her wish to the Sidhe. Make my daughter strong and healthy so that she can succeed and have a better life than mine. As she muttered her wishes an old lady carrying a bundle of sticks passed by and said, "Be careful what you wish for lady, the Sidhe have a mischievous nature and you may not get what you expect". Ciara looked up to see who had uttered the prophetic words but nobody was there just a vague shadow disappearing around the sharp bend obscured by the swirling rain. Ciara walked up to the holy well pump and drew some water and drank it and then poured some more into her cupped hands and dribbled it into Maeve's mouth, finally she wet her finger drawing the sign of the cross on Maeve's forehead. Dermot didn't hold with such beliefs and was a strict Catholic. He would go mad if he knew what she had just done.

Too late now for regrets, it was done! She turned around and started to walk home, only now she was facing the wind and rain head on and it was hard going. Finally, just after midday, Ciara arrived back at the farm cold wet and exhausted. She stripped off her sodden clothes and hung them on the wooden drying horse in front of the fire to dry, made a pot of tea and cut a slice of home-made soda bread. She carefully fixed the bread onto a toasting fork and placed it in front of the fire to toast. While she waited for the bread to toast, she cupped her hands around the steaming mug of tea and let the heat seep into her cold hands. Steam was starting to come off the wet clothes filling the kitchen with a dank musty smell. As she stared into the fire her thoughts drifted back to the Raggedy tree and all those wishes people had made, each one represented by a piece of personal cloth tied to a branch and flapping wildly in the wind creating a unique sound. Was there still magic or was it just mumbo-jumbo. Had she done the right thing or was it wrong? Dermot would say definitely wrong for he was tied hard and fast to the Catholic religion. She snapped out of her daydreaming as the smell of burning toast reached her nostrils and grabbed the toasting fork to pull it away from the hot fire. A knife full of home churned butter spread on the toast completed her lunch. There was little left to eat in the house except a side of smoked bacon and a few root vegetables. Hopefully, Dermot had been successful at market and would be bringing fresh supplies home because they were desperately needed.

She woke suddenly in a panic not realising that she had dropped off in front of the warm fire. Her mind raced, what had woken her, how long had she been asleep, was it Dermot arriving home? She was not halfway through her daily chores. Questions would be asked! As the blur of sleep left her mind, she looked up at the old wooden wall clock the pendulum sending out a reassuring steady tick- tock. She breathed in a huge deep breath as she read the time and then let out a long, slow sigh of relief. She had only been asleep for twenty minutes. A powerful, deep sleep that had restored her strength. She slowly got out of the chair and shook the last remnants of sleep from her body. There was much work to do before Dermot got home.

As spring started to assert itself over the land and the bright yellow, little celandines started to carpet the local woodlands, Maeve's cough started to get better, and by the time the white blackthorn blossom lit up the hedgerows the cough had completely gone. Maeve was becoming a healthy, bonny baby.

The years rolled by and Maeve was constantly by her mother's side helping to care for the animals and the never-ending chores that are part and parcel of small farm life. Maeve loved farm life and had a natural affinity with all the animals both large and small.

One day, just before Maeve's fourth birthday, Dermot was having his usual drink with the other local farmers at the end of market day in Kilkenny. He was merrily chatting to one of his close neighbours, Ted Morris, who remarked that it must be coming up to Maeve's birthday very soon. Dermot told him he was correct and that it was in fact the week after next, and it was her fourth birthday. Tom went on to say that all his children had now grown up and their pony had nothing to do now except eat grass and get fat. Would Dermot like to have the pony for Maeve as a birthday present, as he was sure that the pony would get laminitis if he didn't do some work soon? Dermot was astounded, they had talked about getting her a pony but he and Ciara had both agreed that there were many more urgent things that required what little money they had to spare. A pony for Maeve was sadly out of the question.

Thinking that Ted was trying to sell him the pony, he gracefully declined explaining to Ted that they just didn't have the money to buy a pony for Maeve. Ted burst out laughing saying, "Dermot you great Lumuckse, I'm not trying to sell you the damn pony, I'm offering to give it to you for Maeve's birthday. It's obvious to anyone that isn't blind that she has a great affinity with animals and you would be doing me a favour. The pony needs a job and he has a great pop in him. She could hunt him, and perhaps go jumping in the summer at the local shows when she has grown a bit more. Me and the missus miss the kids now they have all fled the nest, it will give us great pleasure to see her having fun with Sammy the pony. Oh, that's his name by the way".

Dermot felt a tear forming in his eye and could not make up his mind if it were from joy or the embarrassment of misunderstanding Ted's kind offer as he thanked the elderly farmer profusely and accepted his kind offer.

"I hope you won't mind if me and the missus call by occasionally to see how the two of them are getting on?"

"Not at all Ted you and Mary are always welcome at our place, sure you know that anyway", replied Dermot with a big smile on his face. "Will you have a drink with me?" he said as an afterthought, scolding himself for his lack of manners.

Ted, aware of how short money was for Dermot and his family smiled saying, "that's exceedingly kind of you Dermot but I am late already, I must be away now. Some other time maybe, I'd enjoy that. Come and fetch the pony whenever you are ready".

Picking up his hat and his stick he loudly bade goodbye to all the farmers in the bar and strode out of the door with a big smile on his face thinking how good it felt to make someone happy.

When Dermot returned home it was nearly dark. It was early spring and the nights were starting to draw out a little. Ciara had just put Maeve to bed when a smiling Dermot burst through the kitchen door causing the dogs to leap up from in front of the fire and greet him yapping and barking, tails wagging furiously. Dermot squatted down to greet them and give them each a rub and a pat as the dogs licked his hands and face. Ciara turned from the cooker and smiled saying, "any chance of a pat and a cuddle for yer missus, I see I'm still second in line for your affection Dermot Henderson".

He laughed, "no chance of that, you forgot Maeve, that puts you back in third place my love. Is she still awake, have I got time to give her a goodnight kiss?"

He wriggled out of his long heavy coat and hung it on the back of the door before giving her a hug from behind and a peck on the cheek. Ciara brushed him away her hands covered in flour threatening to put her sticky hands onto his face. "Go and give her a kiss good night before she falls asleep. She was hoping that you would be home before she had to go to bed. What kept you?"

He let go of her and whispered in her ear "I have great news". She turned to ask what the news was but he was already at the bottom of the stairs chuckling to himself knowing that the suspense of not knowing the news would be killing her. Ten minutes later Dermot returned downstairs and even before he could close the door at the bottom of the stairs Ciara was asking what the news was!

"I thought I would tell you after we had eaten our evening meal" he said with a cheeky smile. "I'll give you yer dinner over the top of yer head if you don't stop teasing me, so out with it now or no dinner!" "Alright, alright", he held his hands up in surrender knowing full well he had pushed his luck too far with their regularly played, little game. He took his place at the kitchen table; Ciara moved the cooking pots to the side of the range so dinner would not burn and hastily took her place at the other side of the small table with an eager expectant look on her face. Dermot paused to reflect on how beautiful she looked when she was excited about something. "Come on, come on, out with it, you are driving me to distraction Dermot Henderson".
"Well, I met Ted Morris in the pub after market, and was having a chat with him when he came up with this amazing offer to give us their family pony, their kids are now all grown up and there is nobody up at the farm to ride him. Ted thought it would make a nice birthday present for Maeve. Well, what do yer think"?
Ciara was delighted but was convinced that there must be a catch. Dermot assured her it was all straight and above board, the only request that Ted had made was that he and Mary might call by and watch Maeve riding every now and then, because it had been one of their great pleasures in life watching their children having fun riding the pony.

When Maeve's birthday finally arrived, it was hard to tell who was the most excited, the birthday girl, her parents or Ted and Mary Morris who had been invited to join the birthday party. Ciara had been busy baking a birthday cake but this was totally ignored in favour of Sammy the pony which she resolutely refused to get off, much to the delight of Ted and Mary Morris.

By the time Maeve's fifth birthday came around she could catch and put Sammy's bridle on all by herself, she never bothered with a saddle as it was too much trouble. Maeve was happy riding bareback around the farm and often made her way around to visit neighbouring farms as well, much to the delight of Ted and Mary Morris.

As Maeve moved towards her sixth birthday Ted Morris called around to see Dermot and suggested that Maeve could come and join the local hunt when it met at his farm in a few weeks' time. Teds daughter was coming home for the hunt and would be happy to look after Maeve if she wanted to come out with the hunt. Dermot politely declined the offer, as they could not afford to buy proper riding clothes for Maeve to go hunting but Ted just laughed and told Dermot that they had presses (drawers) full of riding clothes to fit all ages and sizes, so that was not a problem and neither was the fee to go hunting because as he was hosting the meet, he could invite a guest free of charge. His daughter Aoife would look after her on a lead rein until she was ready to go home. Unfortunately, Maeve did not want to go home and poor Aoife was stuck with a tear-away child for nearly two hours before she suddenly faded and almost fell off her pony totally exhausted. When Aoife finally found Ciara and handed her over, she was absolutely exhausted. Ciara carried Maeve back to the old car they had recently bought. It was old and rusty but it was their first car and she was exceedingly proud of it. It saved Dermot loads of time and he could take much more produce to the market, get there quicker and be home earlier. She lay Maeve on the back seat totally exhausted and flat out. Dermot on the other hand took the pony and started the long walk back home. In the back of his mind a little seed started to grow, we are going to need some horse transport in the not-too-distant future. But how and where the money would come from, he had no idea.

At seven years old Maeve was going to any local gymkhanas that were in hacking distance and getting placed in competitions. The horse dealing community that were always present at these occasions took note that that there was a new upcoming talent on the block. Ted Morris who was a man of standing in the community let be known that he was her guardian and that any offers to ride other ponies were submitted to him. Quietly Ted protected Maeve from the more undesirable characters of the horse world and got her some nice ponies to ride as she started to outgrow the love of her life, Sammy the pony. Her next season found her with a string of good ponies to compete and rosettes were starting to be won. Her bedroom walls started to change colour as she proudly pinned her red, blue, yellow, and green rosettes up around her bed. Unbeknown to Maeve, Tom with his business wisdom had negotiated with the owners of the ponies she rode to receive a commission on any of the ponies that Maeve had produced when they were sold. He had opened a deposit account in her name and the commissions were paid into the account. Tom, and his wife Mary, also helped discretely with other show expenses such as taking her to shows when Dermot and Ciara were busy on the farm. All the time Tom's business knowledge was being drip fed, to an eager to learn, Maeve.

At home when she was not riding, she worked tirelessly on the farm with her mother and father. By the time she was entering her teens her body had become lithe and strong from carrying bales and buckets of water. Not only was her body strong but so was her mind. She quietly observed everything that went on around her and logging it into her brain. People watching was her favourite and she was wise beyond her age logging everyone into categories for future reference, nobody was going to pull the wool over her eyes. When she had any spare time, she would wander up into the fields and secrete herself in the undergrowth and sit for hours watching nature. As she got older, she travelled further afield onto the neighbouring farms, the farmers were all friends and she knew she would be welcomed if she met up with any of the owners. However, she moved across the land unseen and enjoyed hiding away in it if she spotted someone coming. Sometimes, they would pass close by and never know that she was there. Gradually she knew where hares and rabbits would sit, and the route a fox would take as he searched for prey. She could also identify nearly every bird by it call or song.

One beautiful summers day, she was tucked away out of sight on a neighbouring farm watching the bees harvesting the pollen from the wildflowers. She suddenly became aware of voices and laughter coming her way. She wriggled back into the undergrowth hoping that they would pass without noticing her. It was the farmer's son and a local girl who worked on the farm. To her horror, not twenty yards away from her, they stopped and sat down in the corner of the field, shielded by the banks from prying eyes. It was too late to reveal herself and she watched entranced as they sat and kissed before the lad unbuttoned her blouse and revealed her breasts. After more kissing he removed her jeans and dropped his down to his ankles before lying on top of her. She caught a quick glimpse of his erect penis as he prepared to mount her. Maeve had seen animals mate many times but never humans. The only difference was the humans apparently did it lying down, and animals performed it standing up. After a few agonising minutes of the farmer's son's white bottom bouncing up and down, it was all over, the couple redressed and walked away as if nothing had happened. Maeve made a mental note to avoid this farm in the future. She never mentioned what she had witnessed to a living soul. However, she did keep an eye out for the couple. She never saw them together again. She saw the girl in village quite often and noticed some months later that there was a slight swelling of her stomach. She never saw the girl again. She mentioned the fact to her mother who answered her abruptly saying that had gone away in shame and then her mother suddenly remembered an urgent job that she had to do, giving Maeve no chance to ask awkward questions. Maeve made a mental note to beware of men and their desires because they could get a girl into a lot of misfortune. She was nobody's fool; she knew exactly what had happened and she had very cleverly tricked her mother into confirming her suspicions without her mother even knowing. Boys were very much off her agenda for the foreseeable future.

When Maeve reached her sixteenth birthday, Tom Morris took her to one side and told her that he was getting old and it was time that she started to look after her own affairs where riding was concerned. He told her about the bank account which now, after all those years had built up a healthy balance. There was enough money to buy several young horses to train on and sell. Tom also explained the commission fee system that he had set up with the owners of the horses she was riding. He had informed them all that Maeve would be handling her own accounts from now on but that he would be keeping a close eye on things and woe be tide anyone who didn't abide by the rules.

Maeve was stunned. She had come to think of Tom as the kind uncle, she never had and never considered his age, she thought he would be there for her for ever. She sat stunned and tearful just staring at the ground. Tom reading her mood took her hands and whispered "Maeve, nothing lasts for ever. You are an incredibly talented rider and a wonderful, kind person. I recognised that at an early age and that is why I gave you Sammy and helped you to develop into the wonderful person you are today. There are a lot of bad people in this world and you need to be careful. Think long and hard before you give someone your trust. Think what is in it for them, rather than what you will gain, if you do that, you will go a long way. Pay and be paid, anyone can work for nothing and you are worth more than a pretty penny". Tom took her hand and lifted her to feet saying, "Come I want you to meet another good soul that I have nurtured". He led her across the show ground towards the horsebox park, a young man barely in his twenties was busy washing down a horse tied to an old horsebox. As Tom approached, he looked up and smiled warmly at Tom saying " Tom, how's it going it's great to see yer, and who's the pretty young lady you have with yer". Maeve's stomach flipped she went weak at the knees and she felt a rush of warmth invade her crotch, something that had never happened to her before in her life. She didn't know where to look, she was sure that the good-looking man with his sleeves rolled up and his tousled hair falling all over his face could see everything that she was feeling. She just wanted a hole in the ground to open and swallow her up. "Maeve this is Fergus Murphy, Fergus this is Maeve Henderson, another protege of mine like yourself". Fergus looked her up and down saying "Just a mo' let me finish washing down the mare and I'll be with yee". Carefully Fergus washed the final bits of sweat from the horse's back where the horse's saddle had been and then squeezed the sponge out into the bucket of water very slowly and methodically. The noise of the water cascading down into the half full bucket of water only increased the strange feelings that had invaded her body. She was sure he was doing it deliberately just to make her uncomfortable.

Chapter Two

Fugus Murphy

Thank you and What's Next!

A big thank you for reading my book and I hope you enjoyed it. Writing this book certainly help me cope with the lockdowns and all the uncertainties that the virus has brought to the world.
What next? Writing has become part of my life even though my typing and spelling has not improved. I am still typing with one finger on my iPad but I have managed to speed up a bit. I have decided to have a crack at a fictional thriller as my next project. It has horses at its roots and spans many countries and several decades. The Title of the book is The Raggedy Bush Girl and begins in Southern Ireland in the mid-nineteen-fifties. Although the book is fiction the Raggedy bush is real and has intrigued me since a was shown it in the early nineteen eighties. The central character is Maeve and charts her life as it twists and turns over four decades from the nineteen fifties until the eighties. A period known as "The Troubles" in Ireland. It has horses at its heart, a web of love and deceit in a dangerous time when bombs and assassinations were the order of the day.
Below is the beginning of the tale. I hope you enjoy it.

Printed in Great Britain
by Amazon